Scores to Settle

Scores to Settle

Stories of the Struggle to Create Great Music

for Steven Turpin,
guardian of classical
music in the
airwaves of Indiana,
with Best Wishes,

Norman Gilliland

Norman Gilliland

Sept 22, 2009

NEMO Productions
Madison, Wisconsin

NEMO Productions
P.O. Box 260079
Madison, WI 53726-0079

Publisher's Cataloging-In-Publication Data
(Prepared by The Donohue Group, Inc.)

Gilliland, Norman
Scores to settle: stories of the struggle to create great music /
Norman Gilliland. — 1st ed.

p. ; cm.

Includes bibliographical references and index.
ISBN: 978-0-9715093-3-7

1. Musicians—Anecdotes. 2. Musicians—Biography. 3.
Composers—Anecdotes. 4. Composers—Biography. 5. Music
(Composition)—Anecdotes. 6. Music—History. I. Title.

ML65 .G555 2009
780/.92 B 2009901493

Printed in the United States of America
Cover Design: Zhang Ying

For information about quantity discounts,
please call NEMO Productions at (608) 215-4785,
email us at nemoproductions@hotmail.com,
or visit our Web site www.sandmansions.com

To Vicki Nonn,
Sharing the Air for a Generation.

Acknowledgements

Scores to Settle takes its cue from an earlier book, *Grace Notes for a Year*, which was a collection of stories written for broadcast over public radio stations around the country. Having discovered 366 illuminating and entertaining stories about classical music composers and performers, I thought that the mine was pretty well tapped, but, of course, it was the author that was played out—for the time being.

After a few years of diversion, it dawned on me that there might well be more stories out there, and every now and then I would add one just to keep the broadcast collection fresh. Occasionally, a voice suggested that a second book of stories would be appealing, and that therefore I should stop writing novels and get to work. After a while I paid heed because the voice belonged to my wife.

So here it is.

I'd like to thank some of the other voices responsible for bringing *Scores to Settle* to life.

My gratitude to Andrea Christofferson at the University of Wisconsin Press for putting up with many long phone calls having to do with getting the book out there.

A tip of the hat to Dennis Ryan, Amanda Gilliland, and Vicki Nonn for many valuable hours of assessment and proofing. Thanks to Ross Gilliland for providing so much insight into what it takes to make great music.

Invaluable to the production of this volume were cover designer Zhang Ying, the persistent and thorough Jordan Gilliland, and the patient and indefatigable Li Bo.

Many thanks to the dean of American composers, Gunther Schuller, for setting aside his commissions and autobiography long enough to evaluate *Scores to Settle*. Thanks also to the eminent conductor Edo de Waart, who graciously agreed to look at the book during the rigors of a commute between Amsterdam, Milwaukee, and Hong Kong.

And thanks to you for taking the time to read it.

Preface

Scores to Settle offers only a glimpse of the countless colorful stories behind the creation of classical music. In many cases, the composers and performers are their own best voices. So we hear from the vivid, high-strung letters of Mozart and the contrasting controlled baritone of his father Leopold. We hear the urbane, articulate Felix Mendelssohn and the congenial, business-minded Haydn.

We hear a scattering of letters from Verdi written over the course of forty years that show nonetheless a consistently irascible, iconoclastic side. We hear the now cajoling, now rumbling voice of Beethoven in letters from the middle years of his life.

In the course of a few letters, we glimpse the budding relationship between Robert Schumann and Clara Wieck, who became his wife and the champion of his music.

In the tradition of the novel, the course of the stories sometimes flashes back, so that we see the child Mozart in London after we've met Mozart the mature man. And from the opening story of the financial struggle of the Schumanns, we drift back to Robert's first enchantment with the thirteen-year-old Clara and then several years forward to their struggle to overcome her father's opposition to their marriage. Then we hear from the Clara of later years through her support of the young Johannes Brahms.

We follow New Orleans pianist Louis Moreau Gottschalk during his perilous Civil War travels through the Union states and out of the country to exotic adventures in Peru.

A recurring theme is the culture clash experienced by European musicians who came to America to achieve reputation and fortune—often with amusing results.

All the while, there is a seasonal flow to the succession of stories that unifies this otherwise kaleidoscopic look at some remarkable men, women, and children who live on through their music.

Foreword

Like its predecessor, *Scores to Settle* aims to shed light on the perilous process of inspiration, composition, and performance required to create classical music, whether the final product is a masterpiece or a mess.

Once upon a time, a fledgling radio producer was invited to collaborate in arranging an American performance by a string quartet whose players were members of a certain world-famous orchestra. The orchestra had recently performed in the vicinity, and now four of its players were offering to come back to put on a series of chamber music concerts. The invitation for radio involvement came from an attractive lady of means in a nearby city. She was arranging for the quartet to perform in several nearby venues.

The radio producer jumped at the chance to work with such world-class musicians, and arrangements for the concert went forward. It promised to be a very classy event.

The contact for the quartet was the cellist, a pleasant middle-aged New Zealander. On the eve of the big concert, the producer went up to see him in his hotel room to get some background information that might add color to the broadcast commentary.

He got more color than he bargained for.

After a few pleasantries, the cellist said in a causal way, "Of course, you know that this entire tour is the product of lust."

The producer cocked a brow. "Oh?"

The cellist went on to say that during the recent visit by the world-famous orchestra, the violinist of the future quartet and the lady of means had begun an affair, and the two of them had come up with the idea of the tour in order to pick up where they had left off.

The moral of the story: However lofty the music, it has an earthbound story behind it because it's the product of human experience and expression. It's that human context that *Scores to Settle* intends to illuminate. Here's hoping that you enjoy the stories.

Norman Gilliland

Madison, Wisconsin

April 3, 2009

January 1st
The New Year's Gift

Robert and Clara Schumann started the New Year with high hopes. They had earned so little in 1845 that Christmas had amounted to no more than lighting the tree and giving the children a few little trinkets. They had been unable to afford anything for each other.

But they had arranged a promising all-Schumann concert in Leipzig, and they had invested heavily in it. On New Year's night, 1846, the Leipzig Gewandhaus Orchestra would play Schumann's First Symphony, and Clara was to solo in a performance of his new *Piano Concerto in A minor*. The conductor would be none other than Felix Mendelssohn.

It was to be the concert that would establish Robert Schumann as a major composer.

But after the final rehearsal on New Year's Eve, Clara was dismayed to discover that no posters had been put up to advertise the concert, and ticket sales were meager.

On the big night, Clara played with her usual finesse, but the concerto's lack of virtuoso flashiness left the small audience cold. Nor did the symphony win many admirers. For the Schumanns the concert was a financial disaster.

One listener liked the concert though. Jenny Lind, the famous Swedish Nightingale, offered to sing at the next concert of Schumann's music. Robert wrote:

I'll never forget the first rehearsal—her clear comprehension of music and text at sight. I've never encountered such a perfect concept at the first reading, simple, natural, and from the heart.

Clara, who served as accompanist, remarked that Lind had no "forcing or sobbing or tremolo in her voice, not one bad habit."

Their concert took place in the auditorium of the Vienna Musikfreunde to a full house, and brought in a handsome profit for everyone, but Clara couldn't help lamenting that Lind could bring in more with one song than she and Robert had been able to earn in a year.

As for the generous Jenny Lind, she was quick to volunteer her services for the next Schumann concert.

1

January 2nd

We Need a Mirror

On January 2, 1875, Edvard Grieg wrote about what would become his best-known music to author Bjørnstjerne Bjørnson. He was not altogether enthusiastic:

Peer Gynt *has turned out the way you said it would. It looms over me like a bad dream, and there's no way I can be done with it until spring. It was the need for money—or, to be more exact, the offer of money—that motivated me. Maybe I shouldn't have done it, but the thought of travel and visions of great beauty dangled before me.*

Now I could be so lowdown as to wish that your house would not be finished by summer so that you would have to go abroad again. Yes, if that came to pass I would sweep everything out of the way and follow you wherever you went—all summer, and into the winter too for that matter.

But if you are going to stay home, let me know. I will be delighted to follow your advice as soon as this crisis with Gynt is over.

By the way, the recent performance of Peer Gynt *can be of some value to Christiania, where materialism is threatening to rise up and throttle everything we hold high and holy. We need a mirror, I think, in which all the egotism can be seen.* Peer Gynt *is just such a mirror; then you will come home and rebuild. Because it can't be denied: The people have to see their own ugliness before you can be useful, but as soon as their eyes are opened, you are just the right person to lead the parade. I have this very clear feeling, and I would be very surprised if I am mistaken.*

And then you will be followed by many who are concerned about our homeland, including your faithful friend, Edvard Grieg.

The first performance of Henrik Ibsen's play *Peer Gynt*, with music by Edvard Grieg, took place in Christiania, now Oslo, the following year. On February 24, we'll find out what Grieg thought of it.

January 3rd
The Elusive Moment

Although he enjoyed living in Paris, English composer Frederick Delius was restless and unable to concentrate. He was working on a piano concerto, but had hit an impasse. Thirteen years earlier he had made a musical breakthrough at Solano Grove, his father's orange plantation on the banks of the St. Johns River in Florida. Now, in the winter of 1897, hoping for a second flash of inspiration, he decided to return.

His motive was partly economic. Delius was struggling for financial independence, and, although a series of freezes had destroyed the citrus industry in northern Florida, farmers had turned to raising tobacco, and Delius thought that the old groves might be made profitable.

He returned to find the house still standing and his piano still functional, and reconnected with old friends, many of them former slaves whose work songs, river chants, and firelight dancing had been the catalyst for his *Florida Suite* and his opera *Koanga*. The sounds of nature had been just as important, and he wished that he could have a place like Solano Grove in Europe.

He picked up the piano concerto he had been working on and broke through his writer's block. To his surprise, he also made progress on his orchestral nocturne *Paris*.

And yet, after five months at Solano Grove, Delius found two things lacking.

He still had not received that second flash of insight he hoped for. And he had no one at the plantation with whom he could discuss his work.

He came to the realization that he had to keep trying to bring about that moment of illumination in his music and that to find the combination of solitude and intellectual stimulation he needed, he would have to return to France.

He couldn't afford to travel back and forth to look for his inspiration. This time his departure from Florida would be permanent.

January 4th

Not Good Enough

The young man was one of the most handsome in Boston, seemingly a classical Greek statue that had come to life and put on modern clothes.

He was also spoiled, and all efforts to make him work had failed. An attempt to turn him into a journalist had sent him to India, from which he returned more handsome and more unemployed than ever.

His aunt, poet Julia Ward Howe, famous for writing "The Battle Hymn of the Republic," thought that music might be a good career for the young man. After all, he had a pleasant baritone voice and enjoyed singing the occasional Schubert song with friends. She approached the English conductor George Henschel and asked him to audition her nephew. She and one of the young man's uncles accompanied him to the test.

For once, the young man was enthusiastic. Henschel gave him a thorough audition.

"I had to break to him my conviction that it would be of no use," Henschel remembered. "He could not sing, nor, in my opinion, be made to sing in perfect tune, and must give up all dreams of ever becoming a singer or making a living by music."

The young man was devastated. At the age of twenty-seven he felt that music had been his last hope. His eyes brimmed with tears, apparently seeing nothing but a bleak future.

Trying to come up with something positive, the uncle suggested, "Why don't you write down that little story you told me some time ago of that strange experience you had in India?"

The audition had taken place in January 1882. By Christmas, a novel set in India was sweeping through the United States and Great Britain. It was *Mister Isaacs*, the first of many best-sellers by Francis Marion Crawford. Years later, the prosperous author encountered Henschel in Sorento and reminded him with gratitude of the miserable audition in Boston that had laid the foundation for an outstanding literary career.

January 5th
Sweet Reward

Twenty-first century neurologists have determined that the pleasure a musician derives from playing the climax of a composition compares with the enjoyment of eating chocolate. If they're right, Karl Ditters von Dittersdorf had a double reason to remember a reward he received as a young violinist.

In 1761 Dittersdorf was accompanying the famous composer Christoph Willibald Gluck to Bologna, one of the music capitals of Europe. Years later, when Dittersdorf dictated his autobiography, he recalled an occasion when his playing brought him a particularly sweet return.

A distinguished musician of the day, Giovanni Battista Martini, asked the young violinist to play a concerto in his church during an upcoming service. He asked if Dittersdorf would be satisfied with the usual fee of twelve double ducats. Dittersdorf replied that he would play only on condition that he was not paid.

"What I prized beyond money," he said, "was the honor of being chosen to play by the Father of Music."

During the three-day festival Dittersdorf and Gluck went to church to hear Vespers, which featured music by Martini. Dittersdorf thought it was magnificent. In one Psalm Martini had written the Amen in the form of an eight-part fugue—all the more glorious since the orchestra consisted of 160 people and the chorus was 80 strong.

The next morning Gluck and Dittersdorf went to see Martini, who invited them to drink chocolate with him.

"I think it likely," Martini said, "that yesterday's Vespers and to-day's High Mass will be my Swan Song, because I am already aware that my powers, physical and mental, are beginning to fail."

After Dittersdorf had played his concerto, he and Gluck went home and sat down to dinner, after which the landlord came in and said, "Padre Martini sends you both a few pounds of chocolate."

In a shaky hand, the old priest had written on the packet: "12 pounds for my dear friend Cavalier Gluck and 12 pounds for my dear son Signor Carl Ditters."

5

January 6th
Memory

According to piano virtuoso Ignacy Jan Paderewski, in addition to stamina, dexterity, and an ear for music, a concert performer needs a good memory. During the early years of his career, he found out that memory can take more than one form.

In 1890, for a French colleague, Paderewski agreed on short notice to give a concert of French music. He agreed to play two concertos and a dozen short pieces, all of which he had to learn in the course of two weeks.

By the day of the concert he had learned all of the pieces and could play them all without a single mistake. But ten minutes before he was to perform, he began to doubt his memory.

"It was an agony!" he said years later. "I had to look at the music—the concertos especially—just before I went onto the platform." The concert included established repertory and music by little-known contemporary composers, and he was still consulting the scores at the last minute.

He got through the program to the satisfaction of the audience and the composers who were attending, but three days later he found that he couldn't remember a single piece.

"Not one!" he said in his memoirs. "It was gone."

He came to the conclusion that a big effort of forced memory would achieve only temporary results. "I crammed and I stuffed myself literally like one of the famous Strasbourg geese!" he said, and warned students that reliable and enduring results in learning music are the product of "continuous daily efforts," whereas the result of a single intense effort will be "absolutely sterile."

A musician making a last-minute push to memorize a piece, he said, is like students that "enjoy themselves for a whole year until the time comes for the examination, then they make a supreme effort and acquire superficial, but brilliant knowledge for the moment."

"Very soon," he said, there's "nothing left of it—nothing!"

January 7th
The Gentle Approach

Dimitri Mitropoulos had conducted the Minneapolis Symphony in 1937 in a concert that had turned the usually staid audience into "an excited mob." Now he was back as its music director and everyone was wondering if the magic would hold.

A Minneapolis reviewer had described Mitropoulos' conducting as "punching the air barehanded" and "a weird repertoire of frenzied gestures and scowls and grimaces that registered every emotion from terror to ecstasy."

The reviewer went on to say that the resulting music was full of "great thought and abiding spirit" and the audience agreed. Just days after Mitropoulos' guest appearance in Minneapolis, the orchestra's directors announced that they had hired him as music director for the following season.

Upon his return, he got down to business right away, and the musicians could tell at once that he was different from the stern autocrats many of them were used to. He arrived for rehearsals on time, conducted from memory, and eschewed the use of a baton as if to put himself on a level with the players, whose names he had memorized before the first rehearsal. He also seemed to downplay his importance in leading the orchestra, saying, in effect, to one player or another, "You're more important than I am at this spot, so you set the pace."

"Look," he was quoted as saying, "I am not the boss here. We are working together."

The first concert took place after four days of rehearsals, on January 7, 1938, in Northrop Auditorium, and consisted of three classical works—Haydn's London Symphony, Mozart's Symphony No. 39, and Beethoven's First Symphony, three works that were pleasing but not known for bringing down the house. And yet, Mitropoulos and his orchestra put so much clarity, passion and power into them that at the end of the concert the audience of five thousand stood and cheered.

It was an auspicious beginning, and Dimitri Mitropoulos' year with the Minneapolis Symphony turned into twelve.

January 8th
Mozart's Delayed Homecoming

 Leopold Mozart had been chasing his son, Wolfgang Amadeus, all over Europe—with letters demanding that the twenty-two-year-old come home to Salzburg, where important business opportunities waited—and waited. Christmas passed, then New Year's Day, and still no Mozart. On January 8, 1779, the young genius wrote to his father from Munich:

I assure you, my dearest father, that from the bottom of my heart I am looking forward to returning to you (if not to Salzburg) since your last letter convinces me that you know me better than before! Never was there any reason other than this doubt for my long delay in coming home.

So far as I know, I've done nothing to justify a scolding from you. I'm guilty of no transgression (by transgression I mean something unbecoming to a Christian and a man of honor). In short, I rejoice at the thought of seeing you and I'm looking forward to the most pleasurable and happy days—but only in your company and that of my dear sister.

I swear to you on my honor that I can't stand Salzburg or the people in it (I mean the native Salzburgers). Their language and habits are completely unbearable.

Well, let's discuss something else. Yesterday my good old friend Cannabich and I went to the Electress and presented my sonatas. Her rooms are just the way I'd like mine to be some day—just like those of a private person, very charming and pretty, except for the view, which is horrendous.

We spent more than half an hour with her and she was very gracious. In order to get paid quickly I made a point of letting her know that I'm leaving here in a few days. Well, to summarize, please believe that I have the most aching yearning to embrace you and my dear sister once again. If only it weren't in Salzburg! But if I can't see you without going to Salzburg, I will gladly do it.

January 9th
You Want to Be a Musician?

In 1831 a performance of Rossini's *Otello* convinced thirteen-year-old Charles Gounod that he wanted to be a composer. "I was haunted, possessed," he said later. "I wanted to write an *Otello* myself!"

He poured his energy into writing music. His studies suffered. "I was kept in school," he recalled, "given extra work, imprisoned, et cetera, et cetera." All of which just made him more determined. He put his best effort into his schoolwork, but only for the sake of later being free to write music. To his mother he announced his decision to become a composer. Although she was a pianist and had given him lessons, she was not pleased. She knew how frustrating a musician's life could be.

She took her concerns to the school principal, who assured her that the boy would not become a musician. He and Gounod had a heart-to-heart talk.

"Well, little man, what is this I hear? You want to be a musician?"

"Yes, sir."

"But what are you dreaming of? A musician has no real position at all!"

"What, sir? Is it not a position in itself to be able to call oneself Mozart or Rossini?"

"Oh, you look at it that way, do you?" The principal wrote out some lines of poetry and gave them to the boy. "Take this with you and set it to music for me."

Later in the day Gounod handed the principal the result, a ballad. The principal asked him to sing it. After a fruitless argument about the need for a piano accompaniment, Gounod gave in and sang his composition. When he had finished, the principal said, "Come, we will go to the piano."

"My triumph was certain," Gounod remembered. "I was sure of all my weapons. I sang my little ballad over again." The tearful principal took the boy's face in his hands, kissed him and said, "Go on, my boy. You shall be a musician."

Charles Gounod told the story in his autobiography in 1875.

9

January 10th
The Price of Originality

Not yet nineteen years old, Francis Poulenc was already one of France's promising new composers, but in January 1918, with World War I consuming manpower, France had a more immediate need for soldiers, and young Poulenc would find the two occupations a strange mix.

From the start, Poulenc was at odds with military life. He was wealthy, pampered, and flippant, and within a few months, overstaying a leave in Paris, he pulled a ten-day term in a military prison. He wrote to influential friends, hoping for help, but maintained some sense of humor, asking one friend to spread the word about his incarceration because it was so funny.

While he was still in prison, Poulenc received from the flamboyant avant-garde choreographer Jean Cocteau a proposal for a project to be called *Jongleurs*, and with great enthusiasm he set about writing what he called "a thing of mad melancholy and sensitivity so far unknown in my work."

Jongleurs, meaning "Jugglers," began with a prelude so wild that Poulenc dismissed it as noise. By contrast, he intended the other part of *Jongleurs* to sound "as clear as Mozart," and a well-known dancer of the day moved to it with what was called "melancholy grace."

Poulenc was so concerned with the originality of *Jongleurs* that he passed up the chance to ask his friend Pablo Picasso to design costumes and sets for it because Eric Satie had recently relied upon Picasso's designs for his ballet *Parade*.

His originality would cost him more. The composer came to think of *Jongleurs* as music that was not quite ballet and yet not quite viable outside the theater. And later in life, when Francis Poulenc decided that the more exotic rhythms of his early days were not representative of his true style, he destroyed several works that employed them, including the wild, youthful *Jongleurs*.

January 11th
Parting Waves, Parting Ways

In his 1824 biography of the composer, Stendhal describes an 1818 performance in Naples of Gioachino Rossini's opera *Moses in Egypt.* Stendhal was leery of the opera, thinking that he might be setting himself up to see a musical version of the Inquisition.

Due to no fault of Rossini's, the experience turned out to be much more light-hearted—too light-hearted.

Stendhal was quite taken with the overture, but when the curtain rose on the Plague of Darkness, he burst out laughing at the sight of "wretched little groups of Egyptians" praying furiously as they bumbled around in the dimness of the vast stage.

A bass named Benedetti singing the part of Moses won Stendhal back with the power of his voice, but, during the third act, the special effects tipped from the sublime to the absurd.

The librettist had included the Israelites' crossing of the Red Sea in the opera, which put no small burden on the stage manager. The assignment was all the more difficult because the parting and crossing of the sea was to be accomplished at the front of the stage.

The effect of the resulting stagecraft depended upon the view of the beholder.

Seen from the pit, the Red Sea rose to an impressive height of five or six feet above its theatrical shoreline, but as those in the boxes looked down on tossing waves, they got a peek at the little lower-class Neapolitan stage hands whose job it was to part the sea at the sound of Moses' command.

Apparently, Neapolitan audiences were inclined to make fun of cumbersome stage machinery anyway, and the tossing seas encountered a gale of laughter.

The merriment was so frank and so forthright, Stendhal remarked, that no one had the heart to take serious issue with the clumsy seas.

And besides, he concluded, hardly anyone in the audience was listening to that part of the opera because they were still chatting about the wonderful overture.

January 12th

We Should Hear More

He was a composer and he was a critic. So sooner or later Deems Taylor would face a conflict of interest, and, when the moment arrived, he had to figure out a graceful way to review his own piece of music.

Henry Hadley had recently been appointed the associate conductor of the New York Philharmonic, and, being an American composer himself, Hadley wanted to include in each concert he conducted at least one work by a living American composer. In 1922, when the New York Philharmonic became the orchestra in residence for the city's first outdoor summer concert series, he was in charge of a stadium concert each night for six weeks.

Hadley wanted at least twelve works by living American composers for the concerts that he was to conduct personally, and among those he asked to provide music was Deems Taylor, who sent over a revised version of *Siren Song*, which he had written about ten years previously, a piece that had won the top award of the National Federation of Music Clubs.

When Hadley conducted the premiere of the piece, Taylor was in Europe, but Hadley liked *Siren Song* so much that he included it in a second concert in Carnegie Hall six months later.

Now Taylor was on the spot. Should he review his own piece of music?

In his review for the *New York World* on January 12, 1923, he fell back on a fact that he remembered from his days at NYU. He quoted George Bernard Shaw, who stated that human beings are renewed every seven years, so that reviewing a decade-old piece, was, in effect, evaluating the work of another person entirely, "a posthumous work, written by a young man."

He faulted the piece for its lack of well-defined individuality, but suggested that it nonetheless had a certain simplicity and freshness.

"On the whole," he wrote, "*Siren Song* interested us. We should like to hear more works by the same composer."

January 13th
The Meanest Thing in My Life

In his 1928 autobiography John Philip Sousa describes a concert in which he felt that he had to make a statement.

During San Francisco's midwinter fair in January 1894, the Sousa band was asked to perform in conjunction with Scheel's Imperial Orchestra, which had been playing in a large auditorium to meager audiences, even as the Sousa organization was drawing crowds by the thousand.

The concert was to consist of two pieces by the combined ensembles, two by the ensembles playing separately, and two by soloists from each ensemble. Sousa met with Fritz Scheel, conductor of the Imperial Orchestra, who, apparently, had been told that Sousa would dominate the proceedings if left unchecked.

"What is your piece for the combined orchestra and band?" Scheel asked.

Sousa said he'd conduct the overture to *Tannhäuser.*

"*Nein, nein!*" Scheel protested. He wanted to conduct it.

They got pretty hot under the collar arguing about the piece until the publicity man for the fair convinced Sousa to let it go. Scheel asked, "What is your next piece?"

"The Second Hungarian Rhapsody of Franz Liszt," Sousa said.

Scheel wanted that, too. "What is your opening piece?" he asked.

Sousa turned the tables and asked Scheel what his was. When told it was the overture to *Mignon*, Sousa laid claim to the *William Tell Overture.*

By the time of the concert, the inattention of Scheel's players to Sousa's conducting stirred up such rancor between the two groups of musicians that the Americans threatened fisticuffs if the slight continued. After polite applause greeted the Scheel orchestra's performance of *Mignon*, Sousa's band played an impeccable *William Tell Overture*, and, during a thunderous ovation, Sousa did what he called "the meanest thing in my life." He swept his band into an encore of Americana that ended with a rousing "Dixie" and "Yankee Doodle."

Scheel later forgave Sousa for upstaging him, and for years afterward, whenever they met, they had a good laugh over the incident.

January 14th

I Feel Sorry for All of Them

 On January 14, 1792, Joseph Haydn wrote from London to Luigia Polzelli in Italy a letter that gives some insight into the rough-and-tumble music business:

My dearest Polzelli! I received your letter just now and I'm answering it right away. I'm relieved to hear that you're in good health and that you've found a position in a little theater, not so much because of the money as for the experience. I wish you the greatest success; above all, a good role and a good teacher who works as hard with you as did your Haydn....

I'll be staying in Vienna until the middle of June, not longer, because my Prince and many other conditions make it absolutely necessary for me to return home.

All the same, I'll try to go to Italy to see my dear Polzelli, but in the meantime, you can send your Pietro to me here in London. He'll always be either with me or with your sister, who is now alone and who has been separated for quite some time from her husband, the brute.

She's unhappy, just as you were, and I feel very sorry for her. I see her only rarely because I'm so busy, especially now that the Professional Concert has brought over my student Pleyel to compete with me. But I'm not concerned because last year I made a big impression on the English and so I expect to win their approval this year, too.

My opera was not performed because Signor Gallini, the director of the Italian Opera, didn't receive the license from the King—and never will if the truth were known. The Italian opera doesn't succeed at all right now, and by a stroke of misfortune, the Pantheon Theatre burned down just this very day, two hours after midnight. Your sister was to perform in the last work on the program. I feel sorry for all of them.

January 15th
The Façade

Poetry had prompted William Walton to write the music for *Façade*, but the provocative melodrama propelled the young composer into some very prosaic situations.

The poet, Edith Sitwell, had goaded the reluctant Walton into the project. Her brother Osbert came up with the idea of reciting the words through a kind of megaphone inserted through a curtain.

The first rehearsal took place on a January night in 1922 in a brightly-lit drawing room made all the more cheerful by light reflected from deep snow. But the performers were in no mood to appreciate the setting. They were "puzzled and rather angry with the score" and "so cold that they could hardly use their lips or fingers," one of them recalled. Osbert Sitwell came up with a flask of sloe gin and poured it out in generous quantities, which cheered the musicians considerably.

The premiere of *Façade* took place before a hand-picked audience of twenty, most of them poets, musicians, and painters who were enthusiastic, although Walton recalled that they talked all the way through the performance and concluded that he and Edith Sitwell were mad. A year later, the first public presentation seems to have elicited a quiet disdain. One audience member, Virginia Woolf, wrote in her diary of listening "in a dazed way."

The newspaper critics were all but unanimous in their condemnation of *Façade*, and Osbert Sitwell noted "a sudden unpleasing hush" whenever he and his friends entered a room. Noel Coward lampooned the debut. And when composer Herbert Howells encountered Walton shortly after the performance, he said, "Hullo, William. Still fooling around?" Walton responded by quoting among friends lines he had learned at Oxford: "O Howells, Howells, he's good for the bowels."

Façade would go through many changes in the fifty years to follow and would continue to stir up controversy, but there could be no doubt that it made William Walton a well-known composer at the age of twenty-one.

January 16th

First Hearing

The composer was all caught up in conducting the debut of his first really big work. For several days, Ralph Vaughan Williams had been too nervous to sleep or eat right. He was unaware of friends and musical personages in the audience— Charles Villiers Stanford and the promising composer George Butterworth among them—all of them in Leeds for the performance of *A Sea Symphony.*

The timpanist offered helpful advice to calm Vaughan Williams' nerves. "Give us a square four to the bar and we'll do the rest." The baritone, waiting with the composer before the performance and equally nervous, was less encouraging when he said, "If I stop, you'll go on, won't you?"

Vaughan Williams had lived with the symphony on paper for so long that in rehearsal he had been overwhelmed by his first hearing of it, remarking that the sound of the orchestra playing the first chords and the chorus entering with the words "Behold the sea itself!" had nearly blown him off the podium.

Once the symphony had been performed, Vaughan Williams was suddenly aware of being very hungry and very tired. Some of the singers probably felt the same way. The day after the debut a friend wrote an affectionate thank you note to Vaughan Williams in which she chided him for "expecting human larynxes to adapt themselves to impossible feats and to stretch or contract their vocal chords to notes not in their registers."

Vaughan Williams came to the conclusion that the performance had not been particularly good, and yet musicians and audience alike had recognized the stature of the symphony. A performance at Oxford was arranged almost immediately, and Ralph Vaughan Williams would later find out that many members of the next generation would discover "contemporary" classical music through *A Sea Symphony.*

16

Blunt

Florent Schmitt was an innovative French composer whose 1907 ballet *La tragédie de Salomé* in some ways anticipated Stravinsky's *The Rite of Spring*, and the Russian composer expressed admiration for his works.

His music had what someone called "an aggressive masculinity," and when it came to judging the music of others, Schmitt could be just as blunt.

American composer Daniel Gregory Mason had great respect for Schmitt and thought his music better than that of Claude Debussy. He met Schmitt just once but came away with an impression of an outspoken and unabashed critic.

They attended a Sunday afternoon concert in a stuffy hall. Schmitt grew drowsy during the slow movement of a learned but plodding symphony by his mentor André Gedalge.

"In a quiet passage," Mason reported, "he lost himself a moment, dropping his hard derby hat on the floor with a resounding whack."

Mason was told that after a performance of a symphony by Marcel Labey, Schmitt greeted the composer by saying, "Was it you that wrote that dreadful thing?"

During the 1930s, when he was music critic for *Le Temps*, Schmitt became notorious for his habit of shouting out his verdicts from his seat in the hall. One music publisher pronounced him "an irresponsible lunatic."

He and Stravinsky had a falling out and Stravinsky reversed his endorsements of Schmitt's works.

On the eve of World War II, he became increasingly controversial when he expressed pro-German sentiments. While he was director of the Conservatory at Lyons he was said to have talked parents out of enrolling their daughters of little talent.

"No wonder he lost the directorship," Mason remarked.

Then he added, "But in the midst of the Parisian politesse, a surface under which knives were often concealed, one could not but admire Schmitt for carrying his knife at belt level like an honest pirate, and on occasion using it."

January 18th

Pay Attention!

People who pay to attend a music lecture don't necessarily pay attention while it's in progress. In 1905, music critic Michel Calvocoressi was to do his first public speaking and, due to no fault of his own, he ran into trouble right away. He was to give a lecture on Russian music at a Paris theatrical institution, and he started with a double disadvantage. The date of his lecture was moved up, and he was to stand in for the famous actor André Antoine.

Calvocoressi asked an actor friend to give him some pointers on the art of lecturing. One piece of advice would prove quite valuable.

On the big day, a large audience showed up, most of them expecting the great actor. From an adjoining room Calvocoressi listened in on the conversations in the hall and heard remarks such as, "Oh, not Antoine? What's the lecture about then? Russian music...by whom? Cal-vo-co-res-si....Sounds boring! Let's take off." Then some second thoughts: "Well, lots of things are to be played and sung. As long as we're here, we might as well stay."

But he wasn't off the hook yet.

Calvocoressi entered the crowded, noisy hall and started speaking. Right in front of him, three or four ladies continued to carry on a conversation, rattling handbags and beads, oblivious to his presence. The distraction was bad enough, but Calvocoressi was afraid that their inattention would quickly spread to the rest of the audience unless he took action.

He remembered a pointer from his friend the actor and started lecturing, not to the audience at large, but to the offenders, telling them in a confidential tone about Russian folk songs and their influence on Russian composers. Everyone else in the audience began craning their necks to see who was getting the special lecture, which made the offending ladies very self-conscious—and, suddenly, very attentive.

Michel Calvocoressi tells the story in his memoir *Musicians Gallery.*

January 19th

Repentance

In 1525 Cardinal Thomas Wolsey founded Cardinal College in Oxford and delegated the search for singers to John Longland, the bishop of Lincoln. Longland's search for an instructor of a choir of sixteen boys led him to singer and composer John Taverner, who lived in the Lincolnshire village of Tattershall. But Taverner said he was reluctant because he was already making a good living where he was and had "a good marriage which he should lose" if he moved to Oxford.

Longland suggested that Wolsey hire somebody from his own household and drew up a description of the desired candidate as someone with a good singing voice, an ability to play an instrument, a love of teaching and a knack for it, an ability to work with children, and knowledge of the sacred repertory.

Somehow Wolsey and Longland convinced Taverner to take the job, perhaps by sweetening the deal, since Taverner's salary, plus food and clothing allowances, added up to much more than a singer at Tattershall received.

The days were long and the work hard, but, within two years, Cardinal College had a first-rate reputation.

By then, though, Taverner was caught up in the conflict between Catholicism and Protestantism. Early in 1528 he was among several instructors at the college who were implicated in the circulation of Lutheran literature. He was accused of hiding a Lutheran book under the floor boards in the school. Wolsey took Taverner's involvement in stride, excusing it as the slip of a theologically unsophisticated, unlearned musician.

So the punishment for Taverner was fairly light. He had to walk in a procession while carrying a bundle of sticks as a reminder that a convicted heretic could be burned at the stake. As a final sign of repentance, Taverner and his associates were expected to throw a book into a bonfire.

Soon afterward, the fortunes of Wolsey and his school began to decline, and within a few years John Taverner had become a widower, remarried, and retired in relative comfort.

January 20th

The Experimenter

The work that made Edgar Varèse known internationally was *Amériques*. He finished it in 1921, by which time he was thirty-eight years old. What happened to all the music he wrote before it?

In 1913 Varèse and his wife were living in Berlin, and, after six years of marriage, decided to separate. She left for a theater career in Paris, leaving him to tie up some loose ends before heading to Paris and on to Prague to conduct a concert before returning to Berlin in the autumn. He put his furniture and all but two of his scores and part of his opera *Oedipus* in a warehouse.

As it turned out, he didn't get back to Berlin until 1922, by which time the Sparticist Revolution of 1919 had pitted Bolshevist workers against more moderate Socialists in violence that had included the burning down of the warehouse.

A day or so before the outbreak of World War I, Varèse had sent one of his two remaining scores to Béla Bartók, who never received it. He sent the fragment of *Oedipus* to a friend in Switzerland in 1915 on the eve of his departure for America.

The only remaining complete specimen of his early works was a piece called *Bourgogne*, which Varèse brought with him to New York.

He destroyed that one himself.

Why? The answer lies in America or, more specifically, *Amériques*.

Varèse said later that with *Amériques* he had broken through to a new style, a new idiom toward which his earlier pieces had merely hinted. "I have always been an experimenter," he said, "but my experiments always end up in the wastebasket."

In telling the story, Edgar Varèse's second wife added that the "infanticide" had taken place during a sleepless night when the composer had been depressed, and she wondered if, in more objective moments, he didn't regret destroying the last of his early efforts.

January 21st

Soloists, Choirs, and Ghosts

As the March 14 Florence debut of his opera *Macbeth* approached, Giuseppe Verdi was becoming more and more concerned about the details of its production. Impresario Antonio Lanari had written to him about some of the finer points of hiring soloists and chorus members, which began to get into personalities. On January 21, 1847, Verdi wrote back:

When you receive the music you will see that there are two choruses of paramount importance, so don't be frugal about the number of singers and you'll be happy with the result. In particular, notice that the witches are always to be divided into three groups, the best way to do it being in groups of six, six, and six, for a total of eighteen. Take special care with the tenor who is to sing the part of Macduff. Make sure that the second singers are good, too, because the ensemble needs good voices. And I am greatly concerned about these ensembles.

I can't tell you exactly when I'll be in Florence because I want to finish the opera here in peace. You can be sure that I'll arrive in time. Pass out the solo and choral parts to everyone so that when I arrive we can start with the orchestra after just two or three rehearsals...because we're going to need many orchestral and stage rehearsals.

I find it irritating that the singer who is to do Banquo doesn't want to do the ghost. Why not? Singers have to be engaged to sing and to act, and furthermore the time has passed to get rid of such leniencies. It would be an abomination for someone else to play the ghost because Banquo has to maintain exactly the same appearance when he is a ghost.

Farewell! Write to me immediately. I repeat: I plan to send you more music. In the meantime, give my regards to Romani. I'll write to him soon.

21

January 22nd

The Guide

As organist and choirmaster at St. Luke's Church in the Chelsea section of London, John Ireland was known for nurturing the talent of singers and instrumentalists who came up through the ranks. He was also known for being a fierce disciplinarian who was not above shouting expletives at erring choristers during practices.

No wonder a boy in one of Ireland's choirs was a bundle of nerves when the unthinkable occurred. In the year 1912 or so, Charles Markes was to sing a solo in a work by Mendelssohn, the fervent boy soprano plea "Oh God, hear my cry!"

When the big moment came, he opened his mouth but nothing came out. Just as he was supposed to sing, his voice had broken.

Ireland would occasionally pretend to lose his temper to make a point, but this time his wrath was real. He swept back the curtain that concealed the organist from the congregation. He wanted to know who was responsible for ruining the piece.

The boy retreated to the choir loft, weeping and afraid that he would be thrown out of the choir. Ireland embraced him and whispered, "Don't worry, Charlie. It's something that happens to all of us. Come to church just the same, come up and sit with me."

After the boy had served as a page-turner for a time, Ireland put his talent as a pianist to work and had him trained to play the organ.

Charles' debut as an organist also required additional understanding. Without warning, Ireland told the boy, "You're going to play the next Amen." The novice was so intent upon the two chords of his first public performance that he lost track of the service. At a pause in a long prayer he let forth with a loud and premature Amen.

Ireland yanked the boy's hands off the keys, declaring, "You'll get me the sack!"

But John Ireland was secure in his job, and so was the apprentice organist, who stayed at St. Luke's for many years.

January 23rd

The Salesman

Antonio Vivaldi taught at Venice's Ospedale della Pietà, an institution for orphaned or abandoned girls, but he had further ambitions, and so he also began managing the San Angelo Theater as a producer of operas.

At the same time, he was also a good salesman, and, on one occasion, he sold some music to a visitor and then made a pitch for a way to make some extra money out of it.

Johann Friedrich Armand von Uffenbach had made a big hit with Vivaldi's Opus 3 concertos in 1713 when he had introduced them to some fellow amateur musicians in Frankfurt, and, two years later, he traveled to Venice to meet their composer and found that Vivaldi was a persistent salesman.

Uffenbach went to the theater and saw an opera toward the end of which Vivaldi played a solo violin accompaniment of such virtuosity that the visitor found it frightening. Uffenbach wrote in his journal that Vivaldi "brought his fingers up to only a straw's distance from the bridge, leaving no room for the bow," and played fugues with such speed that Uffenbach was awestruck, even though he didn't particularly care for the sound of the resulting music.

In the month to follow, he attended two more operas, and left word that he would like to see Vivaldi to make a gift of some wine and buy some concerti grossi. One evening after supper, Vivaldi came over and again demonstrated the virtuosity that the German so admired, although Uffenbach thought that the slow movements weren't as lyrical as they should have been.

Three days later Vivaldi came over again, this time with ten concerti grossi that he claimed to have written just for Uffenbach. When the German bought some of them, Vivaldi offered to teach him how to play them right then and there as the first in an ongoing series of lessons.

As far as Vivaldi was concerned, music and commerce were tightly linked.

January 24th

Occupational Hazards

Clara Schumann was one of Europe's great pianists. The widow of Robert Schumann was also the closest friend of Johannes Brahms, and she wrote to him from Vienna on January 24, 1866:

The financial situation here seems to be pretty bad and yet all of the concerts are well attended. I hope mine will be too! My first one is on Saturday the 27th, the second on February 1st. I would be most grateful if you'd send me your Horn Trio, which I want to play on February 4th at Hellmesberger's. He seemed to pounce on it right away and mentioned a phenomenal hornist....

Imagine! I've had another stroke of bad luck because in Brusnwick the other day I took a tumble so bad that I could have broken every bone in my body, and it was at a concert, too, in front of an entire audience. Four temporary steps had been set against the stage because the stage and the steps weren't finished yet, and the steps weren't attached to the stage, just put there to look good.

When I had finished playing and wanted to listen to the Symphony a gentleman led me toward the aforementioned steps, but as soon as I put my foot on them the whole business collapsed with me on top. I was mortified and it was quite a while before I could get up because I had really hurt my foot. In fact I'm still feeling the effects of it and cannot walk but have to drive everywhere.

In the meantime, the sun is doing its utmost to tempt me to go out and I'm feeling rotten for lack of exercise. And yet I don't want to complain about it at all because it really was a miracle that things weren't worse.

January 25th
The Command

In the 1870s Hans von Bülow was one of Europe's great conductors and an outspoken advocate of democracy. When the Russian Musical Society asked him to direct some concerts in St. Petersburg, he found himself on a collision course with Grand Duke Constantine, president of the Russian Musical Society, the brother of the Czar.

Arriving at the Marble Palace, Bülow was presented to the grand duke by cellist Charles Davidoff and treated to a performance that included the grand duke playing the cello. Was the music less than noble or was one of his nervous headaches coming on? For whatever reason, Bülow became increasingly restless during the performance. Suddenly, without a word of explanation, he jumped from his seat, rushed out of the great hall that served as the music room, ran down the grand staircase, and fled the palace.

The grand duke took it in stride, but Davidoff was pale and stammering in his attempt to come up with an explanation. Bülow had gotten into some disagreements with the orchestra, and one of the musicians used his hasty retreat as a way to get back at him.

At dinner he told the grand duke that in rehearsal Bülow had changed a note in the clarinet part of the beloved *Russian Fantasy* of the esteemed Russian composer Mikhail Glinka. Now furious, the grand duke commanded Davidoff to tell Bülow that he was not to change a single note of Glinka's work while it was performed in Russia. At the next day's rehearsal, a nervous Davidoff conveyed the message to the conductor. Bülow burst into laughter and with mock gravity told the clarinetist to change the note back, then made an exaggerated bow to the grand duke.

It's unlikely that the rest of Hans von Bülow's Russian sojourn did much to alleviate his headaches.

January 26th
Almost Everybody Laughs about It

 In the fall of 1830, composer Frédéric Chopin left his home in Poland for a visit to Italy. When he was in Vienna he heard news of an uprising in Warsaw resisting the subservience of the Kingdom of Poland to Russia and opposing the presence of the Russian Tsar on the Polish throne. He also found that something of a musical revolution had occurred in Vienna. On January 26, 1831, Chopin wrote to a friend in Warsaw.

In all senses, the obstacles in my way are much greater now. It's not just that an ongoing series of bad pianoforte concerts has ruined that kind of music by repelling the public, but on top of that, the events in Warsaw have changed my situation, possibly as much to my disadvantage as being in Paris might have been to my advantage.

All the same, I hope that it can be brought about somehow so that my first concerto can be performed during Carnival....

As for your quartet, Joseph Czerny has guaranteed that it will be ready by St. Joseph's Day. He says that he couldn't handle it earlier because he has been publishing Schubert's works, many of which are still waiting for the press. That will probably hold up the publication of your second manuscript. Czerny seems not to be one of the rich publishers here and so can't lavish money on works that can't be played at Sperl's or Zum Römischen Kaiser.

Here they call waltzes works! And Strauss and Lanner, who play them for dancing, are known as Kapellmeisters. Not everybody thinks like that, in fact, almost everybody laughs about it, but only waltzes get printed....

Hasslinger is now publishing Hummel's last mass. He subsists entirely on Hummel, and yet the last things, for which he had to pay him a lot, are not selling well. That's why he's keeping back all manuscripts and printing only Strauss.

January 27th
Crocodile Teeth

A sojourn in Paris was necessary for an aspiring composer, but the cost of living was high, and, toward the end of 1927, Heitor Villa-Lobos was beginning to run out of money. He needed to attract more people to the concerts of his music, and he concluded that the fastest way to do it would be with some powerful publicity.

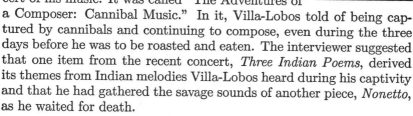

The Brazilian decided to play up his exotic origins. To critic Lucie Mardrus he gave a long interview in which he told a remarkable story.

The resulting article appeared soon after a concert of his music. It was called "The Adventures of a Composer: Cannibal Music." In it, Villa-Lobos told of being captured by cannibals and continuing to compose, even during the three days before he was to be roasted and eaten. The interviewer suggested that one item from the recent concert, *Three Indian Poems*, derived its themes from Indian melodies Villa-Lobos heard during his captivity and that he had gathered the savage sounds of another piece, *Nonetto*, as he waited for death.

Those familiar with the captivity narrative of the sixteenth-century German mariner Hans Staden found Villa-Lobos' account remarkably similar.

In printed programs, Villa-Lobos had already credited anthropologist Roquete Pinto with supplying the melodies for his music.

Nonetheless, the publicity lured plenty of Parisians to the next concerts of *le sauvage brésilien*, but the city's Brazilians found the article offensive and stayed away.

Despite the questionable validity of the article, most of those who attended the later Paris concerts of Villa-Lobos' works found that his music had genuine value and originality. Most prominent among the Brazilian's advocates was critic and composer Florent Schmitt, whose remarks gave a big boost to Villa-Lobos' international reputation.

"We see ourselves in the presence of a youth three-quarters a god," Schmitt wrote, "with teeth like a crocodile and eyes of fire... The art of Villa-Lobos is founded upon the simple native devices that his genius has assimilated marvelously."

Six days after the Hamburg debut of his First Piano Concerto, on January 28, 1859, Johannes Brahms wrote an assessment to violinist Joseph Joachim in Leipzig:

Dearest Friend: Even though I'm still quite stunned by the sublime delights that have assaulted my eyes and ears for the last few days via the sight and sound of the wise men of our musical town, I will force this hard and pointed steel pen to tell you how it happened that my concerto has been here a brilliant and decisive—failure.

First off I have to say that it was really done very well. I played far better than I did at Hanover, and the orchestra was excellent.

The first rehearsal sparked no kind of feeling either in the performers or in the audience. No audience at all came to the second, and not a performer moved a muscle of his face.

In the evening Cherubini's Elisa Overture *was performed, and then an* Ave Maria *by him was sung softly....The first and second movements of the concerto were listened to without the least manifestation of feeling. At the end three pairs of hands were brought together very slowly until an unmistakable hissing from all sides ruled out any such demonstration.*

There's nothing more to say about this episode, for not a soul has said a word to me about the work! With the exception of David, who took a great interest in it, and was very kind and went to a lot of trouble to say something about it....

This failure has made no impression whatsoever on me, and any feeling of depression I may have had evaporated when I heard Haydn's C major symphony and [Beethoven's] Ruins of Athens. *In spite of everything, the concerto will meet with approval when I have perfected its form, and the next one will be quite different.*

January 29th

Insult to Injury

Was it the crowning of the new king, George II, or something in the air that made London audiences tire of Italian music, operas in particular, in 1727? Whatever it was, George Frederick Handel pressed on in spite of it and continued to produce operas until he and his backers ran out of money. As receipts dwindled, the quality of the audiences fell, too. After competing sopranos got into a fistfight during a performance of Handel's *Astinatte*, genteel theater-goers retreated at the first sign of trouble, leaving the theater to those whose pleasure in music was second to their enjoyment of a good brawl.

During Handel's *Richard I* the offending sopranos behaved themselves, but the opera closed after only eleven nights. He tried again with *Siroe, King of Persia*, much of it recycled from an opera he had written twenty years earlier.

It never stood a chance against a new unstoppable force.

The competition was an entertainment called *The Beggar's Opera* and Londoners got their first look at it on January 29, 1728. John Gay's play was a clever satire based on Jonathan Swift's suggestion of a comedy based on the story of London's criminal underclass. It made fun of Italian opera by using ordinary street-wise characters and replacing grand musical themes with popular tunes adapted by Johann Pepusch. The show was outrageous and it was lewd; it drew London audiences in such droves that it threw the city into a carnival mood.

Handel's new opera opened three weeks after the debut of *The Beggar's Opera* It had a wonderful libretto and a sensational cross-dressing role for its lead soprano. After nineteen nights, it folded.

The hot-tempered Handel no doubt went livid when he heard one hit tune from *The Beggar's Opera*. The rousing song of the highwaymen, "Let us take the road," was a standout. And Pepusch had stolen it note for note from Handel's opera *Rinaldo*.

January 30th
An Irresistible Force

 Johann Strauss the Elder and his orchestra had come to London to perform for the coronation of Queen Victoria, but before playing a note, he had been hauled into court over a dispute with an unprincipled hotel proprietor. He won the case, but Strauss was compelled to pay the court costs, which was no easy feat since his valet had meanwhile absconded with all of Strauss' cash.

Strauss had no alternative but to sell some of his new pieces to a London publisher.

Even as his prospects improved, his experiences were mixed. At the Russian embassy, he and his musicians were required to scale a ladder, instruments in hand, in order to reach a second-floor ballroom without rubbing elbows with the guests. But at a ball given by Austrian Prince Schwarzenberg, the prince and the Austrian ambassador linked arms with Strauss and proceeded as a threesome for the entire length of the grand ballroom.

After Victoria's coronation, during which the Strauss orchestra performed eight concerts for the queen and sixty-four other concerts for various public and private occasions, Strauss dragged his flagging musicians back and forth across the country for still more performances that spent almost as much money as they took in.

One day, as summer gave way to fall, the orchestra flatly refused to do one more concert. They wanted to return to Vienna. Somehow Strauss convinced them to go on, even as English dampness wracked instruments and English cuisine knotted stomachs. Travel became a cold, wet, jarring ordeal.

It was no wonder that everyone fell ill, Strauss most dramatically of all. En route back to Vienna, during a concert in France, he collapsed after the third piece of music.

In Paris, doctors told him to stop the concerts at once and return to Vienna to recuperate. Despite his arguments, the orchestra disbanded, leaving the stricken leader to ponder his future. When he returned to Vienna, how would he react to the discovery that his young son was planning a musical career?

That story next.

January 31st
The Next Generation

After a grueling concert tour of Great Britain, Johann Strauss had faced a rebellious orchestra and suffered a physical breakdown. After his return to Vienna to recuperate in the winter of 1839, his shattered health and tattered finances gave him no alternative but to lie in his sickbed and hope to recuperate.

One afternoon he heard violin music coming from another room in the apartment. He left his bed and quietly made his way to the sound, a waltz. He eased the door open and watched silently as his fourteen-year-old son Johann fiddled in front of a mirror, giving his performance all the body language that he himself indulged in as he led his band.

Only grudgingly had the father agreed to let his sons take any music lessons at all—on the piano—an instrument suitable for a young man destined to become a banker.

Meanwhile, the son had borrowed one of the father's discarded violins and begun taking secret lessons on it, lessons given by one of the best string players in the father's band.

As young Johann finished his performance and bowed to the acclaim of an imaginary audience, the elder Strauss, boiling over with rage, rushed into the room, snatched the violin from his startled son, and smashed it on the floor.

And the money for the lessons? Where had that come from, Strauss the Elder demanded.

The boy had earned a little cash by giving piano lessons to a neighbor's daughter.

It was a little too ingenious for the father to resist entirely. Both Johann and his younger brother Josef had already shown their musical ingenuity, playing piano four-hand versions of their father's waltzes.

But music for fun was one thing. Becoming the leader of a dance band was something else; and Father Strauss became all the more adamant that the boy would halt all plans for a musical career and become apprenticed to a banker.

The next day, with the help of his mother, Johann Strauss the Younger, the future Waltz King, secretly appropriated another of his father's violins.

31

February 1st

The Good Times Roll

It was as if Parisians were determined to put the bad times behind them with parties that would drown out the noise of the past. The bloody labor revolt of 1848 had brought in a Second Republic opposed to most reforms. A presidential election had brought in Louis-Napoleon Bonaparte, nephew of the late Emperor, who, not content to be president, had proclaimed himself emperor in 1851. With him came reforms that knocked down much of Paris for the sake of modernization. And as the 1850s progressed, opera composer Jacques Offenbach partied with the best of them, yet never forgot his purpose.

Thanks to growing royalties, he was prospering, and he threw parties that matched his rising station in life, parties that were the talk of Paris. With Gallic drollness, a crowded soiree in February 1857 celebrated the "imminent end of the world." Fellow composer Léo Delibes was so caught up in the merriment that he danced a solo polka. A month later, Offenbach threw an elegant ball that featured a theatrical about a child laborer in which Offenbach had the lead role, famed librettist Ludovic Halévy played the part of a page, and the accompanying pianist was up-and-coming composer Georges Bizet. Friday night revels became a routine chez Offenbach.

And after opening night for every Offenbach opera came more gatherings. In the tradition of French royal dinners, they were known as *Les soupers de Jacques*.

They were not as frivolous as they seemed, though, because Offenbach was one of those composers who thrived on distraction.

Stimulated by all the chattering and laughter, he would take on a faraway look and begin writing music.

During his customary lunches at the Restaurant Peters, as he enjoyed a cigar, an omelet, a cutlet, and a cup of coffee, he took in the talk of his journalist friends and found it as much a catalyst as the goings-on backstage at the theater.

He had his limits though. When the restaurant manager brought in a diversion in the form of a trained bear, Offenbach absented himself from his haunt until the ursine interloper had moved on to another venue.

February 2nd

Pianist on Ice

As the winter of 1893-94 set in, the young Russian pianist and composer Alexander Scriabin was miserable. A year earlier, he was to have undertaken a concert tour, but recurrent pain in his right hand had forced him to cancel. Doctors had prescribed a quiet sojourn in a hot southern climate, a slightly intoxicating drink of fermented camel's milk, and swimming in the Black Sea.

From his sanatorium on the Volga, Scriabin had written to the object of his affections, sixteen-year-old Natalya Sekerina. His letters included a somewhat envious reference to a violinist suffering from hand pain who had gone to Paris for the latest treatments—hypnotism, electric therapy, and massage.

Despite the respite in the south, by the end of 1893, Scriabin's hand was worse than ever. The pain had spread from his fingers up his arm.

When Natalya and her sister met Scriabin for a symphony concert, she found him changed beyond recognition and distracted by his ailment.

When Natalya's piano teacher died, Scriabin asked to take over the lessons, but, not surprisingly, the girl's mother chose someone else.

Maintaining a relationship through music became difficult. Natalya and her sister met Scriabin for a concert, and when a young physics professor joined them in the foyer of the hall, Scriabin "ran around and rubbed his hands together" in an effort to stop any conversation between Natalya and the newcomer. Well ahead of time, he escorted the girls back to their seats.

When Scriabin and the sisters attended the Moscow debut of pianist Józef Hofmann, Natalya was quite impressed, much to Scriabin's displeasure. He refused to let the sisters meet the virtuoso, but Hofmann was an excellent skater, and when Scriabin and the sisters encountered him at a local rink, a mutual friend introduced Natalya to Hofmann, and she and the great pianist sailed around the ice in cheerful conversation while Scriabin winced every time Hofmann paid her a compliment.

February 3rd
Pay It Forward

One day in 1962 world renowned violinist Isaac Stern was at the Paris workshop of celebrated lute maker Etienne Vatelot, a good friend who had written him a letter about a Chinese family of his acquaintance. Vatelot said to Stern, "They have this young boy, about six, seven years old. You should hear him. He's unbelievable."

Arrangements were made for Stern to hear the Paris-born boy perform. His name was Yo-Yo Ma and his cello looked bigger than he was. Stern recalled that hearing the boy play left him "astonished, truly astonished."

When Ma and his family emigrated to the United States, Stern asked the great American cellist Leonard Rose to listen to Ma play, and Rose was fast to take him on as a student. During his studies with Rose, Ma learned important lessons about performing, bow-arm technique, and practice habits. Stern listened to him again and got high-powered artist manager Sol Hurok to sign him up.

In 1977, with violinist Shlomo Mintz and pianist Yefim Bronfman, Ma played the Beethoven Triple Concerto with the New York Youth Orchestra in Carnegie Hall. Years later Stern still remembered the cellist's "turn of phrase and mastery of his instrument that were unsurpassed then or now, and an instantaneous and infectious communicativeness with his audience." He recalled that musicians in the audience would "turn around and smile with delight at one another as they heard the phrases flow forth with beauty and ease from his cello."

After the performance, Stern thought back forty years to a favor the great conductor Pierre Monteux had done for him. He wrote letters to five major conductors asking them to consider inviting Yo-Yo Ma to play as a soloist. All five did invite him, and after the first rehearsal, all five signed Yo-Yo Ma for a return engagement.

Isaac Stern tells the story in his 1999 autobiography *My First 79 Years*.

February 4th
Charisma

James William Davison, music critic for *The Times* of London, was known for his caustic dismissals of celebrated composers and performers.

But when the charismatic young pianist Arabella Goddard came to his attention, Davison changed his tune. At the age of four-and-a-half, the French-born daughter of English parents had played a fantasia at a charity concert. It was said that at seven she played for Chopin in Paris, and, at age eight, for Queen Victoria and Prince Albert.

Arabella was fourteen when she was playing a piece by Mendelssohn and had a memory lapse. She signaled the concert manager to bring her a copy of the music, but he gestured for her to start again from the beginning. At the same point in the piece her memory failed her again, and this time the manager brought her the music. Paying little attention to it, she played the piece with such speed and precision that the often acerbic Davison was more than forgiving:

An anxious desire to take the piece at the tempo indicated by the composer—which she and few beside her can do—and the nervousness naturally consequent thereon were no doubt the cause of her forgetfulness.

He also devoted 2,500 words to her review—twice what he allotted to a performance by an established pianist. He attended all of her performances and invariably gave her rave reviews, describing her physical attributes as well as her musicianship. He wrote that "although she is entirely unassuming, she could not fail to win the most casual observer at a glance."

Arabella's teacher, virtuoso Sigismond Thalberg, turned her over to Davison for further career guidance, and, in 1859, Arabella, age twenty-one, and Davison, twenty-four years her senior, were married.

The union quickly became superficial. Arabella spent years touring the world, making vast sums from her concerts, and becoming known as one of the great pianists of the late nineteenth century. Davison, in the meantime, had long since moved in with his brother.

February 5th

Lost in Translation

As an established concert pianist, Cyril Smith was accustomed to overcoming the routine obstacles that inevitably arose during performances in England. In 1937 he was invited by the British Consul to undertake a six-week swing through Denmark, Sweden, Austria, Hungary, Czechoslovakia, Yugoslavia, and Romania. With the honor of his first tour of the Continent came the responsibility of representing all British musicians, which became a challenge when he encountered a remarkable piano.

By the time he arrived in the Romanian city of Cernauti, winter cold had set in with a vengeance. The piano he was to play was kept in an unheated room in a music shop, tuned just before the concert, and then brought into the warmth of the opera house. When Smith began playing, it became apparent that an hour or two of heat had stretched the strings enough to drop the pitch three semitones. The first piece was in C major, but sounded like A major.

The result was what Smith termed "an agonizing evening."

The last piece on the program was a polonaise by contemporary composer Arthur Bliss, and Smith recalled that "this very modern composition sounded like nothing on earth on my flat piano." The performance was not the desired representation of British music and musicians.

When the end of the concert finally came, the entire audience stood up and hissed.

Smith beat a retreat to the exit, but in the wings somebody intercepted him and pushed him back onto the stage. Even though he sympathized with the displeased crowd, or mob as it now seemed to be, Smith said that he had no desire to go back out and face them again. Then someone explained that the audience wasn't hissing, but shouting "Bis!" by which they meant "Encore!" So with mixed emotions, Smith returned to do battle with the piano again.

Cyril Smith tells the story in his 1958 reminiscence *Duet for Three Hands*.

February 6th
The Rift

The great philosopher was a champion of the great composer until one of them tried to enter the field of the other.

That's the way conductor Hans Richter told the young pianist Ernst von Dohnányi about the rift between Richard Wagner and Friedrich Nietzsche. According to Richter, who was a close friend of the Wagner family, the relationship came to grief with bad music and hurt feelings.

Nietzsche had long been an outspoken admirer of Wagner, and was a frequent visitor to the Wagner home. One day he arrived with a manuscript—a composition of his own, a work for piano duet. Richter and Wagner's wife Cosima obligingly played the work as Wagner sat back in his armchair to listen. As Nietzsche's work unfolded, Wagner's face became more and more grim, and eventually he looked just plain tired. Then, according to the story, Wagner's servant, either reading Wagner's face or drawing from his own knowledge of music, whispered to Wagner in a Bavarian accent, "Herr Wagner, this doesn't seem good to me."

Wagner burst into laughter, and the offended Nietzsche left the house, never to return.

The philosopher's eventual response to the incident was an essay, *The Wagner Case: A Musician's Problem,* published in 1888. "Perhaps nobody was more dangerously connected to or stuck together with Wagnerizing," Nietzsche began. "Nobody tried harder to resist it, nobody was happier to get rid of it."

"Wagner's art is sick," Nietzsche continued. "The problems he presents on the stage are all problems of hysteria—his overwrought effects, his overexcited sensibility, his taste that required ever stronger spices, his instability which he disguised as principles."

Wagner was unable to get in the last word because he died in 1883, and the rift between composer and aspiring composer remained unmended.

February 7th

The Vocal Critic

Casting an opera for the stage and casting it for the movies can be quite different, as was proved by a notable blunder at RCA.

In his 1976 autobiography *Cadenza: A Musical Career* longtime Boston Symphony conductor Erich Leinsdorf tells of recording sessions in Rome in the late 1950s. For a production of Puccini's *Tosca* RCA executive George Marek had cast three of the great singers of the day— Zinka Milanov, Jussi Björling, and Leonard Warren. But for *Madama Butterfly* Marek decided to cast Anna Moffo and Cesare Valletti in the roles of the lovers Cio-Cio San and Lieutenant Pinkerton—two genuinely young attractive singers—instead of what Leinsdorf called the usual "middle-aged, overweight verbal acrobats."

Marek and his associates at RCA were convinced that a few of their singers would accomplish a breakthrough in the movies and become superstars. Apparently they had forgotten that people buy recordings not to look at but to listen to. Pretty faces notwithstanding, the voices of the attractive young singers were too light for the roles.

During one of the recording sessions Leinsdorf, the producer, and the singers were in the control room listening to a playback of the great love duet at the end of Act I when Leinsdorf became aware of a very drunk Jussi Björling at his ear, singing the tenor part the way he thought it should be sung, interspersing his performance with a blistering critique of the recording. For the sake of the singers, the perspiring and embarrassed Leinsdorf tried to quiet the indignant Björling only to make him all the more vocal in his demonstration of the tenor part and his condemnation of the casting.

The intoxicated tenor knew what he was talking and singing about. The album couldn't compete with the *Madama Butterfly* recordings on other labels, and in 1962 RCA tried again with seasoned operatic heavyweights Leontyne Price and Richard Tucker.

February 8th

Condemned!

The premise for the opera was unusual to say the least. The libretto by Gertrude Stein consisted of apparently random sentences and phrases that Virgil Thomson had set to distinctively American music.

As the unconventional *Four Saints in Three Acts* approached its February 8, 1934, debut in Hartford, it began to look like a miracle would be required to get it off the ground.

Since the opera required the illusion of open sky, the set designer had the low ceiling of the stage in the small theater draped in 1500 square feet of looped cellophane. The frustrated lighting designer told her in blunt terms how difficult it was to light, but she refused to listen. She, in turn, had concerns that the skin color of the black performers would clash with her stage and costume colors.

In order to keep their discussions private, Thomson, director John Houseman, and choreographer Frederick Ashton occasionally resorted to conversing in French.

Annoyed by mistakes in the score, hot-tempered conductor Alexander Smallens shouted at Ashton, who stalked out of the theater, but came back as soon as he discovered that the outside temperature was fifteen below zero.

Opening night turned out so well that, two weeks later, the opera went to the 1,400-seat Forty-Fourth Street Theater for a four-week Broadway run.

But just fifty hours before curtain time, a New York City fire marshal put a stop to everything when he cut a strip of the cellophane, lit a match to it, and condemned the set.

A young man from the theater staff suggested coating the entire set and all of the props with a new fire-resistant chemical called water glass. Everything onstage drooped and rich colors paled beneath a thick swath of smelly goo that baked under the bright lights, but the show went on, even as little globs of baked water glass fell to the stage with a sound like falling rain.

February 9th

A Dishonest Teacher

In his 1969 memoirs, English composer Cyril Scott thought back seventy-eight years to a piano teacher who did him a great disservice, and yet played an important part in the development of his career.

When he was twelve years old, Scott and his sister got a new piano teacher. She was not a dishonest person, Scott recalled, but she was a dishonest teacher.

Scott had begun to play the piano before he was old enough to talk, and had long since developed his own haphazard ideas about technique. Had the new teacher been honest, Scott reflected, she would have made him go through the rigors of five-finger exercises for three months, during which he would be forbidden to play anything else on the piano. That was the only approach that would have enabled him to strengthen his fingers and get rid of bad habits.

Instead, she let him go on playing as he had been, when both of them knew that he was only making a show of playing well and would never improve if he went on that way.

So it went for two years. Then Scott had the first great pianistic experience of his life.

His teacher persuaded Scott's mother to let him go to nearby Liverpool for a Sunday afternoon concert by the famous Ignacy Jan Paderewski. The virtuoso was at the height of his powers, and he played with such effect that Scott resolved at once to become a musician. He emulated his new idol, right down to the mop-haired look that was the Polish pianist's trademark.

Within a year, studies in Germany began to mold him into one of the most original writers of twentieth century music.

So while Cyril Scott's teacher didn't make him a great pianist after two years of lessons, during a single concert, she did set him on the path to becoming one of England's great composers.

February 10th

The Fragrant Faust

The producers of Charles Gounod's opera *Faust* had their work cut out for them. The opera had not done so well at its Paris debut in 1859, and now a Hanover premiere was in the works. Although many in the city and the surrounding countryside were excited about the upcoming performance, several newspaper editors expressed suspicion about a  French composer daring to set Goethe's German masterpiece to music, especially since several German composers had failed.

The cast included excellent singers, but the stage manager came up with one special effect that would make this production of *Faust* memorable for everyone in the audience, including King George of Hanover, who was blind.

During the third act, Siebel, a young man in love with Marguerite, is gathering flowers in her garden and asks them to carry his message of love, but, cursed by Mephistopheles, the flowers wither in his hands. Siebel runs to a nearby shrine and dips his hands in holy water, and the flowers he picks now remain fresh.

As the curtain rose on Act III of the Hanover performance, the fragrance of flowers wafted from the stage and filled the entire theater. Attending that night was violinist Leopold Auer, who recalled the impact many years later:

The effect of this faint breeze of fragrance was magical. Throughout the love duo, the artificial flowers on the stage, bound by Mephisto's spell and obeying his command, thus intoxicated not only the lovers but the entire audience as well. This scene assured the success of the work. I have often wondered why so natural and charming an effect has not been employed in other similar scenes—in the balcony scene of Romeo and Juliet *, which takes place in the garden of the Capulets, for instance, or in the second act of* Parsifal *, where the Flower-Maidens dance in Klingsor's enchanted gardens.*

But maybe the fragrant special effect had a charm as ephemeral as the flowers in Gounod's *Faust*.

February 11th

Bad Omens

In June of 1840 the director of the Apollo Theater in Rome invited Gaetano Donizetti to compose an opera for the coming season. Apparently the project was doomed from the start.

For his story Donizetti chose an old libretto, *Adelia, or the Archer's Daughter*, which had been used by several other composers without much success. To suit Roman tastes a new librettist was brought in to provide a happy ending. Donizetti didn't care for the composite result, but he set aside his doubts and put it to music.

The omens were not favorable. First there was the false rumor that the Pope had died, which raised fears that the theaters would close until the election of a new Pontiff. Then there was the abortive storm-wracked voyage from Marseilles to Rome that delayed Donizetti's arrival for several days, and, once he got to Rome, the Tiber River flooding that threatened the theater.

By the time Donizetti's opera was finally scheduled, theatergoers were more than ready for it.

When the big debut came on February 11, 1841, it was a fiasco.

Tickets for the opera were such a hot item that the theater management oversold the house. Of those who managed to get in, few could hear the performance over the racket from those who couldn't. The rattled singers were reluctant to go on.

The conductor stopped the orchestra until the furor died down, only to have chaos break out again when fistfights erupted among the box-holders because a hot-tempered young man overheard insults aimed at the theater directors, one of whom was his uncle.

During the goings-on, the theater director was arrested and carted off to jail along with the cashbox.

When the ruckus had died down, allowing the opera a fair hearing, the verdict was that *Adelia* was a forced marriage of uninspired music and a lame libretto, and Donizetti blamed himself for overriding his better judgment to write it.

February 12th

There Is Just One King!

On a bitingly cold morning on February 12, 1877, an orchestra of professional and amateur players waited in the dining room of the royal palace in Christiania. They were less than enthusiastic about the invitation to perform for Norway's King Oscar II.

The king had recently heard about the success of the *Symphony No. 2 in B-flat* of Johan Svendsen, and had invited the composer to give a concert of his works for a few invited guests at the palace.

Dressed in white ties and tails, the shivering musicians gathered in the empty dining room where they were to perform. There was no orchestra platform, only a bare floor with a distant semi-circle of elegant chairs. The most seasoned of the orchestra members were particularly unimpressed.

On the verge of the king's entrance, Svendsen had a morale problem on his hands.

He jumped onto the cloth-covered conductor's podium and announced, "Gentlemen, when the royal entourage enters this room, there is just one king—and that is—me."

"There were sparks in his eyes," recalled one of the players, "and that caused sparks in our minds as well."

As a result, the orchestra greeted Oscar and his circle with a particularly rousing rendition of the *Coronation March*.

The program continued with Svendsen's Second Symphony and a more rustic Norwegian offering, the orchestral song *Last Year I Was Tending the Goats.*

During the symphony, in the tradition of royalty, Oscar walked around the room talking with his guests as they drank chocolate and ate cakes.

But apparently he was listening to the music. After the concert, he approached Svendsen and said, "Maestro, I consider you one of the greatest composers in the world. I was thinking about giving you the Royal Vasa Order, but everyone who has a medal has that one. You deserve a more distinguished medal, and so I hereby confer upon you Oscar II's Medal of Honor in gold."

Johan Svendsen was the first musician to receive it.

43

February 13th

I Have No Time!

When Wolfgang Amadeus Mozart's sister Nannerl chided him for not writing more often, he sent her a reply that explained where all his time had gone. He wrote on February 13, 1782:

Our father, when he has finished his duties in church, and you, when you're through with your students, can do whatever you want for the rest of the day and write letters containing complete litanies. But not so with me. I described my routine to my father the other day and I'll repeat it to you.

My hair is always done by six o'clock in the morning, and by seven I'm fully dressed. Then I compose until nine. From nine to one I give lessons. Then I have lunch unless I'm invited to some house where they have lunch at two or even three o'clock....I can never work before five or six o'clock in the evening, and even then I'm often kept from it by a concert. If I'm not kept from it, I compose until nine.

Then I go to my dear Constanze, although the joy of seeing each other is often ruined by her mother's snide remarks. I'll explain that in my next letter to my father because that's the reason that I'm yearning to liberate her and rescue her as soon as possible.

At half past ten or eleven I come home, depending upon her mother's darts and my ability to put up with them! Since I can't rely upon being able to compose in the evening...I make a habit, especially if I get home early, to compose a little before I go to bed, but I often go on writing until one—and I'm up again at six.

44

February 14th

Lover or Priest?

The lover or the priest? An incident from early in the life of Franz Liszt suggests that even as a teenager he had the impulses of both.

By the age of sixteen Liszt had long since made a name for himself as one of Europe's great pianists. In Paris he gave lessons to members of aristocratic families, among them Caroline de Saint-Cricq the seventeen-year-old daughter of a count who was finance minister for King Charles X.

The lessons were chaperoned by Caroline's mother, who, in her way, was apparently as charmed by Liszt as Caroline was. The Countess seems to have fanned the couple's hopes to become engaged.

Then she died.

After an emotional reunion at the Countesses' funeral, Liszt went to see Caroline just about every day. They had long conversations about poetry, religion, and music. On one occasion they talked past midnight, forcing Liszt to ask the hall porter to unlock the door to the street.

Unaware that discretion came with a price, Liszt neglected to tip the servant, and the next time he came to the house, the Count was waiting for him.

He reminded Liszt that a mere pianist was no prospect for the daughter of a Count, ended the lessons, and showed Liszt the door.

The distraught Caroline fell sick and spoke of becoming a nun, but finally agreed to marry the son of a wealthy government minister.

Liszt suffered a nervous breakdown and begged to enter a Paris seminary in order to become a priest, but his mother and a spiritual advisor talked him out of it.

Liszt and Caroline never got over each other. During a chance encounter sixteen years later, they reminisced about their broken love affair.

And in his will Liszt left her a signet ring, but since she died in 1872, fourteen years before he did, Caroline never knew about the token of his lifelong affection for her.

February 15th
Oops!

Many a performer has been forced to cancel a concert when the rigors of an intensive schedule led to a physical or emotional breakdown. Occasionally a concert goes awry because of a smaller problem—simple confusion.

Consider a news item in *The Philadelphia Inquirer* regarding the case of Thomas Zehetmair, who was slated to play *Mozart's Violin Concerto No. 4* with the Philadelphia Orchestra on February 15, 2002. Zehetmair allowed himself plenty of time to relax during the afternoon on the day of the eight o'clock concert. Just before two o'clock, he left his hotel room and went for a walk. Somewhere along the way, he had a look at a newspaper and discovered that the concert was not at eight in the evening, but two in the afternoon. At that very moment, 2,500 people were at the Kimmel Center's Verizon Hall waiting for him to perform.

The horrified violinist dashed to his room, threw on his concert attire, and ran to the concert hall, arriving at 2:20 or so to find that the orchestra had just launched into the only other work on the program— the Third Symphony of Reinhold Glière—an eighty-minute musical epic that left no time to tack the Mozart concerto at the end of the delayed concert.

Zehetmair voiced his dismay. "I am very miserable," he said. "I have been performing for twenty-four years or something, and it's really the first time this has happened."

Some audience members were similarly taken aback. One recalled that in sixty years of concerts the only times that performances had failed to go through had to do with a presidential assassination and the discovery of cracked beams in the roof of the concert hall.

Fortunately Thomas Zehetmair did not have to wait long to redeem himself. Of a repeat concert scheduled for the following night—at eight o'clock—he said, "I will certainly be there on time." And he was.

February 16th

Top Notes

In his memoirs Ignacy Jan Paderewski tells of a concert during which he learned a hard lesson about showmanship.

In 1890 Paderewski was making a name for himself as one of Europe's leading pianists, but he discovered that when it came to exciting audiences, a performer needed more than musicianship. After successful performances in Paris, he was in the city of Tours participating in a concert in which he shared the billing with two singers and an actor, an arrangement that required Paderewski to regenerate his concentration and energy during the long intervals between his performances.

A lady singer began the concert, and then a popular actor did a comic monologue that revved up the audience. Next a tenor sang; a mediocre tenor who nonetheless had some impressive high notes that charged up the hall all the more.

Then came Paderewski. He played a Chopin nocturne. He played it very well, but it was a subtle piece, without the thrill of top notes.

"Nobody listened to me," he recalled. "Nobody!"

The lady singer returned and wowed the crowd with trills and cadenzas. Then the actor came back out and repeated his success. The tenor followed, so-so as ever, but with more top notes that drove the audience wild.

After which it was time again for Paderewski, who was to play a series of short solos. In the wake of the excitement, the audience not only did not listen, they talked over his playing. The pianist's only thought was to get through the concert and take the next train out of town.

Backstage, his fellow artists expressed their condolences to Paderewski for his failure. A local resident expressed his outrage at the barbarism of the audience, and, for years to come, attended every one of Paderewski's Paris recitals, after which he greeted the acclaimed pianist with the words, "Well, my friend, this is a little different from Tours, is it not?"

February 17th

Sticking with It

At the age of twelve, Daniel Barenboim was a poised, accomplished pianist with three years of major concerts to his credit. In the summer of 1955, he was taking a conducting class at the Salzburg Mozarteum. The school had brought in a series of guest teachers, conductors who were working at the Salzburg Festival, each of whom would instruct the class for a day.

Among the guest teachers was the formidable George Szell, long-time conductor of the Cleveland Orchestra, who had been given credit for building it into what one critic called "the world's keenest symphonic instrument."

Young Barenboim had met Szell a year earlier, auditioning successfully for him as a pianist. But now the boy was on the spot. On the day that the stern and strict Szell was to teach the class, it was Barenboim's turn to conduct.

Szell was known to enjoy putting musicians into difficult situations to see how they would cope.

He was skeptical when he saw the young pianist. "What are you going to conduct?" he asked.

"Well," Barenboim said, "I have prepared Beethoven's Fourth Symphony." It was one of the works the class had been assigned.

Szell tightened the screws. "I want to see what you will do with the Fifth Symphony," he said.

Even at the age of twelve, Barenboim knew that keeping the orchestra together for the beginning of the Fifth Symphony was a terror for most conductors.

Bravely, he began to lead the orchestra. Very quickly, the whole performance fell apart. With pointed words, Szell advised Barenboim to stick with the piano and become a serious musician.

But Barenboim stuck with conducting, and, thirteen years later, as he was to lead the London Symphony in Carnegie Hall, he was told that Szell was in the audience. The strict lesson for a twelve-year-old paid off. Szell, who was now its Music Advisor, invited Barenboim to become the ongoing conductor of the New York Philharmonic.

February 18th
A Close Shave for the Barber

Giovanni Paisiello had crafted a popular opera from a play by Beaumarchais in 1782, but in 1816 Gioachino Rossini went ahead and wrote his own version of *The Barber of Seville.* Some Roman opera-goers were partial to the Paisiello and considered young Rossini an upstart for thinking he could improve upon it. The name change to *Almaviva* fooled none of the Paisiello followers, who saw at once that this was a reworking of their old favorite.

But on the night of February 20, 1816, when the curtain rose for the first performance, no one could have predicted all that would go wrong with Rossini's opera.

Tenor Manuel Garcia as Count Almaviva broke with convention when he chose to serenade Rosina, not with anything by Rossini, but with a pastiche based on Spanish love songs. And when soprano Geltrude Righetti-Giorgi as Rosina, instead of launching into an entrance aria, merely said to him, "Go on, dear, go on like that," the audience began to express its dissatisfaction. With whistles and shouts, they drowned out the now famous Largo al factotum and the duet between Figaro the barber and the Count.

When bass Zenobio Vitarelli came on as music teacher Don Basilio, he tripped on a trapdoor and cut his face so badly that he nearly broke his nose. He was unable to sing his aria "La calumnia," but by then the audience was out of the mood to hear it anyway.

During the finale a cat wandered onstage and Luigi Zamboni, as Figaro, chased it off, only to have it reappear on the other side of the stage, where it threw itself at bass Bartolommeo Botticelli, who until then had been singing the part of Dr. Bartolo. Mezzo-soprano Elisabetta Loyselet, as Berta the maid, jumped around the stage in an effort to avoid the ferocious feline while the audience cheered it on with a chorus of meowing.

The second performance would stir up just as much pandemonium, and we'll find out about it next time.

February 19th
Broken Windows

On February 20, 1816, a combination of miscalculations and mishaps had brought about a disastrous debut for Rossini's opera *The Barber of Seville.* At the end of the contentious first act, Rossini sat at the piano and applauded the singers, but some in the audience thought he was praising his own opera, which made them all the more volatile.

Then there was the matter of the next night's performance.

On the day after the debut, Rossini and alto Geltrude Righetti-Giorgi sat down and went over the score, and he took out some of the things that he thought the audience had good reason to dislike.

Rossini is said to have stated that for the second performance he decided to stay in his apartment, although he admitted that he couldn't help taking out his watch at curtain time and singing the overture and the first act. When he couldn't stand the suspense any longer, he pulled on his clothes and was on his way out the door when he heard a racket in the street.

According to another account, when Rossini saw that the crowd was carrying torches, he was afraid that they were coming to burn down his apartment house. He slipped outside and hid in a stable, where tenor Manuel Garcia found him and assured him that the opera had been a great success and that the crowd was eager to congratulate him.

The nervous Rossini expressed his scorn for the crowd in such blunt language that Garcia couldn't convey the message in tactful terms and became the target of a fast-flying orange that gave him a black eye. Rossini's landlord showed up, imploring him to speak to the crowd because they were threatening to burn the house down.

After breaking two windows, the crowd finally dispersed and the frazzled composer climbed back into bed, hoping for the time being to forget the frightening second night success of *The Barber of Seville.*

February 20th

The Portent

Because it was politically sensitive, Giuseppe Verdi's new opera *Un ballo in maschera* made the Italian censors nervous. They forced Verdi to change the action to someplace farther from home.

He chose seventeenth-century Boston. The King of Sweden became the Governor of Boston.

When *Un ballo in maschera* came to the United States in 1861, it was quite the rage despite some absurdities, such as Puritans holding a masked ball.

When the opera played at the Academy of Music in New York on February 20, 1861, its audience included President-elect Abraham Lincoln, who was en route from Springfield, Illinois, via Albany and New York to Washington, where he was to be inaugurated as president two weeks later.

It was the first opera Lincoln had attended, and he would become an ardent opera-lover, but he had come to the theater tired and concerned that his presence would detract from the performance.

During the first intermission, he was recognized and received a standing ovation, after which the curtain rose for a rendition of "The Star-Spangled Banner." Isabella Hinkley, the soprano playing the part of Oscar the page, sang the anthem's first stanza half-turned toward Lincoln's second-tier stage box. Then the entire company joined in, while a huge American flag, resplendent with thirty-three stars, dropped from the proscenium.

Adelaide Phillips, who was playing Ulrica the fortune-teller, took up the second verse to vigorous applause. Then came "Hail, Columbia," more cheering, and the continuation of the opera.

During the second intermission Lincoln left the opera and went back to his hotel. Despite his early departure, he was hooked on operas and went on to see eighteen more of them during his time as president, perhaps more than any other Chief Executive.

But he never saw the most controversial scene in *Un ballo in maschera,* the one in which Verdi had accommodated the Italian censors by changing the murder of a European monarch to the assassination of an American head of state.

51

As a student at the Paris Conservatory, Hector Berlioz had experienced at least one run-in with its feisty director, Luigi Cherubini. In his autobiography, Berlioz tells of a second encounter.

He had applied for a professorship of harmony at the Conservatory and received word that Cherubini wanted to see him.

Cherubini explained that Berlioz would surely get the position, but that he had someone else in mind for it.

Berlioz offered to withdraw his application.

"No, no, that is not good," Cherubini said, "because, you see, people would say that I was the cause of your withdrawing."

"Then I'll remain a candidate."

"But I tell you, you'll get the position if you do, and I did not intend for you to."

Berlioz was at a loss. "Then what are we to do?"

Cherubini asked if Berlioz knew that it was necessary to be a pianist to teach at the Conservatory. Not taking himself to be a particularly good player, Berlioz got the hint and offered to withdraw his candidacy on the grounds that he wasn't a pianist.

"Exactly, my dear fellow," said Cherubini. "But I am not the cause of your—"

"No, no, certainly not," Berlioz agreed. "Of course, I have to withdraw. It was stupid of me to forget that only pianists can teach harmony at the Conservatory."

"Precisely, my dear fellow. Now embrace me. You know how fond I am of you."

"Oh, yes. I know."

Cherubini embraced Berlioz "with an almost paternal tenderness" and Berlioz went off and wrote his letter of withdrawal. A week later, Cherubini awarded the position to a certain Bienaimé, of whom Berlioz said, "He was no more a pianist than I am."

It was a neatly executed trick, Berlioz said, and he was the first to get a good laugh out of it, since he was well aware that the director of the Conservatory, the great Cherubini, was himself no pianist.

February 22nd
A Revolutionary Wedding

In the politically charged year of 1848 César Franck was a twenty-five-year-old pianist and composer living in Paris. When his father took him to task for wasting his time dedicating a song to one of his female students, he and his father exchanged harsh words and his father retaliated by tearing the manuscript to pieces.

Franck flew into a rage and declared his intention to move out and marry the student and leave the family to support itself—a scary prospect for his indolent father. The elder Franck alternately threatened and pleaded. He flaunted the name of a notorious wife-murderer, suggesting that Franck would end up like him.

Not long afterward, while the rest of the family was taking a walk, Franck packed his bags and departed, leaving a note saying that he would pay off an 11,000-franc debt his father owed. He moved in with the student and her actor parents. Their house was familiar to him since his prospective mother-in-law had been allowing him to compose there, in defiance of his father's wishes.

Franck and Félicité Saillot planned their wedding for February 22, 1848, at the church of Notre-Dame-de-Lorette. Both families attended.

Their timing couldn't have been worse.

As Franck was hurrying to the church, revolution erupted in the streets of Paris, forcing non-combatants to dive for cover. Student demonstrators chanting "La Marseillaise" and the Girondin chorus advanced toward the Chamber of Deputies, forcing government troops to take up a defensive position there. The revolutionaries grabbed weapons from nearby gunsmith shops and piled furniture in the streets for impromptu fortresses.

The bride and groom used a grill from a church window to climb atop one of the roadblocks, where they were given safe conduct by the revolutionaries and whisked out of harm's way.

In later years, Franck looked back on his wedding day with droll humor. His nickname for his son Georges was "Barricades."

February 23rd

The Peril You Overlooked

Albert Spalding was sixteen years old at the time of his Paris debut. He played the *Violin Concerto in B minor* by Saint-Saëns, the Bach *Chaconne*, the *Romance in F* by Beethoven, and the flashy *Zigeunerweisen* by Pablo de Sarasate. The audience, mostly invited, had nothing but compliments for the young violinist.

But Spalding had misgivings.

He realized that he received just as much praise for his run-of-the mill performances as he did for those that were truly excellent. "Sweet at first to the taste," Spalding said later, "it eventually soured on the stomach."

Spalding's teacher, a man named Lefort, was a voice of dissent. He asked if Spalding knew why he had stumbled in a certain passage. "I will tell you," he said. "Because, depending too much on your natural facility, which in ordinary circumstances is apparently unfailing, you don't take into account the added excitement of public performance." He spoke of the distractions brought on by a thousand pairs of ears and suggested an experiment. He had Spalding write down from memory the passage in question, including the fingering and bowing.

Only after some stops and starts was Spalding able to do it.

"You hesitate," Lefort said. "It is fatal to hesitate in a concert hall."

Spalding muttered something about famous players who had experienced the same problem.

"In the first place, you are not a famous player," said Lefort. He went on to emphasize the danger that came from relying too much on motor memory during a public performance.

Having said that, Lefort smiled and added that in general he was very pleased with Spalding's playing, which had depth and meaning and true virtuoso fire. "Above all," he said, "it sounded like you."

Then he added one more observation. "You have that in your presence which makes audiences want you to succeed. It is like a present from heaven. Only, be careful never to be satisfied with cheap victories."

54

February 24th
Circumstances Beyond My Control

February 24, 1876, brought the debut of a collaboration between Norway's greatest playwright and Norway's greatest composer. Henrik Ibsen's play *Peer Gynt*, with more than an hour of music by Edvard Grieg, became a classic, but in a letter he wrote almost thirty years after the premiere in Christiania, Grieg reflected on the limitations of the first performance and the obstacles to the play's subsequent success.

Unfortunately I didn't get to decide at what points the music would come in and how long each piece would be. That was in the hands of the Swedish theatrical director Josephson, who was then the head of the Christiania Theater, so I had to put together a real patchwork. In no instance was I able to say all I wanted to say, which accounts for the brevity of the numbers.

By the way, the performance of the music by the very modest forces available was anything but good. I didn't hear the first performance because I was living in Bergen at the time, but I was told that the orchestral effects didn't come off particularly well. It really wasn't until the late eighties, after the suites printed by C.F. Peters had come out, that the music achieved its real success.

In the new national theater in Christiania Ibsen's inspired work came back into the repertory a few years ago, and it never fails to draw a full house. The music, which is played by the new orchestra under the direction of our outstanding conductor Johan Halvorsen, now goes well, and the way it's performed now makes a tangible contribution to the success of the play.

If you had the chance to attend one of these performances you would find out that it takes the stage rendition to make the musical intentions clear.

It's really unfortunate that the local color and philosophical tone of much of the dialogue keep Ibsen's work from succeeding outside of Scandinavia.

February 25th

For the Record

The new decade called for a new technology. So in 1920 Adrian Boult agreed for the first time to conduct a performance for a gramophone record. Boult had been signed by the American manager of His Master's Voice, who had liked Boult's performance at the Russian Ballet and asked him to repeat some of the program "for the record."

Boult was to conduct the British Symphony Orchestra in recordings of *A Shropshire Lad* by George Butterworth and two ballet suites— *The Good Humoured Ladies*, based on music by Domenico Scarlatti, and Ottorino Respighi's reworking of Rossini pieces called *La Boutique Fantasque.*

When Boult and the orchestra arrived at the recording studio they beheld a room "so small that it would barely have held a billiard table," let alone the necessary music stands and the huge gramophone horn.

The orchestra placement was not exactly what the musicians were used to. The concertmaster sat in front of the orchestra "with his fiddle so nearly inside the mouth of the horn as he could hold it." A few string players sat on either side of him, but apparently the gramophone horn wasn't good at picking up the low tones of the double bass and so the double bassist was replaced by a tuba player who "puffed away in the furthest corner of the room with remarkable results."

Not long after those first sessions, Boult was conducting a recording of a work by Arthur Bliss. At the end of the performance the impulsive composer shouted, "By Jove, you fellows, that was grand!" Which went right into the hot wax along with the music. Boult was unable to convince the manager that the composer's enthusiastic endorsement would be good for record sales, and so the entire performance had to be re-done.

Undaunted by the early difficulties, Adrian Boult continued to make records for another fifty-nine years.

February 26th
Fantasia

Paul Hindemith was a distinguished composer and music theorist whose works were banned in Germany by Nazi Propaganda Minister Joseph Goebbels in 1936. Like many of his colleagues, Hindemith went to the United States looking for a way to earn a living. By the end of February 1939 he was in Hollywood, where he visited the Twentieth Century Fox and Paramount studios hoping to find a lucrative film contract.

Hindemith-Institut

He pinned his highest hopes on a third visit, to Walt Disney Studios.

Disenchantment came quickly. He watched animators work on a Mickey Mouse production. "Naturally a director oversees all this to make sure nothing original sneaks in," he wrote his wife. He described Walt Disney as "a nice fellow," who was nonetheless "a very cocky guy."

He watched the making of *Fantasia*. Leopold Stokowski's orchestration of Bach's *Toccata and Fugue in D minor* was being played to about 100 frames of film. Disney made some suggestions about the music, and the crew of twelve animators quickly agreed, as did Stokowski. None of the ideas made any sense to Hindemith.

He described the project as a "mishmash" of clumsy rearrangements by Stokowski—*The Sorcerer's Apprentice, Night on Bald Mountain, The Rite of Spring*, and Schubert's *Ave Maria*. He liked the sketches for *The Rite of Spring* but didn't think that they matched the music.

Hindemith talked to Stokowski and got the impression that "the great music god" was insecure and less than thrilled to have a bona fide composer around.

He was further disillusioned at the sight of an arranger cutting and rewriting *Night on Bald Mountain* and *Ave Maria*.

"I finally became convinced," Hindemith wrote, "that the music world could be saved from this evil only by an exterminator."

Nonetheless, the great composer still hoped for a time that a great film could be made with great music and that he would work with Walt Disney to create it.

February 27th

The Shaky Collaborators

Composer Mily Balakirev had scraped up enough money for his Free Music School to put on a series of four concerts in St. Petersburg during the winter of 1879. Colleague Nikolai Rimsky-Korsakov was to direct them, and before they were over, he was a nervous wreck.

One of the concerts was to include the *Polovtsian Dances* and other selections from Alexander Borodin's opera *Prince Igor*, the catch being that Borodin hadn't finished the opera yet, and Rimsky-Korsakov spent no end of time pleading with him to orchestrate the excerpts to be performed in the concert. Borodin taught chemistry and medical courses that took up most of his time, and his home life was so fraught with interruptions that he had few opportunities to compose.

In desperation, Rimsky-Korsakov offered to help Borodin with the orchestrations. Borodin and composer Anatol Liadov came over to Rimsky-Korsakov's house and the three of them flew through the work, hanging up each finished page to dry on a line in Rimsky-Korsakov's study.

Also involved in the concerts was Modeste Mussorgsky, a lover of wine who was given to eccentric behavior. At the rehearsal of a scene from his opera *Boris Godunov*, he listened with exaggerated intensity to the most mundane passages, shaking his shaggy head and raising his hand in a melodramatic gesture. At the end, he bowed low with his arms crossed over his chest.

Nevertheless, for the first three concerts the music of Borodin and Mussorgsky came off well.

The fourth concert of February 27, 1879, was another story.

A pianist named Kimov was to perform Franz Liszt's *Piano Concerto in E-flat*. He missed the rehearsal, but Rimsky-Korsakov gave him permission to play anyway. At the concert he became so nervous and confused that he threw the orchestra off with false entrances and turned the entire concerto into a travesty.

"My mortification was unbounded," Rimsky-Korsakov said in his memoirs, "and I literally cried for chagrin and shame on reaching home after the concert."

February 28th

The Charge

Ludwig van Beethoven spent a good deal of his time concerned with music and money. A letter that he wrote to composer Ferdinand Ries on February 28, 1816, dismisses both matters quickly in order to take up a new preoccupation:

Quite some time ago I wrote to let you know that the trio and the sonata had been sent out. In my last letter, I asked you, since I still had so many expenses to cover, to make sure that Herr Birchall reimburses me for the cost, which comes to at least ten gold ducats. In any event, he got the pianoforte arrangements for next to nothing. And the only reason we let him have the Battle so cheaply is because we didn't think that the Viennese publisher would take so long to publish it.

So I hope, my dear Ries, that you'll rouse yourself a bit so that I may soon receive 140 ducats here in Vienna. In my previous letter I've already told you where to send the money.

Neate left at the beginning of this month and is bringing you the overtures as well as some other compositions.

I haven't been well for quite a while. My brother's death has affected my morale and my nerves. I'm very upset about the death of Salomon because he was a noble-minded man whom I remember well from my childhood.

You have become the executor of a will and at the same time I have become the guardian of the child of my poor deceased brother. You will have nothing like the frustration I have had because of this death. At the same time I have the sweet consolation of having saved a poor innocent child from the clutches of an unworthy mother.

Best wishes, dear Ries. If ever I can be of service to you in Vienna, think of me as nothing but your true friend, Beethoven.

Beethoven and his nephew Karl would try each other's patience for years to come.

February 29th

Violinist of the Hour

 During his final days, the old violinist must have looked back with satisfaction on a career that included, for a time, a close friendship with Beethoven.

George Augustus Polgreen Bridgetower was born in Poland, circa 1780. His father was a valet on the estate where Haydn worked and may have been a runaway slave from Barbados. His German mother was probably a domestic servant at another estate.

As a boy, Bridgetower was such a splendid violinist that the British Prince Regent, later George IV, arranged for him to get lessons from some of the finest musicians in England. During the 1790s he performed often in London and lived as an English gentleman under the prince's protection.

In the spring of 1803 he went to Vienna, where Prince Karl von Lichnowsky introduced him to Beethoven. The two of them performed together in a morning concert that included the debut of Beethoven's ninth violin sonata When Bridgetower threw in an improvised flourish, Beethoven jumped up from the piano, and cried, "One more time, my dear boy!" There had been no time for a rehearsal and Bridgetower had to improvise the second movement by looking over Beethoven's shoulder at the piano part.

The audience was so pleased with the performance that an encore followed immediately.

With characteristic humor, Beethoven dedicated the sonata to "a mulatto lunatic."

In his later years, Bridgetower said that at the time Beethoven was writing his sonata, the two of them were constant companions, but added that they had a falling out when Bridgetower insulted a woman who turned out to be a friend of Beethoven's.

Beethoven rededicated the sonata to Rudolphe Kreutzer, who refused to play it because Bridgetower had already given its first performance and because it was "outrageously unintelligible."

Bridgetower went on to get his Bachelor of Music at Cambridge University and became a member of the new Royal Music Society. He lived to the age of eighty and left a handsome sum to his heirs when he died on February 29, 1860.

March 1st
Everything is in Order

Could it happen today? In the early years of the twentieth century, pianist Harold Bauer was touring in Spain, traveling with a tuner, who was responsible for having Bauer's Erard pianos sent from one venue to the next.

Toward the end of the tour, illness forced the tuner to remain behind, and Bauer had to arrange for the piano transportation himself. After a long train trip, Bauer arrived in Tarragona on the morning of his concert there. The president, vice-president, secretary, and treasurer of the Philharmonic Society met him at the station.

Bauer's first concern: "Is the piano here?"

"Everything is in order," the president assured him. He went on to say that a tuner had been sent from Barcelona and the piano was on the stage, ready for the seven-thirty concert. "The hall will be full," he promised, adding that everyone was looking forward to the performance. He invited Bauer to lunch, after which there would be plenty of time to rest at the hotel.

"We will call you in the evening," he said.

The frazzled pianist relaxed and enjoyed their hospitality. He was too tired to think about practicing.

When he arrived at the theater, he found that it was, indeed, filled to capacity. He walked onto the stage and went behind the lowered curtain to make sure that everything was ready, and, sure enough, the piano was there.

It was standing on its side in a packing crate.

When he had calmed down, Bauer determined that the order to remove the piano from the crate and set it up had gone through so many people that no one had done anything. The tuner had arrived from Barcelona, found the piano crated up, and after a few futile inquiries, had gone home.

After consulting with Bauer, the president appeared before the crowd, explained the situation, and promised a concert the next night.

For which the tuner, the piano, and Bauer were all in top form.

March 2nd
The Downside

 Wealth, fame, and acclaim—Joseph Haydn enjoyed them all during a sojourn in London arranged by Johann Peter Salomon. But there was a downside according to a letter he wrote to Maria von Genzinger in Vienna on March 2, 1792:

I must confess to Your Grace that this is very embarrassing and that on some days I'm down-hearted, especially because, for the following reasons, I cannot send Your Grace the symphony dedicated to you:

First, because I plan to alter the last movement of it and to improve it because it's too weak compared to the first. I was convinced of it myself, and so was the public, when it was played for the first time last Friday, although it still had a most profound effect upon the audience.

The second reason is that I dread the thought of having it fall into other hands. I was more than a little taken aback to hear the unpleasant news of the sonata. By God! I would rather have lost 25 ducats than hear of that theft, and the culprit can be none other than my copyist. Nevertheless, I still hope to be able to replace the loss, yet again through Madam Tost, for I certainly don't want to draw any more scolding from her. So Your Grace must be patient with me until the end of July, when I can have the pleasure of delivering in person not only the sonata, but also the symphony....

My labors have increased with the arrival of my pupil Pleyel, whom the Professional Concert has brought here. He brought a lot of supposedly previously unheard works, but they were composed a long time ago, so he promised to present a new work every evening. As soon as I saw the notice, I knew right away that plenty of people were flat out against me, and so I announced that I, too, would produce 12 different new pieces.

March 3rd
Too Much to Hope For

In 1875 audiences at the Opéra-Comique in Paris were among the most conservative in Europe, and so it was probably too much to hope that they would take kindly to the novel production they were seeing and hearing on the night of March 3.

The day had begun auspiciously for composer Georges Bizet. The *Journal Official* announced that he had been appointed chevalier of the Legion of Honor. Then some wag started the rumor that the authorities had awarded the honor in the morning because they wouldn't have the nerve to bestow it after that night's debut of Bizet's scandalous opera *Carmen*, the sordid story of a seductive cigarette factory worker.

The librettist, Ludovic Halévy, found the music a little different, but he came to believe that the opera would succeed, and his confidence was borne out during the first act, which the audience applauded with enough enthusiasm to bring some of the singers back out for additional bows. During intermission people crowded onto the stage to congratulate Bizet.

Unfortunately, though, the second act didn't fare so well. After the entry of the toreadors, as the realistic opera deviated from the customary format, the enthusiasm chilled, and at the end of the second act, not so many people rushed forward to congratulate the composer. Those who did seemed less sincere in their compliments. In the third act only one aria received applause. And Halévy described the reaction to the final act as "glacial from beginning to end."

When the curtain came down, he said, only three or four sad-looking friends clustered around the composer, offering reassurance.

The unkindest cut might have been the reaction of Bizet's teacher, Charles Gounod, who showered Bizet with praise after the first act, but said in Act III, "That melody is mine! Georges has robbed me. Take the Spanish airs out of the score, and mine, and all that remains to Bizet's credit is the sauce that masks the fish."

March 4th

The Payoff

 Felix Mendelssohn conducted the Düsseldorf revival of Luigi Cherubini's opera *The Water Carrier*. A letter that he wrote to his father on March 4, 1834, shows how hard he worked to get the performance right:

A good performance in the Düsseldorf theater does not find its way to the general public—in fact rarely beyond the Düsseldorfers themselves. But if I succeed in thrilling and rousing my own feelings and those of everybody in the house who's in favor of good music, that's worthwhile too.

The week leading up to the performance of The Water Carrier *was exhausting. Every day we had two long rehearsals, nine or ten hours typically, plus the preparation of the church music for the week, and I was supposed to supervise everything—the acting, the sets, and the dialogue—or the whole thing would've faltered. So on Friday I came from my desk feeling a little worn out. We had been committed to a complete dress rehearsal in the morning, and my right arm was quite stiff.*

The audience hadn't seen or heard of The Water Carrier *for fifteen or twenty years, and had the idea that it was some old forgotten opera, which the committee felt like reviving, and so everyone on stage felt very nervous—which turned out to be just the right mood for the first act. The emotion and excitement were so stirring that by the second piece of music the Düsseldorf resistance burst into enthusiasm, and at one time or another, everyone applauded and shouted and wept.*

It has been quite a while since I have had such a wonderful night at the theater, for I participated in the performance just like an audience member, and laughed and applauded and cried out "bravo" while conducting enthusiastically the whole time.

March 5th

The Pauper

Young André Gretry led the life of a character from Dickens. He was the son of a poor church musician in the city of Liège, Belgium. About 1750, at the age of nine, he became a choir boy, a position that required him to walk a mile each way to attend six services a day. One morning, when he arrived late for the five o'clock service, he was forced to remain on his knees for two hours. In order to avoid  further punishment, young Gretry made a routine of leaving for church at three in the morning, summer and winter, and sitting outside the church door, his lantern in his lap, catnapping until someone came to open the door and let him in.

He applied his energy, self-discipline, and imagination to music. He learned the basics of composition and became a respected church singer who was also a popular performer in local salons.

At the age of seventeen, when his voice broke, Gretry became a composer of symphonies and won a scholarship to study in Rome, where he developed an interest in writing operas—a pursuit that brought him considerable success in Paris in the quarter century to follow. But by the close of the 1780s, Gretry would have to begin another career change. The French Revolution, which led to a government insistence on politically correct operas, inspired only mediocre efforts from Gretry, and the growing taste for massive musical displays was at odds with his relatively simple orchestrations.

So by the turn of the nineteenth century Gretry diverted most of his energy from music to literature, writing his philosophical *Memoirs or Essays on Music* and devoting the last years of his long life to his eight-volume *Reflections of a Recluse*.

The durable and adaptable André Gretry had risen from the cold steps of his boyhood church to the top of the European musical establishment.

The Challenge

By 1754 Francesco Geminiani was known throughout Europe as a composer of concertos. When he was approached by the director of a Paris theater to write theater music, Geminiani took up the challenge.

The Enchanted Forest was a pantomime based on episodes from Torquato Tasso's *Jerusalem Delivered*—a subject that lent itself to splashy special effects, the most exciting that the art of painting and the science of machinery could bring to bear.

The producers kept the plot simple. The story followed events on the Plain of Sharon, near Jerusalem, with scenes set in a Jerusalem mosque and in the camp of a Christian army. In their attempt to bring a new machine into play in their siege of Jerusalem, the Christians are thwarted when the nearby forest, essential for building materials, is enchanted by a magician. Eventually the Christians break the spell and good prevails over evil.

The special effects proved so effective that one marquis scolded their creator for frightening women with his artificial lightning, and prompting others to reach for their umbrellas "for fear of being deluged" by his rain.

Geminiani's music was considered essential to a successful production, and his name appeared on the title page of the program.

And yet, despite all the talent poured into it, *The Enchanted Forest* failed.

The marquis wrote that the producers were capable but that the public was expecting something "quite different" from what was delivered.

How much did Geminiani have to do with the failure? A prominent critic remarked that the pantomime was accompanied by "bad music composed by Monsieur Geminiani that is supposed to represent its various happenings." But Geminiani had made no apparent effort to reflect the onstage events in his music. His accompaniment sounds like a series of well-wrought but abstract concertos.

The Enchanted Forest—Francesco Geminiani's first foray into theater music—was also his last.

March 7th
Radio Won't Wait

According to its producer, *The Ford Sunday Evening Hour* was a way for radio audiences "to feel cultured without really being so." Beginning in 1934 it provided classical music, popular opera arias, familiar ballads, and hymns. Henry Ford hired most of the Detroit Symphony as the house orchestra. The conductors were some of the best—Sir John Barbirolli and Fritz Reiner. The soloists were the finest, although, in the case of pianist Myra Hess, the encounter with radio was not graceful.

Hess was booked to play Edvard Grieg's *Piano Concerto in A minor* for a March 7, 1937, broadcast. A representative of the Ford Motor Company suggested a fee of $3,000.

It was a fortune. "That's ridiculous!" Hess declared.

Taking her surprise for disappointment, the man from Ford said, "All right then. Make it $4,000."

The rehearsal was timed so precisely that Hess got rattled. She went back to her hotel suite, shut herself up in the sitting room, and practiced until it was past time for her to leave for the broadcast. When she got up to go, she found that the door had jammed, trapping her in the room. With the aid of a friend, she forced the door open, did a quick change, and managed to get to the concert hall on time—barely.

The orchestra was already playing an overture as she was led to a small gilt chair on the stage. When the overture ended, she stood up and headed toward the piano, but she was only halfway to it when the time-conscious conductor signaled for the drum roll that began the concerto. She made what was described as "a running dive" for the keyboard and got there just in time to hit the dramatic opening chords.

The ordeal had its compensations. After the broadcast Myra Hess told a backstage policeman that no one had any right to the outlandish fee she was getting for performing the radio concert.

March 8th
Like Bolts of Lightning

Even though he was feeling unwell, Niccolò Paganini didn't want to disappoint those who were eager to hear him perform, and so he went ahead with a Berlin concert for an audience of nine hundred that included Friedrich Wilhelm III, King of Prussia, and all the royal family.

Writing four days later, on March 8, 1829, Adolph Bernhard Marx, the editor of a major German music periodical, was still enthralled:

The man seemed to be enchanted and he had an enchanting effect, not just on me or on this or that person, but on everyone. He came onstage and launched at once into the Ritornelle, in which he conducted the orchestra and shot the orchestral texture through with sparks of tone like bolts of lightning—then passed into the most melting and audacious melody ever to come from a violin.

He sails casually, unconsciously, over all technical challenges with flashes of the most daring and biting satire till his eyes glow with a deeper, darker passion, and the tones become more piercing and headlong so that he seems to be flailing the instrument....Then he stamps his foot and the orchestra plunges in and fades away in the thunderous enthusiasm of the audience, which he hardly notices or acknowledges with a disdainful glance or a smile in which his lips part in a curious way and show his teeth....

There's something curious about this man. The outward aspects of his playing, all the seemingly impossible tours de force, the combination of rapid arco and pizzicato runs, the octave passages on one string—all of those things are just vehicles that actually mean nothing to him. The inward poetry of his imagination, forming the creations before our very eyes—that's what enthralled his listeners.

"This was not violin playing," the reviewer concluded. "This was not music—it was witchcraft—and yet it was still music, but unlike anything else we've heard."

March 9th
The Indian Life

By the beginning of 1911 Italian composer and pianist Ferruccio Busoni had been traveling and performing in America for more than a year, but he was still adjusting to life in the New World. He was often uninspired, but he wrote to his wife about occasional flashes of enthusiasm. On March 9, 1911, Busoni wrote from Kansas City:

I've had to play with fever and pain, and last night was the first time since March fourth that I've had enough of a night's rest.

Now it's improved somewhat. The weather is so pretty that it's possible to sit with the window wide open and enjoy it....

My ideas are dormant. I am morally dulled, physically weak, and depressed in general and everything looks gray.

Nonetheless, Fräulein Curtis received a sleepy letter from me about using Red Indian motives. I believe that my idea of beginning very gradually with them is right, with small experiments at first, like efforts to fly.

It's ridiculous to build a Symphony with Indian melodies, after the Leipzig example—like Dvořák—or an opera in the Meyerbeer style, like the recent one by Victor Herbert. It takes a lot of study to get inside the Indian way of life.

My first thought was to put one or two scenes into one act, with Red Indian ceremonies and actions, very simple, and to link them with the customary "external" stories—mother, son, bride, war, peace, without any subtleties. It takes the greatest subtlety to listen to that kind of music and recreate it accurately.

I owed Miss Curtis some little sketch because she had gone to so much trouble to write out and explain the melodies.

It just might remain a sketch. I've been looking so long for something out of the ordinary and short for my next work.

Ferruccio Busoni did write the sketches in his *Indian Journal* of 1915 and the *Indian Fantasy for Piano and Orchestra.*

March 10th
What If He Had Written Today?

Felix Mendelssohn is sometimes credited with re-introducing the music of Bach in the nineteenth century, thereby establishing the current practice of performing vintage music in concerts. A letter his father wrote to him from Berlin on March 10, 1835, mentions Mendelssohn's teacher Carl Friedrich Zelter as an early advocate of Bach and describes a controversy that arose about new performances of old music:

Zelter was the first person on whom Bach's light clearly dawned because he got to know the works through his activity as a music collector, and, as an artist, shared his knowledge with others. His musical performances on Fridays were a proof that no work begun in earnest and carried out with quiet persistence, can ultimately fail to achieve success. No doubt, had it not been for Zelter, your own musical inclinations would have been completely different.

Your plan to restore Handel to his original form has prompted me to think about his later style of instrumentation. The question comes up from time to time as to whether Handel, if he had written today, would have used all the existing musical options when he composed his oratorios, which really means: would Handel as we know him assume the same form now that he did a hundred years ago, and the answer to the question is obvious.

But the question should be put in a different way: not whether Handel would compose his oratorios now as he did a century ago, but, instead, whether he would compose oratorios at all. The answer is no—not if they had to be written in the same style as those of today.

From what I'm saying you can imagine how eager I am and with what confidence I look forward to your own oratorio, which will, I believe, solve the problem of combining ancient ideas with modern resources.

A year later, Felix Mendelssohn's first oratorio, *St. Paul*, received its first performance and has remained in the repertory ever since.

March 11th
Don't Ever Leave It!

Like many a great musician before him, Argentine composer Ástor Piazzolla went to Paris to take lessons from the celebrated Nadia Boulanger. Although his lessons with her went on for less than four months, long after they were over he would declare that he owed her "absolutely everything."

He was born on March 11, 1921, and so was already thirty-three years old when he came to take his first lesson from Boulanger. She had tutored some of the greatest composers of the twentieth century, and she spoke of them without awe. She dismissed a package in the mail as the latest work by Stravinsky, who sent her a copy of every new work he wrote, and added, "I don't have time to look at them all!"

Piazzolla showed her a hefty stack of his own manuscripts, and as she sifted through them she concluded, "This music is well-written. Here you are like Stravinsky, like Bartók, like Ravel, but you know what happens? I can't find Piazzolla in this."

She asked him what sort of music he played in Argentina.

Reluctantly, he admitted that he played tangos in nightclubs.

"I love that music!" she exclaimed. She asked him what instrument he played.

He confessed that he played a concertina-like instrument called the bandoneón. He had images of her throwing him out of her fourth floor window.

She had heard of the bandoneón. She convinced Piazzolla to play one of his tangos on the piano.

He chose one called "Triumfal." At the eighth bar she stopped him, took him by the hands, and told him in no uncertain terms, "That is Piazzolla. Don't ever leave it!"

It was a formative moment. "I took all of the music I had composed," Piazzolla said later, "ten years in my life, and sent it to hell in two seconds."

March 12th
First Concert

At the age of twenty-seven, Karl Goldmark decided that it was time for him to make his mark as a composer, and so he arranged a concert devoted entirely to his own works.

His colleagues in the Carl Theater in Vienna promised in writing to donate their services. Goldmark recruited an ensemble of instrumentalists and singers and lined up a soloist to sing a ballad. When he had gotten commitments from several singers with the Court Opera Company, he sent out notices advertising the concert and the names of the performers.

Then a setback came in the form of professional jealousy. Seeing the names of the other participants, one by one, the singers withdrew from the concert until just a single soloist remained. Goldmark spent his meager savings on posters, tickets, and renting the hall. He had planned just one rehearsal—to take place the day before the concert, but when he stepped up to conduct it, he found that fewer than half of the orchestra members had bothered to show up, forcing him to cancel the concert and forfeit his funds.

Luckily for Goldmark, he found a patron to cover the cost of a second attempt. The rehearsal was well attended, and the concert took place on March 12, 1858. Goldmark recalled later that the audience reception was friendly, the reviews mixed, and the concert not exactly earth-shattering, although he did benefit from some much needed publicity.

Many years later, Goldmark encountered one of the singers, who mentioned that he still had a manuscript of Goldmark's ballad from the concert. Without success, Goldmark begged him for it, then pleaded at least to have a copy, which was forthcoming, but with Goldmark's solemn ending replaced by a cheerful yodel. Karl Goldmark never bothered to publish the rest of the works from that first concert because he came to recognize their complete lack of originality.

March 13th

Taking the Blame

In the late 1830s and early '40s Gaetano Donizetti had gone through years of grief and bad health. In 1843 his comic opera *Don Pasquale* became an instant international success, and a year later Donizetti wrote another opera, *Caterina Cornaro*. When it failed, he was quick to take the blame. He wrote to a friend:

A fiasco! Then let it be a fiasco! People are saying that the music of Caterina Cornaro *is not mine or that I wrote it in my sleep or that I wrote it to wreak revenge against the management. No!*

I accept complete responsibility, failure, and blame. Why should I have had somebody else compose it? Perhaps because I did not have enough time? Because I was asleep? Perhaps because it's not easy for me to work? For revenge? Could I be so ungrateful to a public which has put up with me for so many years?

No! Maybe genius, experience, and taste deceived me, or maybe I lack them completely. But descend to loathsome things, sleights of hand—never! I would have thought that certain pieces should not have stirred up so much commotion—for example, the duets, the quartet....

But what's the point of mentioning it now? All I do is to pour out fresh blood from an old wound.

Donizetti was equally forthright in a letter to another friend:

You will have read about the fiasco of my Caterina in Naples? It hurts me a good deal because I thought I had composed something worth-while. It hurts to lose the effort of a few months, but it's the same rule for everyone, and I bow my head in humility.

He was in the twilight of his life, but a few months later Gaetano Donizetti would find a triumph in the Naples revival of his opera *Maria di Rohan.*

March 14th
Burning Ambition

 After the success of his Second Symphony in Germany, Norwegian composer Johan Svendsen received encouragement from a representative of Leipzig publisher C.F. Peters, who thought that a third symphony would be lucrative for both of them. In the fall of 1882, after several years had passed without Svendsen producing the symphony, the representative sent him a reminder, to which Svendsen replied that he would be honored to have his new symphony published by Peters—as soon as he could get around to writing it.

Sometime in the winter of 1883, Svendsen wrote the symphony.

Then he ran into a serious problem.

According to his friend John Paulsen, the handsome and charming composer was constantly pursued by admiring women who sent him letters and flowers. After one of his concerts, a celebrated Christiania beauty sent Svendsen a big bouquet of roses. Tucked among the pink blossoms was a love letter.

The bouquet and the love letter fell into the hands of Svendsen's American wife, Sally, who was not amused.

From a desk drawer, she took the manuscript of Svendsen's freshly finished Third Symphony and threw it into the fire.

When Svendsen told Paulsen the story, his friend asked, "What did you do to her then? She deserved to be killed on the spot."

The composer stroked his black mustache as he recalled the scene. "Believe me," he said. "I was firm."

Knowing how mild-mannered Svendsen was, Paulsen persisted. "So what did you do? Did you divorce her at once?"

"No, not that," Svendsen said. "But in a commanding voice, I did tell her, 'On your knees!'"

The story made its way around Christiania to Henrik Ibsen, who used a version of it for a key scene in his play *Hedda Gabler*.

Svendsen was unable to respond so creatively to the crisis. Although he lived for another twenty-eight years, he was unable to compose more than a few scattered pieces of music.

March 15th
Composer, Conductor, Confrontation

Serge Koussevitzky had studied conducting with the great Arthur Nikisch, founded his own orchestra in Moscow in 1909, and published the music of several prominent composers of the day, so he had reason to feel that he had some control over the way the music was performed.

One of the composers whose music he had published was Alexander Scriabin, who invested his works with an intensity verging on religion, so it was inevitable that the two would clash.

An omen of future discord came in 1911, during rehearsals of Scriabin's symphonic poem *Prometheus*. Scriabin's original idea was to accompany the performance with a light show activated from a color-coded keyboard, a plan that had to be abandoned for technical reasons, but the music was complicated enough as it was.

A percussion player who had an important stroke on the tam-tam at a key point in the performance was afraid of missing his cue from the conductor amid the complex fury of the music, so he asked the player next to him for an extra signal, a preliminary nod of the head followed, after the appropriate number of beats, by a decisive downbeat of his arm. In the excitement of the first public rehearsal, the tam-tam player became confused and slammed his hammer down not on the tam-tam but on his neighbor's head, resulting not in the prescribed percussion, but a piercing scream.

Although the March 15 debut of *Prometheus* was a boon to the reputations of both Koussevitzky and Scriabin, the two soon fell into a series of personality clashes and a public quarrel over the amount Koussevitzky paid to publish Scriabin's music.

Another bone of contention was probably Koussevitzky's assumption that he had the right to interpret and modify Scriabin's music as he saw fit, while the composer believed that the intentions of the creator trumped everything else.

Despite the falling out and Scriabin's defection to another publisher, Koussevitzky continued to conduct and champion his music for upwards of twenty years.

March 16th
Respect Me!

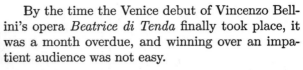 By the time the Venice debut of Vincenzo Bellini's opera *Beatrice di Tenda* finally took place, it was a month overdue, and winning over an impatient audience was not easy.

Librettist Felice Romani was part of the problem. He was slow to deliver and, apparently, stood Bellini up at least once, because the composer wrote to him:

Dear Romani, having worked like a dog, I assure you that it is too cruel for me to come all the way to your house only to find that you are not there. Since we agreed that I'll always be there by four at the latest, I beg you that if matters more important than the libretto require you to leave home, you will send me word before three o'clock, when I am always in. I hope that today you will have me find everything that is missing from the first act because I have promised to deliver it to the copying office tomorrow or the day after.

The "slacker of a poet" made Bellini despair of completing the opera in time for the debut, and when an inadequate singer had to be replaced and his part rewritten, he had no option but to apologize to his audiences and postpone for another month, to the very end of the opera season.

On opening night, March 16, 1833, those in the audience were unforgiving—cool to the introduction and loud in their accusation that Bellini had borrowed from his previous opera, *Norma*. They were still muttering their disapproval as soprano Giuditta Pasta began a duet. She turned and faced the audience for the line, "If you cannot love me, respect me!"

It is said that the audience got the hint and responded with vociferous applause. For the five performances that remained before the close of the season, the crowds were friendlier, and for the last two, *Beatrice di Tenda* almost doubled the money it made on the night of its contentious debut.

March 17th

He's as Good as They Say

Francesco Geminiani spent much of the 1730s in London and Paris, giving concerts and selling, or attempting to sell, subscriptions to a proposed book of music instruction. In 1737 he went to Dublin and stayed for three years. It was probably inevitable that he would meet the greatest of Irish harpers, Turlough O'Carolan. According to Joseph C. Walker, writing in 1789, Geminiani couldn't resist conducting an experiment:

And it is a fact well ascertained, that the fame of Carolan having reached the ears of an eminent Italian music-master in Dublin, he put his abilities to a severe test and the issue of the trial convinced him how well founded everything had been, which was advanced in favor of our Irish Bard. The method he made use of was as follows.

He singled out an excellent piece of music, and highly in the style of the country which gave him birth; here and there he either altered or mutilated the piece, but in such a manner as that no one but a real judge could make a discovery. Carolan bestowed the greatest attention upon the performer while he played it, not knowing, however, that it was intended as a trial of his skill; and that the critical moment was at hand, which was to determine his reputation forever.

He declared it an admirable piece of music; but, to the astonishment of all present, said, very humorously, in his own language tá sé air chois air bacaighe, *that is, here and there it limps and stumbles. He was prayed to rectify the errors, which he accordingly did. In this state the piece was sent from Connaught to Dublin; and the Italian no sooner saw the amendments, than he pronounced Carolan to be a true musical genius.*

At the end of his long career, the famous harpist had proven that his reputation as a great musician was well-founded.

March 18th

Water Music

Louis Spohr Self Portrait

Louis Spohr was an innovative musician, the first in London to use a baton to conduct an orchestra. He might have wished it was a magic wand during an incident in Vienna.

In his autobiography Spohr tells of emerging from a rehearsal at the Theater an der Wien during a heavy downpour and finding the street to his house flooded as the Wien River and the Danube overflowed. He doubled back long enough to grab his violin case and returned to a street now knee-deep in flood waters.

At home, his landlord's family was racing to the top floor loft of the house with everything they could carry, and within a few hours the water was lapping at the front door. The streets became rivers sweeping along an unlikely assortment of household goods, drowned cattle, and a cradle containing a screaming infant that was rescued by someone floating nearby.

As the onslaught of flotsam subsided, the streets filled with boats, some of which carried enterprising merchants selling food, while others ferried businessmen home from the sodden heart of the city.

As long as daylight made it possible to see through the torrents of rain, Spohr found the scene intriguing, but as night fell, the uncertainty turned to anxiety. While his wife and children slept on a sofa, Spohr made a point of staying awake by working on a song that required occasional trips to the piano.

His landlord's family found the music less than comforting. "That Lutheran heretic will bring even greater misfortune upon us with his unchristian singing and playing," lamented the lady of the house. But the night passed without further incident, and within a day the streets were again passable on foot.

The Theater an der Wien was not quite so fortunate, however. It remained closed for eight days while it dried out.

Soon afterward, on March 18, 1815, Louis Spohr and his family left waterlogged Vienna to embark on a long concert tour in drier regions.

March 19th
What They Lack

In 1859 composer Georges Bizet was a twenty-year-old student studying in Rome. He had already written a masterful *Symphony in C*, a major sacred work, and his comic opera *Don Procopio*, and he had strong opinions about his fellow composers. He wrote to his mother in Paris on March 19:

You attribute to feeble libretti the string of failures that has plagued our best writers for the past several years. You're right. But there's another reason. Not one of those writers has a well-rounded talent. Some of them—Massé, for example, fall short when it comes to style and a grand design. Others—including David, I suppose—lack the musical basics and spirit.

Even the best of them lack what a contemporary composer needs to make himself understood by today's public—the motif, which is usually and quite wrongly called the idea. One may be a great artist without using the motif, in which case he has to abandon all hope of money or acclaim. But one may be a man of great talent and have that precious gift as well.

Think of Rossini. Rossini is the greatest of the lot because, like Mozart, he has every attribute—elevated ideas, style, and the motif.

I have no doubt about what I'm saying and it gives me hope. I know my business very well and I'm very good at orchestration. I'm never commonplace, and at last I have discovered this open sesame that I've been looking for. In my opera I have a dozen motifs, but real ones, rhythmic and easy to remember, and yet I haven't made any concessions as far as taste is concerned.

I wish you could hear it all. You would see that I have found a little of what I was lacking.

March 20th

From the Ashes

Georg Solti's career as an opera conductor was nipped in the bud in 1938 when German troops marched across the Austrian border, making life unsafe in Hungary. Solti left Hungary for the security of Switzerland, where he conducted two more opera performances. For the duration of World War II, with conducting jobs scarce, he got by as a pianist, hoping all the while to get back to leading an orchestra.

As the war in Europe came to a close, he learned that a friend, Hungarian-American pianist Edward Kilényi, was helping the U.S. Army to rebuild musical life in Munich. With the German postal system in a shambles, Solti asked an acquaintance to hand deliver a letter to Kilényi, offering his services as a conductor anywhere in Germany.

Kilényi's reply was prompt. He told Solti to be at a specific German border crossing at eight o'clock on the night of March 20 to meet an American jeep that would take him to Munich, to the Bavarian State Opera, which was in desperate need of a conductor.

On the appointed day, he waited in the cold, half-hoping that the jeep wouldn't arrive because he had heard rumors about German snipers shooting indiscriminately among the ruins of Munich.

But, at the last minute, the jeep showed up, and a long, freezing overnight ride to the bombed-out city made Solti question all the more his desire to go there.

When Solti arrived at the theater that was a substitute for the devastated opera house, the general manager said to Kilényi, "Why did you bring him here? We don't need him."

Furious, Kilényi arranged a less important job for Solti in Stuttgart: conducting a performance of Beethoven's *Fidelio*, which was familiar to Solti only as a piano score. After five days of perusing the score and just two rehearsals, Solti conducted the opera with such success that the manager in Munich changed his mind and offered him a contract.

March 21st
One of a Kind

In 1774 Carl Philipp Emanuel Bach wrote a description for a biographer of his late father Johann Sebastian:

The first thing he would do when trying out an organ was to joke, "Above all, I have to find out whether the organ has good lungs." He'd pull out all the stops and play in as many voices as possible, making the organ builders turn white with fear. The precise tuning of the instruments and of the whole orchestra got his undivided attention. No one could tune and quill his instruments to suit him. He did everything himself.

He had a perfect understanding of the placement of an orchestra. He knew how to use any space. He knew at a glance any idiosyncrasy of a place. Here's a notable example. He came to visit me in Berlin and I showed him the new opera house. Right away he perceived its strengths and weaknesses with regard to music. I showed him the great dining hall in it. We went up to the gallery that skirts the upper part of the hall. He looked at the ceiling and, without studying it ahead of time, he said that the architect had accomplished something without intending to and without anyone knowing it, which is to say, if someone whispered a few words up the wall in one corner of the rectangular hall, then someone else standing diagonally in the other corner facing the wall would hear it quite clearly, whereas people standing in the middle or in other places wouldn't hear a thing. Until now a very rare and marvelous architectural accomplishment!

He heard the slightest wrong note in the richest texture. As the greatest judge and connoisseur of harmony he enjoyed playing the viola most, with appropriate dynamics. From his youth into his later years, he played the violin with a clean, penetrating tone, and in so doing, kept the orchestra more precise than he could have done with the harpsichord.

March 22nd

Sweet and Sour

The popularity of his music was waning and he was in debt and ailing, but during his last days, John Bach enjoyed life.

After twenty years of eclipse, the eleventh son of Johann Sebastian Bach had restored his reputation as an opera composer by succeeding with *La Clemenza di Scipione*. His friend Thomas Gainsborough painted a portrait of the composer, showing a dynamic man in his mid-forties.

Each spring Bach went with the Court of George III to their palace at Kew to the southwest of London. In 1781 the diversions there included afternoon boat processions on the Thames that accompanied the eighteen-year-old Prince of Wales to the promenade at Richmond. Friends of Bach owned a decked yacht, "elegantly and conveniently fitted up," and often hosted Bach and his wife, Cecilia. Another frequent guest was a young singer, a Miss Cantelo, whose career Bach was eager to advance, and during the cruises, she sang often with Cecilia, whose voice was said to sound beautiful on the water.

Morning and evening musical parties included the King's Band of Musick and, with a friend, Bach played fortepiano duets. The Prince of Wales, later to become George IV, was a good singer and cellist. He joined in the quartet parties and adapted music for them.

In that jovial environment, Bach enjoyed a good joke. He bet oboist Johann Christian Fischer five guineas—a hefty sum—that he couldn't play his own minuet on his own instrument. The confident Fischer was quick to take up the bet. He sat down and began playing. After a few bars, Bach stood in front of him and started chewing a lemon, allowing the juice to trickle down his chin. Fischer's mouth began watering, putting a damper on his performance and forcing him to concede the wager.

In ways large and small, John Bach made the most of the last of his forty-six years.

March 23rd

Spontaneous Inspiration

For Spanish pianist and composer Enrique Granados, writing music was mostly a matter of the moment. He was not one to work out a formal scheme for an extended composition, but when inspiration struck, he was impulsive and completely absorbed until he had turned his feelings into notes.

A variety of situations could spark his inventiveness. Granados' student Frank Marshall was turning the pages as Granados played a recent piece called "El pelele" when it became clear that Granados was playing something other than what was in the manuscript. The audience thought the piece was wonderful and insisted on hearing it again, but when Granados obliged, he played what was written.

So far as anyone knows, the first piece, the one that had captivated the audience, never saw print and disappeared into thin air after its first and only hearing.

Although he often paced through his house trying to coax ideas to come and jotted them down when they did, he also carried a pencil to write down his ideas when they came without warning, and, when they did, he pursued them single-mindedly. A visiting conductor who found Granados touching up a manuscript was promised that the composer would join him in a moment. The moment turned into an hour.

In an instant, his immediate surroundings could turn into music for Granados. He was improvising at the piano in a friend's house, and when asked what he was playing, he replied, "the garden, those flowers, the blue and orange sky at sunset, the peace of the jasmines."

But the most frequent and dramatic source of inspiration for Granados may have been illustrated by an incident in Barcelona. As he sat talking with friends, a tall, beautiful woman walked by. The composer broke off the conversation and hurried upstairs to the nearest piano. A friend who followed him said that right on the spot Granados improvised "a romantic, passionate, tender, and inflamed melody."

March 24th
Doubtful Loyalty

 During the Civil War, New Orleans-born pianist and composer Louis Moreau Gottschalk was a Union sympathizer. During a concert tour of the northern states he wrote in his journal on March 24, 1864:

Concert at Washington. The President of the United States and his lady are to be there. I have reserved seats for them in the first row. The Secretary of State, Mr. Seward, accompanies them. Mrs. Lincoln has a very ordinary countenance. Lincoln is remarkably ugly, but has an intelligent air, and his eyes have a remarkable expression of goodness and mildness. After an encore I played my fantasia, "The Union," in the midst of great enthusiasm. Lincoln does not wear gloves. I played very badly and was furious with myself, which, however, did not prevent many of my friends from coming to congratulate me on my success. One of them who was present at the first concert (at which, by the way, I played very well) said to me, "Well and good, you are in the vein tonight, for at the first concert one saw that you were badly prepared."

March 26—Concert at Washington. Crowded from top to bottom— every place taken. Lieutenant General Grant and all his staff were present. Grant, the most fortunate of all our generals, is a small man, of ordinary appearance, slender, modest. He has taken more than one hundred thousand prisoners and captured five hundred cannons in two years and a half. The title of lieutenant general, which has just been decreed to him by the government, is at the least equivalent to the marshal [of France]....

Madame Variani sang "The Star-Spangled Banner," each stanza of which was applauded to the skies and encored. The enthusiasm nevertheless is confined to the gallery filled with soldiers; the parterre, the boxes, and orchestra seats abstain from demonstration. You are not ignorant that Washington is of very doubtful loyalty and that her most influential families sympathize with the South.

March 25th

The Bitter Ballet Battle

Apparently Erik Satie felt that his fellow French composers were lining up against him.

In 1924 Francis Poulenc received good reviews for his ballet *Les Biches* and so did his friend Georges Auric shortly afterward for his ballet *Les Fâcheux*. Most vocal among their admirers was Louis Laloy, who had been a good friend of the late Claude Debussy.

Enter Satie, a generation older than Auric and Poulenc, and a sworn enemy of Laloy's. He sent a letter to Poulenc warning him to have nothing to do with Laloy.

He closed it with a compliment to Poulenc: "Don't forget that you are a thousand times superior to him."

But when Auric wrote a lukewarm review of Satie's new ballet *Mercure*, the vitriolic Satie wrote a response that pitted him against both Auric and Poulenc:

All right, my little friend, let him go on. Let him Laloy himself as much as he wants. Then we'll see what we shall see. What crime have I committed? I don't care for his cobbled together, trussed up Fâcheux. *Those who tell me that this former friend of mine is merely an old flat-foot are overstating his merits. He is merely an Auric (Georges)— which is more than enough for a man, if he is a man, to admit.*

Soon afterward, Poulenc was in a Paris shop looking for some playing cards when he caught sight of a child's rattle crafted into a bearded head that looked like Satie. He told Auric, who bought the rattle and sent it to Satie.

Satie did not take the implied insult well. Six years earlier, feeling slighted, he had sent an insulting letter to the dying Debussy, and, in 1925, when Satie was on his deathbed, and a mutual friend of the feuding composers tried to bring about a reconciliation, the unyielding Satie said, "What can be the use of seeing them again? Debussy himself died without my seeing him again."

March 26th

Depend on Yourself

 He was determined and innovative and, at twenty-two, California-born Henry Cowell was also trying to establish his musical reputation. His mentor, John Varian, who was quite a nonconformist himself, advised young Cowell that "you will have to depend on yourself and very few other musicians to develop your music...you will have to forget the public and their demands altogether and only write to your best idea."

It was the summer of 1919 and Cowell the innovator took some of his music to an unlikely appraiser, the famous neo-romantic pianist and composer Sergei Rachmaninoff, who had just moved to Menlo Park. Cowell took a stack of manuscripts to Rachmaninoff's house, but the Russian, once described as a six-foot scowl, opted to look at just one of them. It was a piece called "Fleeting" that, more than any of Cowell's other pieces, resembled Rachmaninoff's own style.

Cowell recalled later that Rachmaninoff "looked at it intently with no comment for two hours, upon which he marked tiny red circles around forty-two notes, saying, 'You have forty-two wrong notes.'" Seeing that the young composer was taken aback by the criticism, Rachmaninoff added, "I too have sinned with wrong notes in my youth, and therefore you may be forgiven."

Cowell asked what was wrong with those forty-two notes. Rachmaninoff informed him that they "were not within the rules of harmony."

Cowell asked if composers still needed to feel bound by those rules, to which Rachmaninoff replied, "Oh yes. Those are divine rules."

Cowell spent the rest of 1919 working out a new set of rules, the result being a slender book called *New Musical Resources*. When he finally got it published, sales of the book fizzled; and yet it went on to be considered one of the most influential books on composing written during the twentieth century.

March 27th

A Mass in Time of War

Dissatisfied with the quality of teaching at the Paris Conservatory, Vincent d'Indy and two colleagues had founded the Schola Cantorum in 1894 as a way of raising the standard of music education in France.

He was not about to let anything close it down, including a German bombardment.

In March of 1918, as World War I began to turn against them, the Germans launched a last-ditch offensive along the entire Western front, putting more and more pressure on Paris. From seventy-five miles away, they pounded the French capital with giant howitzers known as "Big Berthas" and rattled the city further with bombing raids.

During his walks through the city, d'Indy became fascinated by falling incendiary bombs and the rumbling reply of the defensive guns, which he compared to an organ pedal-point. He was in the Square de l'Observatoire when a shell exploded nearby. As if to demonstrate his calm, he went over and measured the crater, determining it to be four or five meters in diameter.

Despite the danger, he kept the Schola open.

When the police dispersed an audience that had gathered for a performance of Beethoven's *Missa Solemnis*, d'Indy was quick to see the irony. "The sabotage of Beethoven by the krauts," he scoffed, "that's original."

He scolded inattentive students exhausted after spending nights in underground shelters, saying, "You would be much better off in your bed. At least there's no risk of getting rheumatism."

But his soldierly resolve faltered when a shell hit the roof of St-Gervais-et-St-Protais Church and killed a hundred people attending a concert, including a student from the Schola.

After consulting with his staff, he decided, nonetheless, to keep the Schola open. He expressed his gratitude to all of his colleagues who had remained at their posts and replaced any staff members and students who had fled the city.

March 28th
I Don't Know How You Do It

Lehman Engel was a successful composer and music director for the stage in New York, but when the United States entered World War II, he took a less predictable job as a yeoman, third class, in the Navy.

Engel was put in charge of organizing a symphonic concert band at the Great Lakes Naval Training Station. He got in touch with draft boards around the country and rounded up some of the finest instrumentalists in the world.

The largest group performed weekly concerts in a modern auditorium and worked with some of the top soloists of the day. But a smaller ensemble was put to a less glamorous use—performing in the Victorian bandstand in the admiral's front yard. Even though many of the musicians outranked him, Engel was supposed to march them to the bandstand, which required on-the-job training. In his first attempt, much to their amusement, he motioned them forward with the very unmilitary order, "Come on, fellows."

The admiral's concerts took place each week in all kinds of weather as long as the temperature didn't dip below 40 degrees, whether the admiral was home or not and without any indication that anyone was actually listening to them. One damp 40-degree day, when the instruments were out of tune and the surly band members were deliberately playing wrong notes in Wagner's *Tristan* Prelude, Engel caught sight of the commandant's wife, wrapped in furs, sitting on a bench and listening to the concert. Embarrassed, he approached her to make some excuse for the abysmal performance, but before he could speak, she said, "Oh, Mr. Engel, I don't know how you do it, it's so wonderful!"

As one of the lowest-ranking men in the Navy—and one of the more discreet—Lehman Engel was not about to argue.

March 29th
They Wouldn't Stop!

A great composer isn't always a great conductor, even when leading a performance of his own music. That was the upshot of an extraordinary occurrence involving Claude Debussy.

In 1909 Debussy was in London to conduct several of his works at Queen's Hall. He was delighted to be there, thinking that Londoners appreciated his music even more than Parisians did. He received a warm welcome, and his English counterpart, Henry Wood, had rehearsed the orchestra thoroughly before Debussy's arrival.

The concert included the second of Debussy's Nocturnes, a movement called *Fêtes*, suitable for such a festive occasion, a piece in which the time signature changes often. According to Wood, Debussy was not a great conductor in the first place, and as he conducted the piece he somehow lost his place—and the beat. Apparently he decided that the only way to salvage the performance was to stop and begin again. He tapped on the conductor's desk. Wood continues:

Then the most extraordinary thing happened. The orchestra refused to stop. It really was an amazing situation. Here was a famous composer directing a work of his own and, having got into difficulties, was asking the orchestra to stop and was being met with refusal. They obviously did not intend to stop. They knew that the audience would think the fault was theirs. Moreover the work, which they liked immensely, was going beautifully and they meant to give a first-rate performance of it, which they proceeded to do and succeeded in doing.

The audience was aware of the orchestra's dilemma and responded with applause that demanded an encore of the piece, an encore that went off without incident. "They wouldn't stop," Debussy told Wood afterward in the artists' room.

"I fancy," Wood said later, "that he went back to Paris with something to think about."

The Contented Listener

Although London conductor Henry Wood had led orchestras through all kinds of difficulties, he wasn't quite prepared for an engagement with the Queen's Hall Orchestra at the Hippodrome in 1909.

Wood first noticed the problem during rehearsal. "I noticed an appalling smell of fish," he recalled. He wondered where it was coming from, especially since it got worse as the rehearsal went on. At the end of the rehearsal Wood sought out the manager for an explanation.

"Oh yes," the manager said. "That's the sea-lion."

Wood must have thought he was speaking a foreign language. "The sea-lion?" he repeated. "What sea-lion? Where is it?"

"In a tank," was the answer. "Under your stage."

"That accounts for it," Wood said. "I thought I heard some splashing, but I never knew a sea-lion smelled like that."

"Oh, he doesn't smell," said the cheerful manager. "It's the fish we feed him. But come downstairs and have a look at him."

On the way to see him, the manager explained that although some animals had been moved for the concert, the sea-lion had to be left in his tank under the stage.

"Unless we keep feeding him," he warned, "he will bark and spoil your music."

"With which knowledge I had to be content," Wood recalled. He went on to describe the peculiar challenge of the performance:

All through the concert, especially as the hall became warmer, the smell of fish was really beyond a joke. Indeed, I was quite sorry for people who had paid to sit in the front rows. During the soft passages I could hear the sea-lion splashing about in his tank and expected every movement to hear him bark; but he was so busy eating that he kept silence.

It's quite possible that the sea-lion was, after all, one of the more satisfied members of the audience.

The riots that erupted in Paris after the 1913 debut of Igor Stravinsky's *The Rite of Spring* made the ballet famous, but that year of musical chaos didn't begin with Stravinsky. Two months before the Paris debacle, the same sort of thing had already happened in response to an orchestral concert in Vienna.

Schoenberg Archives, USC

On the evening of Monday, March 31, 1913, the program at the big Musikvereinsaal included the *Kindertotenlieder* of the late Gustav Mahler, *Songs with Orchestra* by Alexander von Zemlinsky, the symphonic poem *Pelléas and Mélisande* by Arnold Schoenberg, and works by his protégés Alban Berg and Anton Webern.

Avant garde works by Webern sparked hisses and laughter that his supporters drowned out with applause. The Zemlinsky songs, more conventional, brought calm, but Schoenberg's *Chamber Symphony*, several years old by the time of the concert, brought a protest expressed with rattling keys, which persisted through loud clapping.

At the sound of songs by Berg, the audience lost all control, and a shouted threat by Schoenberg to call the police just made things worse. From his box above the fray, Webern bellowed that the troublemakers should be ejected from the concert hall, and received an answer that anyone who liked his kind of music should be hauled off to the local lunatic asylum.

A policeman who came in was powerless to stop the proceedings. Someone went to the conductor's stand and pleaded for quiet so that Mahler's work could be heard, but was quickly forced to use his fists.

The frenzied crowd poured onto the stage, where the musicians sat too frozen with fear to leave the hall. Half an hour passed before the combatants finally left.

A resulting lawsuit included testimony from a doctor who stated that the effect of "such music" was "enervating and injurious to the nervous system."

Although he would become a major force in twentieth century music, Arnold Schoenberg would continue to struggle with detractors for the rest of his contentious career.

April 1st
The Fireworks Orchestra

Not everyone appreciated the jokes, and English conductor Thomas Beecham had plenty of them up his sleeve.

In 1909 Beecham took his newly-founded symphony orchestra on tour, and within weeks it was notorious among railway officials. Whenever the orchestra's train pulled into or out of a station, orchestra members threw lighted firecrackers onto the track, startling passengers and porters alike. The practice reached its climax in Birmingham, when the first cellist used a time fuse to set off a giant firecracker under a baggage trolley just before the train pulled out. The blast was so big that the station master had the train stopped and backed into the station. He stormed aboard and threatened to have every member of the orchestra arrested.

Beecham's outfit soon became known as the Fireworks Orchestra.

On one occasion when fireworks were unavailable Beecham resorted to other devices. Late at night in a Liverpool hotel, he and his accomplices climbed the spiral stairway from the lounge and collected high wattage light bulbs from each landing. They bundled the bulbs into a blanket, carried them to the top floor, and launched them over the balustrade, admiring the explosions that blossomed on the ground floor. In the resulting chaos, hall porters pursued the perpetrators up stairs and through corridors.

By the time they laid the blame at Beecham's feet, he was ready to call it a night.

His tired reply: "Put it on the bill."

But he had one more trick up his sleeve. It was customary at the time for hotel patrons to set their shoes outside their doors at night for polishing. Beecham got up early in the morning and switched the shoes around, taking particular glee in the fact that many of the guests were about to sail for the United States.

For Thomas Beecham, any day could be April Fool's Day.

April 2nd
Square One

As World War I ended, Romanian composer Georges Enesco had two reasons to be worried.

He had turned his concert earnings over to his father to invest, thinking that the earnings would enable him to retire to the country and spend his time writing music.

The elder Enesco had invested the money in land, and the deterioration of the Romanian economy during the war had wiped out his savings. And then land reforms promised by King Ferdinand resulted in the confiscation of much of his father's estate. Financially, Enesco was back to square one. He would have to go back to the concert stage and build up his savings all over again.

A bigger concern came from a curious mishap with his music.

In the summer of 1917 the beleaguered Romanian government had sent its gold reserves to London for safekeeping via a train to Moscow. Traveling with the bullion was an assortment of crates containing documents, including a large wooden box labeled "Musique Manuscrite Georges Enesco." The box contained a generous collection of the composer's compositions, some of them going all the way back to pieces he had written as a child. The box contained the only copies of his Second Orchestral Suite, his Second Symphony, and his opera *Oedipe*, which he was planning to finish now that the war was over.

A revolution was brewing in Russia. As soon as the box arrived in Moscow, it disappeared. Seven long years passed.

In 1924 conductor Bruno Walter made an appeal to the Soviet authorities on behalf of the distraught composer. Playing, perhaps, on their war experiences, he likened Enesco to "a father who assumes his sons are missing in action," and offered to bring the box back to Enesco personally.

After more delays, someone found the missing box in the Kremlin and returned it to Paris with the help of French diplomats, and a greatly relieved Georges Enesco was reunited with his music.

April 3rd

The Uninspired Student

Carl Czerny counted many great pianists among his students and at least one pianist who, apparently, was not so great, but whose uncle knew something about music and sent Czerny a letter in an effort to make the lessons go more smoothly. In 1817 Czerny received a letter from Ludwig van Beethoven:

My dear Czerny! Please be as patient as you can with our Karl, even though at the moment he may not be making as much progress as you and I would like. If you are not patient, he will do even less well because (even though he must not know this) his undesirable schedule for lessons has put him under unnecessary stress. Unfortunately we can't do anything about that right now. So just treat him with as much affection as you can, but be firm with him. That will improve the chances of success despite this difficult situation for Karl.

As far as his playing for you is concerned, as soon as he has learned the proper fingering and can play a piece in the correct time and the notes, too, more or less accurately, then please concentrate on the interpretation with him, and when he has gotten to that point, don't let him stop playing just because he makes minor mistakes. Instead point them out to him when he has finished playing the piece.

I've done very little teaching, but I've always worked on that principle. It soon develops musicians, which, after all, is a major objective of this art, and it is less wearing for both master and student....

I hope that you will entertain these suggestions in the spirit in which I have presumed to make them and would like to have them considered.

April 4th
The Devious Employee

The most capable employee does not always make the most compliant one, as will be apparent in a letter that Mozart wrote from Vienna to his father in Salzburg on April 4, 1781, while he was employed by the Archbishop of Salzburg:

I can assure you that I was very pleased with the Viennese public yesterday when I performed at the concert for the widows of the Kartnerthor Theater. I had to begin all over again because the applause never let up. So how much do you suppose I'd make if I were to give a concert of my own now that the public knows who I am? But this arch-clod of ours won't stand for it. He doesn't want people to take any kind of profits, only losses.

Well, he won't succeed there because if I have even two students I'm better off in Vienna than I am in Salzburg. Nor do I need his room and board.

Now get a load of this. Brunetti said today at the table that according to Arco, who was speaking on behalf of the archbishop, he was supposed to inform us that we were to receive coach fare and be out of here before Sunday. But anyone who wanted to stay (oh, how shrewd!) could do so, but would have to live at his own expense because he would no longer get room and board from the archbishop....

When they asked me what I intended to do I answered, "I have yet to find out that I have to leave because until Count Arco himself tells me I won't believe it. When he does, then I'll make my intentions known, and if you don't like it, you can lump it." Bomike was there and grinned.

To be sure, I'll probably play some tricks on the archbishop and I'll be delighted to do it. I'll do it with such civility that he won't even know the difference. Enough of this! In my next letter I'll be able to tell you more.

Mozart's later letters show that his tribulations with the Archbishop continued.

Rough Play

In the years leading up to World War I, concert disturbances sparked by clashing musical tastes became commonplace in Europe, and Italy was no exception.

A patron asked Alfredo Casella to conduct a concert of contemporary music in the Teatro Augusteo. He prepared works by Jean Roger-Ducasse, Albéric Magnard, the first Italian performance of Ravel's *Daphnis and Chloe Suite No. 2*, his own *Notte di maggio*, and Stravinsky's *Petrouchka*—a rather risky program to put before Roman audiences of the day.

The first several pieces encountered a "glacial" reception, but *Petrouchka*, which had forced Casella to fight the orchestra's resistance during rehearsals, elicited a more friendly response.

An attempt to protest the modernisms failed when someone yelled, "Down with Wagner! Cheers for Stravinsky!"

By the spring of 1915, another cause of musical disruption had emerged in Italy—the dispute between those who favored the country's entry into the war and those who wanted Italy to remain neutral.

The Café Aragno was a focal point of life in Rome, and became the setting for nightly skirmishes between the factions. It became routine for chairs and other furnishings to take wing until the police arrived and shut the place down.

Casella thought it was safe to give a piano recital at the Sala Pichetti until one night when he was playing the *Variations on a Theme of Rameau* by Paul Dukas. As he played, he heard an ardent pro-German professor exchange words with some young men who retaliated by driving him out of the hall. As Casella played the Interlude, a fight broke out in the back of the hall, and he stopped, waiting for the din to die down.

An agitated young man rushed through the main door and shouted to him, "Play the Royal March!"

Thinking that it might restore order, Casella obliged, much to the amusement of two front row attendees who had already seen their share of concert disturbances—ballet impresario Serge Diaghilev and composer Igor Stravinsky.

April 6th

The Long Struggle Back

Although he had established himself as one of England's finest keyboard players and conductors, Samuel Wesley was beset by physical and emotional difficulties and often was at odds with his family. In 1816 the death of an infant son threw him into a state of depression, and while he was en route from London to Norwich to earn some money, he collapsed and had to return to London destitute.

Facing arrest and imprisonment for debt, he worked as best he could, made some money playing the organ, taught, and wrote church music, but within a few months, he was again in a desperate way. At his mother's house, he fell under the delusion that his creditors were closing in on him and jumped out an upper-story window. He sustained such dire injuries that he wasn't expected to survive.

On the advice of doctors, he was sent to a private asylum to recover, and by June 1818, when he was discharged, his career was in a shambles.

He was offered a commission from the Philharmonic Society to score a symphony for a few pennies a page. He held out for more, saying that he could do a lot better by running errands, and the Society doubled his fee. After a year's absence, he returned to playing the organ for a series of oratorios at Covent Garden.

He scraped up whatever jobs he could find as a copyist. He arranged music for a barrel organ. In 1822 he returned at last to serious composing with a Magnificat and Nunc Dimittis that completed the full morning and evening service for the Church of England that he had begun fourteen years earlier. Two years later, he completed his return by securing a modest but stable position as organist at the newly-built Camden Chapel. He re-entered the circle of London composers and performers.

He capped off his return by writing to correct an article in the *Dictionary of Musicians* stating that he had died back around 1815.

April 7th

The Master

At age twenty, Franz Liszt was already a spectacular pianist. Paris had plenty of virtuosi, but seeing a spectacular violinist perform took him to a new summit of musicianship.

In April 1832 Liszt attended a benefit concert for cholera victims. The performer was Niccolò Paganini, who, to Liszt's way of thinking, not only played the violin better than anyone else, but played the instrument as well as it could be played, and seemed to be at one with his violin.

The stunned pianist wrote a letter to his student, Pierre Wolff, Jr., attributing to Michelangelo an utterance generally believed to have come from Correggio:

For two weeks now my mind and my fingers have been working like two lost souls. Homer, the Bible, Plato, Locke, Byron, Hugo, Lamartine, Chateaubriand, Beethoven, Bach, Hummel, Mozart, Weber are all around me. I study them, meditate on them, devour them with fury. Besides this, I practice four or five hours of exercises (thirds, sixths, octaves, tremolos, repetition of notes, cadences, etc., etc.) Ah! As long as I don't go mad, you will find an artist in me. Yes, an artist such as the one you desire, such as is required these days.

"And I too am a painter!" cried Michelangelo the first time he beheld a masterpiece. Your friend, though insignificant and poor, can't stop repeating those words ever since Paganini's recent performance. René, what a man, what a violin, what an artist! Heavens! What sufferings, what misery, what tortures in those four strings!

As far as his expression and his style of playing are concerned, they come from his very soul!

Liszt's new goal was to create a piano repertory that would enable him to emulate some of Paganini's most dramatic effects—leaps, glissandos, and bell-like harmonics. But from watching Paganini on that spring evening, he also learned that the artist himself could become a work of art. Next we'll see how Liszt dazzled concert-goers with his showmanship....

April 8th

Showmanship

In 1832, after attending a concert by Niccolò Paganini, twenty-year-old Franz Liszt had been inspired to raise the level of his virtuosity by applying Paganini's violin techniques to the piano. At the same time, Paganini's charisma made Liszt realize that showmanship would take him to even greater heights. A description of a Liszt concert of ten years later shows that the pianist had taken his lessons to heart.

On April 8, 1842, Russian critic Vladimir Stasov attended a Liszt concert at the Assembly Hall of the Nobles in St. Petersburg. He described a stage in the middle of the concert hall on which stood two pianos facing in opposite directions.

Liszt, noticing the time, walked down from the gallery, elbowed his way through the crowd, and hurried toward the stage. Instead of using the steps, he leapt onto the stage. He yanked off his white kid gloves and tossed them on the floor, under the piano. Then, after bowing low in all directions to a din of applause such as probably had not been heard in St. Petersburg since 1703, he sat down at the piano. A hush fell over the hall at once. He went straight into the opening cello phrase of the William Tell Overture. *As soon as he finished, while the hall was still ringing with applause, he rushed to the second piano facing in the opposite direction. Throughout the concert he alternated pianos, facing first one, then the other half of the hall.*

He played the Andante from Lucia, *his fantasy on Mozart's* Don Giovanni, *piano transcriptions of Schubert's* Ständchen *and* Erlkönig, *Beethoven's* Adelaide, *and ended with his own* Galop chromatique.

Never in our lives had we heard anything like that; we had never been in the presence of such a brilliant, passionate, demonic personality, at one moment rushing like a whirlwind, at another pouring out cataracts of pure beauty and grace.

April 9th

The Reluctant Teacher

In 1874 Georges Bizet was caught up in writing what would become his masterpiece, his opera *Carmen*. So it's understandable that he was preoccupied and temperamental when he had to take time out to give piano lessons. An American girl living in Paris at the time had vivid memories of the reluctant teacher.

He was supposed to come at three o'clock....We would wait, wait, wait; and I was always glad if I thought he was not coming, for I was afraid of him....Not that he ever scolded, but the way he would look at you through those eye-glasses! Our apartment had several rooms strung along one after the other. When Monsieur Bizet arrived he would often have to knock at all the doors and hunt us up....One day he became impatient at finding no one, and we heard him stop in the adjoining room....and rap on the floor with his cane, exclaiming, "Can anyone hear me? What am I supposed to be doing here? Do you think I have time to waste like this?"

During the lessons Bizet would pace about the room, looking everywhere except at the piano, but at the slightest slip in fingering he would turn and declare: "I am not sleeping! I am not sleeping!" He never touched the piano, choosing instead to hum the way the music should go. His young student recalled:

When I would come to the crowning passage in Chopin's Second Scherzo he would become half mad. He would rush up and down the room, crying out to me: "This is the climax! Throw your whole soul into it! Don't miss a note! Play as if you were saying something."

Although Bizet was tense at the student's apartment, when the lessons moved to his home, Bizet was at ease. He would talk, show pictures, bring in his wife and baby, play the piano, and occasionally leave the lesson and retreat to his studio to work out his latest inspiration for *Carmen*.

April 10th

The Curse

In 1935, when John Houseman needed music for a Negro Theater Project production of *Macbeth*, he turned to Virgil Thomson, who had recently produced *Four Saints in Three Acts*, an all-black opera, on Broadway. Also involved was nineteen-year-old Orson Welles. It would be a strange collaboration with an even stranger aftermath.

Set on an island resembling Haiti, this *Macbeth* had three witches that were real voodoo priestesses and a team of authentic African drummers, led by a genuine witch doctor named Abdul.

Thomson was to provide incidental music for the pit orchestra plus sound effects from a backstage percussion group with a bass drum, a thunder sheet, a wind machine, and gongs. For the banquet scene he arranged Viennese waltzes by Joseph Lanner, plus trumpet fanfares and military marches.

Although Welles wanted original music, he had such specific ideas for it that, out of pride, Thomson refused to write note for note what the teenaged director dictated.

When Thomson and Houseman complained to the drummers that the voodoo music didn't sound wicked enough, the Africans finally admitted that they were just playing some spells to ward off beriberi because real voodoo music was too dangerous.

On opening night, April 10, 1936, two detachments of band musicians from the Benevolent Protective Order of Elks paraded through the streets of Harlem to stir up excitement about the debut.

The play racked up a total of 144 performances, but Abdul took exception to a caustic broadside from *Herald Tribune* critic Perry Hammond. The witch doctor asked Welles if the critic was a bad man and when told he was, asked Welles, "You want me to make beriberi on this man?"

Welles shrugged. "Go right ahead. Make all the beriberi you want to."

After that evening's performance, the drums and chanting in the Lafayette seemed to go on all night. Ten days later, critic Percy Hammond, age sixty-three, took ill and died of what was reported to be lobar pneumonia.

April 11th
Make It a Hit

Although few people in France knew it at the time, Hector Berlioz was one of the country's great composers. In order to supplement his income, he turned to musical journalism, writing newspaper articles and commentaries, many of which combined facts with fanciful embellishments. In 1852, in another attempt to make money, he published a collection of whimsical sketches called *Evenings with the Orchestra*. It includes an encounter with a musical hack who makes a fortune by having "killed and skinned the works of celebrated composers."

One day a musician named Corsino encounters the arranger Marescot dressed up in a brand-new frock coat, high boots, and a white tie.

"Good heavens!" Corsino exclaims. "Have you been so unfortunate as to lose a rich American uncle or have you become the collaborator in a new opera by Weber?"

Marescot says that he doesn't need a collaborator, thanks to a lack of international copyright laws. He's published an instrumental arrangement of an aria from Weber's opera *Der Freischütz*.

His cash cow is Agatha's prayer in Act III of the opera. "As you know, it's in three-quarter time," he says, "at a lulling tempo, accompanied by syncopated horn parts that are very difficult and about as stupid as they can be. I said to myself that by speeding the song up in six-eight time, marking it allegretto, and by accompanying it intelligently with a suitable rhythm (a quarter note followed by an eighth note, with the drum rhythm in quick march) it would make a pretty piece, which would be a great hit."

"In that style," Marescot concludes, "I wrote my piece for flute and guitar and published it, leaving Weber's name on it. Now it has become a hit, and I'm selling it, not by the hundred, but by the thousand, and its sales go up every day. That song alone will make me more money than the entire opera did for that dolt Weber...."

Hector Berlioz' *Evenings with the Orchestra* did the same for him. It became a bestseller.

102

April 12th
The Backwater

Between the high cost of living in Sweden and supporting his wife back in Prague, Bedřich Smetana found it necessary to add to his income as the director of a music school in Göteborg, and so he accepted an invitation to become the conductor of the Göteborg Society for Practicing Classical Choral Music. The society soon joined forces with the languishing Harmonic Society, and the merger gave Smetana the chance to broaden his experience as a conductor.

Broadening the musical tastes of his musicians and audiences would not be so easy.

Smetana's homesickness was alleviated by a fellow Czech named Josef Czapek who had been conductor of the instrumental section of the Harmonic Society, and he took over the leadership of the combined instrumental forces while Smetana took responsibility for the choral section.

After weeks of nervous tension and exertion that left Smetana sick, the first concert turned out to be a success. But Smetana came to the conclusion that he was working in a cultural backwater. To Franz Liszt, the financial backer of his music school, he complained that the musical inclinations of the locals were far behind the times. "Mozart is their idol, but not yet understood," he wrote. "Beethoven is feared, Mendelssohn declared indigestible, and newer composers are unknown!"

He added, "You can scarcely imagine what it's like to prepare a score with singers who are untrained or amateur, with runaway soloists, and an orchestra made up partly of unpracticed dilettantes and partly of the military."

Smetana's conducting was hampered all the more by his limited command of Swedish and his quick temper.

And yet, at the end of his three years in Göteborg, as he prepared to return to Prague, his students showered him with such gratitude and affection that he wrote in his diary, "I was so deeply moved that I could only express my thanks in a few words."

April 13th

To Be or Not To Be

The barest encyclopedia entry implies a hard life for the English composer Havergal Brian: "Self-taught composer of 32 symphonies, five operas, and various choral works, all on a very large scale and mostly unperformed." In 1914, believing that his wife had been unfaithful, the composer fled from Staffordshire to London hoping to make a new beginning, but only by chance did he avoid coming to a bad end.

After settling in a set of cheap rooms, he came up with a plan to compose and to make his earlier works known to critics while he looked for employment as a proof-reader for a publisher. The plan ran into trouble at once. He didn't have the money to mix with other musicians or even to attend their concerts, and friends who had previously arrived in London had come with paying jobs already lined up.

It was hard just to get through the night, let alone compose. On one occasion Brian was awakened by a violent fight in the apartment above his, a set-to that his landlady attributed to "some theatricals being behind with their rent." He was cold and hungry and his professional contacts proved disappointing.

At last, Brian decided that to die would be better than prolonging his rejection and poverty. On Fleet Street he had seen a shop window lined with firearms, and he went there to buy a weapon with which to end his life.

Once again he had failed—the shop was closed. He wandered away and later had only a vague recollection of where he had been or what he had been thinking, but something, apparently, had driven him to live because when he returned home he became aware that he held in his hand, not a revolver, but a roasting chicken. Havergal Brian would turn his life around and live to the age of ninety-six.

April 14th
The Poet and the Prophet

Georgette Leblanc, the wife of poet Maurice Maeterlinck, expressed her "ardent desire" to sing the part of Mélisande in the opera Claude Debussy had based on Maeterlinck's play *Pelléas and Mélisande*. Debussy expressed some enthusiasm for the idea, but not long afterward, Maeterlinck read in the newspaper that rehearsals for the opera were proceeding with Scottish prima donna Mary Garden as the lead.

He blew his top and vowed to stop the production.

During legal wrangling Debussy claimed that he had never outright offered the role to Leblanc, and he emerged victorious. Brandishing his cane, Maeterlinck confronted Debussy in his apartment, but the composer's wife threw herself between them and convinced him to leave. After talk of a duel, Maeterlinck redirected his wrath at Opéra Comique director Albert Carré, leaving Debussy free to rehearse the opera, which he did, forty-one times, while writing additional entr'acte music demanded by conductor André Messager.

Maeterlinck, in the meantime, went to a clairvoyant to determine how the struggle was going to come out. After going into convulsions and speaking in the voice of a little girl, the clairvoyant assured him he would need to take no further action, that Carré would soon die "covered in blood." Although Carré did soon fall ill and require an operation, he stubbornly refused to fulfill the prophecy and, on April 14, 1902, Maeterlinck resorted to firing off a disgruntled letter to *Le Figaro*, which he concluded:

In short, the Pélleas *in question has become strange and hostile to me, practically an enemy, and, deprived of all control over my work, I resort to wishing its immediate and decided failure.*

Albert Carré later cast Leblanc for the title role in another opera and, Maeterlinck "released" the future from its promise to kill him off, but he never forgave Debussy. In 1909 he attended a performance of *Pélleas and Mélisande* at the Manhattan Opera House in New York. After the first act, he walked out.

April 15th
The Shuffle

It's not unusual for players and conductors to get slightly lost in the score during concerts, but a Boston Symphony timpanist suddenly found himself completely out of the loop during a performance of Richard Strauss' massive *Domestic Symphony.*

The guest conductor for the occasion was the formidable Fritz Reiner, called the last of the conductor tyrants, who had fired so many musicians that he was later said to have dismissed two pallbearers at his own funeral. In fact, the stories about Reiner were so full of nastiness, cold sarcasm, and cruelty to musicians that during its first rehearsal with him the orchestra was braced for a scolding from him and was almost disappointed when Reiner stopped them and said, "Gentlemen, I'm enjoying myself immensely."

But during the concert the timpanist risked raising Reiner's wrath. He discovered to his horror that the middle page of his score was missing. Just then one of the violinists turned a page and found the missing timpani part in his music. He looked over at the frantic timpanist, who was using a few bars of rest to rifle through the rest of the pages of music on his stand.

The violinist picked up the missing part and sprinted over to the timpanist, coattails a-flutter, brushing past four viola players, a pair of oboists, a contrabassoonist, and three trumpeters, and got to the kettledrums at the last second. Reiner and the orchestra assumed that the runaway violinist had simply lost his mind, and the conductor said later that he thought of stopping the musicians and running for safety.

As for the misplaced page of music, the timpanist had only himself to blame. Before the concert he had taken his score over to the first violins to confirm a cue and had absentmindedly left it there.

Longtime Boston Symphony and Boston Pops associate Harry Ellis Dickson tells the story in his 1969 memoir *Gentlemen, More Dulce Please!*

April 16th
Humble But Powerful

During a long concert career, English pianist Ivor Newton found that page-turners have more power than audiences realize. In a job that requires agility, quick thinking, and musicianship, they're in a position to make or break a performance.

Newton found that, on the one hand, a dispassionate page-turner could sap his enthusiasm, and on the other, a page-turner who was too caught up in the music could distract him with heavy breathing.

During a Paris concert with cellist Gregor Piatigorsky, Newton asked the house manager to find a page-turner for him. Just as the performance was due to begin, "a fluffily dressed, extremely voluptuous" young woman appeared and said that she was going to be turning the pages.

Newton thought that she would be more distracting than helpful and told her that Piatigorsky insisted on having the pages turned by a man.

Bristling with indignation, the young lady informed him that she was a top prize-winner at the Paris Conservatory and that her father was a person of considerable importance. She complained to Piatigorsky, who bowed, kissed her hand, and said, "We shall be charmed, Mademoiselle. With your assistance we shall play as we have never played before."

He was right. Newton put up with one mishap after another as the eye-catching page-turner blundered her way through the entire performance. Her puffy sleeves got in his way, her long pearl necklace clacked on the piano keys, and more than once, she brushed the music from the stand.

During World War II, in one of London's East End air-raid shelters, there was no music stand at all, and Newton asked if someone would hold the music while he played. The alluring young woman who volunteered was very capable, but her tattooed arms, with images that disappeared above her sleeves, broke Newton's concentration because he couldn't help wondering "what curious pictures might be just out of sight."

April 17th
Szymanowski vs. America

Like many European visitors to the United States, the Polish composer Karel Szymanowski had mixed feelings about America and Americans.

One of his three traveling companions, the pianist Arthur Rubinstein, was already a veteran of tours in America by January 1921 when Szymanowski sailed from Liverpool. During their last day aboard ship, the group steeled themselves with a drink before their foray into prohibition country. Szymanowski was bowled over by the skyscrapers that reminded him of medieval castles, by the lights in Times Square, and by what he called "the strange, unintentional beauty of Broadway."

He rubbed elbows with the famous of the day. At the Metropolitan Opera he was introduced to singer Mary Garden, whom he later described as "a horrible old hag." At the Ritz Hotel he had lunch with Sergei Prokofiev, noting, "He seems very pleasant." He went to a movie, enjoyed the jazz of the Haitian Blues, and indulged in clandestine drinking bouts at the apartment of an American friend.

He wrote home, "to come here for a short time for the dollars—fine! But to live here—not for all the treasure in the world." Of his apartment on East Thirty-Fifth Street, he said, "We live—horrors—on the twentieth floor. We have a wonderful view, but I prefer the ground floor!"

When the wife of a heavy-drinking acquaintance began pursuing Szymanowski, apparently with her husband's approval, the composer jumped at the chance to visit Miami and Havana.

In the Everglades Szymanowski and his friends stopped by a Seminole Indian village to see an experiment with anesthetized alligators—twice. They went to Tampa, went fishing off the coast near Miami, and saw Charlie Chaplin in *The Kid.* They admired the long bridges connecting the Florida Keys, but never got over a feeling of alienation that Szymanowski expressed in two novels begun in America.

When he emerged from his American adventures, Szymanowski had a clearer sense of his identity as a Pole and an artist.

April 18th
Why He Quit

Two weeks after the successful debut of his oratorio *The Celestial Country*, composer Charles Ives did something surprising. He swore off any more public performances of his works.

The Yale graduate had benefited from the teaching of a major American composer of the day, Horatio Parker, who had done his best to bend Ives' unorthodox ideas into the conventions of symphonic form.

Ives had been a church organist in Danbury and New Haven, Connecticut, from the age of fourteen and was well acquainted with traditional music for Sunday services, and yet he couldn't resist the occasional foray into fresh harmonies or an allusion to a tune that didn't quite belong.

A roommate of Ives' recalled, "I am sure that various members of the congregation were in a state of continual quandary whether Charlie was committing sacrilegious sin by introducing popular and perhaps ribald melodies into the offertory...but the melodies were so disguised that the suspicious members of the congregation would never be sure enough to take action."

After fourteen years of sour looks from the pews, Ives was getting a little tired of fighting for something new. Nonetheless, on April 18, 1902, he produced a seven-movement cantata based on a plodding work by Parker, with a few original touches, such as ragtime rhythms in the first and last sections.

After the performance, reviewers for the *New York Times* and *The Musical Courier* praised the scholarly good intentions of the composer.

Finding neither conventionality nor faint praise to his liking, Ives responded by resigning his position as church organist and giving up his effort to write music that people wanted to hear.

The cantata was the last of his works to be performed in public for twenty years. For the rest of his life Charles Ives continued to experiment, supporting himself handily with a career in the insurance industry while he wrote music that would eventually make him one of the first American composers to have an international reputation.

April 19th
The Mother-in-Law

The celebrated violinist and his admirer were forty years apart in age, but they had more than music to bring them together. They had Mrs. Angelina Chapman Thorp.

The Norwegian virtuoso Ole Bull was world-famous by the time he arrived in Madison, Wisconsin, in 1868. Tickets for his Madison concert were going for ten dollars apiece, five times what most men could hope to earn in a day. Money was of no great interest to Mrs. Thorp, though. As the wife of a wealthy lumberman from Eau Claire, she had plenty of it. She was drawn to the spectacular musicianship and strong good looks of the fifty-eight-year-old Norwegian widower, and was eager to have him as her son-in-law.

Despite her husband's objections, Mrs. Thorp encouraged the relationship between Bull and her eighteen-year-old daughter Sara, and, in 1870, when Bull returned to Madison, Mrs. Thorp arranged for him to stay with the family at their elegant Gilman Street house and saw to it that Bull and Sara had opportunities to be alone. When Bull invited mother and daughter to accompany him on a trip to Norway that summer, Mrs. Thorp was quick to accept.

Bull's ardent love letters to Sara and the idyllic visit to Bull's estate culminated in a secret marriage.

When the newlyweds settled in Madison, Mrs. Thorp wasted no time in gaining control of her new son-in-law—or trying to. Bull soon developed such a strong dislike for her that he ducked out of the parties she had in order to show him off, preferring the company of a friend on State Street with whom he liked to eat anchovies and talk Norse mythology.

The mother-in-law who did so much to bring Ole Bull and Sara together could hardly have done more to drive them apart, but the marriage held for ten years, and in 1880, when the violinist died, his wife Sara was at his side.

April 20th

A Russian Retreat

English soprano Clara Novello's prime reason for her 1839 visit to Russia was to gain the favor of the Czarina, who could prove a powerful patron, but when she arrived in St. Petersburg, the Czarina was ill. In western Europe Novello could count on great composers—Rossini, Mendelssohn, and Schumann—to promote her concerts. In Russia, without the help of the Czarina, she was on her own.

Those Russians who did befriend Novello left something to be desired. Behind the formal façades of their mansions she found foul-smelling air and unwashed squalor. "I learned," she wrote, "to know by the evil smells when rooms were bedrooms." Social events consisted of endless card-playing and countless cups of tea in stuffy quarters. When Novello and her mother went for a walk to the Neva River, sleighs, fog, ice, and soldiers in uniform came across as a dull wash of cold gray landscape.

Novello's attempts to get fresh air resulted in a sore throat that made it impossible for her to sing for weeks. She was planning to retreat to Germany when she finally received word that the Czarina would see her. The Czarina gave Novello a warm welcome, expressed regret at not being able to see her sooner, and vowed to make up for lost time, which she did by having Novello sing a favorite song over and over again.

The frazzled soprano informed the Czarina that her health required her to leave Russia at once, to which the Czarina replied, "Not when the Czarina wishes you to remain, *mon enfant.*"

All the more desperate and determined to go, Novello employed the British Embassy to get permission to leave the country, but her retreat was as perilous and undignified as her sojourn had been. On an embankment near the Polish-German frontier the coach toppled, dumping Novello, her mother, and their baggage onto the icy ground.

April 21st

Proving Themselves

R. Nathaniel Dett
1882—
Drummondville, Ont.

In 1930 R. Nathaniel Dett was composer and conductor for the Hampton Institute near Hampton, Virginia. The Negro school had just changed its name from Hampton Normal and Agricultural Institute, and the choir that Dett led to Europe that year would go even further to change the school's image.

On April 21, en route to New York, the forty-voice choir sang for President Hoover on the White House lawn. Two days later, they were sailing third-class aboard the French steamship *De Grasse*. Their fellow passengers took the choir to be some kind of flamboyant "Negro show." In his account of the tour, Dett told of how the singers broke the stereotype and set them straight.

"None drank wine, spoke dialect, or indulged in gambling," he wrote. "These young people were reserved in their dancing, orderly at games, unobtrusive at meals, and friendly to strangers without making advances."

The other passengers nonetheless expected them to sing current popular songs or "characteristic race tunes," such as "Ol' Man River," but when the choir agreed to sing for the passengers as a benefit for the Marine Welfare Society, they did so without deviating from their more classical repertory.

During a six-week tour of seven countries, the choir performed for British Prime Minister Ramsey MacDonald and sang at Queen's Hall and Royal Albert Hall. In Paris they made two recordings for the Pathé Talking Machine Company. They performed in Berlin and Vienna, where a reviewer compared them to the best Viennese choirs.

In Salzburg a former choral director and orchestra conductor offered to show the choir around the city. In the Salzburg Cathedral, where a number of people were praying, their guide said, "You may sing, but please don't sing any jazz."

The choir sang an Ave Maria in Latin.

"That is a most beautiful Ave," said the guide, "but I don't believe I ever heard it before. Whose is it?"

As soon as they were outside, Dett whispered, *Mine!"*

112

April 22nd
Haughty Beauty

By the time Muzio Clementi had collected a good deal of Beethoven's music, he was determined to bring Beethoven the man into his circle of friends. He wrote to his business partner, William Collard on April 22, 1807:

By a little management, and without committing myself, I have at last made a complete conquest of that haughty beauty, Beethoven, who first began at public places to grin and coquet with me, which of course I took care not to discourage; then slid into familiar chat, till, meeting him by chance one day in the street— "Where do you lodge?" says he; "I have not seen you this long while!" Upon which I gave him my address.

Two days later I find on my table his card, brought by himself, from the maid's description of his lovely form. This will do, thought I. Three days after that, he calls again and finds me at home. Conceive then the mutual ecstasy of such a meeting! I took pretty good care to improve it to our house's advantage, and therefore, as soon as decency would allow, after praising very handsomely some of his compositions— "Are you engaged with any publisher in London?"

"No," says he.

"Suppose then, you prefer me."

"With all my heart."

"Done. What have you ready?"

"I'll bring you a list."

In short, I agreed with him to take in manuscript form three quartets, a symphony, an overture, a concerto for the violin which is beautiful and which, at my request, he will adapt for the pianoforte with and without additional keys; and a concerto for the Pianoforte: for all which we are to pay him two hundred pounds sterling.

Beethoven was equally delighted with the arrangement, writing to a friend a few weeks later, "By this means I may hope even in my early years to achieve the dignity of a true artist."

April 23rd

The Assassin

As the Civil War swept the eastern United States, New Orleans pianist and Union sympathizer Louis Moreau Gottschalk made a concert tour of the northern states. He then left New York on a steamship bound for San Francisco and was off the coast of California on April 23, 1865, when he wrote in his journal:

A steamer in sight! It is the Golden City, which left San Francisco two days ago. The captain comes on board, and, in the midst of questions from all passengers who crowd the staircase, hurls these words like thunderbolts: "Richmond is taken, Lee has surrendered, Lincoln is assassinated."

The news, more or less true, which has been transmitted to us since the commencement of the war, has rendered us incredulous. Nothing is more probable than that Lee has surrendered, since, on the morning of our departure from New York, the news of the taking of Petersburg was confirmed—but the death of Lincoln! Some ask for the papers; a passenger has mounted in the rigging and has been requested to read with a loud voice.

Alas! There is no longer any doubt Lincoln is dead. We do not know the details of the horrible outrage—the name only of the assassin is mentioned—Wilkes Booth. I remember having seen him play a year ago in Cleveland. I was struck at that time with the beauty of his features, and at the same time by a sinister expression of his countenance. I would even say that he had something deadly in his look.

A literary lady among my friends who knew him told me that he had as much natural talent for the stage as his brother Edwin, but that his violent and fantastic character would not permit him to polish the natural brutality of his manners any more than to restrain the fury of his acting within the ordained limits of art.

Gottschalk's voyage to San Francisco continues....

April 24th

Music for the Circumstances

Having heard the news of Abraham Lincoln's death, Louis Moreau Gottschalk and some of his fellow passengers en route to San Francisco came to terms with the loss. He wrote in his journal on April 24, 1865:

We are to have a meeting on board to give official expression to the sentiments of grief, which, with merely two or three exceptions, are felt by all the passengers. I have said with merely one or two exceptions, because a lady whose opinions are Secessionist, has pushed her forgetfulness of the respect due to humanity so far as to qualify the assassination of Lincoln as a judgment from God; and one or two other female parrots (a species of female dolls, who are dying for sorrow in not having put on their last new dress), who are exclaiming, with philosophic profundity, that "Lincoln would have had to die sooner or later!"

Where now are those frivolous judgments on the man whom we are weeping for today? His ugliness, his awkwardness, his jokes, with which we reproached him: all have disappeared in presence of the majesty of death. His greatness, his honesty, the purity of that great heart which beats no longer, rise up today and in their resplendent radiance transfigure him who we called the "common rail splitter."

O Eternal Power of the true and beautiful! Yesterday his detractors were ridiculing his large hands without gloves, his large feet, his bluntness; today this type we found grotesque appears to us on the threshold of immortality, and we understand by the universality of our grief what future generations will see in him.

After the meeting, the Italian singers who are on board sing the Hymn of the Republic, which I accompany on the piano. Miss Adelaide Phillips sings with electric feeling the patriotic song "The Star Spangled Banner." I play my piece, Union. The enthusiasm aroused is without doubt less owing to our music than to the actual circumstances.

April 25th
That Won't Kill Me

 When it came to criticism, Felix Mendelssohn could take it or dish it out. In April 1834 he wrote from Düsseldorf to his friend Ignaz Moscheles, who had been rehearsing Mendelssohn's *Fair Melusina Overture* for an upcoming performance.

I agree completely with what you say about Berlioz' overture Les Francs Juges. *It's a prosaic shambles, although more modest in concept than some of his others....His orchestration is a horrible mishmash, such a disjointed muddle that a person should wash his hands after handling one of his scores. And besides, it really is a waste to set nothing but murder, misery, and caterwauling to music. Even if it were well done, it would merely preserve the abominations for us. At first it depressed me a good deal because his evaluations of others are so cool and correct. He seems so completely reasonable, and yet he doesn't realize that his own works are such irrational balderdash.*

And so, dear Mrs. Moscheles, the people of the Philharmonic didn't care for my Melusina? Never mind. That won't kill me. I felt discouraged when you told me, and played the overture through right away, to see if I would dislike it also, but I liked it, and so there's no harm done. Or do you think that it would cause you to receive me less cordially during my next visit? That would be a shame, and I'd regret it. But I hope that won't happen. And maybe it will be liked someplace else, or I can write another one that will be more successful?

What I want most is to see something take form on paper, and if, on top of that, I'm lucky enough to get kind words about it such as those I had from you and Moscheles, it has been well received and I'm able to continue working in peace.

April 26th

Royal Crush

Frederick, Prince of Wales, son of George II and heir to the British throne, was so at odds with his father that he would do whatever he could to oppose him. Caught in the crush between father and son was the country's greatest composer, George Frederick Handel.

Frederick didn't confine his quarrel to politics. The king sponsored Handel's opera productions at the King's Theatre in Drury Lane, so Frederick founded a rival company, Opera for the Nobility, largely for the purpose of ruining Handel.

In 1733 Opera for the Nobility bankrolled a formidable cast of competitors, beginning with composer Nicola Porpora, who was then the talk of Europe. The Italian launched a talent raid that gutted the King's Theatre. Before he knew it, Handel was deeply in debt.

At the end of the year, as Handel was scraping together a production of his opera *Ariadne*, Opera for the Nobility beat him to the stage with Porpora's opera of the same name. The prince and his retinue attended Porpora's opera at Lincoln's Inn while the furious king and queen watched Handel's version from the royal box at the languishing Haymarket Theater.

Then the prince and his friends moved in for the kill and bought the lease of Handel's opera company, which left the composer out on the street.

He maneuvered for a comeback only to find that the prince and his cronies had unleashed a secret weapon in the person of the castrato Farinelli, whose voice combined feminine sensitivity with masculine power.

At the end of 1734, now allied with successful producer John Rich, Handel moved to the new theater at Covent Garden, where he fired back with *Ariodante* and *Alcina*, lighter operas written more for the public taste than for his own. They couldn't compete with Farinelli.

With a bold new oratorio, *Alexander's Feast*, he succeeded at last.

Then a second success changed everything, and in a strange way, turned into defeat. We'll hear about it next. . . .

April 27th
The Cruel Reversal

After being ruined by competition with Opera of the Nobility, a company founded by the unruly Frederick, Prince of Wales, Handel had finally begun to reverse his losses with his oratorio *Alexander's Feast*, which had been a great success of 1736.

Frederick's company had brought in celebrated singers, mostly Italian, to sabotage him, but Handel had the advantage of local talent, a nineteen-year-old tenor named John Beard. The words for the oratorio had come from the neighborhood, too, from the respected seventeenth-century poet John Dryden. Soprano Cecilia Young rounded out the homegrown success.

In the fight of the rival opera companies, Handel had the support of Frederick's father, King George II. What could go wrong?

Reconciliation.

On April 27, 1736, the Prince of Wales was to marry sixteen-year-old Augusta of Saxe-Gotha, and a wedding anthem from Handel was inevitably part of the royal ceremonies. It was played so well that at the final chords from the organ, the prince declared his approval to everyone at hand, although he didn't pass his praise on to Handel.

The occasion inspired Handel to compose an even more ambitious work, the opera *Atalanta*, which had a sumptuous debut within two weeks of the wedding. The pastoral fantasy was so suffused with love and tenderness and the outdoors that the prince began to reconsider his effort to break the composer.

He sent for Handel and made peace with him.

Then events took a strange twist. The king was still at odds with his wayward heir, and reasoned that any friend of the prince's was not worthy of royal support. He pulled his money out of Handel's theater and stopped attending.

"Where the prince goes," he sniffed, "I am not seen."

The high-living Prince settled down and became a devoted family man, and Handel went into solitude, eventually to struggle toward a new reputation as a composer of oratorios.

April 28th

Healthy Pessimism

Thanks to a decree from the Central Committee of the Communist Party, Soviet music took some hard knocks in 1948. Four major composers were accused of writing "formalistic" music that didn't serve the needs of the people, the result being that their music was blacklisted from performance.

The four were Dmitri Shostakovich, Sergei Prokofiev, Aram Khachaturian, and Nikolai Miaskovsky.

The accusations were so serious that after conducting Shostakovich's Fifth Symphony for what he presumed would be the last time, Evgeny Mravinsky kissed the score and held it high above his head.

The reasons for the condemnation were nothing secret. Shostakovich had written an opera that dictator Joseph Stalin didn't like. Prokofiev had emigrated to the West for a time and was quite popular there. Khachaturian had headed the politically suspect Soviet Composers Union. Miaskovsky was accused of writing works that were too tragic.

The faultfinding trickled down into every aspect of music.

At the time, pianist Dmitry Paperno was a student at Tchaikovsky Moscow State Conservatory. At first, he and his classmates found it entertaining to see professors accusing each other of kowtowing to the West, but after a while it became apparent that awful things were going on before their eyes. Often as not, the charges came from people who knew nothing about music. Often the accusers had something to gain from bringing down the accused.

Paperno particularly admired Miaskovsky, a greatly respected composer and teacher accused of writing music imbued with "a pessimism void of ideas." He grew angry as he heard the charges repeated by accusers who obviously had been rehearsed.

The dreary litany came with only one moment of comic relief, when a fellow musician, slightly tipsy, made his way onstage, stamped his foot, and said to the audience, "You see, comrades, his isn't the kind of pessimism to condemn—it's our healthy Soviet pessimism."

Dmitry Paperno tells the story in his *Notes of a Moscow Pianist*.

April 29th
Scandal!

His career and his family relationships were bumpy; how could his love life be any different? During his courtship of Constanze Weber, Mozart hit plenty of rough spots. He reacted to one of them in a fervent letter he wrote to Constanze on April 29, 1781:

In spite of all my pleas, you've dumped me three times and told me to my face that you don't want anything else to do with me. I—to whom it means more to lose the object of my affections than it does to you—am not sufficiently hot-headed, impulsive, and dull-witted to accept my dismissal. I love you way too much to do so.

So I'm pleading with you to consider and think about the reason for this unhappiness, which came up because I was annoyed that you were so thoughtless and inconsiderate as to tell your sisters—and in my presence to boot—that you had allowed a young dandy to measure the calves of your legs.

No woman who cares about her honor would do such a thing. It's a good saying that one should do as one's companions do. At the same time, there are other considerations. For example, are only close friends and acquaintances present, whether I am a child or a marriage-able girl, and in particular whether I am already engaged. But above all, whether people of my own class, my social inferiors—or more important still—my social superiors are in the company?

If it's true that the Baroness herself allowed it to be done to her, the situation is quite different because she's already past her prime and there's no way that she can still attract anybody. And anyway, she's inclined to be promiscuous. I hope, dearest friend, that even if you don't want to become my wife, you'll never lead a life like hers.

If it was completely impossible for you to resist playing the game, then for heaven's sake, why didn't you take the ribbon and measure your calves yourself?

120

April 30th
Judgment Day

At the age of twenty-five, Nicholas Slonimsky found out that playing the piano could save his life.

As the Russian Revolution became increasingly deadly, he became determined to emigrate to Paris. The only way to Europe was through British-occupied Constantinople, and, on the boat from Yalta, he was heartened to hear his fellow passengers say that "the outside world" had a big demand for musicians to perform in restaurants and movie theaters.

But not all of the arts were in such high demand.

When they arrived in Turkey, an interviewer questioned each refugee about his or her skills. The selection system was simple. An order to proceed to the right meant acceptance. Being sent to the left meant rejection and deportation to Russia.

A poet was sent to the left. A painter, having clarified that he was a modern art painter rather than a house painter, was also sent to the left. A journalist who admitted that he couldn't write in French or English likewise was dispatched to the left.

Then it was Slonimsky's turn. He declared his profession. The interrogator asked if he could read music, and Slonimsky declared with rising pride that he could, even difficult music. He was about to quote composer Alexander Glazunov, who had said that his playing was full of elegance and taste.

But the official cut him off and told him to go to the right.

A few more musicians and people with manual skills joined him there, but most were sent to the left.

"The scene suggested the Last Judgment," Slonimsky noted, "with the sheep led to the right and the goats to the left. I was a sheep and qualified to enter Heaven."

Within a few years, Slonimsky headed for the United States, where he became a leading proponent of contemporary music and the editor of a major music encyclopedia, a job that he held until four years before his death at the age of a hundred and one.

May 1st
Large Scale

Conductor Theodore Thomas wielded the baton over a massive music festival that took place in New York in May 1880, and the size of the ensemble required him to be alert with his eyes as well as his ears.

The Philharmonic Orchestra was the largest, and in his opinion, the best orchestral organization the country had ever heard. Their efforts for the year culminated in a five-day collaboration with seven choruses from New York and six other metropolitan areas—for a combined total of three thousand singers.

There were upwards of three hundred instrumentalists, all of whom had been members of Thomas' orchestra in previous years. It was a grand reunion of players who had performed together over the past twenty years or so.

The monster ensemble made it necessary for Thomas to keep track of a lot of instruments and voices, and during one rehearsal Thomas impressed everyone with his perceptiveness.

They were playing Wotan's Farewell from Wagner's *Die Walküre*. There were thirty-six cellists and the last stand was about eighty feet from the conductor's desk. Thomas was aware that a passage in the cello part began in the bass clef and continued in the tenor clef, and he knew that cellists would sometimes miss the transition and continue playing in the bass clef. When they came to the passage in question, Thomas heard the predictable oversight, stepped quickly to a last stand cellist, and pointed out the mistake.

The orchestra members were amazed that Thomas could tell which of the thirty-six had made the mistake. Over the years, the incident was reported far and wide with increasing inaccuracy.

Years later, in his autobiography, Thomas set the record straight with a simple explanation.

Being familiar with the mistake, when he heard it, he glanced at the cellists and saw that one of them still had his hand in the bass clef position, and that visual cue had enabled him to single out the erring player so quickly.

May 2nd
Managing the Manager

In 1904, when cellist Pablo Casals undertook his first American tour, he had to rely upon a manager to keep track of his money. The manager told Casals that he could get bigger fees if he would wear a hairpiece. Casals had no interest in that kind of superficiality, and so the manager sent out press releases explaining that the Spanish virtuoso had gone bald so young because of favoring so many female admirers with locks of his hair.

Although Casals had never liked handling cash, he had a keen eye for counting it in a ledger. His agents set up contracts that Casals okayed and deposited his income in one of his accounts. During the tour, Casals began to suspect that his New York agent was collecting more money than he was reporting and skimming off the difference, as much as two or three hundred dollars a concert.

Casals kept a silent watch on the books, and, at the end of the tour, set up a conference with the agent in the lobby of his hotel, guaranteeing him that it wouldn't take long.

The agent found Casals waiting for him in one of two chairs he had placed next to a small table near the entrance of the hotel. By way of making small talk, the agent asked how Casals' tour had been.

It had gone well enough, Casals replied, except that his management had been taking him to the cleaners. He went on to say that he knew exactly how much his management had siphoned off.

The agent blanched and got to his feet, sputtering some kind of protest, and Casals shoved him into the revolving door and began spinning it. He got it going as fast as he could, and when it broke, the agent scrambled free and ran down the street.

Ever mindful of costs, Casals returned to the lobby and paid for the damage.

May 3rd
Love in Time of War

It began the way many love stories have begun ever since young men began giving music lessons to young women. In 1910, a wealthy St. Petersburg family, the Meshcherkys, welcomed nineteen-year-old Sergei Prokofiev into their musical gatherings as an alternative to the straight-laced young men in uniform who were prospective suitors to their elder daughter Talya.

Before long, Prokofiev became attracted, not to Talya, but to her fourteen-year-old sister Nina.

In the spring of 1914 Prokofiev was giving piano lessons to Nina, and a romance developed. Prokofiev likened their relationship to the long-forbidden love between composer Robert Schumann and his piano student Clara Wieck—a relationship that eighty years earlier had weathered the disapproval of Clara's father and resulted in marriage.

In a letter to a harpist friend, Prokofiev referred to being involved in "a bitter war" in which he was fighting like a madman. No doubt taking his cue from the real war that had erupted that spring, he referred to his heart as "a miserable little town" in his territory, a town that was being occupied by an outside force.

Prokofiev asked Nina to marry him. Assuming an authoritarian air, he insisted that she declare their relationship to her parents and leave for Italy with him that very day, or the next at the latest.

The revelation of the relationship caught Nina's father by surprise. He was adamant that Nina's marrying an "artist" was out of the question, and a head-on argument with the unyielding Prokofiev convinced the stubborn young musician that the only alternative for Nina and him was to elope.

Nina was caught trying to sneak out of the house, and after an angry confrontation, her parents moved her to a city in the far south of the Russian empire.

Prokofiev traveled alone to Italy, where he began to develop a reputation that made him known throughout Europe. Although they spoke on the telephone, he and Nina never saw each other again.

Slightly Different

No one doubted that Domenico Dragonetti was one of the greatest bass players the world had ever seen. There was some disagreement, however, as to whether he was a true eccentric or just a performer with a sense of promotion and a highly developed sense of humor.

Dragonetti left his hometown, Venice, in 1794, having gotten a paid leave of absence to perform for a year with the King's Theatre orchestra in London. He quickly became famous in England and obtained a four-year extension of his leave. He overstayed his extension by forty-eight years.

He never married and had no close family, but kept a large collection of baby-sized dolls. His favorite was a black doll that wore a tartan-patterned cotton dress, a head scarf, and pearl-buttoned shoes. When visitors came to call, the dolls would move over to make room for them and, at his concerts, he would sometimes see to it that the dolls got front-row seats.

His dog Carlo was also a frequent concert attendee. Carlo made a habit of sleeping under Dragonetti's chair during performances, and if a tenor was involved in the concert, Carlo was inclined to wake up and howl.

It was said that Dragonetti blended languages into such a garble that an attempted conversation with Napoleon prompted the exasperated emperor to tell Dragonetti to fetch his double-bass and make his statement with music.

How eccentric was he? Although the doll collection was probably a genuine hobby—Haydn, too, had a doll collection—Dragonetti might also have been using it as a publicity device, just as Carlo the dog added zest to the novelty of a double-bass performance. His colorful use of language might also have been part of the pose.

Whether his eccentricities were genuine or contrived, at a time when many performers fell by the wayside after short careers, Domenico Dragonetti was still performing for English audiences after the age of eighty.

Next—Dragonetti meets Beethoven.

May 5th

The Test

In the spring of 1799, Domenico Dragonetti was on his way back to London after visiting his hometown, Venice. He stopped in Vienna, where he went to meet Beethoven.

A mutual friend wrote a note to Dragonetti, saying, "tomorrow morning at eight o'clock precisely, go to Prince Lichnowsky's. You will breakfast at his house, and he will take you to Beethoven's himself to get him to fulfill your wishes...and be sure that I'll be praying for you as I wait. I'm counting on seeing you after tomorrow morning to find out the result."

Years later, Dragonetti described his encounter with the twenty-eight-year-old Beethoven. Having heard that Dragonetti could play virtuoso cello music on the double bass, Beethoven indicated that he'd like to hear a sonata. Dragonetti sent for his bass and Beethoven selected his *Cello Sonata in G minor*, Opus 5, No. 2. As Beethoven played the piano part, he watched Dragonetti closely, and in the finale of the sonata, where arpeggios come in, Beethoven was so pleased with Dragonetti's performance that he jumped up and threw his arms around both Dragonetti and his bass.

In 1813, when he rounded up the best musicians for a performance of his battle piece *Wellington's Victory*, Beethoven chose Dragonetti as his bassist.

But how influential was Dragonetti when it came to Beethoven's subsequent writing? Bassists of the time were convinced that in 1824, when Beethoven wrote the prominent bass recitative in his Ninth Symphony, he had Dragonetti in mind, although he, apparently, was hoping that the whole bass section would play the difficult passage.

According to one account, Dragonetti didn't play in the London debut of the symphony because he wanted too much money, but nevertheless claimed that Beethoven had written the entire symphony for him.

A tantalizing question turned up in the conversation books Beethoven used after he had become deaf: "Were you thinking of Dragonetti in the recitative of the D minor symphony?"

Unfortunately, Beethoven's answer wasn't written down.

May 6th

A Tactful Approach

In his memoirs librettist Lorenzo Da Ponte takes credit for using tact to bring about the debut of Mozart's masterpiece *The Marriage of Figaro.*

[Mozart] asked me how hard it would be for me to make an opera of a comedy by Beaumarchais, The Marriage of Figaro. *I liked the idea a lot and promised him to write one. There was a major obstacle though. Just a few days earlier the emperor had forbidden the German company at the theater to perform that comedy, which he thought was too off-color for a self-respecting audience.*

How could I suggest it to him for an opera?

Da Ponte decided to write the libretto in secret and show it to the theater directors—or to the Emperor himself—so that they could see how tastefully the play could be adapted for opera.

I went to work, and as fast as I wrote the words, Mozart set them to music. In six weeks everything was ready. The Opera was in need of scores just then and, taking the opportunity, I went to the Emperor to offer him The Marriage of Figaro.

"What?" he said. "Don't you know that even though he's a marvelous writer of instrumental music, Mozart has written only one opera, and nothing special at that?"

"Yes, Sire," I said softly, "but without your Majesty's good will, I would have written just one drama in Vienna."

"Maybe so," he answered, "but this Marriage of Figaro—*I have just forbidden the German company to use it!"*

"Yes, Sire," I replied, "but I was writing an opera and not a comedy. I had to leave out many scenes and trim others extensively. I've left out anything that might offend good taste or public decency at a performance over which the Sovereign Majesty might preside. And if I may say so, the music seems absolutely beautiful."

"Very well. If that's the way it is, I will rely on your good taste regarding the music and on your wisdom regarding the morality. Send the score to the copyist."

The Marriage of Figaro had its debut in Vienna on May 1, 1786. Next, the story of their first collaboration from Mozart's perspective.

May 7th
Our Poet

On May 7, 1783, Mozart got around to writing from Vienna to his father in Salzburg a letter in which he introduced the man who would collaborate with him on some of the greatest operas ever written.

I have looked at a least a hundred libretti or more, but I have barely found a single one that's satisfactory, by which I mean that so many changes would have to be made here and there that even if a poet would try to make them it would be easier for him to start from scratch with a new text—which indeed is always the best thing to do.

Our poet here is now a certain Abbot Da Ponte. He has a tremendous amount to do with revising pieces for the theater and he's committed to writing an entirely new libretto for Salieri, which will take two months. He has promised to follow that with a new libretto for me. But who knows whether he'll be able to keep his word—or will want to? For, as you know, these Italian gentlemen are very courteous to your face. Enough! We know them!

If he's in cahoots with Salieri I'll never get anything out of him. But I really want to show what I can do in Italian opera! So I've been thinking that unless Varesco is still quite put out with us regarding the Munich opera, perhaps he would write me a new libretto for seven characters. Basta! You will know best if it can be worked out. In the meantime he could make some notes, and when I come to Salzburg, we could work through them together.

Lorenzo Da Ponte would go on to write the texts for three of Mozart's greatest operas—*The Marriage of Figaro, Don Giovanni*, and *Cosi fan tutti*. Then he would fall on hard times and get help from an unlikely person. We'll get that story in December.

May 8th

The Catalyst

During the course of a long career, Malcolm Arnold developed a reputation as a composer of classical music and film scores with a strong current of humor, but during the dark days of World War II, he struggled with tragedy.

In 1941, as war raged in Europe, Arnold's brother Philip, a pilot in the Royal Air Force, was reported missing, and, after several months, confirmed dead. Arnold continued to work as a musician until 1944, when a second blow made him alter his course.

In the summer of 1943 Arnold's wife Sheila became pregnant, and in January a girl, Kate, was born, but she lived for only a short time after the delivery. Something in the confluence of those sad events made Arnold decide to join the military, a decision that put him at odds with his parents, who had lost one son to the war and had another risking his life among Arctic convoys.

After being turned down by the navy, Arnold tried to join a parachute regiment, which turned him down because he was too small. The infantry accepted him and, after putting him through basic training, placed him in the army band. He sat down and cried.

"I could not believe that I had given up a reserve occupation, and they put me in the band," Arnold said later. He went to the latrine, took off his boots, placed a biscuit barrel under his foot, aimed his rifle at his big toe, and fired. The self-inflicted wound could've gotten him shot as a deserter, but a sympathetic and insightful psychiatrist got him a discharge from the military, and the next unit he joined was the BBC Orchestra.

Within a few years, Malcolm Arnold would be one of the most sought-after composers in England, and would go on to compose music for eighty films, including the monumental tribute to British military endurance, *The Bridge on the River Kwai.*

May 9th
Resurrection

In 1965, twelve years after his last stage appearance, virtuoso pianist Vladimir Horowitz felt again the urge to "communicate directly" with the audience. He decided to perform at Carnegie Hall.

The sixty-one-year-old Horowitz worried about being physically up to resuming his concert career and feared that his memory would fail him during a performance. He selected a new Steinway, had it delivered to the hall, and practiced for a couple of months without committing himself to scheduling a concert. Finally he settled on Sunday, May 9.

He worried that not many young people would come to the recital, and he insisted that plenty of $3 student tickets be made available. He was astonished to hear that hundreds of people, many of them young music students, had waited four abreast through a cold rainy night to buy tickets. He arranged for the entire crowd to have coffee and received a grateful telegram from a hundred of them.

Horowitz chose a tough program—Robert Schumann's *Fantasie in C* and Alexander Scriabin's Ninth Sonata, plus the Bach-Busoni *Toccata and Fugue in C*, with short pieces by Chopin, Debussy, and Schumann for encores. In his bedroom he practiced bowing. As the day for the recital approached, he diverted himself with mundane details. He chose a formal cutaway jacket with handkerchief, black pants with faint white stripes, white shirt, gray vest, and silk tie.

He walked onstage to a standing ovation and shrugged with upturned hands as if to say, "I haven't even played yet." In an emotional whirlwind, he played the Bach-Busoni piece too fast and hit wrong notes. Sweat in his eye made him miss notes in the Schumann. During the Scriabin he aimed for grandeur and lyricism rather than speed, and by the end of the encores the response was deafening. The audience refused to leave until the stage lights were dimmed and the piano lid closed.

"I don't know what to call it," Vladimir Horowitz told a friend. "Resurrection, I think, is all right...."

May 10th

Why They Really Built the Railroad

The celebration marking the completion of the Transcontinental Railroad on May 10, 1869, was about uniting a country torn by Civil War, but long before that event, French composer Hector Berlioz suggested, tongue in cheek, why Americans were really so eager to unite east and west by rail. In his 1852 bestseller *Evenings with the Orchestra*, a character assures a friend that it was all about music, and about one performer in particular.

We simple Europeans had thought it was to be built just to facilitate the travel of the explorers of the New El Dorado. We were wrong. Quite the contrary, the idea was more artistic than commercial or philanthropic. Those hundreds of miles of iron roads were voted by the States to enable the pioneers wandering among the Rocky Mountains and on the banks of the Sacramento to come and hear Jenny Lind without wasting too much of their time over the indispensable pilgrimage.

But because of some odious conspiracy, the work was far from finished, was hardly begun in fact, when she arrived. It's hard to come up with the right word to describe such carelessness on the part of the American government, and one can only imagine that she, as humane and caring as she is, complained bitterly about it.

And so these poor seekers after gold, of every age and gender, had to make the long and dangerous continental crossing while already exhausted from their arduous toil, on foot, by mule-back, and to go through unprecedented sufferings. Placer mines were abandoned, gaping excavations sat untouched, the buildings in San Francisco remained unfinished, and heaven only knows when work was resumed.

This may be the cause of very serious disruptions in the commercial relations of the entire world.

Berlioz notes that, in the meantime, Jenny Lind withdrew from her contract with promoter P. T. Barnum, married a pianist, and retired from the frenetic world of musical stardom.

May 11th
You Are Playing That Wrong

Pianist Harold Bauer had never heard of the young woman dancing at the home of an acquaintance and took no notice of her name. But he watched with fascination as she gestured and posed to the sound of familiar classical music. He had never seen a performance quite like it. Her gestures seemed to illustrate the dynamics of the music, and he hit upon the idea of letting his gestures at the piano bring forth corresponding dynamics in the music.

His first efforts to bring tone out of gesture were ridiculous, but he persisted and eventually used the approach whenever he played.

Thirty years later, after he had given a recital in Los Angeles, his friend, violinist and composer Eugène Ysäye greeted him in the artists' room by introducing a companion. "Of course you know Isadora," he said.

"Isadora who?" Bauer asked.

"Isadora Duncan," said Ysäye.

When Bauer realized that she was the dancer from all those years ago, he told her how greatly she had influenced his method of performing, and, before long, the two of them planned to give a concert together.

It was to be entirely pieces by Chopin, and while rehearsing the *Etude in A-flat*, Opus 25, No. 1, they had a falling out.

"You are playing that wrong," Isadora said. She explained that the crescendo had to continue to the very end of the phrase and be softened later.

With some annoyance, Bauer said that he was playing the piece the way it was printed on the page.

Isadora didn't care. She said that the music had to build to a climax at the end of the phrase or else she'd have nothing to do with her arms. "Anyway," she insisted, "you are quite mistaken."

After a long discussion, Bauer gave in for the sake of allowing her the indispensable dramatic gesture.

Afterward, when he had a look at Chopin's original manuscript of the piece, he found that it had the precise dynamics the dancer had instinctively required, and he played it that way ever after.

May 12th
But We Shall Have Tonight

Puccini's opera *Tosca* tells of revenge and murder—both of which were also in the air backstage after a notorious Saturday night performance at the Metropolitan Opera.

On the evening of the performance Met General Manager Schuyler Chapin went to see Franco Corelli, who was singing the part of Cavaradossi, and found him at his dressing table, staring into the mirror, brooding over his enmity for conductor Carlo Cillario.

Chapin pointed out that the conductor would not be returning for the next season.

Corelli remained uneasy. "But we shall have tonight," he said.

After more reassuring words, Chapin went off to his box to enjoy the opera with friends.

The pleasure was short-lived.

At the end of two key arias Cillario tried to rush the orchestra over the applause. When Corelli slowed him down in one aria by hanging onto two long notes, the conductor retaliated by quickening the tempo, forcing the tenor to keep up.

In Act III the disgusted tenor flipped his thumb between his teeth in a gesture of defiance and left the stage, forcing Dorothy Kirsten, as Tosca, to sing to the empty space where he was supposed to be.

When Corelli returned in time to ascend the steps for Cavaradossi's execution, one property man expressed regret at not putting real bullets in the rifles. As the shots rang out, several people backstage applauded.

As soon as the curtain came down, Corelli ran toward the orchestra pit, yelling insults. When Cillario emerged, Corelli pounced and did his best to strangle him. It took Chapin, the artistic administrator, and three big stage hands to pry the two apart.

Shouting over the mixture of applause and boos from the audience, Chapin commanded Corelli to go out and take a curtain call, which he did.

Chapin suggested to Cillario that it would not be a good time to take a solo conductor bow.

May 13th

The Poisoned Referral

During the late nineteenth century, nationalism became a force in music, and a leader in the cause of Russian music was composer Mily Balakirev. He was one of the five nationalistic composers known as The Mighty Handful. He thought that fellow Russian composer Anton Rubinstein had turned his back on Russian music in favor of German influences. He said that Rubinstein's music was mere accompaniment, building toward a resolution but never providing it, and without melody. When a patron approached Balakirev with an offer, the Russian nationalist turned it into a joke at Rubinstein's expense.

Balakirev's servant Adrian brought him the calling card of a famous member of a Guards' regiment. Balakirev was perplexed.

"This isn't for me," he told Adrian, "Tell him the midwife lives on the next floor up." But the officer was insistent and so Balakirev agreed to see him. The dapper guardsman came in carrying an expensive green leather portfolio. An important friend had sent him to Balakirev for advice. He apologized for disturbing the composer.

Balakirev was still puzzled. "I'm quite incompetent in military matters," he said.

"It's purely a musical matter," the guardsman assured him. "You see, I've written an opera."

Balakirev became wary. "An opera? Then you must have studied. But where?"

"Oh, yes," the officer said. "I've done a lot of studying abroad."

"Well, that's interesting," Balakirev conceded, "but I still can't help you. I have very little influence in theatrical circles."

The guardsman cut him off. "This isn't about staging. I've come to ask your advice as to whom I could commission to write an accompaniment for my opera."

Balakirev looked his visitor in the eye and, with a straight face, suggested, "I think you should ask Rubinstein and nobody else. That's his specialty."

Mily Balakirev's student A.A. Olenin tells the story in his memoir *My Recollections of Balakirev.*

May 14th

Too Much to Ask

Although Antal Dorati would become a world famous conductor, he was a ten-year-old pianist in 1916, when he first encountered his musical idol, and, thanks to his father's excessive enthusiasm, the occasion called for a hasty retreat.

Antal Dorati conducting Ballet Russes Australian Tours
By Permission of the National Library of Australia

Dorati's father was a violinist in the Budapest Philharmonic, and the boy grew up with a keen awareness of Hungarian classical music. The luminaries of the day were Zoltán Kodály, Leo Weiner, and—the giant of them all—Béla Bartók. Dorati and his father were on their way into the Franz Liszt Academy of Music when his father stopped to greet "a small, thin, gray-haired, clean-shaven gentleman."

"Good day," the man said in a whisper.

"Good day, Professor Bartók," said the elder Dorati.

Young Antal was amazed. He had imagined the great Bartók as someone larger than life, and yet he was not disappointed. He determined that his idol had to look that way—frail, small, and gray-haired, although he was only about thirty-five. The boy was struck by the composer's eyes—"large, knowing, penetrating, transforming—the eyes of a prophet, just stepping out from the Bible."

"Good day," Bartók whispered to the boy. After a prompt from his father, the bashful Antal returned the greeting.

"That is your son?" the great composer asked.

"Yes."

"Is he musical?"

"Yes, he plays the piano."

As it was, the boy thought that his father was saying too much, but he didn't stop there. "He always plays your pieces," he added.

"Well, sometime he shall play for me, maybe?"

"Certainly, he will be honored to do so—won't you, Toni?"

Dorati recalled that at that point he was already running up the stairs, "very scared, my ears red like two small traffic signs."

135

May 15th

First and Last, a Composer

Although he came from a musical family, Swedish composer Franz Berwald had trouble fitting into the musical scene in Stockholm, so in the spring of 1829 he pursued his art in Berlin, where he wound up in a profession that had little to do with operas and symphonies.

In Berlin a friend introduced Berwald to Felix Mendelssohn, who was politely unenthusiastic about Berwald's new opera and didn't particularly care for Berwald either.

Before long Berwald was broke, but he somehow borrowed enough to pursue his second great interest—orthopedics. He opened a clinic in Berlin, specializing in the treatment of spinal abnormalities in children, prospered, won considerable admiration for his compassionate and effective treatment, and invented equipment that would be in use for decades.

Once he had saved up some money, Berwald couldn't resist returning to music, and during a sojourn in Vienna he wrote plenty of it, achieving modest success although he had to pay for some of the concerts out of his own pocket. After more than a decade away from Sweden, he went back to his homeland and eked out a living as a composer and teacher, but he felt compelled to return to the Continent, where success proved so elusive for the composer that he had to borrow money from the King of Sweden just to get home again.

He was never far from writing or teaching music, but for the rest of his life Berwald had to rely on "day jobs" to support him—managing two glass factories and a sawmill. In the spring of 1868, while revising the Swedish Chorale Book, Franz Berwald succumbed to an attack of pneumonia. In a later century he would become Sweden's best known symphonist, but he died so destitute that a benefit concert and the contributions of friends were needed to pay for his funeral.

May 16th

Some of It Seems to Have Turned Out Well

It was as if a floodgate had opened. Suddenly composer Henry Cowell was immersed in music. He rehearsed a band, taught musicianship to about 200 students a day, corrected papers and correspondence course lessons, played the flute and the violin, wrote a book on melody, and composed. The burst of productivity was perhaps not unusual, but the workplace was. Henry Cowell was an inmate of San Quentin.

In 1936, after being convicted of engaging in homosexual activities, Cowell entered the largest prison in a penal system rated the second worst in the country.

As he awaited sentencing he worked in the prison jute mill. The sentence was fixed at the maximum—fifteen years—and he was assigned to work with the bandmaster of the San Quentin Education Department. He put together band concerts that were a combination of popular and "serious" pieces, although the avid musical theorist rarely included so-called modern music.

He did his best to accommodate the musical tastes of his fellow inmates. He wrote Oriental and Celtic and Mexican-inspired pieces and a band suite called *How They Take It* that touched on various ethnic styles, reflecting the diversity of the prison population. He also wrote experimental pieces, including "elastic" compositions that could be expanded or contracted according to the wishes of the performer.

Within three years Cowell had developed a full-fledged school of music in San Quentin, including a small orchestra and a chamber music series in which he played duets with a violinist who had been convicted of writing bad checks.

The testimony of medical experts and exemplary behavior reduced Cowell's sentence to ten years, and with less than half of the sentence served, he was paroled in 1940.

Looking back on his work in San Quentin, Henry Cowell said, "Some of it seems to have turned out well."

May 17th
The Only Problem

It looked like a lucky break or a big favor done for one composer by two others. The National Society of Music in Paris was putting on a major concert and composer Vincent d'Indy asked Ernest Chausson to withdraw one of his pieces from the program in order to make room for a work by a newcomer, Maurice Ravel.

Ravel aspired to write an opera based on *A Thousand and One Nights*, and his first orchestral piece, *Shéhérazade*, was to be the overture for it. For the big concert of May 17, 1899, Ravel provided detailed program notes describing the structure and story of the overture.

D'Indy was to conduct, but had to back out at the last minute, providing a triple opportunity for Ravel, who would now get to have his conducting debut directing the first performance of his first orchestral work.

The only problem was Ravel's inability to conduct. He lacked the assertiveness necessary to impose his interpretation on the orchestra. Neither the structure nor the descriptive details of the resulting performance lined up with the meticulous program notes.

The audience began to give voice to their frustration.

A few of Ravel's friends tried to rally support for him with cries of *bravo*, which brought a backlash of catcalls and whistling.

The critics were even more outspoken in their condemnation of the piece. The son of a prominent composer suggested that Ravel had a powerful imagination—if he believed that his overture conformed to classical models.

After a while, Ravel agreed. His conducting career continued without distinction. At the end of one concert, he laid down the baton and sighed, "My God! I had no idea what was going on."

He never wrote his opera. *Shéhérazade* disappeared for three-quarters of a century and was rediscovered in time for a performance marking the centennial of Ravel's birth in 1975.

May 18th
Such a Marvelous Gift

Ludwig van Beethoven is said to have proposed marriage to Therese Malfatti, a supposition supported by the tender tone of a letter he wrote to her in May 1810. He referred first to something he had sent her, quite possibly a copy of a piano piece dedicated to her, later to become famous as "Für Elise:"

In this letter, beloved Therese, you are receiving what I promised you, and, in fact, if it weren't for some very powerful hindrances, you'd be receiving even more, if only to prove that I always do more for my friends than I promise. I have every confidence that your avocations are every bit as charming as your entertainment is pleasant....No doubt I'd be expecting you to esteem me too highly if I were to say of you, "People are united not just when they're together, even the distant one, the absent one, also being with us."

Who would apply a saying like that to our whimsical Therese, who has such a carefree approach to all of life's situations?

As far as your pursuits are concerned, be sure not to neglect the pianoforte or music in general. You have such a marvelous gift for music. Why don't you develop it seriously? You have so much feeling for everything that's beautiful and good. Why not apply it to finding in such a glorious art that which is fine and perfect, attributes that in turn radiate beauty upon us?

My life is very lonely and quiet. Even though here and there, some poet would like to awaken me, all the same, ever since you left Vienna, I feel an emptiness that not even my art can fill.

Your pianoforte has been ordered and you'll soon have it. I wonder what difference you'll find between a theme that was improvised one evening and the way I recently wrote it down for you. Work it out for yourself, but please do not drink punch to help you.

May 19th

The Talk of the Town

Londoners were accustomed to visits from great musicians, but in the spring of 1764, king and commoner alike were astonished by an eight-year-old named Wolfgang Amadeus Mozart.

Young Mozart's fame had come before him, thanks to his performances in Vienna and Paris. He arrived with his father Leopold and his sister Nannerl, and almost at once they were summoned to the royal residence at Buckingham House, where they were greeted with what Leopold called "indescribable" hospitality. Riding through St. James Park a week later, they were recognized from the royal carriage, and, forgetting regal decorum, twenty-six-year-old King George III let down the window sash and nodded and waved heartily to the prodigy.

During Mozart's second visit to the palace on May 19, the king tested the boy's ability to play music by popular composers of the day—Handel and Karl Friedrich Abel—at sight. He played the organ and the harpsichord, accompanied Queen Charlotte as she sang an aria, and improvised a melody based on a tune by Handel. On June 5 Mozart and Nannerl played a public concert in the Spring Gardens Room, and within three weeks Mozart was being promoted as "the most extraordinary prodigy and most amazing genius that has appeared in any age."

About then Mozart met the Queen's Music Master, the twenty-eight-year-old Johann Christian Bach, who had settled in London three years previously and now went by the name John Bach. The two took to each other at once. They played a harpsichord duet, taking turns playing a bar at a time, with Mozart sitting on John Bach's lap, and then Bach started a fugue that Mozart finished.

But the relationship thrived on more than novelty. After a year in England, Mozart picked up vocal and symphonic techniques from John Bach. He wrote his first six piano concertos based on Bach's sonatas and learned to subordinate theatrical effects to sheer beauty of phrase.

140

May 20th
The Upgrade

By the early twentieth century, Granville Bantock had become one of England's most respected
composers, but at the end of the nineteenth century,
he was the Musical Director of the New Brighton
Tower, a job that required him to conduct an open-
air band and a ballroom orchestra. He had no intention of devoting his career to light music, and
yet he wasn't in a position to buck the authority of
the directors, and so he devised a subtle strategy to
improve the repertory.

Bantock's first move was to become friends with the orchestra members, which he did by throwing parties that went well into the night.
He was quick to convince the management that he could conduct the
frothy kind of music they wanted, and, once he had gained their confidence, he suggested that putting on a slightly different kind of concert
would upgrade the music at New Brighton Tower. With the help of a
sympathetic director, Bantock slowly added string players and other
instrumentalists until he had a full orchestra.

Before they knew it, couples at afternoon events at the ballroom
were dancing to waltzes by Tchaikovsky, Beethoven, Dvořák, Liszt,
and Brahms. For one concert Bantock had the outdoor band playing
his arrangements of excerpts from Wagner's *Parsifal*. Once he pushed
things even further by having the orchestra practice the Prelude to
Wagner's *Tristan and Isolde* when they were supposed to be rehearsing
for a pops concert.

Within a year Bantock had a Sunday afternoon concert series underway, with works by major composers on the programs, and, before
long, music-lovers from nearby Liverpool were taking the ferry across
the Mersey River to attend. All of which encouraged Bantock to take
an even bolder step—inaugurating a concert series in which prominent
composers of the day would come and conduct their own works, among
them Jean Sibelius and Edward Elgar. And soon the New Brighton
Tower Orchestra became famous as a major force for performing first-
rate classical music.

May 21st

Vampires

In his 1978 reminiscence *My Many Years*, pianist Arthur Rubinstein describes an early confrontation with the innovative composer Igor Stravinsky.

Just after World War I, Rubinstein and the cash-strapped Stravinsky were in a Paris recording studio. The composer asked the pianist, "Did you play in your concerts my Piano Rag Music?"

Rubinstein replied that, while he was proud to own the manuscript of it, the piece didn't suit his preference for music of "the old era." He added that it was written "for percussion rather than for my kind of piano."

Stravinsky argued that Rubinstein didn't understand the piece. To demonstrate, he banged it out on the piano—about ten times—which made Rubinstein balk all the more.

Stravinsky raged. "You think you can sing on the piano, but that is an illusion. The piano is nothing but a percussion instrument and it sounds right only as percussion."

Rubinstein blew his top. He said that the public neither liked nor understood Stravinsky's music and that his orchestra was too loud for them, as had been proven by the riot at the debut of *The Rite of Spring*. "But for some mysterious reason," he said, "when I play your music on the piano, it becomes clearer to them and they begin to like it." He played some of Stravinsky's *Petrouchka* and demanded, "Does it sound like percussion or like music?"

Stravinsky was so taken with the playing that he forgot all about their quarrel. He said that he would write a sonata for Rubinstein. The two embraced and went to dinner. When the hard-up Stravinsky heard that Rubinstein had been making good money, he complained that pianists became millionaires by playing the music left to them by starving composers—"the starving Mozart and Schubert," he said, "and the poor mad Schumann, the tubercular Chopin, and the sick Beethoven."

"He was right," Rubinstein reflected. "I always felt that we were vampires living off the blood of these great geniuses."

May 22nd
The Wrong Answer

One day in the 1770s the Prince of Asturias was eager to hear the latest quintet by Luigi Boccherini, and with a simple lapse of tact the composer turned the honor into a catastrophe.

The story might well have been exaggerated for the sake of good gossip, but the confrontation between the composer and the prince was clearly tense enough to leave a lasting impression.

According to the story, the prince began to play the first violin part of the quintet and found it extremely monotonous, the notes do si, do si alternating on and on for half a page. The prince launched into his part with vigor and, not noticing the general harmonic effect of the work, got impatient and began to exaggerate the repetition of his part, then lost his patience completely, jumped to his feet and voiced his annoyance. "Any novice could write stuff like this—*do si, do si!*"

Boccherini remained calm and deferential. "Sire, will Your Highness be so gracious as to observe the modulations that the second violin and the viola are expressing, and the pizzicato to be heard in the part for the violoncello while the first violin repeats itself? The sameness of the first violin ceases to be monotonous as soon as the other instruments enter and participate in the dialogue."

But the prince was not to be pacified. *"Do si, do si!* And it goes on that way for half an hour. Some delicious dialogue! It's the music of a novice—and a bad novice at that!"

Boccherini couldn't resist a comeback. "Sire, before making such a judgment it is necessary to understand music."

That was enough for the prince. From then on the palace was off limits to Luigi Boccherini. It was forbidden to mention his name at court, and he soon became a nonentity there.

May 23rd

A Pleasant Interlude

As one of Europe's leading composers and performers, Felix Mendelssohn was also an astute judge of the talents of others, including his best friends. On May 23, 1834, he wrote to his mother of an encounter at a Music Festival in Aix-la-Chapelle after a rehearsal of Handel's oratorio *Deborah:*

Who should trip right into my arms but Ferdinand Hiller, who was so glad to see me that he almost hugged me to death. He had come from Paris to hear the oratorio, and Chopin had skipped out on his students to come with him, and so we met again.

Now I had everything I could want from the Music Festival, because the three of us stayed together, and got a private box in the theater where the oratorio is performed, and, of course, on the following morning we went to the piano, where I found the most enjoyment. Both of them have improved greatly in their playing, and as a pianist Chopin is now one of the very best. He comes up with new effects the way Paganini does with his violin, and pulls off previously implausible passages.

Hiller is also a commendable player—powerful and yet light. Nonetheless, both tend to fall into the passionate, flamboyant Parisian style, often losing track of tempo and sobriety. On the other hand, maybe I don't fall into it enough. So all three of us naturally learn and improve each other, making me feel a little like a school teacher and they like French dandies.

After the festival we traveled together to Düsseldorf and spent a very enjoyable day there, playing and talking about music. Then I accompanied them yesterday to Cologne. Early this morning they set out for Coblenz by steamer. I took off in the other direction and the pleasant interlude was over.

May 24th

The Wayward Bach

Johann Sebastian Bach fathered four sons who became prominent composers, but he had other musical children, including a black sheep named Johann Gottfried Bernhard.

In 1736, when a position opened for an organist at St. Mary's in Mülhausen, Bach put in a good word for the twenty-year-old Bernhard, who was impressive enough at his audition to get the job.

Much like his father thirty years earlier, young Bernhard had a way of annoying church officials. One of them complained that his overlong preludes cut short the time available for the services, and another warned, "If Bach continues to play this way, the organ will be wrecked in two years and most of the congregation will be deaf." They later suggested that the organ be checked for damage.

With shaken self-confidence, Bernhard asked his father to help him find another job, and the result was another church organist position, this time in the village of Sangerhausen.

After less than a year in the new job, Bernhard disappeared, leaving behind debts that a Herr Klemm called to Sebastian's attention.

In a letter of May 24, 1738, Sebastian reminded Klemm that he had already paid several of his son's debts and added:

So you will understand that I am distressed to learn that he has again been borrowing money on all sides, has in no way changed his lifestyle, and has taken off without giving me the least idea of his whereabouts. What more can I do or say, my warnings having been ineffective and my loving care having accomplished nothing? I can only bear my cross patiently and commend my wayward boy to God's mercy.

Bach asked that the position be kept open until the young man's return, but Bernhard showed up next at the University of Jena, where he planned to study law.

Less than a year later, the story of the wayward Bach ended when he died of a fever at age twenty-four.

May 25th

A Team Effort

In the spring of 1782, Mozart was a busy twenty-six-year-old composer with music and matrimony on his mind. On May 25 he wrote from Vienna to his father Leopold in Salzburg, and the letter was a team effort between Mozart and his intended. Mozart wrote:

This time I really do need to steal a moment, so that you don't have to wait too long for a letter. Tomorrow our first concert takes place in the Augarten, and at half past eight, Martin will be bringing me in a carriage and we still have to make six visits, which I need to get out of the way by eleven because then I have to go to see Countess Rumbeck. After that I'll be lunching with Countess Thun—in her garden at that. In the evening we will be rehearsing the concert. The performance will include a symphony by Van Swieten and one of mine. An amateur singer, Mademoiselle Berger, is going to sing. A boy by the name of Turk will be playing a violin concerto. And Fräulein Aurnhammer and I will be playing my E-flat concerto for two pianos.

Mozart was in such haste that his fiancée, Constanze Weber, finished the letter, saying:

Your dear son has been called away to Countess Thun's at this very moment, and hasn't had time to finish this letter to his dear father, much to his regret. He has commissioned me to inform you since today is posting day, he doesn't want you to be without a letter from him. He will write more to his dear father the next time. Please forgive me for writing to you. These few lines cannot be as agreeable to you as those from your son.

In the months to follow, a skeptical Leopold Mozart and his optimistic son would continue to cross letters about Mozart's musical and marital plans.

May 26th

A Bad Business for Me

When Confederate general Stonewall Jackson defeated forces led by Nathaniel Banks at the Battle of Winchester, Virginia, pianist and composer Louis Moreau Gottschalk was in Philadelphia. Although he was a Union sympathizer, he realized that the war could be dangerous for him regardless of his stance. He wrote in his journal for May 26, 1862:

The news received yesterday, Sunday, of the defeat of Banks by Jackson has aroused patriotic enthusiasm, which the rapidly succeeding victories of the last two months had weakened by inspiring an exaggerated serenity. The Seventh New York Regiment, composed exclusively of young men belonging to the aristocracy of that metropolitan city, leaves tonight for Washington. It numbers twelve hundred able-bodied men. Seven other regiments leave New York tomorrow.

The State of Massachusetts will send ten or twelve thousand more in a few days. They fear that the Confederacy, taking the offensive, plans to march on Washington. There was a riot yesterday in Baltimore. The people wanted to hang a man who expressed secessionist sentiments. An imposing police force guards the streets.

A bad business for me, who ought to give a concert there in two days. I understand very well how to fill the hall, but it is dangerous. It would be to announce that I would play my piece called "The Union" and my variations on "Dixie's Land." In the first I intercalate "Yankee Doodle" and "Hail, Columbia." The second is a Southern Negro air of which the Confederates, since the beginning of the war, have made a national air. It is to the music of "Dixie's Land" that Beauregard's troops invariably charge the soldiers of the North. At the point at which men's minds are now the hall would be full of partisans of both sections, who certainly would come to blows. But I should make three or four thousand dollars. It is true that in the tumult I might be the first one choked.

Like many, Gottschalk was unaware that "Dixie" was attributed to Daniel D. Emmett, a Northerner.

May 27th

The Guardian

By May of 1816 Ludwig van Beethoven was the guardian of two concerns—his music and his nephew, and he wrote about both in a letter from Vienna to Charles Neate in London:

Mr. Ries informed me of your plan to give a concert for my benefit. For such a triumph of my art in London I would be beholden to you alone. But an even healthier influence upon my practically destitute life would be to have the profits generated by the undertaking. You know that in a sense I am now a father to the handsome boy you saw with me. It's all I can do to live alone for three months on my annual salary and now there's the added load of supporting a poor orphan. You can imagine how much I would welcome any legal way to improve my situation.

As for the Quartet in F minor, *you may sell it to a publisher right away and indicate the date of publication because I'd like for it to come out here on the same day. Feel free to do the same with the two sonatas, Opus 102, for pianoforte and violoncello, but there's no hurry.*

I leave it completely up to you to determine my reward for the quartet and the sonatas. The more the better.

Please write to me at once for two reasons: so that I don't have to shrug when I'm asked if I've gotten letters from you and so that I can know how you're doing and if I'm still in your good graces. Answer me in English if you can give me happy news (for example, about a concert in my benefit) and in French if the news is bad.

Maybe you can find some music lover to whom the trio and the sonata with the violin or the symphony arranged for the harpsichord might be dedicated, and from whom one might expect a gift.

May 28th
The Magician, the Musician, & the President

Would the composer and the president catch on to the trick? In 1914, at an evening's entertainment for the German Sailors Home and the Magicians Club of London, after the Ritz Carlton orchestra's performances of excerpts of Puccini operas, the agenda moved on to the great magician Houdini.

Houdini began with some simple close-up illusions—changing the colors of silk handkerchiefs and turning water into wine, and he noticed that sitting next to composer Victor Herbert was a very intent Theodore Roosevelt. He was sure that the former president had been able to see through every trick—so far.

The magician proposed a spiritualistic slate test "in the full glare of light."

Houdini invited the audience to seal into envelopes questions they wanted answered from the spirit world. When Roosevelt began to write his question with the paper in the palm of his hand, Houdini took an atlas from the ship's library and offered it to him as a support.

Thinking that Victor Herbert was onto the ruse, the magician gave him a wink.

"Turn around," Herbert told Roosevelt. "He'll discern what you write from the movements of the pencil."

After Houdini had collected all of the questions, he said, "I am sure that there will be no objection if we use the Colonel's question." The audience readily agreed.

He had Roosevelt place his sealed question between two blank slates and asked him what his question had been.

"Where was I last Christmas?" the Colonel replied.

Houdini opened the slates and held them up for all to see. One slate had a detailed map in colored chalk of Brazil's River of Doubt in the Amazon. The other slate contained the message, "near the Andes" and was signed by W.T. Stead, a spiritualist journalist who had drowned when the *Titanic* sank.

The next morning, when Roosevelt asked Houdini if the whole thing had been spiritualism or sleight of hand, the magician confided, "It was hocus-pocus."

May 29th

The Shortcut

In the spring of 1592 John Bull left London for Bristol, leaving his work as organist at the prestigious Chapel Royal to a subordinate. In a curious way, his leave of absence would provide a great opportunity to an undistinguished musician named William Phelps.

For reasons unknown, Bull took his time getting back to London, riding north through Gloucestershire, perhaps stealing a bit of a vacation from his employer, Queen Elizabeth, who was known to keep a short leash on her favorite musicians. He seems to have been on his way to visit friends in Worcester when he took the road along the Severn River to Tewkesbury.

During the night, William Phelps was returning home to Tewkesbury when he encountered two dismounted men, bending over someone lying beside the road. As he rode forward to investigate, the two took to their horses and galloped away.

The man lying beside the road was John Bull, dazed, bleeding, and battered, his clothes riffled and torn. Phelps brought him home and took care of him for several days until he was able to ride again. He seems also to have forwarded Bull's description of his attackers, because two days after the robbery, two suspects were arrested as they tried to leave Bristol by sea. One of them was a Spaniard named Goula, who worked for the Duke of Feria, the Spanish Ambassador in France, and the other, Dubois, was a member of the French Catholic League. During an attempt to resist arrest, Goula fell into the harbor and drowned.

Bull invited Phelps to accompany him to London, where Bull had an audience with the queen. Apparently Elizabeth was grateful for the safe return of her Master of Music, because although Phelps was a musician of no great note, on May 29, 1592, he was quickly and unanimously appointed as Gentleman Extraordinary to the elite Chapel Royal on the grounds that "he did show a most rare kindness to Mr. Doctor Bull in his great distress."

May 30th

The Million Dollar Trio

They were three of the world's most formidable musicians, and in 1949 they were invited to perform together during a series of four concerts in Chicago's Ravinia Park. Their togetherness would be short-lived.

Pianist Arthur Rubinstein, cellist Gregor Piatigorsky, and violinist Jascha Heifetz drew huge admiring crowds at Ravinia, and the newly-formed threesome was so successful that one critic referred to them as "The Million Dollar Trio."

Rubinstein disliked the nickname so much that he couldn't wait to drop out of the ensemble, but when RCA invited the trio to make a recording of their concert repertory, he agreed to participate.

The rehearsals took place in 1950, mostly at the home of clarinetist Max Epstein, and apparently they became opportunities for Rubinstein and Heifetz to engage in personality clashes. Phrasing, tempo, and any other aspect of music interpretation became grist for their growing feud, and their quarrels became so rancorous that the rehearsals sometimes ground to a halt while the two artists cooled off.

Rubinstein reported later that Heifetz was particularly perturbed by the billing in the concert programs because Rubinstein's name always came first, followed by Heifetz and then Piatigorsky.

Heifetz wondered why the billing couldn't rotate so that each of them would be mentioned first at one time or another.

"I don't mind," Rubinstein supposedly replied, "but as far as I know, all trios are written for piano, violin, and cello, and traditionally one advertises the names of the players in exactly that order."

Heifetz argued that he had seen some trios for violin and cello with piano accompaniment. Rubinstein doubted it; Heifetz insisted.

Rubinstein lost his temper, "Jascha," he shouted, "even if God were playing the violin, it would be printed Rubinstein, God, and Piatigorsky, in that order!"

When RCA printed the record jackets, the names of Rubinstein and Heifetz appeared side by side on the top line, but the two never performed together again.

May 31st
The Special Effect

The crossing from Europe to New York left Igor Stravinsky with hours to fill and so he prevailed upon cellist Gregor Piatigorsky to work with him on a cello and piano transcription of his ballet *Suite Italienne.* Violinist Nathan Milstein also had some time on his hands and so he came along and watched as Piatigorsky made daring suggestions and defended them as Stravinsky listened.

One of Piatigorsky's most brilliant effects came about by accident.

Tea was served aboard the SS *Rex* at 4:45, and Milstein and Piatigorsky attended regularly, enjoying the company of various attractive young women who were drawn to the charming cellist. One day when the two musicians were expecting a particularly alluring young lady, Stravinsky got more involved than ever in the transcription and showed every indication of working right through tea.

Piatigorsky was a nervous wreck. He had no intention of missing his date, but he couldn't work up the courage to tell Stravinsky that their time for working on *Suite Italienne* was limited.

As he played the suite, Piatigorsky became so tense that the bow popped out of his hand and slipped behind the bridge of the cello, where it made a strange whistling sound.

Stravinsky jumped up. "That's it! Marvelous! I like it!" he cried. "How do you do it?"

After some tinkering, Piatigorsky was able to recreate the effect and they decided to write it into the transcription.

Milstein was impressed that the stubborn and opinionated Stravinsky was so quick to pick up on the new sound and use it. The composer was delighted with their accidental discovery, and so were Milstein and Piatigorsky, who got to tea in time for their rendezvous with the young lady.

Nathan Milstein tells the story in *From Russia to the West*, the 1990 memoir he co-authored with music journalist Solomon Volkov.

June 1st

Rabin

The violinist had achieved spectacular feats of virtuosity as a child, but as a young adult he had been shaken by a series of personal and professional difficulties, and now he was dependent upon a powerful sedative that helped him to cope with his latest crisis—the fear of falling off the front of the stage.

During his years as a child prodigy, Michael Rabin had said more than once that nervousness was never a problem for him, but by the time he was in his mid-twenties, he had begun taking "the little yellow pills" to quell the anxiety he had begun to feel before each concert. Only gradually did it become apparent that the pills were addictive and that their withdrawal symptoms included a loss of coordination.

And larger and larger doses were necessary to achieve the same calming effect.

Rabin was also taking a second prescription drug, a diet tablet with side effects that included the very things Rabin was trying to overcome with the sedative—nervousness, dizziness, and insomnia.

In 1962 he pulled himself together to give a major performance— the first concert in Philharmonic Hall, later called Avery Fisher Hall, in New York's newly-built Lincoln Center. He played the Brahms *Sonata in D minor*, Bach's unaccompanied *Partita in D minor*, and a sonata by the late American composer Robert Kurka.

New York Herald Tribune critic Harold Eyer wrote Rabin off as an overgrown prodigy who had let his intonation and technique go sloppy.

At the urging of friends, Rabin consulted a series of general practitioners who prescribed another smorgasbord of sedatives and dietetics, a course that led to concert cancellations, hospitalizations, and an erratic withdrawal from the drugs. During the next several years, Rabin gradually made his way back to the concert stage.

But twilight came early in the troubled life of Michael Rabin, and, at the age of thirty-five, he died alone in his apartment, apparently as the result of a fall.

June 2nd

Discord

He joined the Nazi Party in 1935 and closed his letters with *Heil Hitler*, but in 1939 conductor Herbert von Karajan began a dramatic break with Hitler's government.

At thirty-one, Karajan was the musical idol of Germany, especially among the young. He was particularly successful in 1938 with a State Opera performance of Wagner's *Tristan and Isolde*.

On June 2, 1939, he conducted two performances of Wagner's *Die Meistersinger* with the Berlin Opera. The first of them was a State Gala in honor of Prince Paul of Yugoslavia. Karajan won praise from all for the clarity of the music, his youthful vigor, and the amount of freedom he allowed the singers.

The second performance did not go so well.

According to one account, bass baritone Rudolf Bockelmann, singing the part of cobbler Hans Sachs, was feeling the effects of drink and made a mistake that disoriented Karajan, who was conducting from memory. The singers ground to a halt and the curtain came down while things could be sorted out.

It would've been a forgettable mishap except that one audience member was there just to see the famous Karajan for the first time. Adolf Hitler was a big fan of Bockelmann, and flew into a rage to see his pet singer embarrassed just because Karajan had the audacity to conduct without a score. He declared Karajan a lightweight who was incapable of making Wagner sound sufficiently German.

Karajan continued to have problems controlling the State Opera. Two years later, during a Rome performance of *Die Meistersinger*, when he tried to make the part of the clerk Beckmesser more humorous, singer Eugen Fuchs turned away with the pronouncement, "My Führer does not wish me to change anything in this part."

The gap between Karajan and the Party widened even more a year later when he married Anna Maria Güttermann, who was one-quarter Jewish.

154

June 3rd

Good Intentions

The road to disaster was paved with good intentions. In 1915 or
'16 famed pianist Sergei Rachmaninoff came to the St. Petersburg
Conservatory to perform a benefit concert for the widow of composer
Alexander Scriabin. Not everyone appreciated the gesture, and a notable musician who attempted a compliment caused a rift that lasted
for years.

Rachmaninoff's entire concert consisted of works by the late composer, but some difference of opinion arose as to just how his music
should sound. In one of the front rows of the hall an assortment of
people chatted and whispered throughout the performance. One of
them was a thin man of twenty-five or so with pendulous lips and an
oversized blond head. His name was Sergei Prokofiev.

Rachmaninoff was the musical idol of Moscow, whereas Scriabin
had been the hero of a small group of fervent aspiring mystics and
philosophers that dismissed Rachmaninoff as the representative of out-
moded romanticism. Prokofiev was their musical spearhead. He and
his music were powerful, tough, and direct. His friends in the audience that night were surprised by Rachmaninoff's tribute to Scriabin
but were quick to express their disdain for his methodical, less than
mystical approach to Scriabin's visionary music.

After the concert they had nothing but scorn for Rachmaninoff's
playing.

Except for Prokofiev, who thought that Rachmaninoff had done a
good job. He went to the artists' room and with typical bluntness told
the celebrated pianist that his performance was "not bad, not bad at
all."

It was not what Rachmaninoff wanted to hear. "What do you
mean—not bad?" he demanded. He turned his back on Prokofiev.

Although it took many years, the two Russian greats were able to
get on better footing during a chance meeting on an ocean liner, where
they met again not at a concert, but over a chessboard.

Nicholas Nabokov tells the story in his 1942 memoir *Old Friends
and New Music*.

June 4th

Water Power

Debt-ridden and feeling battered by his critics, Jean Sibelius liked the offer from America. Composer Horatio Parker was offering him $1,200 to participate in Yale University's Norfolk Festival, at which he would conduct his new symphonic poem *The Oceanides* and a few of his shorter works.

Five weeks later Sibelius was on a steamship bound for New York, revising the poem as he got more and more experience with the sea.

At the first Carnegie Hall rehearsal, festival organizer Carl Stoeckel had the impression that the orchestra found *The Oceanides* perplexing, but he was impressed at how rapidly each successive rehearsal made it more musical.

Sibelius, too, threw himself into the performances of *The Oceanides*. "It is as if I find more and more of myself in it," he wrote to a friend. "The ocean has really inspired me."

The concert of Sibelius' music, which took place in a huge wooden structure called The Music Shed, in Norfolk, Connecticut, on June 4, 1914, was the crowning moment of the festival. Rather than counting strict time, Sibelius made broad poetic sweeps of his arms as he conducted some of his best-known works—*Pohjola's Daughter*, the *King Christian II Suite*, *The Swan of Tuonela*, *Finlandia*, *Valse Triste*, and then the new work, *The Oceanides*.

According to critic Olin Downes, the effect was of great waves crashing.

At the end of the concert, the audience gave Sibelius an ovation that Stoeckel said he had never seen equaled anywhere.

A few days later, Sibelius would again encounter the power of water when his host took him on an excursion to Niagara Falls. Sibelius was deep in thought as they approached the foot of the Falls in a small steamboat. He later confided to his host that he had been trying to come up with a way to convey the experience musically, but had concluded that Niagara Falls was "too solemn and too vast to be represented by any human individual."

156

June 5th
Master of the Comeback

Fritz Kreisler was a master of the comeback, large and small. After World War I, the Austrian violinist had to win back his American audiences, and did so by playing concert after concert with irresistible virtuosity and taste. In 1935, when he admitted that many of the Baroque masterpieces he played were actually his own compositions, he rode out the scandal by defending his actions in the press and continuing to perform. His resilience was put to the test again in 1941 when he stepped off a New York curb and was hit by a truck.

After nearly a month in a coma, Kreisler began the slow process of recovery, which included listening to classical music on the radio and attending a concert in Carnegie Hall featuring the New York Philharmonic led by Leopold Stokowski. But Kreisler had not recovered yet. He had to cancel all twenty-six of his remaining engagements for the 1941-42 season

A few months later he ventured a performance in Philadelphia for an audience of orchestral players and sound engineers, and then played a cautious concert in Albany in which he performed a familiar but demanding program of Grieg and Bruch and some of his own compositions.

Three months after that success and eighteen months after the accident, Kreisler performed a full-fledged Carnegie Hall comeback recital that began with a standing ovation. The enthralled audience included violin virtuoso Jacques Thibaud, who was so involved in Kreisler's playing that he subconsciously fingered every note against his cheek.

Fritz Kreisler was also a master of the little comeback. When a socialite engaged him to perform a private concert for a fee of a thousand dollars and added, "We ask that you not mingle with the guests afterward," Kreisler replied, "In that case, madam, my fee will be five hundred dollars."

June 6th
Khachaturian

Young Aram Khachaturian had aptitude and a strong desire to study music. At the age of nineteen he was gambling that they would be enough to get him into a first-rate music school. Khachaturian was born on June 6, 1903, in Tiflis, in the Republic of Georgia, where he grew up improvising Armenian folk songs on the piano. He was a biology student when he heard his first symphony orchestra in the Great Hall of the Moscow Conservatory in a performance of Beethoven's Ninth, a performance that he said "shook him to the depths."

Khachaturian's closest advisor at the time was his brother, who steered him toward a career in biology, a discipline that became more and more at odds with Khachaturian's inclinations. "What, after all, did I know about biology?" Khachaturian reflected in later life. "I must admit it was difficult for me to get used to the subject I had to study, to the laboratory work and to dissecting frogs."

Khachaturian decided to put his musical inclinations to the test by applying to the Gnessen Music School, a small but important family-run institution in a cramped old house on a Moscow side street. "I faced the admissions committee without even the most elementary knowledge of theory," Khachaturian recalled later. "To demonstrate my voice and ear I blithely sang a soulful romance that caused the members of the committee to smile."

To show his piano aptitude, Khachaturian fell back on his familiarity with Armenian dance tunes and easily passed the tests for ear, rhythm, and musical memory, although this was the first time he had taken such a test.

The committee decided unanimously to enroll Aram Khachaturian in the school. He would go on to become a teacher there on his way to becoming a major composer of the twentieth century.

June 7th
Reconciliation

Arthur Friedheim was worried. His former teacher and longtime friend, Franz Liszt, had promised a pupil a concert appearance at the 1886 Carlsruhe Music Festival. Friedheim considered the pupil a disaster, but, perhaps because the young woman in question was a protégé of Empress Augusta of Prussia, Liszt saw fit to go ahead and put her on the program.

At a time of competing musical factions, Friedheim was concerned that a bad performance would be a setback for the festival and for the cause of innovative music. He pleaded with Liszt to reconsider, but to no avail.

He argued with festival conductor Felix Mottl until they were able to thrash out a compromise. Instead of accompanying the questionable soloist with the orchestra, Mottl would perform with her as a second pianist. Just before the performance, still full of misgivings, Friedheim approached Liszt again and found him unyielding.

"If she isn't nervous," Liszt said, "she'll get through all right."

"But you know full well that she will be nervous," Friedheim said. "She's going to wreck everything that we've accomplished."

The performance turned out to be as bad as he feared. From the second piano, Mottl did his best to drown out the offending novice.

By opposing Liszt and winning over Mottl, Friedheim had offended his former teacher, and when Liszt left for London and Paris on what he half-jokingly referred to as his last tour, instead of accompanying him as usual, Friedheim remained in Weimar. But suddenly he felt that he had to see the old virtuoso again. So he hurried to a Liszt festival in Liège, Belgium, hoping somehow to restore their relationship.

"You are inclined to come too late," Liszt said with a frown. "Beware of missing chances, otherwise it may be altogether too late someday." Then, seeing how downhearted Friedheim was, Liszt smiled and embraced him, and their friendship was mended, a blessing for Friedheim, because a few weeks later, his old teacher died.

June 8th

The Bullet

Composer Georges Onslow was a master of the string quintet, and he applied that mastery to one of the most remarkable string quintets ever written—a description of an accident that nearly took his life.

Onslow was born in France in 1784 to a father banished from England because of a homosexual scandal. Onslow spent much of his youth in London receiving the education of a gentleman, and became a capable cellist. After two years of travel in Germany and Austria he began composing, specializing in string quintets for two violins, viola, and two cellos.

The quintet that most fascinated his contemporaries describes an accident that nearly ended Onslow's composing and his life.

In 1829 Onslow and some companions were hunting a long-elusive wild boar, but—ever the composer—Onslow brought along a book of music paper just in case inspiration came during the hunt. Book in hand, he took up an assigned position and waited for his fellow hunters to drive the boar his way. After a while, the quiet woods roused Onslow's musical imagination and, forgetting his friends, he wandered deeper into the woods, found a stump, and sat down to work on his latest quintet.

A shot rang out and Onslow fell bleeding to the ground.

A bullet had cut through his ear and lodged in his neck. His recovery was slow, painful, and partial. He roused himself by continuing his work on the quintet that had distracted him in the woods, only now it became a recollection of the accident. To the second movement minuet he gave the title "Suffering, Fever, and Delirium." The next movement he called "Convalescence." And the finale became known as "Recovery."

The bullet in his neck was never removed and he eventually went deaf in the affected ear, but despite the high cost of his "Bullet Quintet," Georges Onslow said often that he would not have wanted to miss the opportunity to write it.

June 9th
Fun While It Lasted

As World War I spread through Europe, the famous Australian-born pianist and composer Percy Grainger described himself variously as a conscientious objector or a coward. He had arrived in New York from London as the United States was entering the war. Because of what friends considered his unpatriotic attitude, he couldn't go back to England. So he took a perfectly logical next step.

He bought a saxophone.

On June 9, 1917, he walked to Fort Totten and enlisted as a bandsman in the U.S. Army. He was fitted for a uniform, his billowy hair was cut to military specifications, and the following day he was transferred to Fort Hamilton, South Brooklyn, where he became a member of the 15th Band of the Coast Artillery Corps.

The only catch: The virtuoso pianist couldn't play the saxophone. And, as it was, the band already had plenty of saxophonists, so he was given an oboe, and got by well enough to be promoted to Bandsman 2nd Class.

The brilliant but eccentric Grainger would later describe the first few weeks in the army as the happiest time of his life. He was paid $36 a month to study all kinds of brass and reed instruments and even got to conduct the band a few times. He was most pleased with the anonymity the army gave him and the freedom from the pressure of playing professional concerts.

The idyll was not to last though. Before long a reporter caught sight of him performing in one of the band concerts, and soon the New York papers revealed that one of the world's great pianists was masquerading as a humble bandsman.

He was reassigned to be a star pianist for Red Cross benefit concerts and Liberty Loan and War Bond drives.

But at least his army experience helped him to make up his mind about one issue. Within three weeks of joining the band, Percy Grainger applied to become a U.S. citizen.

June 10th

Driving Each Other Crazy

Sir Thomas Beecham was known for his practical jokes, but when Arthur Rubinstein played one on him, the celebrated conductor was not amused.

One hot morning, as they rehearsed Beethoven's *Piano Concerto in G* in the Hollywood Bowl, both Beecham and Rubinstein were in a bad mood. The piano was at the edge of the shell, and after playing the opening phrase of the concerto, Rubinstein settled in for the duration of the long orchestral section to follow. Beecham became increasingly impatient with the orchestra, stopped them after every bar, and singled out one musician after another for criticism, making them play the same passages over and over again.

He more or less forgot about Rubinstein sitting there in his short-sleeved shirt, broiling in the hot sun.

By the time he finally got to play again, Rubinstein was "pretty boiled up in every way." For the rest of the rehearsal, he and Beecham said little as they pressed on, openly hostile toward each other.

When it was finally over, and a sunburned Rubinstein was in the parking lot settling into his new Fleetwood Cadillac, Beecham appeared out of nowhere and asked for a lift. Rubinstein put on a friendly demeanor and said, "Certainly, Sir Thomas." As they headed into the streets of Los Angeles, Rubinstein said that it would be an honor to give Beecham a ride because he had gotten his license that very morning.

As Beecham blanched and shrank into the seat, Rubinstein made a point of becoming more and more nervous and inept.

"Look out, look out," Beecham bellowed, "there is a red light!"

"Thank you, Sir Thomas. I didn't see it."

And so it went for forty-five minutes. When they finally reached his destination and Sir Thomas stumbled out of the car, he gave Rubinstein a baleful look as he whispered "Thank you."

The lover of practical jokes had become the victim of one. Rubinstein had been driving for two years.

Beecham reacted to another joke at his expense in a more convivial way. That story on September 23.

June 11th
Budget Cuts

Czarina Catherine the Great was a big spender. When she wanted music she brought in the best performers and composers. In 1787 she brought in composer Domenico Cimarosa for what would prove a rocky sojourn in Russia.

The Czarina was eager to audition her new music master, and shortly after his arrival in St. Petersburg, she asked him to sing while accompanying himself on the harpsichord. He passed with flying colors and was deemed worthy of teaching the two grand dukes who were the sons of the heir to the throne.

She was less impressed by one of Cimarosa's first compositions for the Russian court, a comic opera that she dismissed as worthless and performed by singers who were "detestable."

Then a larger problem arose. Catherine's lavish lifestyle began to drain the royal treasury, forcing the Czarina to impose spending cuts. The most obvious way to reduce expenses was to dismiss some of the more costly musicians, but Catherine refused to do so, and during the next two years, Cimarosa wrote two new operas for the Russian court, one of which seems to have been quite successful since it was translated into Russian and, in its Italian version, remained in the St. Petersburg repertory for fifteen years. Cimarosa also had two earlier operas performed and went on to provide a multitude of other works.

By the spring of 1791, though, the imperial theater management had laid off most of their Italian company. Cimarosa's sense that the Czarina regarded his work as mediocre and his disapproval of what he saw as the Russian court's barbarity inspired the composer to leave the country with his wife, two children, and Italian servants.

The leave-taking, apparently, was friendly enough. As a gesture of goodwill, the Czarina presented the departing composer with a fine English fortepiano.

June 12th
Remembrance

After their 1989 concert tour of Japan, marimba player Keiko Abe and recorder virtuoso Walter van Hauwe went to the Columbia studio in Tokyo to produce a CD of the repertory they had played.

When van Hauwe arrived for the last day of recording, he was obviously depressed. When Abe asked him what was wrong, he explained that his wife was very sick. She had already been in the hospital when van Hauwe had flown to Japan for the tour, but her illness had since become much worse.

Abe suggested that he return to Holland at once. She could explain the situation to Columbia, and, anyway, the final studio session was to consist of free improvisations. They could easily enough do the recording later.

She had convinced him. Van Hauwe put his recorder back in the case. But then he had second thoughts. "Keiko, let's play now," he said. "Just one or two times."

As they played, Abe became aware that something special was happening. "The music angels came—and I simply followed the feeling," she recalled. She didn't think about the marimba, just followed the music as it passed from soft and tempered to strong and passionate, letting her imagination follow her feeling as she and van Hauwe improvised.

After they had played two pieces, van Hauwe packed up and flew to Amsterdam. A week later Abe got a phone call from him. He asked if they could put his wife's name on one of the improvised pieces. He had been thinking of her as they played, and the piece had since become connected to her memory. Soon after his return home, she had died.

Columbia was just about to release the recordings with titles of their own, but Abe was able to get to the producers just in time to have them change the title of one of the pieces to "She died, my water lily Tonneke."

164

June 13th

The Necessary Detachment

In his memoirs, violist William Primrose reported that during moments of crisis a certain detachment and a well-developed sense of humor saved him from disaster. At such times, he felt a curious sensation of viewing things from the outside. But if the situation became desperate enough, he was inclined to "giggle inwardly," and had to struggle to keep the giggle from becoming audible.

A performance of Bartók's complex *Viola Concerto* was particularly challenging. Primrose was soloing with a major American orchestra led by a celebrated conductor. The rehearsals had gone well, and the concerto went along smoothly—up to the forty-first measure of the first movement. At that point in the concerto, conductors sometimes subdivide the beat for greater clarity, and the conductor in question was doing just that when some misunderstanding arose between him and the orchestra and things began to fall apart.

In its efforts to recover, the orchestra bogged down into what Primrose could only call "heartbreak."

He could hear "a little toot on a flute, a tentative scrape on a cello or violin," and the tense, sweaty, desperate conductor calling out bar numbers.

Primrose felt the giggle coming on even though he knew that the concerto would get back on track as soon as the players got to a point at which the whole orchestra was to play together. He managed to avoid laughing out loud.

After the concert Primrose told the apologetic conductor to give the catastrophe no further thought because the performance had come out all right, and, since this was the first time the orchestra had played the piece, it was likely that few in the audience were aware of how much the piece had come unglued.

He was right. The day after the concert, a leading critic wrote about the "extraordinary meshing" of the solo viola and orchestra during the troubled section of the concerto's first movement.

Primrose reflected that without his outrageous sense of humor, his entire performance might have fallen apart.

June 14th

A Rare Specimen

 A friend had played the joke on Dmitri Shostakovich. Given the opportunity, Shostakovich couldn't resist perpetrating it on a conductor he found irritating.

Shostakovich grew up during the early years of the Soviet state. When he was about twenty he and some friends were obligated to take a test on Marxism-Leninism. Taking the test ahead of them was a young academician named Ivan Ivanovich Sollertinsky who reported that the test questions were incredibly hard. He said, for example, that the examiners wanted to know how Sophocles exemplified a materialist tendency. Young Shostakovich and his friends were scared to death until they realized that Sollertinsky was joking.

Somewhat later Shostakovich used the joke himself. Conductor Alexander Gauk and his wife were to be made Honored Artists of the Russian Republic. The title was bestowed upon very few, and Gauk and his wife gave a series of receptions to celebrate their new status. Shostakovich and Sollertinsky attended one of the parties, and amid the eating and drinking, Sollertinsky stood and gave a toast, congratulating his hosts and hoping that they would pass the test and be confirmed in their new titles.

Gauk froze and asked. "What test?"

Sollertinsky feigned surprise. Didn't his hosts know that passing a test on Marxism-Leninism was a prerequisite to receiving the title? In the sudden quiet Shostakovich and his friend finished eating and drinking, then departed, leaving the gloomy conductor and his wife at an empty table.

It was a cruel joke to be sure, but Shostakovich had an ax to grind. Gauk had lost the manuscripts to Shostakovich's Fourth, Fifth, and Sixth Symphonies, and in response to the composer's objections, had replied "Manuscripts? So what? I lost a suitcase with my new shoes, and you're worried about manuscripts?"

In his memoirs Shostakovich referred to Gauk as "a rare specimen of stupidity."

166

June 15th
Advances

In June 1852, chronically destitute Richard Wagner wrote from Zurich to the influential Franz Liszt in Weimar:

Dearest of friends, a request! I am working hard and hoping to finish the poem of my Valkyrie within two weeks. Then I'll be in urgent need for some kind of relaxation, such as a holiday, all the more so since I'd rather not finish my final poetic work, the great prelude, here in Zurich, where the sameness of these familiar surroundings oppresses me, and tedious visits tend to put me in a bad mood. I need to go up into the Alps and get at least a taste of the Italian border, where I might be able to stay for a while. But I can't afford that kind of extravagance on my basic income.

For next winter I have a few extra earnings to look forward to: (Tannhäuser in Leipzig and most likely also in Breslau.) Most of all, though, I'm depending upon the receipts you'll provide me from The Flying Dutchman *in Weimar. No doubt, I may expect 20 or 25 louis d'or? What do you say to sending me that much in the form of an advance?*

If Ziegesar is not yet back in charge of business, I'd rather not approach the box-office directly for this advance on my fee, but perhaps there's some well-intentioned person who wouldn't refuse you that amount in the form of an advance?

At the same time, you would be the best guarantee that such receipts would actually accrue, since your enthusiastic backing will see to it that The Flying Dutchman *is performed this winter in Weimar.*

The advance would be a source of great pleasure for me! But—I need the money before the end of the month at the latest! See if it's possible to bring this about.

Liszt arranged for an advance, and Wagner relaxed with a four-week walking tour of the Alps.

June 16th

The Human Flood

Harrisburg, Pennsylvania, June 16, 1863. New Orleans pianist and composer Louis Moreau Gottschalk found himself in one of the most dangerous places in the world as a Confederate invasion of the North spread panic in the streets. He wrote in his journal:

One train leaves at five o'clock, another left at two o'clock. I doubt the one promised us can accommodate the constantly increasing crowd of four or five thousand persons which presses into and around the station. Litters are provided for the sick. Many are occupied by wounded soldiers who will not be left here. Immense trains of merchandise continue to arrive. The panic increases. It is no longer a flight, it is a flood, a matter of everyone for himself. It would seem, in view of the speed with which the inhabitants abandon their city, that the rebels already were in sight. Trunks, boxes, bundles of clothes, furniture, mattresses, kitchen utensils, and even pianos are piled pell-mell on the road.

Carriages, carts, chariots, indeed all the vehicles in the city, have been put in requisition. The poor are moving in wheelbarrows. A trader has attached to his omnibus, already full, a long file of spring carts, trucks, and buggies, whose owners probably have no horses, and drags them along to the great displeasure of his team, which sweats, froths, and falls under the increased weight of the load. A long convoy comes in, with ten locomotives in front. It brings cannons, caissons, and many steam engines under construction, which have been sent to Harrisburg to prevent their falling into the hands of the enemy. The confusion is at its height. Cattle bellowing, frightened mules, prancing horses, the noisy crowd, the whistling locomotives, the blinding dust, the burning sun....

Harrisburg remained in Union hands. Gottschalk traveled on to Philadelphia and points north as Confederate and Union armies moved toward a confrontation near a town called Gettysburg.

June 17th

Why I Took the Job

Did doubts about the job's merit prompt Antonio Vasselli to take his brother-in-law to task for accepting a position in Vienna? Or was he more concerned about losing an Italian composer to the Austrian Emperor at a time when Italians were asserting their national identity? One way or the other, Gaetano Donizetti felt compelled to justify himself.

With enthusiasm he had written to a friend in June 1842, just before his appointment was confirmed:

You should know (and this is a secret for now and I implore you to keep it one) that I was called to Court to find out if I would accept the post that Krommer, Mozart, and Kozeluch, and others had held, namely, Kapellmeister to His Majesty the Emperor, accountable only to him through the Grand Chamberlain. I would be expected to direct concerts in the royal apartments only two or three times a year, with additional pay for every cantata that might be commissioned, every year having five or six months off, with an honorarium of three thousand a year. I said if His Majesty wished, I would serve for nothing.

Donizetti accepted the position gladly, thinking that his place in music history was secure.

When Vasselli rebuked him, Donizetti was quick to defend his decision:

Faulting me for accepting the most honorable post is unfair. Six months off are a fine thing; a thousand lire a month at Vienna and away are not to be sneezed at. Do you know that in Bologna they only wanted to give me three months off at a time? Are you aware that I would have to be in Bologna on Saint Petronio's Day? That it would not suffice to write new music, that I would be wanted there in person?

Are you aware, for that matter, that the position was Mozart's? That His Majesty expects only two concerts a year and that if I am commissioned to write music, I am paid for it?

June 18th

Achilles Heel

 Bringing his opera *Savanarola* to the stage was an uphill struggle for English composer Charles Villiers Stanford. The premiere was set for London's Covent Garden as part of the German Opera season, on June 18, 1884, but when the lead soprano pulled out of the performance, it had to be postponed for nine days. A replacement soprano couldn't master the part and also backed out, leaving Stanford to muster what optimism he could, even as he weighed the alternatives—hazard a bad performance or postpone again and risk losing credibility with the public.

The production was postponed again.

A third soprano learned the part in a week, and *Savanarola* had its shaky debut on July 9. Its most immediate problem wasn't musical. The opera was performed in German, and, because of a copyright suit, the libretto and story line were available only in German, in Gothic script that few in the audience could decipher.

Nonetheless, a critic for the London *Times* was astute enough to determine that the opera suffered from an "almost total absence of any dramatic qualities."

Composer Hubert Parry maintained that although the music was "clean and well-managed," its lack of excitement produced very little applause except from Stanford's personal supporters.

The opera's large chorus, elaborate sets, and splendid costumes couldn't save it.

The main problem was that, as an opera composer, Stanford had an Achilles heel: He could write dramatic music if the libretto called for it, but in the case of *Savanarola*, librettist Gilbert A'Beckett had written a plodding story weighed down with pseudo fifteenth-century language. Stanford had been unable to see that the libretto had no drama in it.

Not that the music was without shortcomings. Stanford's inconsistent use of character motifs and reliance upon borrowed Wagnerian harmonies produced an opera that made Savanarola's martyrdom at the stake an ordeal for the audience, too.

With his last four librettos—and the resulting operas—Stanford would be luckier.

June 19th

The Trouble with the Movies

At the age of twenty-two, composer Benjamin Britten learned some important lessons about composing—by going to the movies.

The year was 1935, and a producer working for the British government film unit asked Britten to write music for a series of documentaries. Already working for the unit were some of the great literary luminaries of Britten's generation—W.H. Auden, Louis MacNeice, and Christopher Isherwood. An added benefit for Britten was the discipline that came with having to work quickly to specifications, even when inspiration was lacking.

Britten also learned how to write for small ensembles and how to create unusual musical textures since he was sometimes called upon to help make sound effects.

While he was working for the government film unit, Britten was commissioned by an outside producer to write music for a feature film, *Love from a Stranger*, starring Basil Rathbone and Ann Harding. From that experience he quickly learned about the darker side of writing film scores. For weeks at a time, the director kept him on standby at the studio and then expected him to write something on short notice only to have it scrapped when the director changed his mind.

Britten finished the feature film score on time, but the ordeal soured him on writing anything else for feature films. His one weakness was for the books of Arthur Ransome, and the author did approach Britten about writing a score for him, but the project never materialized, and although Benjamin Britten received many other offers to write for the movies, he turned down every one of them.

At the age of twenty-two, Benjamin Britten had learned all he needed to know about the bright and the dark side of composing for films.

The story is told in the 1986 biography *My Brother Benjamin* by Beth Britten.

June 20th

Very Exaggerated

Erik Satie was well known for his eccentricity by June 1920 when his ballet *La Belle Excentrique* turned up on the stage of the Théatre des Champs-Elysées in Paris. He had a devoted following among composers and other artists in the know, but was all too familiar with the complaints of audiences and the barbs of critics, one of whom he had battled with his fists and walking stick.

Elizabeth Toulemon, known to friends as Elise and as Caryathis onstage, was to do the dancing. After several false starts in her search for a costume, she asked Jean Cocteau to come up with something, saying, "You know, Jean, Satie is clarity, order, and reason personified. He knows how I ought to be dressed, extravagantly, of course, but intentionally absurd." Cocteau obliged with a skirt of multi-colored tulle, long sleeves, diamond-studded shoes, a heart-shaped patch of black velvet in a "strategic position," and a black velvet corsage. The outfit hid all of Elise's face except for her heavily made-up mischievous eyes and, fluttering up from her hip, was a white ostrich feather curling into a question mark.

Satie thought it was just the thing.

As Elise danced to the music of various French composers, someone at the back of the theater, later identified as artist André Derain, shouted, "What a shame the costume looks like a public lavatory!"

And then came Satie's music for *La Belle Excentrique*. "The Waltz of the Mysterious Kiss in the Eye" was to be "very exaggerated," perhaps as a spoof of music hall numbers. There was a "Grande Ritournelle" before which the dancer was to "vamp until ready," a "Franco-Lunar March" with a nursery tune running through it; and a "Grand Worldly Cancan" that brought up the rear.

Elise became so identified with her role that she titled her autobiography *The Joys and Sorrows of a Belle Excentrique*, and maintained that she alone had understood Erik Satie, whom she called "the exceptional man, so different from all who surrounded him."

June 21st
No Conductor in the World

During the summer of 1921 Igor Stravinsky was in London, where his *Symphonies of Wind Instruments* was to be performed for the first time as part of a program conducted by the distinguished Serge Koussevitsky. Stravinsky dedicated the work to the memory of Claude Debussy, but he didn't expect any great popular success with the symphony because he had written it to appeal to the intellect rather than attempting to please his audience by  playing on the emotions. He later described the work as "an austere ritual" that consisted of "short litanies" between groups of instruments that didn't provide any great dynamic contrast.

And for listeners enthralled with Stravinsky's *The Rite of Spring*, the soft chanting of flutes and clarinets was likely to come off as less than revolutionary.

Stravinsky was prepared for all of those objections from the audience. He was counting on being able to reach the few who would be receptive to music that didn't rouse their emotions.

But on the night of the performance, unforeseen circumstances made it all but impossible for the symphony to appeal to the intellect.

Part of the problem was the context. The work followed richly orchestrated marches from Nikolai Rimsky-Korsakov's *Golden Cockerel*. As soon as the marches were over, the players not involved with Stravinsky's work left the stage, leaving the twenty wind players in the back rows of the large Queen's Hall stage, with a lot of empty chairs between them and the distant conductor.

The resulting effect was distracting for the audience and difficult for the conductor.

To conduct or control a group of instrumentalists at such a great distance was an exceedingly arduous task, Stravinsky observed. It was all the more difficult, he added, because the music required particular attention to detail in order to hold the audience's attention.

In an autobiography published in 1956, Stravinsky came to the conclusion that both his symphony and Koussevitsky were the victims of unfortunate circumstances that no conductor in the world could have made good.

June 22nd

The Missing Ingredient

In 1889, one M. P. Byelyayev decided to promote Russian music at the Paris Universal Exposition. He arranged for two symphonic concerts of Russian music at the Tocadéro Hall to be conducted by Nikolai Rimsky-Korsakov. Also participating would be a pianist named Lavrov and the impressive young composer Alexander Glazunov, who would be represented on the program by his second symphony and a symphonic poem.

The French orchestra was excellent and the music included some of the best new works Russia had to offer—including Rimsky-Korsakov's own Antar Symphony and major compositions by Tchaikovsky, Mussorgsky, and Borodin, among others.

The audience responded with ample applause during the concerts of June 22 and 29, but according to Rimsky-Korsakov a key ingredient was missing.

He noted that "while advertisements for all kinds of institutions were being displayed at every street corner, shouted everywhere, carried on people's backs, printed in newspapers in large type—Byelyayev confined himself to modest announcements."

The impresario had a curious attitude toward advertising. He reasoned that anyone who was interested in the concert would find out about it and come, and that those who were not interested would not bother to find out and not come. As far as he was concerned, those who would come only because they had nothing else to do were not welcome at all.

"With such ideas," Rimsky-Korsakov remarked, "no large audience was to be expected."

And then he pointed to a deeper cause of the scant audiences—for foreigners, Russian music was simply not important enough.

At the same time, he said, concert-goers craved the familiar and fashionable and could be lured to new music only by popular artists and appealing advertisements.

Byelyayev lost a lot of money on the Russian Symphony Concerts at the Exposition—and had expected to—but according to Rimsky-Korsakov, his opportunity to make Russian music better known was also lost because he failed to advertise.

June 23rd

Even One Note

It wasn't that Pablo Casals was always kind. After all, the fiery-tempered Spaniard had once punished a double-dealing manager with some rough turns in a revolving door. But when it came to judging students, the celebrated cellist could be gentle almost to a fault.

In the late 1920s he was staying at the Berlin home of Francesco von Mendelssohn, a distant relative of composer Felix Mendelssohn, who invited up-and-coming cellist Gregor Piatigorsky to come over and meet Casals and another guest, the young pianist Rudolf Serkin.

Casals said that he always enjoyed meeting young, talented musicians. He wanted to hear Piatigorsky and Serkin play. The two twenty-something musicians were nervous enough as it was, but being asked to perform together for the great Casals when they had just met made them all the more ill-at-ease. With reluctance they took on Beethoven's *Sonata in D.*

Somewhere in the middle of it, they gave up.

"Bravo!" cried Casals, clapping.

Then they played Schumann's cello concerto and some things by Bach, both badly.

Casals embraced Piatigorsky. "Splendid, Magnifique!"

Piatigorsky left confused, wondering why such bad playing had elicited apparently sincere praise from Casals.

Several years later, Piatigorsky met Casals in Paris. They played cello duets long into the night, and, feeling relaxed, Piatigorsky reminded Casals of his praise for the bad playing in Berlin.

Now the Casals temper came out. He snatched up his cello and played a phrase from the Beethoven sonata. "Didn't you play this fingering? Ah, you did! It was novel to me...it was good...and here didn't you attack that passage with up-bow, like this?" He went on to point out what he liked about everything Piatigorsky had played that night.

"Leave it to the ignorant and stupid who judge by counting only the faults," he said. "I can be grateful, and so must you be, for even one note, one wonderful phrase."

June 24th

The Impoverished Romantic

 Félicien David is remembered as one of France's great romantic composers. At the age of twenty-one, he already had a strong sense of romanticism and the hardships that came with trying to make a living from it.

In 1831 David was writing a comic opera, but his financial situation was no laughing matter. He had just lost the financial support of his uncle and was penniless in Paris. David managed to find a few students in harmony and piano, and fell in love with one of them, which left him "dreaming, timid, wondering, and more than a little confused," according to a friend.

David longed for the recognition that would come with winning the prestigious Prix de Rome, but didn't apply for it because he feared the loss of self esteem that would come with the failure he thought inevitable, given the back room scheming that affected the outcome of the competition.

When he began to lose pupils, David expressed his romanticism in a worried but light-hearted letter to his sister and brother-in-law:

Unless my luck gets better, I'll be as naked as a rat at the morgue. For some reason my mind has been rather fallow of late, maybe because of my persistent piano practicing. I'm working on some piano pieces—not sonatas—that term is too old. You understand that I'm a romantic. That's what everyone tells me, even my teachers. Entre nous, it's true. I have little patience with theory. I'd be delighted to be romantic like Beethoven and Weber—new and original. That's where my romanticism is. I hope it won't detract from my severe principles. You would marvel at my chin—dark with a black beard. It's the secret emblem of the romantic—or at least those who intend to be so.

Félicien David would go on to make a comfortable living as one of France's great romantic composers.

176

June 25th
Shifting Allegiance

Although he was born in Glasgow of an English mother, Eugène d'Albert never considered himself an Englishman. His father, who was a ballet master in London's King's Theatre and at Covent Garden, was German-born, but was of French and Italian descent, and had among his forebears two eighteenth-century composers, Giuseppe Matteo Alberti and Domenico Alberti.

If young d'Albert had a constant in his life, it was probably music. His first teacher was his father, who, apparently, was quite effective because at the age of twelve the boy won a scholarship to the new National Training School for Music, where he became well-known not just as as a bravura pianist, but also as a capable composer, and by the age of seventeen he was credited with writing the overture to Gilbert and Sullivan's comic opera *Patience.*

During the same year, 1881, d'Albert won a scholarship that enabled him to study in Europe, where he made the acquaintance of Liszt and Brahms. Under the spell of Wagner's *Tristan and Isolde*, he moved to Germany and changed his name from Eugène to Eugen. He said that one hearing of Wagner's opera had taught him more than everything he had learned from his father or the National Training School of Music.

A year later, at eighteen, he became the youngest soloist to perform with the Vienna Philharmonic when he played his own piano concerto.

After years of international touring, d'Albert devoted more and more time to composing, and produced a total of twenty-one operas, the seventh of which, *Tiefland,* found a permanent place in the repertory.

In 1914, at the outbreak of World War I, d'Albert's longstanding favoritism toward Germany made him a controversial figure in England, and he later softened some of his statements, saying with a curiously foreign syntax, "The former prejudice which I had against England, which several incidents aroused, has completely vanished since many years."

Eugen d'Albert's personal allegiance also tended to drift. In 1932, having long since become a Swiss citizen, he died in Riga, Latvia, where he had gone to divorce his sixth wife.

June 26th

A Summer Prank

Muzio Clementi was one of the most diverse musicians of his time. He was a celebrated pianist. He manufactured and sold pianos. He was a major composer. He was a publisher. And if one account is true, Clementi was also focused to a fault.

In his memoirs, oboist William Parke wrote of a hot summer day in 1796 and an outing during which Clementi and a cellist named John Crosdill went swimming while visiting the estate of the Earl of Pembroke. Hearing of Clementi's absent-mindedness, Crosdill decided to test it. While Clementi continued to swim, Crosdill sneaked off with his shirt and took it into the house and let Lord Pembroke in on the joke. Parke continues:

At the expiration of half an hour Clementi returned, perfectly dressed as he believed, and while he was expatiating largely on the pleasure he received by his immersion, a gentleman and his lady (friends of the peer) arrived on an evening visit. After the usual introductions had taken place, the lady expressed a desire to hear Clementi play one of his own sonatas on the pianoforte, to which he readily assented.

Having taken his seat, and fidgeted a little in his peculiar way, he played the first movement of one of his most difficult pieces, and was about to begin the adagio, when, being oppressed with heat, he unconsciously unbuttoned nearly the whole of his waistcoat, and was proceeding, when the lady, greatly surprised, hastily retired to the furthest part of the room while Lord Pembroke, almost convulsed with laughter, apprised Clementi of his situation, who, staring wildly, darted out of the room, and could not by any entreaties be prevailed on to rejoin the party.

The absent-minded Muzio Clementi was also known for going out in the morning wearing one black and one white stocking.

June 27th

Into the Smoke

On June 27, 1847, Giuseppe Verdi was in London, hoping to further the cause of his operas, when he wrote to Giuseppina Appiani:

Glory to the sun, which I have always loved so much, but which I now worship, since I've been dwelling in this fog and smoke, which chokes me and blinds my spirit! Nonetheless, what a magnificent city! It has things that stop you in your tracks. But the climate ruins all the beauties. Oh, if only there were a Neapolitan sky here, you'd have no need to wish for Paradise.

I have yet to begin the rehearsals for my new opera because I haven't yet had time to do anything. Not a thing. That's it in a nutshell! By the way, Jenny Lind still makes the same impression on me: I am the very embodiment of loyalty!...If you laugh, by heaven, I'll blow my top.

The theaters are crowded to overflowing. The English enjoy such performances—and they pay so many lire! Oh, if only I could stay here for a couple years, how I'd like to carry off a bag of those oh-so-holy lire! But there's no point in getting ideas like that into my head, because I couldn't tolerate the climate. I can't wait to go to Paris, which holds no particular charm for me, but which I will enjoy greatly from the start because there I'll be able to live as I please! When I consider that I'll be several weeks in Paris without getting tangled up in musical business, without hearing anyone talk about music (I shall throw all publishers and impresarios out the door), I all but lose my senses, and the thought is so consoling.

My health is not half bad in London, but I'm always afraid that some misfortune will swoop down on me. For the most part, I stay home to write (or at least intend to write). I go into society very little, very little to the theater, to avoid the annoyance.

June 28th

A Whimsical Beginning

Felix Mendelssohn never wrote a significant opera, but, while trying to, he kept his good spirits. On June 28, 1834, he wrote a whimsical letter to librettist Karl Klingemann. At the top of the page the gifted composer—and painter—drew a cartoon of noisy trumpets and kettledrums.

Here you have a fanfare for the beginning of the opera. Have you really begun it? Send me right away the first line at least, or better still, everything that's done. In all seriousness, my dear boy, I am very grateful to you and I beg you to stay with it now, so that for once in my life I'll have a chance to write an opera. Will you please send me by return post a copy of the general outline as you have put it down so far?

I have plenty of ideas for the last act, but I can't arrange them until I know—at least the basic outline—how you want to get the plot going. But those ideas might come in handy if I could work on them now. Let me know what you've kept from your notes and mine, and what you dropped so that I can complete my part. I had several suggestions for the first act, each of them in two different styles, and in order to continue with the third, I need to know which of them you'd like to pick up. The third act will be the most difficult, but unless I'm wrong, it will be the most novel and appealing of the entire work.

Thanks, thanks, old boy! And tell me what kind of overture I should write for the opera? A fairy-tale style or otherwise fantastic? And in what key? I believe that if you can get the libretto to me this year, I can bring the finished score to England next spring, because I know I'll hit my stride....

So, God willing, we shall get together early next year, play over our opera, have a happy, happy time and enjoy life. Stay well, work hard, and let me hear from you soon.

June 29th

None of These Men Will Compare

At the age of twenty-three, Robert Schumann was a keen judge of his fellow pianists, and he got to know most of the virtuosi in Leipzig not long after his arrival in the city. But he was most impressed by one of his students, a thirteen-year-old prodigy, and he wrote about her in a letter to his mother in June 1833:

Now that I am acquainted with all the principal virtuosi except Hummel, I'm beginning to realize that my own achievements were once considerable. These great people, instead of offering us something new or original, as we expect, are too fond of giving us our own dear old errors under the label of respected names. I assure you, a name is half the battle.

In my opinion, none of these men can compare with the two girl artists, Mlle. Belleville and Clara.

Clara, who is as fond of me as ever, is the same wild and fanciful little person, skipping and tearing around like a child one moment, and full of serious sayings the next. It's a pleasure to watch the increasing speed with which she unfolds the treasures of her heart and mind the way a flower unfolds its petals. The other day as we came home from Connewitz together—we do a two- or three-hour trek almost every day—I heard her say to herself, "Oh, how happy, how happy I am!" Who doesn't love to hear that?

Along this same road there are some very unnecessary stones in the middle of the path. It turns out that I have a way of looking up instead of down when I'm talking, so she walks just behind me, and gently pulls my coat before every stone to keep me from falling, and stumbles over them herself in between.

Within three years, Robert Schumann and Clara Wieck would become engaged, despite her father's strident objections. That story next.

Unacceptable Conditions

Robert Schumann and Clara Wieck wanted to marry, and when Clara's father, Friedrich Wieck, raised objections, most of them having to do with money, Schumann wrote to a Leipzig attorney named Einert on June 30, 1839:

A few weeks ago, to our surprise, Clara received his written permission with certain conditions, which I hope will not give you the wrong impression of me:

1. That we should not live in Saxony during his lifetime, but that I should make an effort to earn as much elsewhere as I do through editing a musical paper here.

2. That he should keep Clara's money, paying four percent interest, and not paying the capital until five years from now.

3. That I should have the statement of my income, as submitted to him in September 1837, legally verified and place it in the hands of an attorney of his choice.

4. That I should make no attempt to communicate with him verbally or in writing until he so desires.

5. That Clara should give up all claim to inherit anything from him after his death.

6. That we should be married by Michaelmas.

We cannot agree to these conditions, except for the last one, and so we are resorting to legal remedies.

Schumann added that he and Clara wanted the matter settled as quickly as possible and were willing to make another attempt to reason with Friedrich Wieck if it seemed advisable. "Failing that," he concluded, "we shall apply to the court, which cannot refuse us permission since our income is assured."

A year later, after taking the matter to court, Robert and Clara married, despite Wieck's objections. Three years afterward, Clara's father initiated a reconciliation.

July 1st
Sometimes Cannons Are Enough

When Peter Tchaikovsky described his *1812 Overture* as "noisy," he had no idea how loud—and dangerous—it could get.

In 1998, more than a hundred years after Tchaikovsky wrote and disdained his overture, the *Seattle Times* carried the remarkable story of Paolo Esperanza. Esperanza was the bass trombonist with the Simphonica Mayor de Uruguay. He was performing in an outdoor children's concert and hoped to add a little excitement to the sixteen cannon shots that punctuate the finale of the 1812. His good intentions were unaccompanied by good physics.

Esperanza decided to add to Tchaikovsky's pyrotechnics by inserting a large firecracker, equivalent to a quarter-stick of dynamite, into his aluminum straight mute, which he then stuffed into the bell of his new Yamaha in-line double-valve bass trombone.

From his hospital bed, through bandages on his mouth, Esperanza explained to reporters that he had expected the bell of the trombone to funnel the blast away from him while firing the mute in an arc high above the orchestra.

The laws of propulsion physics were not on his side. A superheated shaft of air shot backwards from the blast, burning his lips and face. The explosion split the bell of his trombone, turning it inside out and launching the trombonist backwards from his perch on the orchestra riser. The hot gases shooting through the trombone forced the slide from his hand, hurling it into the back of the head of the third clarinetist, knocking him out.

Because Esperanza didn't have time to raise his trombone before the concussion, the mute went low, shooting between the rows of woodwinds and violists, and caught the conductor in the stomach, propelling him into the audience, where he knocked down the first row of folding chairs in a kind of domino effect.

It was probably the first performance of the *1812 Overture* in which the cannons were upstaged.

July 2nd

The Outsider

George Gershwin had come to write an opera about the inhabitants of Folly Island, South Carolina, but in June 1934, when he arrived for a five-week stay, he wasn't ready for what he found.

Folly Island was not the kind of vacation spot he was used to. "It looks like a battered old South Sea Island," he wrote to his mother. The urbane composer, used to the rapid whirl of Manhattan, found himself ten miles away from the nearest telephone. Instead of traffic he was seeing crabs and giant turtles. Instead of car horns and rumbling subways he heard the bellowing of alligators.

When librettist DuBose Heyward arrived, he was pleased to see Gershwin immersing himself in island life. The spirituals of blacks from a nearby island provided powerful inspiration. Heyward said that for Gershwin the songs and body language of the locals were "more like a homecoming than an exploration."

At a prayer meeting on a nearby island, Gershwin joined into the "shouting," the complex rhythmic pattern beaten by feet and hands. To the amusement of the congregation, he upstaged the champion "shouter."

He composed on an old upright piano hauled down from Charleston.

He walked the beach, "bare and black above the waist," according to a reporter, "wearing only a two-inch beard and a pair of once-white linen knickers."

And yet, for all his mixing with the locals, Gershwin felt like an outsider, sensing that many of his neighbors were suspicious of him as "a Yankee" and someone who was a little too slick.

During his several weeks on Folly Island he had written little, but after he got back to New York, the notes began to flow. By December he had played some of the opera, *Porgy and Bess*, for several influential friends, and wrote to Heyward, "If the opera is so successful as these people think, we have an exciting event ahead of us."

184

July 3rd
Taking It in Stride

How did Hector Berlioz cope with the pressures of life as a composer and conductor? With a lively sense of humor. It comes out in a letter he wrote from London to Theodore Ritter on July 3, 1855.

A ghastly rehearsal at Exeter Hall yesterday. Glover's cantata in a piquant style, but difficult, and I was sweating enough to engorge the gutters in the Strand, and the finale of my Harold in Italy, *a ferocious concerto by Henselt played by Mr. Klindworth in a free style, which kept me dancing on a slack rope for an hour, and Cooper, our first violin, who couldn't take it any more, sang out, "Sempre tempo rubato!"*

...Glover gave a soireé at which Meyerbeer was expected. The great man sent his regrets, pleading a terrible colic...then, finally, he shows up just as everyone had finished regretting his absence. Congratulations on the end of his colic. Moseying through the streets of London in the moonlight, I go to Ernst's house to join my wife....

Wagner has gone, after the esteemed Mr. Hogarth had introduced him to Meyerbeer, asking the two celebrities whether they were acquainted. Wagner's delighted to be leaving London, a new salvo of ranting against him from the critics after the latest concert in Hanover Square. It's true that he conducts in a free style, like Klindworth playing the piano, but his ideas and conversation are enchanting. We went to drink punch with him after the concert. He reassured me as to his friendship, embraced me ferociously, saying he used to have all kinds of prejudices against me. He wept, he capered around, and no sooner had he left than the Musical World *published the passage in his book in which he cuts me to pieces with wry wit.*

July 4th

Music and More

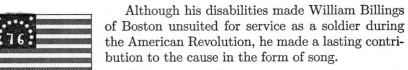

Although his disabilities made William Billings of Boston unsuited for service as a soldier during the American Revolution, he made a lasting contribution to the cause in the form of song.

By 1770, when he wrote his collection *New England Psalm Singer*, tensions were already high between American colonists and their English rulers. As a composer, Billings had been affected by the Stamp Act of 1765 and the Townshend Acts of 1767 and 1770, which raised the cost of paper. Massachusetts instituted a policy of barring the importation of all goods subject to the duties, and so a combination of patriotism and necessity caused Billings to delay his book's publication until he could get American paper.

The British occupation of the city from 1775 to 1776 inspired him to write "Lamentation for Boston," an Americanized version of Psalm 137 published in 1778 in the collection *The Singing Master's Assistant*. In the same collection he republished his song "Chester" in 1778, making his revolutionary sympathies clear:

> *Let tyrants shake their iron rod,*
> *And Slav'ry clank her galling chains,*
> *We fear them not, we trust in God,*
> *New England's God forever reigns.*

And so on, for five verses, celebrating the defeat of British General Burgoyne at the Battle of Saratoga in October 1777; the mistakes of General Howe, who let George Washington's army slip from his grasp after the Battle of Long Island; the blunders of General Henry Clinton, whose Carolina campaign was called off after he led a disastrous attack on Fort Sullivan at Charleston; the embarrassment of General Richard Prescott, who was captured by rebel raiders in 1777; and the errors of Cornwallis, whom George Washington outmaneuvered at Princeton and whose surrender at Yorktown in 1781 would signal the ultimate American victory.

The Singing Master's Assistant was the first tunebook published in America after the outbreak of the Revolution, and as an American book for American voices, it offered comfort to its readers in dangerous times.

July 5th

The Day Job

When violinist Leopold Auer was a little-known Düsseldorf concertmaster, he managed to line up a performance in Wiesbaden, a big step toward a solo career. With new confidence, he put up in one of the town's best hotels and wasted no time going to the casino, where he ran into an acquaintance, the famous violinist Henri Wieniawski.

Wieniawski confided to Auer that he had a sure-fire gambling system. He and Moscow Conservatory director Nikolai Rubinstein had come from St. Petersburg and had recently worked the system in Caen, with such certainty that he expected to break the casino at any moment. He and Rubinstein had pooled their money, and since Rubinstein was the cooler-headed of the two, he was doing the actual gambling.

The two planned to go on to other cities, where they would make a good deal more money gambling than they could by concertizing. No longer would they have to spend all that time practicing.

Wieniawski had also decided that his new vein of wealth would enable him to devote his spare time to composing, and that he could afford to play just for his own pleasure.

For the next several days the system worked so well that the two invited Auer into their arrangement, and, looking forward to shedding the drudgery of practicing scales, Auer gladly gave them his money.

As the cash rolled in, they lived in light-hearted luxury, and Auer considered quitting his job in Düsseldorf so that he could settle down near the casino, where he could live off the system, while accepting only a few select highly-paid performance engagements.

Then he and Wieniawski encountered Rubinstein out for a walk. He was so crestfallen that even his cigarette seemed to droop.

"It's all over," he said with characteristic calm. "I lost all of our capital in a few turns of the wheel."

After a dinnertime consultation, the gamblers decided to go their separate ways and resume their former occupations.

July 6th

Sour Success

With the acclaimed debut of his First Symphony just a few weeks behind him, Dmitri Shostakovich was in for a different experience when it played elsewhere. On July 6, 1926, the nineteen-year-old composer wrote from Ukraine to his mother in Leningrad about a performance by an orchestra in Kharkov.

The concert took place in a garden. As the conductor prepared to start, some nearby dogs began barking. The longer he waited, the louder they barked, much to the merriment of the audience. When the symphony finally got underway, the trumpeter botched his opening phrase and the bassoonist chimed in with a jumble of wrong notes. The dogs came back in and added their voices throughout the rest of the first movement. The outdoor acoustics made the strings thin, the piano inaudible, and the timpani overpowering.

At the beginning of the second movement, the carefully rehearsed cellos and double basses came to grief, and the clarinets started playing out of tempo. In order to get everyone back together, the conductor gave up on the dynamics. The bassoonist returned, playing in a way that caused Shostakovich "dire distress."

The middle of the movement dragged into a muddled confusion. It was all Shostakovich could do to keep from bursting into tears. The piano sounded like a toy harpsichord, one that was out of tune.

Nonetheless, at the end of the second movement, the audience applauded.

Despite percussion that overpowered everything else, the third and fourth movements went much better.

At last it was over. From the front row, a reluctant Shostakovich bowed to the clamoring crowd.

At their insistence, he climbed onstage and bowed again.

The audience was clapping out of habit, Shostakovich deduced, but at least they weren't booing. The conductor declared the performance a success and complimented the orchestra.

For Shostakovich, the words struck a sour note because he felt that the orchestra had "spattered his symphony with dirt."

July 7th
Unforeseen Advantages

In 1941, as Europe waged war, English composer Gerald Finzi wanted to do something for the war effort.

He was offered a job at the BBC that he described as "the usual sort of thing, where one would have been involved with a little music and much, much office work, concert agency, and all the BBC schmozzle!" He turned it down, saying "I would really prefer to be in the army than do that sort of thing."

Soon afterward, Finzi joined the Ministry of War Transport, where he was put in charge of South American Shipping. He expressed his enthusiasm to his wife, saying, "To think that I who wrote *Proud Songster, Dies Natalis,* and *Farewell to Arms* am to become a Principal in the Foreign Shipping Relations Department of the Ministry of War Transport. How fantastic! How unbelievably fantastic!"

But in a time of convoys and submarines, the job was no pushover. Among his colleagues at the Ministry, the stressed composer was referred to as "Frenzy," and within three weeks the novelty was beginning to wear off. The days were long and laden with paperwork so tiring that he had no energy left over for composing. "Anything more than a month old is quite definitely old history," Finzi observed. "Thank Heaven in real life my job deals with more permanent values."

Despite his frustrations with the job, Gerald Finzi stuck it out for the duration of the war and probably benefited from it in ways that became clear only much later. He developed greater confidence and interpersonal skills, plus the ability to keep on task and deliver on deadline. He wrote twice as much music, and for much larger ensembles, in the ten years after the war than in the fifteen years before his stint in the Ministry of War Transport.

It

 Eighteen-year-old Sergei Rachmaninoff was hoping that his opera *Aleko* would make his reputation as a significant composer, but that major effort was quickly overshadowed by a miniature piece of music—his *Prelude in C-sharp minor*.

The year was 1891, and as a recent graduate in music theory from the Moscow Conservatory, Rachmaninoff was scrambling to make a living. He had no great confidence in his opera, and the delay of payment for its publication had made him glad to accept an invitation to play a set of piano pieces for the Electrical Exposition in Moscow for a fee of 50 rubles. He played the first movement of Anton Rubinstein's D minor piano concerto and a group of solo pieces, including a Berceuse by Frédéric Chopin and Franz Liszt's transcription of a section from Charles Gounod's opera *Faust*.

But one piece from the concert went on to attract attention to last a lifetime. It was one of Rachmaninoff's own—his slender *Prelude in C-sharp minor*.

A reviewer remarked at the end of his commentary that the prelude "aroused enthusiasm." It continued to do so. With its powerful opening of descending chords and Slavic brooding, it quickly became an international favorite in concert performances and piano lessons alike. Rachmaninoff dismissed its creation, saying, "One day the prelude simply came to me and I wrote it down. It came so forcefully that I couldn't shake it off despite myself. It had to be and so there it was."

The more audiences demanded the *Prelude in C-sharp minor*, the more Rachmaninoff began to resent the piece, which he started referring to as "It." At the end of a concert, yielding to the audience's demand for the prelude, he would pound "It" out with a violence borne by resentment, which only made the prelude that much more memorable, so that "It" soon became synonymous with Sergei Rachmaninoff.

July 9th
The Surreptitious Composer

At the age of twelve, Edward Elgar had his debut as a composer—much to his father's displeasure.

Elgar's father was a piano tuner and a dealer in sheet music. Young Edward grew up surrounded by scores, and at an early age he became fascinated by the process of turning a printed page into music. The child could improvise on the piano and organ, but he became eager to demonstrate his powers as a composer, and the 1869 Three Choirs festival gave him the chance to do just that.

The annual event, which rotated from his hometown in Worcester to Hereford to Gloucester, was his first experience with choral and orchestral music on a grand scale. Elgar's father performed among the second violins, his Uncle Henry among the violas. Elgar attended his first festival in 1866, at the age of nine. It featured Beethoven's *Mass in C*, which inspired young Edward to tell a friend, "If I had an orchestra under my own control and given a free hand I could make it play whatever I liked."

Three years later he would do something very much like that.

At the 1869 festival Handel's *Messiah* was to be performed. The parts were to be supplied by Elgar's father's firm. The boy had written a little tune and was very proud of it, so proud that he thought the public should hear it.

While his father labored over the printed parts, Elgar also went to work, copying out his tune and inserting it into the score of Handel's *Messiah.*

"The thing was an astonishing success," Elgar recalled years later, "and I heard that some people had never enjoyed Handel so much before! When my father learned of it, however, he was furious!"

Despite his successful, if unauthorized, debut as a composer, young Elgar was more attracted to playing the violin. After he had mastered a part in *Messiah*, he proved such a natural fiddler that his father started taking him along for monthly performances by the local Glee Club.

July 10th

A Summer Song

In the summer of 1876, English baritone and composer George Henschel was vacationing on the German island of Rügen in the Baltic Sea. The day after his arrival, Johannes Brahms came up to visit him, and Brahms led Henschel to music in an unexpected place.

On July 10 Henschel bought a hammock and hung it between two trees in a beech forest with a view of the sea. "We both managed to climb into it simultaneously, an amusing, though by no means easy task to accomplish," Henschel recalled.

Henschel remembered an idle hour or two as Brahms, in a cheerful mood, "went from one charming, interesting story to another, in which the gentler sex played a not unimportant part."

Then they went looking for one of Brahms' favorite places, a frog pond, that eluded them for a while since Brahms' sense of direction left something to be desired. After walking across long stretches of "waste moorland" and not seeing another person, they finally found a small pool in the middle of a wide field of heather.

Listening to the call of the bullfrogs, Brahms asked, "Can you imagine anything more sad and melancholy than this music, the indefinable sounds of which for ever and ever move within the pitiable compass of a minor third?"

The enchanted composer went on. "Here we can realize how fairy tales of enchanted princes and princesses have originated. Listen! There he is again, the poor king's son with his yearning, mournful C-flat!"

Brahms and Henschel stretched out in the low grass, lit cigarettes, and lay listening for half an hour.

Henschel noted that the songs Brahms wrote about that time made frequent use of the interval he heard in the call of the bullfrogs.

George Henschel tells the story in his 1918 memoir *Musings and Memories of a Musician*.

July 11th

A Concert for Summer

During a tour of Europe, Boston hymnist and music educator Lowell Mason was enchanted by an outdoor concert that took place near Berlin at an Elbe resort called Linchen Erben. In his journal for July 11, 1837, he described a radiant summer evening in which the music and the surroundings blended perfectly.

He described a house with several acres of grounds, walks, shade, and groves, and tables and seating for several hundred amid booths, tents, and small houses. Wandering about the lawns were men, women, and children "of all sizes" and many dogs. Many of the men were smoking pipes or cigars or taking snuff. Old men and little children were playing, and most of the women were knitting, reading or writing. Children rode on a railroad built for horses and carriages.

Seated among fresh blooming roses or in shady bowers, clusters of picnickers enjoyed cakes and tarts and confections and drank a variety of beverages, the favorite being beer.

A man approached Mason with a plate in his hand and said something in German. Not knowing the language, the American was perplexed until a woman came by and dropped a few copper coins on the plate, saying, "de music."

He found a place at a table and ordered a beer and a large piece of cherry pie, which entitled him to his seat for the entire afternoon.

At five o'clock, in a gazebo, an orchestra played a program of opera overtures and ballet music by various recent composers.

"A better concert of this kind I have not often heard," Mason concluded, "perhaps never. They played admirably....I was highly delighted—the more so as I would walk about them and hear them at different points—be close to them, look over the music to some of the instruments, etc., and between the pieces could go and sit at my table and sip my beer."

July 12th
The Guest of Honor

 One of the highlights of composer Victor Herbert's life was a music festival that took place in Zurich in 1882. Herbert, a young cellist with the Royal Orchestra of Stuttgart, was among those chosen to attend. The five-day event was largely a tribute to Franz Liszt, who had fostered the careers of many composers to follow, ranging from the celebrated Richard Wagner to a dazzling new American pianist named Edward MacDowell.

The first four days of the festival included formal and informal performances by various composers and performers Liszt had championed, plus a presentation of his oratorio *The Legend of Saint Elizabeth*, but for Herbert the memory of a lifetime came on the final afternoon, July 12.

A gathering in honor of Liszt took place at an estate outside the city, and a steady rain made getting to it an ordeal, but Herbert was hardly aware of the soaking because he was so overwhelmed by seeing Liszt play the piano.

At age seventy, Liszt had not been above dozing during the orchestral and choral performances at the festival, but when he sat down to play the piano, he came to life with the power of a young virtuoso. In a duet with composer Camille Saint-Saëns, he played his famous *Mephisto Waltz*, and, speaking twenty years later, Herbert recalled:

We were afraid every moment the piano would go to smash under Liszt's gigantic hands that came down like very sledge hammers. He played primo and Saint-Saëns secundo, and though Saint-Saëns had the more powerful end of the piano, Liszt soon overpowered his bass notes completely.

Not that there weren't distractions, including one that would become all too familiar to concert-goers today. In addition to great music, the festival also gave Herbert his first look at a telephone. "I will always remember how we marveled at this telephone," he reflected, "and every few minutes set the bell ringing just for the pleasure of hearing the voice at the other end."

July 13th

Roads Not Taken

Malcolm Arnold's music for David Lean's 1957 film *The Bridge on the River Kwai* earned him an Oscar, but he described composing it as one of the worst jobs he'd ever had.

He had only ten days to write thirty-five minutes of music for an enormous orchestra that included three marimbas, a large section of untuned percussion, and a military band. He wrote through the night as couriers waited to carry the score to the copyists. "It gave all the people working on it a very great headache," Arnold recalled, adding that he was "lucky to be alive the way I had to work on the film, but I did it because I liked the picture."

David Lean left the musical decisions up to Arnold, and the result pleased the director immensely. In a letter to Arnold he wrote that Arnold's score brought him the only moment when he looked at his own work and thought, "that is really good."

The triumph was bittersweet for Arnold, though, largely because of three minutes of music that he did not write. Arnold set the jaunty "Colonel Bogey March," written by Kenneth Alford in 1914, against his own "River Kwai March," leading to some confusion as to what was Arnold's and what was not.

Another annoyance for Arnold came when the marching and whistling on the screen failed to match the studio recording Arnold entrusted to the film editors.

When David Lean suggested another collaboration that would include Arnold, William Walton, and composer Aram Khachaturian, Arnold and Walton sat down to view the film after a liquor-laden lunch and found it laughable and overloaded with camels. They turned it down, and Maurice Jarre won an Oscar for writing the score for what proved a blockbuster, *Lawrence of Arabia.*

Arnold never saw David Lean again and went on to turn down two Stanley Kubrick films that became classics—*Dr. Strangelove* and *2001: A Space Odyssey.*

July 14th

The Ironical Genius

On July 14, 1836, Felix Mendelssohn wrote from Frankfurt to his mother and his sister Rebecca in Berlin about the cultural and geographical landscape:

Early yesterday I went to see Ferdinand Hiller, and sitting there I found none other than Rossini. Big, fat, and in a sunny mood. I know very few men who can be as amusing and clever as he is when he feels like it. He kept us laughing the whole time. I promised that the Cecilia Association would sing the B minor Mass for him and several other works by Sebastian Bach. It will be all too entertaining to see Rossini obliged to admire Sebastian Bach.

But he thinks "different countries, different customs," and is determined to howl with the wolves. He says he finds Germany fascinating, says that once he gets his hands on the wine list at the Rhine Hotel in the evening the waiter has to show him the way to his room or he'd never be able to find it. He tells uproarious tales about Paris and all the musicians there, and also stories about himself and his compositions and how he has the greatest respect for all the men of today, so that you might actually believe him if you had no eyes to see the irony in his face.

Intellect, imagination, and wit sparkle in all of his features and in every word, and anyone who doesn't believe that he's a genius should hear him holding forth that way, in order to change his opinion.

I like the scenery around Frankfurt right now more than anything else—such fruitfulness, the richness of the greenery, gardens, and fields, and gorgeous blue hills as a backdrop! And there's a forest on the other side. To wander in the evening under the magnificent beech-trees among the countless herbs and flowers and blackberries and strawberries. It's a delight for the heart.

July 15th
I Will Surely Die Here

Inspired by the musical experiments of his teacher, Arnold Schoenberg, Anton Webern was starting to write works that broke new ground. But being an avant garde composer didn't earn Webern a living, and so he did his best to support himself as an opera conductor.

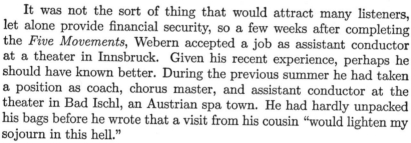

A spring holiday in 1909 enabled him to write his modestly titled *Five Movements for String Quartet,* which broke sharply with tradition by emphasizing short, often explosive, phrases and color instead of striving for an overarching connectedness and a sense of a home key.

It was not the sort of thing that would attract many listeners, let alone provide financial security, so a few weeks after completing the *Five Movements*, Webern accepted a job as assistant conductor at a theater in Innsbruck. Given his recent experience, perhaps he should have known better. During the previous summer he had taken a position as coach, chorus master, and assistant conductor at the theater in Bad Ischl, an Austrian spa town. He had hardly unpacked his bags before he wrote that a visit from his cousin "would lighten my sojourn in this hell."

"My activities are awful," he wrote. "What a service would be done to mankind if all operettas, farces, and folk-plays were destroyed."

A specific incident might have set him off, or he may simply have resented duties that kept him from the more creative pursuit of composing. In Innsbruck his emotions again ran high as he wrote to his teacher:

"My God, dear Mr. Schoenberg, it's impossible for me to stay here. It would be a sin against the Holy Ghost...Oh, my God, do I really have to perform all this slime?" He closed the letter with the lament: "I will surely die here. I'm being murdered here."

Webern broke away long enough to climb a mountain in East Tyrol, which restored his spirits for the time being. He wrote to Schoenberg. "Up there in the heights is where a person should stay."

July 16th
The Children

It was to be a combination of youthful innocence and Celtic grief. When the London Sinfonietta commissioned a work from John Tavener, the composer found his atmosphere in the brooding landscape of Ireland, his structure in the traditional requiem, and poignant symbolism in children's games.

Tavener built his work around the story of a girl named Jenny Jones who is forced by her peers to pass from life to death. From a book about singing games, Tavener learned that hopscotch was originally a representation of the soul's progress through life to death, from Purgatory to Paradise. His composition, to be called *Celtic Requiem*, would be a theater piece for children that would include a game of hopscotch played on the stage. Also included would be a swing because swinging games were once part of extended rituals intended to gain the release of souls from Purgatory.

Children and their games representing death would be in the foreground of the *Requiem*. In the background would be two contrasting adult responses to death—a forthright Irish balladeer and the ritual of the Catholic Church.

From the nearby village of Little Missenden, Tavener recruited sixteen children, ranging in age from seven to eleven.

During the debut in London's Festival Hall on July 16, 1969, the audience in the packed auditorium scarcely noticed the more traditional forces on the stage—the orchestral players and the adult singers. They were looking at the children, who whispered to each other as they passed through the audience on their way to the stage.

The *Requiem* unfolded with a mixture of games, poetry, twisted nursery rhymes, and a dizzying blend of music that included scat singing and electric guitar, all in the structure of a traditional requiem mass. At the end, four giant spinning tops hummed magically as the singing of the retreating children faded into the distance. Then the tops keeled over, leaving the audience in silence that was broken by a long ovation.

July 17th
The Elusive Muse

Although he was one of the world's great composers, Giacomo Puccini sometimes despaired as he searched for the subject of his next opera. Two years after the success of his 1910 masterpiece *La Fanciulla del West*, he considered basing an opera on another American subject, Washington Irving's *Rip Van Winkle*. He tinkered with the idea of using the fragmentary novel *A Florentine Tragedy* by Oscar Wilde. He thought about working with George  du Maurier's wildly successful 1894 Gothic novel *Trilby*, which in 1896 had become the first book to be adapted for film.

In a letter to Luigi Illica, who had written the librettos of three of his greatest operas, Puccini confided his difficulties and aspirations:

I still want to make people weep: That's what it's all about. But do you think it's easy? It's extremely difficult, dear Illica. First of all, where is a person to look for a subject? And will our imagination find one that's universal and enduring? We don't have to take off in completely new directions nor do we bend over backwards to come up with something original. Love and grief were born with the world, and we who have passed the half-century mark are familiar with both of them.

So we have to find a story that grips us with its poetry and its love and grief, and inspires us enough to make an opera of it. But I repeat to you (not that I doubt you in the least—not ever!) I feel a little shaken in my faith and it begins to abandon me!

Do you think that during all this time (since the final note of Fanciulla*) I have sat with my hands folded in my lap? I have tried everything and anything....I feel tired and in despair.*

Five years later, Puccini would produce his next opera, *La Rondine*, which would lead to a burst of creativity that would carry him through his final years.

July 18th

No Excuses

English violist William Primrose made a policy of never making excuses for his performances, no matter how difficult the circumstances surrounding them.

While he was a member of the prestigious London String Quartet, the ensemble was scheduled to perform at New York's Town Hall. The program included works that had particularly hard viola parts—the B-flat Quartet by Brahms and the Debussy quartet.

Before the concert, Primrose stepped outside to relax. While taking in the fresh spring air, he decided that a cigarette would be just the thing, so he lit a match. But he neglected to close the cover, and the whole book of matches went up like a torch, giving his left hand a severe burn.

He hurried to a drugstore to kill the pain and got some medication that made the hand feel somewhat better, but the stuff was so sticky that when he played, the ball of his left thumb kept getting stuck to the viola. The process of getting his thumb stuck and unstuck was so noisy that Primrose could imagine everyone in the audience, back row critics included, squirming at the sound of it.

The friction against a burn between his first and second fingers caused him considerable suffering every time he played a half step.

Nonetheless, at the post-concert reception, he received nothing but praise and congratulations for his execution of the difficult viola parts.

But cellist Warwick Evans took him to task for being rude, especially while talking to the ladies at the reception. "You've had your left hand stuck in your pocket all evening," he said.

Primrose reminded him about the burn and explained that he wasn't trying to hide it for appearance's sake, but because he didn't want people to think of it as an excuse and deduce that the performance wasn't as good as it might have been under better circumstances.

Primrose tells the story in his 1978 memoir *Walk on the North Side.*

200

Monster

American bandleader Patrick Gilmore came to England to recruit performers for a giant concert to be part of a World Peace Jubilee. Gilmore had in mind an ensemble of 20,000 that would "whip creation" in size and sound.

Not everyone was thrilled by the so-called "monster concerts" that swept through nineteenth-century America. One participant, singer Erminia Rudersdorff, wrote to critic Joseph Bennett from Springfield, Massachusetts, on July 19, 1872:

Altogether the festival has been a terrible humbug and failure. It was a hideous nightmare, and all are awaking, and trying to believe it never took place. A.B. will tell you of my own glorious successes, and of that never-to-be-forgotten scene when I sang "God Save the Queen." It is my almost only pleasant recollection, for what do I care for all my other encores and recalls in such a place?

But that frantic recall, that rising of the mass to wave their handkerchiefs and hats, their insistence upon an encore, and that shout for England when I brought on Dan Godfrey to play for my encore, I shall never forget. It was the best thing at the Jubilee, although Gilmore spoiled the beginning by making the organ play the first part twice over. The chorus came in, and it was awful till I came to the rescue. Godfrey can tell you of that scene.

The real Bostonians were immensely disgusted with this big show. All the gentlemen's houses were shut up, and all real musicians left the city. The Music Committee were never once called, and Gilmore and his private secretary made the programs.

Such programs! See what John Dwight says. Upon my word, had I not my £1500 in my pocket (my only excuse) I should never hold up my head again for having been concerned in such a "thing." Dear Mr. Bennett, such gigantic outbursts are really and truly distressing!...There was great discontent among the chorus, and he will never get them together again. Thank God.

July 20th
The Desirable Ordeal

 Attending the Bayreuth Festival became all the rage for musicians in the late nineteenth century. The annual tribute to Wagner's operas drew performers and composers from all over the world. But it took a toll on its attendees, as composer Hugo Wolf wrote to Melanie Köchert on July 20, 1891:

Fortunately the first performance is over. I nodded off from time to time during Acts 1 and 3, and I'm just glad that I was able to take in most of the work. Bayreuth has put me in the worst of moods, and I'm not about to surrender myself again to the local environment, which is dreadful beyond compare. I hardly eat anything anymore, and even the beer tastes bad.

As for sleep, what's that? It's impossible to get to sleep before 2 a.m., and at 4 or 4:30 a person is jolted awake by all kinds of racket. Believe me, I'm a complete wreck, and would like nothing better than for this Bayreuth pilgrimage to come to a swift and peaceful conclusion for me. All of the people here disgust me (except perhaps for Humperdinck, who is mulling over a review for the Frankfurter Zeitung *and every now and then urges me to hurry).*

My round-trip ticket has me seething with anger. What idiocy it was to set out on the trip by way of Nuremberg when it's possible to do it easily in one day via Weiden. Now I'll actually have to stay overnight in Nuremberg if I'm not permitted to go via Weiden....

I can't report much about the Parsifal *performance because I participated with half-open eyes and ears. People said it was very beautiful, and so it probably was.*

Today it's Tristan. *May God keep me awake... Now you should thank God you're not in Bayreuth. Soon I'll be able to be human again and enjoy eating, drinking, and sleeping—ah, sleeping! Who cares about all those spiritual pleasures when the body is a wreck?*

July 21st

Communication Failure

The Liverpool Philharmonic Society had suffered from a shaky performance of Mendelssohn's incidental music to *Athalie*, and when a blistering review prompted the infirm conductor to resign, the Society invited German composer Max Bruch to take over the helm. Bruch accepted the job. An oversight would make him regret the decision.

Bruch had already served as a guest conductor for the Society, leading successful performances of his own oratorios in 1877 and '78, and so he had good reason to trust that his permanent appointment as Musical Director would be equally harmonious, and in the spring of 1880 he left his position as a choral conductor in Berlin to take the job in Liverpool.

Although Bruch could write English fairly well, he was not so good at speaking it, and his thick German accent put him at odds with the choir. During Bruch's second season, one member of the Society went so far as to write a letter of protest to Society secretary Henry Sudlow:

We should be very grateful if you will kindly do something to put an end to the incessant talking and rude remarks, to which we, in the front row, are at present victims. If anything, the annoyance is worse than last season, one young person—I cannot call her a Lady—appearing to delight in making all the ridicule possible of our conductor, and that in such a loud and insulting manner, it is quite painful to us to hear.

Although he stayed in Liverpool for a total of three years and conducted thirty-five well-received concerts, Max Bruch returned to Germany under a cloud. Years later he wrote that he had made a mistake when accepting the post in Liverpool, noting, "If you live there and you wish to achieve something, then you must become anglicized...for me it was quite out of the question."

July 22nd

The Accused

At the end of World War II in Europe solid facts were almost as hard to come by as solid food. In Allied-occupied Vienna the distinguished Hungarian composer Ernst von Dohnányi suddenly found his career threatened by a rumor.

During the war Dohnányi had done what little he could to help the victims of the German regime, signing his name to petitions to free concentration camp prisoners and refusing to obey laws limiting the number of Jews who could be employed at the Hungarian Academy of Music. He had disbanded the Budapest Philharmonic rather than following orders to fire the Jewish members of the orchestra.

So in the summer of 1945, on the day before he was to conduct a performance at the Salzburg Festival, Dohnányi was shocked to receive a letter from Salzburg stating that the performance had been canceled because of allegations that Dohnányi was a war criminal.

The accusation appeared to be the work of musicians in Russian-occupied Hungary, who viewed his return as a threat to their own professional ambitions. Among them was a man freed from a concentration camp through Dohnányi's anonymous influence.

"I will fight them," Dohnányi told his wife. "You know I like to fight. The greater the injustice, the more I shall defend myself against it."

Armed with a supportive letter from a sympathetic American colonel, he went to Salzburg to see the American officer in authority, who promised to give Dohnányi a chance to clear himself, but first put on a radio announcement repeating the war crimes charge against him. When Dohnányi finally confronted his accuser, the officer refused to discuss the accusation.

Most of a year would pass before the composer's efforts and those of persistent friends would be able to go over the officer's head and secure a certificate by which all four Occupation powers in Austria gave Ernst von Dohnányi permission once again to appear on stage.

The composer's wife Ilona tells the story in the 2002 biography *Dohnányi, a Song of Life.*

July 23rd
Desperate Departure

Sir Henry Wood was one of England's most distinguished conductors of the early twentieth century. In 1888, though, he was a nineteen-year-old
student whose departure from the Royal Academy
of Music was anything but dignified. He told the
story in his 1938 autobiography.

During the Handel Festival at the Crystal Palace
in London, Wood heard his ideal of the great
organist—W.T. Best—play a newly-edited concerto
in B-flat with an elaborate and complicated cadenza upon which Wood
had been working for some weeks with the intention of playing it at
one of the Royal Academy concerts. Wood's performance of the concerto was scheduled for a Friday rehearsal. After the first few bars,
the principal of the Academy turned to an organ student and said,
"You can conduct this. You are an organist and should know Handel's
concertos."

It turned out that the student had never conducted before. As a
result the orchestra bogged down several times in the first movement—
much to Wood's disgust, because he had expected the principal to
conduct, and thought that the merits or deficiencies of his playing
would be judged by his performance under the direction of an expert.
Getting angrier by the moment, he went through the first and second
movements and began the third. In his wry way, Wood described what
happened next:

*When we came to the finale, although the principal was doing his
best in dumb-show to keep conductor and orchestra together, I completely lost my temper, jumped off the seat, and fled from the hall. It
was not until I had gone some distance that I realized I had left my hat
and coat behind. For all I know, they are there now. Perhaps they kept
them as a memento of my bad temper?*

Sir Henry remarked that he undoubtedly had completed his musical
education by then anyway, and added that despite his desperate departure, he and the principal of the Academy remained lifelong friends.

July 24th

Transformed into Singing Voices

In July 1825 Franz Schubert was traveling through Upper Austria, enjoying mountain scenery and the company of friends. From the picturesque city of Steyr he wrote to his parents:

In Steyreck we stayed with Countess Wiessenwolf, who is a great admirer of my humble self, owns everything I have written, and sings many of the things very beautifully too.

The Walter Scott songs impressed her so favorably that she made it patently clear that she would not object at all if I were to dedicate them to her. But as far as they are concerned, I intend to break with the customary publishing procedure, which brings in so little profit. I feel that these songs, since they bear the celebrated name of Scott, are likely to pique more interest, and—if I add the English text—should make my name better known in England too. If any honest dealing were possible with these infernal publishers. But the wise and beneficent regulations of our Government have seen to it that the artist shall remain the eternal slave of these wretched money-grubbers....

I have come across my compositions all over Upper Austria, but especially in the monasteries at St. Florian and at Kremsmünster, where, with the assistance of an excellent pianist, I gave a very successful recital of my Variations and Marches for four hands. The Variations from my new Sonata for two hands met with special enthusiasm. I played them alone and not without success, for several people assured me that under my fingers the keys were transformed into singing voices, which, if true, pleases me a good deal because I can't stand the blasted hacking of the instrument to which even first-rate pianists are addicted. It pleases neither the ear nor the heart.

July 25th

Last Visitor at Troldhaugen

Australian pianist and composer Percy Grainger grew up hearing the piano pieces of Edvard Grieg, and by the time he was in his twenties he had put the Norwegian "in the firmament of my compositional stars." He had no idea that the admiration was mutual.

A friend of Grieg's had shown him Grainger's settings of Irish and Welsh folksongs. Grieg liked them so much that he sent a signed photograph of himself inscribed "To Percy Grainger with thanks for your splendid choruses."

Two years later, in May 1906, Grieg was in London, where his wife Nina was to give two concerts of his music at Queen's Hall. The Griegs were the guests of a financier, but the "Miniature Viking" as he was known, was not one to mingle lightly. He spent much of the time sitting in the hall wearing his hat and coat, not saying much of anything to anyone. When his host asked him if there was any musician in London he'd like to meet, Grieg said, "No, thank you, I feel so weak and sick that I just want to get the concerts over with and go home." Then, as an afterthought, he added, "There is one person I'd like to meet—this young Australian composer Percy Grainger."

Grainger was invited over for dinner. The twenty-four-year-old and the sixty-three-year-old hit it off right away, partly because Grainger spoke Norwegian. He gave a sparkling performance of Grieg's *Peasant Dances*, recent pieces unappreciated in Norway. Grieg invited the young Australian to visit him at his summer villa, Troldhaugen.

On the evening of July 25,1907, Grainger arrived. Grieg had been laid low by asthma, sleeplessness, and hallucinations. Grainger's presence brought him around. He proposed a grand concert tour for the next year.

Grainger was the last guest at Troldhaugen. Three weeks after his departure, Grieg was on his way to England for the Leeds Festival when he became ill and died.

July 26th

A Disturbing, Chaotic Life

After a heavy bombardment, Vienna had fallen to Napoleon's army on May 10, 1809, and life became difficult for the city's residents. In a letter to Leipzig publisher Breitkopf and Hertel, Beethoven wrote on July 26:

You are quite wrong to assume that things have been going well for me. The truth is, we've passed through a heavy concentration of misery. Since the fourth of May I've produced very little coherent work, no more than a fragment here and there. The entire course of events has affected me body and soul. Nor can I give myself over to the enjoyment of country life, which is so crucial for me. My position, only recently attained, rests on a shaky foundation. Even in the short time I've had it, not all of the promises made to me have been kept. From one of my patrons, Prince Kinsky, I have yet to receive a single farthing, just at a time when the money is most necessary.

Heaven only knows what's going to happen. I'll probably have to change my residence. The confiscations are to begin today.

What a disturbing, chaotic life I see all around me—nothing but drums, cannons, and human misery of all kinds. My present situation again forces me to bargain with you. So I am inclined to think that you could surely send me 250 gulden at the current rate for the three major works. Be assured that by no means do I consider this an excessive sum, and right now I really need it because I can't count on what was promised me in my certificate of appointment. So write to me and let me know if you will accept this offer. For the Mass alone I could get a fee of 100 gulden at the current rate.

You know that in matters of this kind I'm always forthright with you.

July 27th
Milestone or Millstone?

Ravel had *Bolero*, Rachmaninoff had his *Prelude in C-sharp minor*, and Constant Lambert had *The Rio Grande*—a work so popular that it overshadowed everything else he wrote. Like Ravel and Rachmaninoff, Lambert came to resent the public's partiality to one of his works above all others. Unlike them, Lambert became best known for what is probably his best piece of music.

Lambert came from an aristocratic London background and early on was drawn to American jazz. In 1927 a poem by Sacheverell Sitwell inspired the twenty-two-year-old Lambert to write a work for solo piano, chorus, and an orchestra without woodwinds. The poem was about a South American port on carnival day and had nothing to do with jazz, but provided a convenient vehicle for Lambert to use in writing something jazzy.

Arranging a performance of *The Rio Grande* turned out to be a challenge because it was so different from the sort of things that English choral societies were trained to sing. Those that did take it on found it hard to get into the right spirit. They tended to end Lambert's evocation of a South American carnival with a full-voiced contralto wearing a lavish evening gown.

Performers did what they could with it. A chamber performance featured an all-boy choir that gave a strange and unintended twist to the sensuous words and music. After a BBC performance a reviewer complained that the price of colonization was the black influence upon western poets and musicians.

The difficulties were largely forgotten in 1929, when Lambert conducted the first concert performance of *The Rio Grande* in Queen's Hall in Manchester. A newspaper headline summarized the concert with the words: "Sudden Fame for a Young Composer. Queen's Hall in a Frenzy. Jazz Changed into Music of Genius."

And Constant Lambert was changed into an international celebrity.

July 28th

The Daring Recitalist

Just after the turn of the twentieth century, as he arrived to play in a Western mining town, English pianist Harold Bauer was in for a culture clash.

He traveled with Pop Bacon, a piano tuner who knew him well and warned him, "These people don't understand sarcasm and they don't like it." He suggested that using it might prompt some large person to punch the pianist.

The town was, to Bauer's way of thinking, "very wealthy and very crude." The Opera House was packed to capacity and rang with the banging of seats being turned down as ushers hawked peanuts, chewing gum, and candy.

Bauer appeared onstage to a torrent of applause—and whistling, which he had always thought was an expression of disapproval.

All through the first piece, the racket of seats and selling continued. When Bauer finished, he waited for the applause and the excess noise to die down before continuing with, so far as he could recall, the Moonlight Sonata.

By the middle of the first movement, loud as ever, the ushers were peddling their peanuts again and the seats banged down fortissimo for latecomers.

Bauer stopped playing and, to more applause, advanced to the footlights, trembling with rage—and brimming with sarcasm. He apologized for disturbing the audience with music, for not personally turning down the seats ahead of time, and for not passing out the refreshments himself.

Backstage, Pop Bacon assured him that an attack was imminent.

Bauer played the rest of his concert to wild applause.

As the audience left and a group of solemn men approached Bauer, the piano tuner retreated upstage. A spokesman for the group made a courtly motion, referred to Bauer's acidic lecture to the audience, and said, "We thank you, sir, for your generous gesture, but we cannot permit you to assume the blame."

Although Bauer's sarcasm resulted in no assault, the tuner was correct in his assertion that the locals didn't understand it.

In Love with Life

Peter Tchaikovsky never met his patron Nadezhda von Meck, but in the summer of 1880 he stayed at her estate in Ukraine, and he wrote her a letter expressing his pleasure at two aspects of life there:

At sunset I had tea and then wandered alone by the steep bank of the stream behind the deer park, and drank in all the deep delight of the forest at sundown and freshness of the evening air. Such moments help us to bear with patience the many minor grievances of existence. They make us in love with life. We are promised eternal happiness, immortal existence, but we do not realize it, nor shall we perhaps attain it. But if we are worthy of it, and if it is really eternal, we shall soon learn to enjoy it. Meanwhile, one wishes to live, in order to experience again such moments....

Today I intended to leave for Simaki, but as I write to you a terrific storm is raging, and it is evidently going to be a wet day, so perhaps I shall remain here....

Dear friend, today I have committed a kind of burglary in your house, and I will confess my crime. There was no key to the bookcase in the drawing room next to your bedroom, but I saw that it contained some new books which interested me greatly. Even Marcel could not find the key, so it occurred to me to try the one belonging to the cupboard near my room, and it opened the bookcase at once. I took out Byron, and Martinov's Moscow. Don't worry, all of your books and music remain untouched. To quiet Marcel's conscience...I gave him a memorandum of what I have taken, and before I leave I will return to him the books and music to put back in their proper order.

July 30th

The Crossroads

On July 30, 1830, Robert Schumann wrote from Heidelberg to his mother in Zwickau about the crossroads he had reached:

My entire life has been a twenty-year struggle between poetry and prose or, if you prefer, between music and law. In things practical my ideals were just as high as they were in art. My ideal was, in fact, to have a practical influence, and I hoped to wrestle in a broad arena. But what's the likelihood of that, particularly in Saxony, for a commoner with no powerful patron or fortune and no real fondness for the begging and scraping that are part of a legal career!

At Leipzig I was oblivious to plans for the future. I went my merry way, dreaming and hanging around and really doing nothing of value. Since I got here I've done more work, but in both places my attachment to art just keeps getting deeper and deeper. Now I've come to the crossroads and I think with terror: Which way do I go now?

If I follow my instinct it will lead me to art, and I believe that's the right path. But, in fact—and don't take this wrong, I say lovingly and in a whisper—it always seemed to me that you were blocking my way in that direction for worthy maternal reasons that are as clear to me as they are to you: the "uncertain future" and "unreliable livelihood" as we used to call it.

But what's going to happen now? The most tormenting thought a man can have is the prospect of an unhappy, lifeless, and superficial future of his own making. On the other hand, though, it's not easy to choose a way of life that's at odds with one's early upbringing and disposition. It requires patience, confidence, and fast training.

I'm still in the youth of my imagination, capable of being cultivated and ennobled by art, and I believe that with hard work, patience, and a good teacher, I'll be the match of any pianist.

July 31st

Tell Me When It's Over

Many audience members at classical music concerts are not sure when to applaud. Even in the most sophisticated and controlled circumstances, premature applause can create an awkward break in a performance. One person who knew first-hand was President John F. Kennedy.

According to Kennedy social secretary Letitia Baldrige, on more than one occasion during East Room concerts at the White House, Kennedy was uncertain as to whether a concert was over and found himself clapping at the wrong time. Even when he was following a printed program he had trouble keeping up with the procession of movements within a single work.

The resourceful social secretary hit on a plan.

The distinguished violinist Isaac Stern was scheduled to perform, and Baldrige worked out a code by which she could subtly inform the president that each piece was about to end. As the last piece of the Stern concert was about to end, she would open the central door to the East Room from the outside, about two inches, just enough for the president to glimpse her rather prominent nose.

The code worked brilliantly during the Stern performance and the two used it for every other concert. As soon as Kennedy saw that the door was ajar, he knew that the last piece had begun. He would wait for the applause, join in enthusiastically, take Mrs. Kennedy by the arm, and escort the honored audience members to the stage to congratulate the musicians.

Both John and Jackie Kennedy were very impressed with Baldrige's musical knowledge and sophistication, but she had a secret.

She knew even less about classical music than they did. During each concert she had one of the White House Social Aides stay with her at the door, an aide who was a capable musician and could cue her when it was time to cue the president.

August 1st

Entangling Alliances

Richard Strauss admired the music of Richard Wagner, and so he felt honored in 1893 when he received an invitation from Wagner's widow Cosima to conduct during the consummate Wagnerian event, the Bayreuth Festival.

But the honor would come with strings attached.

Part of Cosima's motive for the invitation came from the formation of a rival festival in nearby Munich. The director of the Munich festival put it into direct competition with Bayreuth by announcing a new production of Wagner's *Lohengrin*, the same opera Bayreuth had presented on its season's opening night.

The Munich director also invited Strauss to conduct two of their operas.

His willingness to work with the competition put Strauss at odds with Cosima's increasingly resentful son Siegfried, a composer who also did some conducting. Strauss was not reluctant to voice his criticisms of Cosima and her family. He and Siegfried had a quarrel about artistic control that prompted Strauss to break off his association with the Wagners. Cosima asked that Strauss not return to Bayreuth as a conductor.

In August 1896 he did return—as an audience member—to hear Siegfried conduct Wagner's Ring Cycle for the first time, and he found the Wagners amiable, although he thought that Siegfried's conducting was awful.

Siegfried rekindled the animosity by publishing a letter in which he stated that the ultimate authority in the theater at Bayreuth was the stage director, who got to give orders to the director. Strauss took the letter as a personal insult.

But despite his break with the Wagners and his condemnation of Bayreuth as "the ultimate pigsty," Strauss remained steadfast in his admiration of Wagner's music and saw the festival as its greatest safeguard, in fact, the consummate safeguard of all German art. And in 1933, after the deaths of Siegfried and Cosima, when the invitation came to conduct again at Bayreuth, neither the needs of his own music nor the grim Nazi politics of the times kept him from accepting it.

214

August 2nd

Tenuous Encounters

The two composers would be major forces in late nineteenth-century music and great friends, but not before some preliminary missteps.

In 1857 Camille Saint-Saëns began seeing small notices announcing Paris performances by an unknown Russian named Anton Rubinstein. Rubinstein was unknown in Paris for a very good reason—he avoided press coverage. His Paris debut took place in an elegant hall—without a single paying listener in attendance.

With power and artistry, Rubinstein wowed his first audience, and for his next performance the hall was, as Saint-Saëns put it, "crammed to suffocation." In his memoirs, Saint-Saëns gushed, "I was bowled over, chained to the chariot of the conqueror!"

Despite his admiration, Saint-Saëns avoided meeting the great pianist. The twenty-two-year-old was terrified at the prospect, despite Rubinstein's reputation for kindness and gentility. For a year, mutual friends continued to invite Saint-Saëns to meet Rubinstein, but Saint-Saëns turned them down. The following year, though, during Rubinstein's next visit to Paris, Saint-Saëns finally got up his courage for an introduction and the two hit if off at once.

They got together often to play flamboyant piano duets. Saint-Saëns was taken not only with Rubinstein's artistry, but also with his lack of jealousy when it came to his fellow musicians. Rubinstein planned to solo in performances of some of his works for piano and orchestra and invited Saint-Saëns to conduct. Again reluctant, Saint-Saëns eventually agreed, and found the experience to be his primary education as a conductor.

It was a baptism by fire because Rubinstein paid no attention to the orchestra and sometimes drowned them out, forcing Saint-Saëns to follow him by watching his hands. And Rubinstein provided scores that were marked up beyond comprehension because he found it amusing to see Saint-Saëns conduct his way into and out of trouble.

During later Paris visits, the bold, broad-shouldered Anton Rubinstein and the shy, delicate Camille Saint-Saëns became almost inseparable friends.

August 3rd
Why I Left Paris

Richard Wagner and his first wife Minna had fled Riga, Latvia, and come to Paris to escape their debts, but the French capital also held promise for an opera composer, and Wagner managed to complete two of his operas, *Rienzi* and *The Flying Dutchman* while he was there. And yet, after spending 1840-1 there, Wagner was eager to leave the city known for its free lifestyle, as he reports in his autobiography:

My own painful experiences and my disgust for all the mockery of that kind of life, once so attractive to me and yet so foreign to my upbringing, had quickly driven me away from having anything to do with it.

It's true that the production of The Huguenots *that I heard for the very first time dazzled me considerably. Its beautiful orchestration and the meticulous and effective staging gave me a grand idea of the possibilities of such perfect and precise artistic resources. But, strange to say, I never felt like hearing the same opera again. I soon tired of the extravagant execution of the singers, and I amused my friends no end by mimicking the latest Parisian style and the vulgar exaggerations packed into every performance.*

In addition, the composers who aimed at success by adopting the style that was then fashionable couldn't help provoking my sarcastic criticism.

The last scintilla of esteem that I tried to retain for the "first lyrical theater in the world" was, in the end, rudely obliterated when I saw how such an empty, totally un-French work as Donizetti's Favorita *could achieve such a long and important run at that theater.*

During the entire time I was in Paris, I don't think I went to the opera more than four times. The cold productions of the Opéra Comique and the degenerate quality of the music produced there had repelled me from the beginning, and the same lack of enthusiasm shown by the singers also drove me from the Italian opera.

August 4th

The Price of Originality

Claude Debussy wanted to prove that he could write something completely different from his opera *Pelléas and Mélisande*—a wish that drew him into the dark corridors of the House of Usher.

Debussy had been attracted to the writings of Edgar Allan Poe for several years, saying, "I'll have to find its equivalent in music." He began with Poe's satirical story *The Devil in the Belfry*, planning to have the devil whistle instead of sing, with most of the vocal roles going to members of a crowd. As his satirical idea developed, Debussy decided to include a companion piece for contrast—*The Fall of the House of Usher.*

With single-mindedness worthy of a Poe character, Debussy threw himself into the project. "There are times," he said, "when I lose the awareness of my surroundings, and if Roderick Usher's sister were suddenly to walk into my home, I wouldn't be the least bit surprised." For most of a year, he forgot about the outside world—or tried to— saying that "the heirs of the Usher family gave me no peace."

In February 1908 he broke off his work on the opera to conduct some of his music in London. By the time he finally got back to *The Fall of the House of Usher*, bad health was slowing him down. "I do as much as I can," he told an impatient friend. But by 1914 he had written only about a half hour of *The Fall of the House of Usher.* As for *The Devil in the Belfry*, he destroyed every note.

He had set himself too high a mark in his quest for originality, driven by a fear that he would prove his critics right by reusing ideas from *Pelléas and Mélisande.* "No doubt they realize," he said, "that if such a thing were to happen, I would immediately devote myself to growing pineapples, because I think it's quite disastrous to repeat oneself."

August 5th
Bodyguards

When Soviet pianist Sviatoslav Richter came to America, his government took no chances on losing him.

In 1960, when he arrived in New York for the first time, Richter was accompanied by a bodyguard named Anatoly, a young veteran of the NKVD, the Soviet security service. Anatoly was pleasant enough, but he was supervised by another bodyguard named Byelotserkovsky, who was always bossing him around. "Follow him; keep an eye on him," Byelotserkovsky would say repeatedly to his young charge, "Listen to what he says. See who he meets."

One day when Richter was leaving the Art Institute of Chicago, he found Anatoly hiding behind the door. "It's him," said the flustered young bodyguard. "He's the one who sent me. It was him!"

And Byelotserkovsky didn't stop at pestering Anatoly. He made a habit of saying to Richter, "Your job is to perform," the implication being that to take in any of the American scenery or culture would be unacceptable.

One day, at the end of a rehearsal of Beethoven's First Piano Concerto with the Boston Orchestra, Richter was so moved by the orchestra's playing that he kissed the hand of conductor Charles Munch. Afterward, Byelotserkovsky vented his disapproval. "How can a Soviet artist sink so low as to kiss the hand of a foreign conductor?" he complained. And when they were invited to the home of Russian émigré Efrem Zimbalist, Byelotserkovsky tried to persuade the aging violinist to return to Russia, where he'd be offered a fine apartment—and a lavish funeral.

On a later trip to America, Richter's escort was a former director of the Leningrad Philharmonic, who persuaded concert organizers to give expensive gifts to Richter, which he would intercept and keep for himself. Richter put his foot down, and from then on, his "guardian angels" gave him no more trouble.

August 6th
The Most Personal

"The last thing on my mind was that it would have wide appeal." So said Andrew Lloyd Webber of the requiem he wrote in 1984. The composer of wildly successful musicals wrote his requiem in response to several deeply-felt experiences.

In 1978 the director of arts programs at the BBC had approached Lloyd Webber with the idea of writing a requiem for the victims of violence in Northern Ireland. His experience with requiems was limited but powerful: At the age of thirteen he had attended the first London performance of Benjamin Britten's *War Requiem*, and three years before that, the Westminster Abbey memorial service for Ralph Vaughan Williams had left a lasting impression on him.

In 1982, when his father died, Lloyd Webber returned to the idea of writing a requiem. Four months later a young journalist friend was killed by an IRA bomb in Harrods Department Store. The composer was further moved by a *New York Times* report about a Cambodian boy who had been forced by terrorists to kill his sister.

The resulting requiem was described as "a rough barbaric score with moments of great tenderness." The "Pie Jesu" from it hit the British Top Ten and became the only single issued by the HMV Classics department, prompting the astonished composer to remark, "When I wrote *Starlight Express* I really worked hard to produce something that would contain a collection of pop singles, and they all failed. This thing comes out in Latin and in ten days it's at Number Three."

At the same time, Andrew Lloyd Webber said that *Requiem* was the most personal of his scores, and for its world premiere in New York he insisted on flying in the same singers who had participated in the recording—his wife Sarah Brightman, boy treble Paul Miles-Kingston, Placido Domingo—and the entire Winchester Cathedral Choir.

August 7th
The Transformation

The burgeoning career of teenaged cellist Janos Starker had come to a rough halt when World War II broke out in Europe. As German and Russian troops vied for control of Budapest and American planes laid down a carpet of bombs, Starker's music had lost priority to a fight for survival.

In November 1945, a few months after the end of the war, when Starker was in Bucharest to perform, he was invited to visit composer Georges Enesco.

Starker had never met Enesco, but he had heard Romanian musicians praising his violin virtuosity with something akin to reverence. The venerable composer lived in a grand house in the city. Bent and soft-spoken, he welcomed Starker into his studio, and after a few questions about Starker and his life, suggested that they play some Brahms together. The celebrated violinist brought out the score of the E minor cello sonata and sat at the piano, and they played through it.

When they had finished, Enesco said, "I still remember hearing Brahms playing it." Then, without music, he began the F major sonata and Starker joined in. At the end of the performance, Enesco remarked that he had played it with Pablo Casals twenty years ago. "His playing was stunning," Enesco said. He invited Starker to come back the next day, when he'd be playing three Beethoven violin sonatas with some friends.

Starker joined about a dozen elegantly-dressed guests for the occasion. After tuning, Enesco and his pianist began to play Beethoven's Spring Sonata. Starker was shocked. As Enesco scratched and sawed, out of tune, the young cellist gritted his teeth and tried to put his mind somewhere else.

Then, suddenly, as if some kind of inner conflict had ended, Enesco began playing like someone else entirely, a master with a beautiful tone and exquisite phrasing.

In his memoirs, Starker wrote, "It was probably the only time in my life that listening to music has brought tears to my eyes."

August 8th

Doctor's Orders

In August 1889, as the great Hungarian violinist Leopold Auer was on his way from St. Petersburg to Bayreuth to hear two Wagner operas for the first time, he came down with what was diagnosed as malaria. Not one to let illness get in his way, he continued on to Bayreuth.

He and a friend began with *Die Walküre*, after which Auer's illness flared up so much that he sent for a doctor, who prescribed several days of bed rest.

Auer was reluctant to comply. *Tristan and Isolde* and *Die Meistersinger* were to be conducted by the foremost Wagner interpreters of the day—Hans Richter and Felix Mottl, who had personally set aside tickets for him.

He decided to attend *Tristan and Isolde*, but the music seemed slow to him, and even key moments in the opera seemed to drag. The heat in the hall was stifling, and he felt a headache coming on. By the time the curtain finally came down, his chest and head seemed to be on fire. He hurried outside for fresh air and caught sight of a friend, cellist David Popper, who hailed the house doctor. After a cursory examination, he, too, recommended bed rest.

But Auer felt compelled to go back for the second act, during which he felt even worse. "I was suffering such tortures," he wrote in his memoirs, "that I felt like shouting to Tristan and Isolde to hurry up and finish their love duet as quickly as possible so that I could go home to bed."

After a second examination, the doctor said that Auer might have typhoid fever, and only after twelve days did he authorize Auer to get out of bed—to continue his cure at mineral baths in Bohemia.

Before Auer departed, a rumor circulated through the hotel that "a dying Russian" in one of the rooms had made a killing on the sale of his tickets.

Pulling It Together

Having left Germany with his family in 1933, Otto Klemperer had landed a job as musical director of the Los Angeles Philharmonic, only to have his eccentricities wreck his reputation in the city and force his resignation.

An invitation to conduct a series of Bach concerts at the New School for Social Research offered him a chance to pull his career back together, but Klemperer made life difficult for everyone, including himself.

Arriving only a few days before the first performance, he took out what appeared to be a revolver, actually a squirt gun, and put it on his desk. Then he ordered that all of the rehearsal conductor's score markings be erased. Excepting only the cellists, he demanded that everyone stand to play. He chased an unsatisfactory musician all the way out to the street.

The first performance went well, but at one point Klemperer walked among the orchestra members. He grabbed a forgetful cellist by the arm and yelled, "E-flat major!"

The following three concerts came across hurried and heavy-handed. The New School did not invite him back.

But the Federal Music Project, a Depression-era program for employing musicians, invited Klemperer to conduct the New York City Symphony Orchestra, which he whipped into shape for a favorable rendition of Beethoven's Fifth Symphony, although their performance of Klemperer's turgid choral work *Trinity* came across as a bewildering hodgepodge.

Klemperer showed up for a second concert in stale dress clothes smeared with chocolate and read a long rambling defense against an accusation that he was programming works by anti-Semitic composers.

Despite the incidents, the concert and the one to follow were successes, and Klemperer was engaged to conduct four more performances in Carnegie Hall.

But his resistance to employing a full orchestra for a performance of Wagner's *Siegfried Idyll* led Klemperer to boycott one of the concerts, and from then on, the discredited musical director of the Los Angeles Philharmonic was also unemployable in New York.

August 10th

The Earthquake

Louis Spohr had heard unflattering things about the famous Sistine Chapel choir performances of *Miserere* by the seventeenth-century composer Gregorio Allegri, but he was eager to judge for himself. After a visit to Rome, he wrote in his journal for August 10, 1817:

These simple sequences of harmony, almost entirely in triads, this blending and sustaining of the voices, sometimes building to the loudest forte, at another fading away into the softest pianissimo; the constant and lengthened sustaining of single notes to an extent attainable only by the lungs of a castrato, and then in particular, the soft introduction of a chord while the chord of other voices is still softly sustained, gives this music, for all its defects, something so strange that the listener can't help feeling attracted to it.

So now I can easily understand that in former times, when the choir was much better, how this must have made a huge impression upon foreigners who had never heard pure vocal music and the voices of castrati....

At the end of the ceremony, the servants, scraping and walking upon the foot-boards, made a very unpleasant noise for musical ears, which greatly disturbed and then wiped out the impression of the music, to which one would gladly have given oneself over a little longer. I'm told that the noise is intended to represent an earthquake!

On the second evening I managed to arrive at the chapel right at the beginning of the real singing, and at the putting out of the last taper. The crowd was so large that I had to remain standing for a while at the entrance surrounded by Englishmen, who, during the entirety of the music, talked to each other in very loud voices and couldn't restrain themselves despite signs for silence.

On top of that, the singers sang much more carelessly than they had the day before, and often were so false that I was glad when the earthquake put an end to the ceremony.

August 11th
Independent

He was a master organist and player of the early keyboard known as the virginal. John Bull was one of Queen Elizabeth's favorite musicians. Like her, he knew what he wanted and persisted in pursuing it, but he paid a heavy price.

According to the account of a contemporary, Bull would have gotten a doctorate in music at Oxford, "had he not met with clowns and rigid Puritans that could not endure church music." And so Bull applied to pursue the degree at Cambridge, which, through an administrative change, later led to the Oxford degree he wanted.

In 1597, on the recommendation of the queen, he was elected the first Public Reader in music at Gresham College in London. College rules required him and his fellow teachers to give public lectures in Latin and English. But Bull was a fierce proponent of the English language. He resisted the rule and received the queen's special permission to give all of his lectures in English.

The rules at Gresham College also required that its readers be unmarried men, and in 1607, Bull's independent-mindedness cost him his lucrative job and his lodgings when he "got one Elizabeth Walter with child" and had to marry her.

A commission to build an organ for an Austrian Archduke held some promise for income, and when it started to fall through, he offered to build the organ with his own money. His plan took him to Madrid and, on the way back to England, he was attacked by pirates who took his money, making him unable to fulfill the commission.

Then he fell into a serious scandal, a charge of adultery, and the assertion by the Archbishop of Canterbury that Bull had "more music than honesty and is as famous for the marring of virginity as he is for the fingering of organs and virginals."

Having no hope for a favorable outcome, one of the country's great musicians left England in August 1613 and never returned.

August 12th
Escape

Czech composer Bohuslav Martinů was in Paris in June 1940 when German armies entered the city. He left the city in a hurry, leaving behind his manuscripts and most of his personal possessions. He and his wife fled south to keep one step ahead of the Germans, and the experience made him feel that "a great vacuum had opened into which all humanity was being drawn."

In Aix-en-Province he tried to make up for lost time, composing a fantasia and a toccata for piano. When he applied for an American visa at the United States consulate, the consul asked him for proof that he was an artist, and Martinů was at a loss for words but blurted out, without any knowledge that it was true, that he was on a list of artists blacklisted by the Nazis. Calling his bluff, the consul pulled out a book and began searching for the composer's name. As Martinů stood breathless, waiting for the worst, the consul nodded and said, "Yes, you are down here" and sent him straight to an office to receive his American visa.

Arranging for transportation to America required frequent travel to and from Marseilles. Martinů bought the last sheets of music paper available in the city and during the long train rides, sketched a sinfonia that he completed in November while bundled in his coat and gloves in an unheated room.

While the French Vichy government dithered about granting crucial exit visas and the paperwork for a Spanish transit visa dragged, the Martinůs' boat sailed from Lisbon. Martinů diverted himself by writing a cheerful sonata da camera and planned other works, and eventually his patience and perseverance paid off. Three months later, Bohuslav Martinů and his wife arrived at last in the New World—a place where he could compose in safety.

August 13th
Turning Point

Even during his career as a civil servant in the French Ministry of the Interior, Emmanuel Chabrier was never far from thoughts of music. He wrote piano pieces and entertained his friends with playing so wild that he reminded one witness of an enraged bull.

And yet there was a deeply serious side to Chabrier that became apparent in 1880 when he attended a Wagner opera at Bayreuth. Composer Henri Duparc recalled:

You can scarcely imagine how much it meant to him to be hearing Tristan, *which he didn't know then, and was almost afraid to get to know, as if some inner voice was warning that it was going to transform his entire life. There had been some excellent performances in Munich, and I had gone to hear the first; it was on a Sunday, and I was so excited that I went back to Paris to persuade a few friends to come for the second performance the next Sunday.*

One of those friends was Chabrier, whom I went to see at the Ministry. He hesitated for quite a while, and raised a lot of objections; but apparently I was able to convince him, and at last he promised to come along with us.

Everyone was delighted, because that meant that the journey would be entertaining...He was so overcome by the opera that, although he was usually so gay and chipper, he left us after the performance and shut himself up in his room. You know, until then he didn't intend to devote himself entirely to music; Tristan *made him realize his true vocation, and by the time he returned from Munich he had made his decision....*

Although Wagner inspired Chabrier to quit his civil service job and devote himself to music, Chabrier soon joined a growing line of French composers determined to break away from Wagner's influence and write music that was inherently Gallic.

August 14th

Mutual Admiration

In the early twentieth century, many Spanish composers traveled to France for training, and a fair number of French composers went to Spain for inspiration. The friendship of Manuel de Falla and Claude Debussy is a prime example.

When Falla arrived in Paris from Madrid in 1907, he soon met a host of celebrated musicians from various countries.

The most renowned of them all was Claude Debussy, whom Falla failed to recognize at first because he was dressed more like a sailor than a famous composer, but it didn't take long for the Frenchman's well-known sardonic sense of humor to manifest itself.

"It is I," Debussy assured the Spaniard. "It is I myself."

In an effort to get a conversation going, Falla said that he had always liked French music.

"Well, I haven't," said Debussy.

Having been notified by composer Paul Dukas that "a little Spaniard dressed all in black" was coming to see him, Debussy asked Falla to play his opera *La vida breve* on the piano. Debussy listened attentively to the whole thing and had good things to say about it.

The two became good friends. After seven years in Paris, Falla returned to Spain and entered the most productive stage of his composing career. In 1920, not long after Debussy's death, Falla wrote an article for *Revue Musicale* in Paris in which he alluded to a reciprocal relationship between the music of Spain and France:

[Debussy] unquestionably, I venture to say, unconsciously, created Spanish music the likes of which aroused the envy of many who knew it all too well. He crossed the border only once, and stayed for a few hours in San Sebastian to attend a bullfight—little enough experience indeed. But he retained a vivid memory of the unique light in the bullring, the amazing contrast between the side flooded by sunlight and the one in shadow.

"He has paid us back so generously," Falla concluded, "that it is Spain who is today the debtor."

August 15th
Excellence or Precedence

During his sojourn in Paris in the 1920s, composer George Antheil decided to investigate a claim made by his teacher back in Philadelphia. It alleged that Debussy, Ravel, and Satie had stolen their impressionistic technique from a largely forgotten Italian composer named Ernest Fanelli.

Antheil tracked down the composer's widow and grown son and daughter. Posing as a critic eager to write an article about the composer's "true worth," he received the family's cordial invitation to have a good look at Fanelli's music.

He discovered that the claim was true—Fanelli had anticipated the technique of Debussy, Ravel, and Satie by many years.

On the other hand, Fanelli's work wasn't as polished as those of his three more famous contemporaries.

Antheil asked Fanelli's widow if the three composers had ever visited Fanelli and borrowed his scores.

"Oh, yes," was the answer. Young Debussy had been very enthusiastic about her husband's work.

Antheil faced a dilemma. He felt obligated to write the promised article, but who in Paris would want to read that the city's most beloved composers had borrowed from a foreigner? And was touting the less-inspired music of Fanelli worth incurring the wrath of Parisians?

He wrote a wishy-washy article about Fanelli without mentioning the borrowed scores.

A few days after it came out, he found at his hotel room door a calling card wrapped in a handbill advertising a cure for sexual impotency. The card was from Fanelli's son and, in French terms, the insult implied by the handbill was a challenge to a duel.

Antheil felt his temper boil, and, being an expert marksman, he decided to go out and fight.

As he passed the concierge, she asked if he had gotten the card, and went on to explain that to keep it clean, she had wrapped it in the first thing at hand.

As he thought about the "true worth" of Ernest Fanelli, a relieved George Antheil concluded that "art is not a matter of precedence, but of excellence."

August 16th

The Breakthrough

In 1841 Anglo-Irish composer Michael Balfe was down on his luck. He was in Paris, about to finish an opera tailor-made for soprano Giulia Grisi, when arrangements fell through, leaving him with little but his music and his optimism to sustain him.

Pierre Erard of the piano manufacturing firm offered to lend his salon for a benefit concert devoted entirely to Balfe's music. He went on to say that he would invite various influential personages from the Paris musical establishment.

The "Grande Concert Balfe" attracted a full house of those expecting to be entertained by the failure of an Englishman rash enough to put together an entire program of his own works.

As Balfe played the piano and sang in his light baritone with an ensemble of volunteer musicians, one piece after another provoked encores. "His music was sparkling," wrote one audience member, "and flashed like a splendid brilliant that gives out radiant colors from a thousand facets, and astonishes and captivates by its beauty."

At breakfast the next morning Balfe was interrupted by a mysterious visitor cloaked and wrapped as if for winter. He declined to give his name, and refused to leave until Balfe had seen him.

"You are Balfe," he said. "I am Scribe, and I've come to ask you to write an opera with me."

Eugène Scribe, the librettist for operas by Rossini, Auber, Meyerbeer, Cherubini, and other major composers, had attended Balfe's concert the previous night.

Balfe agreed at once. As he worked, his wife made sure that he saw none of the sarcastic journal speculations about the Englishman who was writing an opera for Parisian audiences.

Although it has since been forgotten, the opera, called *The Wellsprings of Love*, suited the tastes of the time. It was so successful that some of the doubters were quick to point out the French elements of Balfe's musical training, and King Louis Philippe had a special gold medal struck in his honor.

229

August 17th

The Music Seeker

English music critic Edward Holmes set out for the Continent in 1827, eager to experience the cultural excitement in cities where great composers had lived. When he reached Vienna, he was in for some surprises. He wrote in his travelogue:

At the smaller theaters in the Leopold Stadt and the Joseph Stadt nothing in a musical way is produced worth notice, though a Kapellmeister is there employed to beat the time to songs which are in the regular Astley and Sadler's Wells style.

My English proprieties were somewhat scandalized at finding a number of young ladies introduced on the stage here in short tight jackets without tail, silk breeches, and stockings equally tight, a dress calculated to delineate the form with excessive accuracy; and I would leave it to casuists to settle whether the gentleman in black, whom, out of respect and ceremony they will not engage for the Freischütz, would conduce half the mischief to public morals and decency by appearing on the stage, that these abandoned and profligate exhibitionists do.

In the suburban theaters laughter reigns supreme, and the unities of time, place, etc., are all sacrificed to it; thus, the most sober morning conversation may be interrupted by the entrance of Apollo, or Mercury, or some such unexpected visitor; as for a ghost, it is impossible to know when one may not be expected, and a thing of that sort is as well understood when it comes, and excites no more surprise, than does a banker's clerk in Cheapside at twelve o'clock in the day.

After the theater, which is soon over, the sound of various bands of music invites the passenger to take his supper in open gardens. No place of refreshment, from the highest to the lowest, is without music; bassoons and clarinets are as "plenty as blackberries," and in the suburbs, at every turn one alights upon fresh carousing, fresh fiddling, fresh illuminations.

Wrestling with the Medium

In 1950 Gian Carlo Menotti directed the film version of his opera *The Medium* in Rome—his first film directing assignment. The crew also included a conductor who had never recorded a note of music and a cast of singers who had never seen a film studio.

"It would be highly inaccurate to say that I enjoyed making my first film," Menotti said almost thirty years later. "I missed all along the spontaneity of the stage and its immediacy of expression." He came to think of the camera as "a merciless Medusa that petrifies all freshness before it."

So he rarely looked at his scrupulously prepared script, and found that the improvised shots not only took less time to set up but also proved more satisfactory. As he looked at the rushes, the unedited film from each day of shooting, he felt like a novice composer surprised by the first hearing of what he has written.

But there was one stricture he couldn't avoid. He had to shoot the scenes to conform to a recorded sound track.

And then there was the star—Marie Powers, who felt slighted when the Genoa debut of the opera had someone else in the lead. She did everything she could to drag out the filming so that Menotti wouldn't be able to attend, but Menotti got her under control by threatening to go to Genoa anyway and bringing in another director to finish the film.

The film version of *The Medium* opened to mixed reviews, and Menotti was equally ambivalent about his experience as director. He compared himself to a surgeon, saying, "The patient is still alive, and even looks a little better than before."

His preference would have been to write an opera expressly for film, an opportunity that never arose, but within a year after his debut as a film director, he became the first composer to write an opera for American television—the Christmas favorite *Amahl and the Night Visitors.*

August 19th

How to Listen

As a critic, Michel Calvocoressi appreciated an analytical mind, so he particularly admired composer Vincent d'Indy, the author of *Treatise of Composition.*

One of the things he liked most about d'Indy was the apparent contradictions in his thinking.

Calvocoressi found it intriguing that within the space of just four years, d'Indy could have written both the sensuous, unabashed *Symphony on a French Mountain Air* and the cerebral, constrained First String Quartet. Similarly, he said, at times d'Indy endorsed the headlong, emotionally charged music of Liszt, and at others he seemed to disapprove of it.

Calvocoressi concluded that d'Indy was having trouble making up his mind between feeling and reason. Hearing d'Indy talking about Claude Debussy's *Pelléas and Mélisande*, Calvocoressi determined that what he was saying didn't tally with what he had written about the work.

He pressed d'Indy about the apparent inconsistency and was surprised by the answer.

"Oh! You see, two very different points of view are possible," d'Indy said. "The first time I heard *Pelléas and Mélisande*, I listened to it as to 'music' in the ordinary sense of the word, to 'music' as I conceive it. As such, it meant very little to me."

He went on to say that, after thinking about it some more, he concluded that he had been wrong, and should have listened to Debussy's work as something completely different and new.

"So I went to hear it again," he continued, "and in that new light I was able to admire it."

In his article, d'Indy had written that *Pelléas and Mélisande* was neither an opera nor a lyric drama because music played a subordinate role in it, much the way illuminations in medieval manuscripts enhance the all-important text.

Calvocoressi deduced that d'Indy's reason had led him to approve of *Pelléas and Mélisande*, and that his feelings were the source of his appreciation for the music of Liszt.

August 20th
That Terrible Year

In 1869 Emperor Napoleon III launched three music competitions in Paris, and Jules Massenet was fast to enter all three. The contenders were to write music for the cantata *Prometheus*, the opéra-comique *Le Florentin*, and the opera *La Coupe de Roi de Thule*.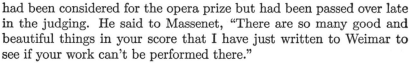

Massenet won nothing.

Camille Saint-Saëns had won the cantata competition. He knew that Massenet had competed and had been considered for the opera prize but had been passed over late in the judging. He said to Massenet, "There are so many good and beautiful things in your score that I have just written to Weimar to see if your work can't be performed there."

Composer Ambroise Thomas introduced Massenet to Michel Carré, who had worked on the librettos for his operas *Mignon* and *Hamlet*. Carré gave Massenet a libretto called *Méduse*.

From the summer of 1869 to the spring of 1870 Massenet labored on the opera, and soon after it was finished, Carré made an appointment to meet him at the Paris Opéra. His plan was to tell the director that Massenet's work should be produced and that he would provide the money to make it happen. Massenet saw the future brighten before him.

At their meeting, Carré took his leave with the words, "Until we meet again on the stage of the Opéra."

Massenet's joy lasted until the next morning, when the newspapers announced the declaration of war between France and Germany.

Massenet never saw Carré again. His hopes for a production in Weimar were crushed, and in the upheaval to follow, any production at the Paris Opéra was also out of the question.

Massenet joined the army. When he wrote his memoirs, he skipped over what he called "that utterly terrible year," saying, "I do not want to make such cruel hours live again."

During the thirty years to follow, Massenet would reuse much of his thousand pages of languishing orchestration in the composition of subsequent works.

August 21st
Second Notice

As if the money problems weren't bad enough, now Heinrich Schütz had to put up with disrespect. For thirty-five years he had been music director for Johann Georg, Elector of Saxony, and now, in 1652, the sixty-seven-year-old Schütz wanted to retire, but the signs were not good.

The elector had fallen on hard times, and salary payments to his court musicians had fallen behind. More than once, Schütz had written eloquently on their behalf, asking for some kind of financial relief. He wrote of a highly-respected bass singer, long in the service of the court, who had been forced to pawn his clothes and now "paces about his house like a beast in the forest."

But now Schütz was finding his reputation under attack. On August 21, 1653, he wrote to several court patrons, voicing his dismay at having been commanded to pick up the mundane responsibility of providing music for the regular Sunday services. He was supposed to share the chore with the crown prince's music director, one Giovanni Andrea Bontempi, whom Schütz described as "a man a third my age and castrated to boot," and to compete with him for the approval of biased and largely unqualified audiences and judges.

Two days later, Schütz wrote to the elector's son, the crown prince, to defend himself against the accusation that he employed too many Italian musicians. The rapid promotions of the Italians and the fact that they were Catholics serving in a Lutheran court, was stirring up resentment among the German musicians. More than a little resentful himself, Schütz pointed out that most of the Italians had been hired by the crown prince.

And so it went for several years, with the defensiveness and the pleas for money becoming increasingly strident, until 1656, when Johann Georg died, and his son, Johann Georg II, allowed arrangements that eased the plight of the court musicians and enabled Heinrich Schütz to retire in comfort.

August 22nd
Surviving The Queen of Sheba

Karl Goldmark had poured his best efforts into his opera *The Queen of Sheba* and had high hopes for it. He was in for some shocks.

He submitted it to the Vienna Court Opera for the 1873 season. *The Queen of Sheba* went to the directors of the Court Opera, who took a dim view of it. They were already critics and rivals of Goldmark.

Next the opera went to the institution's three conductors. One of them complained about its discords. The second, a frail old man, said that he was too sick to look at such a novel and difficult composition. He promptly proved his point by dying.

"I had this consolation," Goldmark quipped. "My score was not responsible for his death."

The third conductor liked the opera but wasn't influential enough to push it.

Along the way, the Vienna newspapers caught wind of the opera and began to clamor for its production. Facing dwindling receipts, the Director-General of the opera, Prince Hohenlohe, decided that *The Queen of Sheba* might be just what the doctor ordered. Told that the director was balking at the idea of putting it on, he declared, "I will break his neck if he doesn't produce the opera."

It proceeded on a limited budget. By the time of the dress rehearsal the singers were worn out. The thing dragged on for four hours in a half-empty house.

"In a word," Goldmark recalled, "The performance was as heavy as lead. Nothing seemed to go; everything we tried failed."

The prince asked Goldmark to come into his box. "For God's sake," he said, "you've got to chop the opera down to size. It's impossible to produce the way it is."

The next night Goldmark and some of the directors went to a restaurant to gather strength for the cutting. There at the table the frazzled Karl Goldmark fainted dead away.

August 23rd

Repressed Delight

Because young Charles Burney admired the music of Thomas Arne, he was excited to meet him when Arne returned to London in August 1744 after two years in Dublin. He was all the more delighted when Arne offered to accept him as a student, tuition free.

A legal contract bound the eighteen-year-old Burney to Arne for seven years.

In exchange for room and board and learning his trade, Burney was expected to transcribe the music that Arne wrote for the Drury Lane theater, to teach it to the minor performers, to give lessons to Arne's students, and to play in various orchestras. During Lent of 1745, Arne also farmed Burney out to perform in oratorios for Handel.

Whatever money Burney and his fellow students made went to Arne, but in the excitement of getting to know some of England's great composers, performers, and actors, Burney didn't mind.

But as he became more and more driven to develop his abilities as a composer and to make a name for himself, Burney found that his initial "inexpressible delight" began to wear thin. He wrote later that Arne's pettiness made life all the more frustrating. He recalled:

He was so selfish and unprincipled, that finding me qualified to transcribe music, teach, and play in public, all which I could do before I was connected with him, he never wished I should advance further in the art. And besides not teaching or allowing me time to study and practice, he locked up all the books in his possession, by the perusal of which I could improve myself.

Burney also discovered that Arne was so consumed by lust that he couldn't pass a woman on the street without trying to seduce her.

In 1746, with five years of subservience still ahead of him, Burney met the high-living Fulke Greville, who bought his apprenticeship from Arne.

Free from the grip of an oppressive master, Charles Burney developed into one of the great music historians of all time.

August 24th
An Emotional Maelstrom

By the time he was in his thirties, composer Jules Massenet avoided public performances of his operas because the excitement was more than his nerves could take. In 1875, at the debut of his music for the mystical play *Eve*, he was in for a set of surprises that would throw the high-strung Frenchman into an emotional maelstrom.

Massenet had been heartened by what he described as "the superb general rehearsal," which he had attended only because the theater was empty. Even so, during the debut he waited in a small café nearby as a friend brought him progress reports. After each part of the play his friend ran across the street. The news from parts one and two was encouraging. After the third part it was still encouraging, and his friend told Massenet that the whole thing was over and that the audience had gone home. He convinced the composer to go to the theater and thank the conductor. In his memoirs Massenet describes what happened next:

I believed him, but what a fraud he was! The minute I reached the musicians' foyer I was blown like a feather into the arms of my cohorts, which I hung onto for dear life because I now understood the trick. But they set me down on the stage in front of the audience, which was still there and still applauding and waving their hats and handkerchiefs. I got up, bounced like a ball, and vanished—furious!

Massenet was in for a second shock that night when a servant appeared at the concert hall and informed him that his mother was desperately ill. The distraught composer hurried to his mother's residence only to be met by his sister with word that their mother had died.

Jules Massenet tells the story in his autobiography *My Recollections*.

August 25th

Occupation and Liberation

During the German occupation of Paris, French musicians had to make a choice: perform for the enemy or risk all by remaining loyal to the Resistance and refusing. Among those who dared to refuse was organist and composer Jean Langlais.

Langlais thought it was particularly gratifying that the liberation of Paris by Allied troops came on August 25 since that was the feast day of St. Louis, the patron saint of the city. But liberation on that day in 1944 was dangerous. The city was still infested with rooftop snipers as the Germans retreated. Langlais described a performance that could have become deadly for all who attended it.

Hearing of the German retreat from the city, Charles de Gaulle, leader of the Free French, said that a Te Deum would be performed at Notre-Dame Cathedral. Langlais and two friends walked over and found the cathedral strangely quiet. The bells weren't ringing.

As de Gaulle approached the cathedral, he was fired upon, and so were Langlais and his friends, who ran inside and threw themselves onto the floor. Those who had come to sing remained silent until the organist was authorized to play.

The organist began a Magnificat. The only singer to respond was de Gaulle, who was answered eventually by the rest of the attendees, still lying on the floor, singing *et exultavit spiritus meus*—and my spirit shall rejoice.

As the gunfire continued outside, the singers got through the entire Magnificat.

When de Gaulle left the cathedral, he was fired at again, and so were Langlais and his friends, as many wounded or dead were brought out on stretchers. On their way home, Langlais and his friends threaded their way home through a gauntlet of shooting. When they reached a store, the firing stopped abruptly, suggesting to Langlais that the Resistance had killed all of the rooftop shooters.

But he couldn't be sure because, from the age of two, he had been blind.

238

August 26th
Music of the Future

One of the last letters by Rossini shows that the seventy-six-old composer was keenly aware of the latest trends in music—and had strong opinions about them. Referring to composers touting "music of the future," he wrote to a friend on August 26, 1868:

There is no such thing as progress or decadence in the latest novelties. They are sterile inventions, the product of perseverance rather than inspiration. Once and for all, let them find the courage to throw off convention and embrace with light hearts and complete confidence those aspects of Italian music that are divine and genuinely charming—simple melody and variety of rhythm.

If our young colleagues follow these principles they will achieve the fame they desire and their compositions will have the long life enjoyed by those of our predecessors—Marcello, Palestrina, and Pergolesi, which is certainly fated for today's celebrities—Mercadante, Bellini, Donizetti, and Verdi.

You've no doubt noticed that I've intentionally left out the word imitation for the benefit of young composers in that I've referred only to melody and rhythm. I will remain forever steadfast in my belief that Italian music—vocal music in particular—is entirely ideal and expressive, never imitative, as certain materialist philosophers suggest. Permit me to assert that the feelings of the heart may be expressed but not imitated.

If imitation is accompanied by elevated artistic feeling and a touch of genius—with which nature is not generous—then even though genius rebels against the rules, it will be as it has always been, in a single gesture, the creator of beauty!

August 27th

The Bluff

One summer day, circa 1760, young Karl Ditters von Dittersdorf rushed in late to perform in a concert for his employer, a prince who took a dim view of tardiness.

On top of that, he had to fill in for the ailing leader, but he impressed the prince and his guest, the Venetian ambassador, with his performance, which he followed by improvising an accompaniment to the singing of the ambassador's wife.

The ambassador told the prince that, as a professor of violin himself, he'd like to hear Dittersdorf play a solo. With a sinking feeling, Dittersdorf realized that in his haste he had forgotten to bring any music, a fault that the prince disdained even more than tardiness.

Dittersdorf hit on a plan. He asked his younger brother to make up some kind of accompaniment in G, and when he got the "dreaded order to play," he casually walked to a table full of scores and pretended that one of them was his *Sonata in G*. It turned out to be a symphony in E. Supposedly reading the score, Dittersdorf played his sonata from memory as his brother dutifully faked an accompaniment.

Then the ambassador and another Italian got up and started reading over his shoulder.

Dittersdorf was about to confess and ask the ambassador not to tell the prince about the trick, but as the ambassador commented on the music, Dittersdorf determined that the supposed violin professor was a phony. Emboldened, he began to throw in all kinds of flourishes, much to everyone's admiration.

The next day, having found out about the ruse, the prince demanded to see him. He gave Dittersdorf a plate with several biscuits on it and told him to eat. Under the third biscuit Dittersdorf found a tidy sum, ten ducats.

"It is because you got out of the scrape so cleverly yesterday!" declared the prince.

Dittersdorf deduced that presence of mind was the quality the prince most valued.

August 28th
A Tough Act to Follow

By the age of twenty-five, Johann Nepomuk Hummel already had a career that would've been the envy of a much older musician. As a child he had lived with Mozart and taken free keyboard lessons from him for two years. By the age of thirteen he had given a concert tour of Europe. He had just written a groundbreaking trumpet concerto.

It was 1804. Haydn was retiring as Kapellmeister for Prince Esterházy in Eisenstadt, and he recommended the young pianist to be his replacement.

The job turned into one of the greatest struggles of Hummel's life.

Replacing Haydn was the hardest part. The old man was loved and admired. Several senior members of the musical staff had been passed over for his job in favor of the strident, cocky young keyboard virtuoso. On top of that, the blunt and tactless Hummel had no administrative experience, so he was unprepared to handle the inevitable back-biting and petty politics of a provincial court.

During the seven years to follow, Hummel seemed to butt heads with just about everyone. The indulgent prince kept him on, largely because he liked the masses Hummel wrote. Hummel continued to push the envelope. He spent more and more time moonlighting. He even had an opera produced in Vienna.

For seven years the prince put up with his insubordination. Then one day Hummel wrote, "Whether the prince likes my composition (as he pretends) or not is no proof that my works are valuable or not....Since the prince is no connoisseur of music, he is not able to judge a work of art."

That did it. The prince fired him.

Perhaps the experience helped Hummel to become more tactful and cooperative because after a few years of teaching in Vienna, he became Kapellmeister at Weimar and kept the job for the rest of his life. It gave him the freedom to compose on the side, and to pursue copyright protection and pensions for musicians.

August 29th

The Hornet

Carl Maria von Weber had admired the lyrical poetry of Helmina von Chézy, and when the Vienna theater commissioned him to write an opera, he asked her to write the libretto. For her story, Chézy chose *The Tale of the Virtuous Euryanthe*, which was based on the timeworn device of a wager about a woman's virtue.

The rambling, complicated, supernatural plot defied staging. After eleven revisions, Weber diverted himself with performances of his recent success, *Der Freischütz*, in Prague and Vienna. When he returned home to Dresden, he took walks in the woods, repeating Chézy's poetry in an effort to set it to music.

Within about sixty days, he had the whole score of *Euryanthe* in his head and had written down all but the overture by August 29, 1823.

In the meantime, the hard-up Chézy wanted to be paid for all the revisions. The "hornet," as Weber called her, wrote to say that if he didn't send her 600 thalers, she would come to Vienna and forbid the production. He replied that he would pay her as soon as he had fulfilled his current engagements. She responded with an ultimatum: she must have the money or a guarantee by the next morning.

Weber took some comfort from hearing that Chézy was generally considered to be a crackpot, but he sent her a fraction of the money as "a gift." When he went to Vienna to conduct the October 25 debut, she was making the rounds, telling everyone that she was refusing his money and was planning to take him to court.

At performance time, she burst into the theater, shouting, "I am the Poetess! Let me through! I am the Poetess!" The audience replied with cheerful jeers and somehow passed her hand to hand over the heads of those who were seated.

For the sake of keeping the peace, Weber made an effort to get her token payments from all theaters and publishers who purchased the ill-fated *Euryanthe*.

242

August 30th
Domestic Strife

His family life was a good deal less harmonious than his music. This is Mozart writing from Vienna to his father Leopold in Salzburg at the end of August 1782:

You want to know how I can flatter myself that I'll be the music master for the Princess? Well, Salieri can't teach her to play the clavier! He can only try to hamper me by recommending somebody else, and it's entirely possible that he's doing just that!

On the other hand, the Emperor knows me, and the last time the Princess was in Vienna, she would have been happy to take lessons from me. Furthermore, I know that my name is in the book of the names of those who have been selected for her service.

I don't know where you got the idea that my highly honored mother-in-law is living here too. You can be sure that I didn't marry my sweetheart in such a rush just to lead a life of aggravations and arguments, but to enjoy peace and happiness.

Since our marriage we have visited her twice, and during the second visit the arguing and needling started up again, so that my poor wife began to cry. I cut off the quibbling right away by telling Constanze that it was time for us to go. We haven't been back since...and have no intention of going back until we have to celebrate the birthday or name-day of the mother or one or two of the sisters.

You say that I've never told you the day on which we got married. Pray excuse me, but your memory may be playing tricks on you because if you'll look at my letter from August 7th, it will confirm that we were married on Sunday, August 4th. Or maybe you never got that letter— but that's unlikely because you received the march that was enclosed with it and also replied to several things in the letter.

August 31st

The Maelstrom

The situation did not look good. The opera had the benefit of an ingenious librettist and a brilliant composer and yet, as the August 31, 1928, debut approached, few would have given more than two cents for *The Threepenny Opera*.

By midnight of opening day a visitor to the Berlin theater found the stage "filled with shouting people wildly gesticulating, yelling at each other," their only point of agreement coming in the form of threats to the director, who reacted by shouting them down. "Smoke filled the air," the visitor observed. "Crumpled papers, empty bottles and broken coffee cups littered the floor."

Performers rebelled. One lead took issue with the shortening of his part, packed his bags and planned to leave town. A player with a bit part threatened to halt the debut unless his pay was tripled. Arguments erupted over the set design. The actor playing Macheath got into a running dispute with practically everyone about the tie he insisted on wearing.

The dress rehearsal went on until six in the morning. When the frazzled performers finally were told to go home, many fell asleep in their dressing rooms, backstage, or on the set. Composer Kurt Weill, librettist Bertolt Brecht, and the impresario stayed at the theater, rehashing the script, surrounded by people who wanted to call the whole thing off. The impresario was later heard asking if anyone knew where he could find a new play in a hurry.

When he found out that his wife's name had been left off the program, the usually cool Kurt Weill blew his top and had to be talked into letting her go on.

Lotte Lenya recalled that the opening night audience seemed "cold and apathetic, as though convinced it had come to a certain flop," until the "Kannonen-Song," at which point the mood suddenly changed, making it "wonderfully, intoxicatingly clear that the public was with us."

For Kurt Weill, Bertolt Brecht, and their cast, the persistence had paid off in the runaway success of *The Threepenny Opera*.

244

The Subversive

Eugene Luening had come through some hard times, and in 1908 he accepted a one-year appointment as director of the Music Department at the University of Wisconsin in Madison. He soon found that he would have to give up some of his freedom, but he never gave up his sense of humor.

When his young sons asked Luening what he would be doing in his new position, he replied that he would recruit an orchestra of eighty-five and a chorus of 300 from the university students to produce Mendelssohn's *A Midsummer Night's Dream*. "We'll do it on the lake," he continued, "the soloists in canoes, the chorus on rafts. The orchestra will be on a barge."

University President Charles Van Hise did not find Eugene Luening so amusing. In a budget request Luening asked for $5,000 to finance top-notch concerts with brilliant soloists, a large chorus and a big orchestra, and promised not to embezzle any of the money. Most of the requests were turned down. Luening's performance of Haydn's *Creation* was accompanied not by an orchestra, but by a pianist.

When Van Hise insisted that Luening teach counterpoint, Luening replied that the students weren't ready for it, but Van Hise insisted. "Harvard offers counterpoint," he said, "Yale offers counterpoint, the University of Wisconsin must offer counterpoint." So Luening obliged, but the highest grade he gave was a 48. When Van Hise called him to task, Luening replied, "I was being generous. Bach gets one hundred. I myself don't get more than a 75."

Eugene Luening was removed as director of the Music Department and replaced by a PhD from Harvard. As consolation he was offered tenure, but by then he had other ideas. He moved his family to Germany and became a vocal coach. His son Otto went on to become an independent—and durable—composer who lived from 1900 to 1996 and told of his father's struggles in his 1980 autobiography.

September 2nd

First Impressions

Russian pianist and composer Sergei Rachmaninoff would eventually become an American citizen, but his first impression of America and America's first impression of him were not entirely promising.

By 1909 Rachmaninoff was enough of an international celebrity to follow in the path of many famous performers who had done well in America, a prosperous nation hungry for European culture and willing to pay top dollar for it, and yet Rachmaninoff had his misgivings about his three-month concert tour of the New World.

Many of them would be justified.

The critics were not particularly impressed by Rachmaninoff and his music. Richard Aldrich of the *New York Times* granted that Rachmaninoff was "perhaps the tallest known pianist" and went on to suggest that in recent years his Second Piano Concerto had been performed more times than its "intrinsic merits" called for. He conceded that the pianist could convey plenty of effects on the instrument, but concluded that "a beautiful and varied tone is not conspicuous among them."

A Boston reviewer dismissed the Second Concerto as "of uneven worth."

Rachmaninoff's Russian melancholy prompted the reviewer of a recital to remark that "towards the end of the program many of the listeners began to feel as if they were prisoners bound for Siberia."

The homesick Rachmaninoff wavered between boredom and anger.

The highlight of his exhausting three months in America was playing his new Third Piano Concerto with the New York Philharmonic under the direction of another composer sojourning in America—Gustav Mahler. Rachmaninoff noted that Mahler insisted on rehearsing the orchestra to the point of perfection, his attitude being that every detail of the score was important. It was an attitude, Rachmaninoff said, that was all too rare among conductors.

Rachmaninoff called American audiences "amazingly cold"—even while mentioning that they demanded as many as seven encores from him—and complained that local newspapers used the number of encores as a gauge of talent.

September 3rd

Excuses

In 1886 American composer Horatio Parker had been hoping for a performance of his string quartet by an important Boston ensemble. When the performance fell through, his colleague George Whitefield Chadwick wrote a cheerful letter explaining what had gone wrong:

In the first place, Kneisel gave me an excuse for not playing your Quartet that so many people wanted to hear the Brahms Sextet that he was obliged to put it on the program to the exclusion of the great American work! And in the second, Brother Gericke told the astute critic of the Transcript *that he was so exhausted by his arduous labors with the flute and oboe player that he could no longer read a score, in which the astute critic doubtless sympathized with him!*

That, however, he saw no reason why he could not play it next season and also that he could do it early in the season.

This, I think, will be much better for you than to have it half played. I would select the Allegro in B-flat which you can easily call "Venetian Overture," which is not only a good tune but a good name also, which is rather to be chosen than great riches.

I have made some new songs for one and four male voices, scored my Dedication Ode, *and am at present at work on a string quartet in D major, which I hope to show you completed when you come. Whiting has done nothing! Niento! Gar Nichts! Says he hasn't any ideas. Perhaps I haven't either, but I don't mean to forget how to make notes, etc., while I am waiting for some. I want to see that opera of yours. That it will be funny I have no doubt.*

September 4th
The Misfit

 As a composer he mastered vast thundering symphonies and sublime sacred choral works, but as a man Anton Bruckner was awkward and bumbling, especially with women.

When it came to the fair sex, the lifelong bachelor was a man of impulses. Once, while visiting a town to give an organ recital, he saw a beautiful girl in church. The next morning he asked for permission to marry her.

During a vacation in the Alps he was working on his Sixth Symphony, which shows no particular influence of the lofty mountains, but the diary he kept sports a long list of girls he found appealing.

Bruckner's interest in a woman lasted only so long as he believed that she was honest and would make a suitable wife. If she passed his initial scrutiny, he would hound his friends to find out about her character and her family.

He also made a point of asking about the girl's dowry. He wanted her to have enough money to guarantee a dignified marriage, and he was well aware that if he died he would have nothing to leave a widow.

In 1890, knowing that Bruckner considered forward women to be symbols of sin and damnation, some of his cohorts decided to play a trick on him. Conductor Hans Richter and some friends took the sixty-six-year-old composer to a restaurant that employed waitresses, a possible indicator that the place had a dubious reputation. One or two at a time, the friends withdrew until Bruckner was alone with the waitress, who was in on the joke.

Without warning, she sat on Bruckner's lap.

The horrified composer jumped up and shouted in his best Latin, "Satan, get thee behind me!"

The stunt was not entirely without provocation. After Richter had conducted one of Bruckner's symphonies in a rehearsal, the absent-minded composer had tipped him a dollar.

248

September 5th

Smoke-Filled Rooms

Although he wrote a sublime *German Requiem*, Johannes Brahms knew all about the earthly—and earthy—side of music.

Brahms grew up in Hamburg in the 1840s in a family so poor that he had to go to work at the age of thirteen. Because he had remarkable talent, young Brahms had no trouble finding jobs playing the piano in local taverns and restaurants, and he soon became so popular that proprietors would call him away from home at all hours to play at dances for free drinks and a little money.

His mother, who also had gone to work at the age of thirteen, believed that honest work was healthy as long as the home environment was wholesome, and she suggested that as long as young Brahms kept in good health and stayed morally straight, he would get through that difficult time in his life.

But Brahms was wearing out. He was being pulled in two different directions—toward the career of a virtuoso under the guidance of Hamburg composer Edward Marxsen on the one hand—and, on the other, by the need to make fast money playing dance music in smoke-filled night spots. Brahms later recalled that his two-sided life made him so anemic and nervous that he could walk along an avenue only by "staggering from tree to tree."

In 1847, when Brahms was fourteen, his luck changed. His father made the acquaintance of Adolf Giesemann, the owner of a paper mill in the village of Winsen on the Luhe, who invited the boy to spend the summer with him in order to give piano lessons to his daughter Lieschen. The experience was so redeeming that forty years later, when Lieschen asked Brahms to help obtain a music scholarship for her daughter, Brahms offered to pay the girl's tuition himself.

September 6th

Missing!

On September 4, 1915, a *New York Times* headline broke the story: *Godowsky Missing.* And so began one of the strangest disappearances in music history.

The celebrated Polish pianist Leopold Godowsky had been working at a fever pitch to complete a set of thirty piano adaptations for the Arts Publication Society's *Progressive Series of Piano Lessons.* A series of interruptions at home had made the work slow going. On September 1 Godowsky had left home in Avon, New Jersey, telling his wife that he was taking the train into New York to deposit $1000 in the bank. Godowsky was wearing an expensive suit, a very expensive watch with a diamond monogram on the back, a diamond fob, and a valuable stickpin.

When Godowsky failed to return that night, his wife Frieda began telephoning friends, but failed to find him. The search expanded to hospitals without results.

The next day it was determined that Godowsky had never been to the bank. But he had been to a music store on East Forty-Third Street and he had visited his hairdresser, having left in time to catch the train back to New Jersey.

Frieda Godowsky went to the police, convinced now that her husband was either suffering from amnesia or had been the victim of foul play. Detectives scoured the city and watched ships sailing for Europe.

Friends of the family brought in a clairvoyant, who proclaimed that Godowsky was suffering from sleepwalking or amnesia and would soon be found wandering the city with his mind blank.

Further investigation revealed that Godowsky had left his hairdresser with the words, "I've just about enough time to catch my train," and had begun walking in the direction of Pennsylvania Station.

Then events took a strange and sinister turn. Next—the rest of the story of the missing pianist.

September 7th
The Mystery Remains

Polish piano virtuoso Leopold Godowsky had disappeared.

On September 4, 1915, Godowsky left his home in Avon, New Jersey, telling his wife, Frieda, that he was going to New York to deposit $1000 in the bank. When he failed to come home, Frieda contacted the police, who determined that Godowsky had never been to the bank, although he had been to his hairdresser and had left saying that he was on his way to Pennsylvania Station to take the train back to New Jersey.

Godowsky had been missing for five days when events took a darker turn. A friend remembered the pianist saying that his $130,000 worth of life insurance would make him more valuable dead than alive.

Harbor police dragged the waters of the North and East Rivers.

The newspapers were full of speculation. Various crackpots came up with solutions of their own.

On September 6, five days after the pianist's disappearance, the telephone rang in the Godowsky home. A caller claiming to be the pianist said that he was quite all right and would return home when his work was done. He said that he had left a letter explaining his absence. Then he hung up.

Was it Godowsky? No one was quite sure.

On the evening of September 7 the police commissioner announced that the investigation was at an impasse.

Half an hour later Frieda Godowsky received a letter.

It was from a mortified and contrite Godowsky, writing from Hackensack to explain that he had been in seclusion for six days, working to finish his piano adaptations, and had just seen the newspaper stories about his disappearance.

He insisted that he had left a letter for Frieda explaining his intentions, but none was ever found.

Although the case of Leopold Godowsky's disappearance was closed, some of the mystery would remain.

September 8th

Pure Persistence

For music, it was the worst of times. In September 1940, as German planes began bombing London, the main thing on everyone's minds was survival, and yet an important part of surviving was music.

At Queen's Hall, after audiences for several performances were kept away by alerts that ran far into the night, conductor Sir Henry Wood was forced to announce that the popular Proms concerts would have to be suspended. Before long, there was no nighttime classical music in London.

The National Gallery and a few other places continued daytime concerts, but the advent of daytime raids required crowds to wait for an All-Clear signal before they could enter the building, and delays ran as long as four hours. By early September daylight raids forced all of the Gallery's concerts downstairs to the shelter room, where the first concert, an all-Bach program, accommodated an audience of 120. Pianist Kathleen Long played brilliantly even though she had just lost her home and all of her possessions. After fifty-seven consecutive days of bombing, even the Gallery management had to curtail their concerts.

Pianist Myra Hess lived away from the heart of the city, but the war found her. Across the road from her house, on Hampstead Heath, six anti-aircraft guns pounded away all through the night as incendiary bombs fell and flares illuminated nearby houses bristling with rooftop guns. One bomb obliterated the house across the road. Hess gave up her customary nighttime practicing, and, during the worst raids, used her piano as a shelter, crouching under it as she sorted through letters from aspiring musicians and planned upcoming concerts.

In addition to music, her British sense of humor surely helped Myra Hess endure the danger. As she and her niece tried to get some sleep during a night of deafening barrages, she said, "I do hope my snoring won't keep you awake."

Free Spirits

In 1904 nineteen-year-old Alban Berg entered the Austrian civil service as an accountant, keeping tabs on the sale of pigs and the productivity of distilleries, but he was most devoted to classes in music theory taught by the innovative Arnold Schoenberg.

Like Berg, Schoenberg had been forced by poverty to leave school at sixteen to become a bank clerk. Schoenberg had forfeited that job by signing a customer into the account books under the name L. van Beethoven.

When an aunt died and left Berg's mother a modest inheritance, Berg ended his stint as a government accountant by absolving all farmers in his jurisdiction of their debts and then resigning.

After a few years of concentrated study with Schoenberg, Berg was ready for the concert debut of his first published work, an avant garde piano sonata, and the big event took place in Vienna in 1911, in a program that included works by others connected with the Society for Art and Culture. A Viennese newspaper critic wrote of the event:

The Society against Art and Culture went through its usual exercises Monday evening in Ehrbar Hall. The group's leaders, lacking talent, imagination, and taste...have identified the director of the Viennese cacophony, Mr. Schoenberg, as their patron and have taken up the cause of his youthful followers...Mr. Berg had written a piece for the piano, presumptuously called Piano Sonata, that shows traces of talent and musicianship. But the joke has stopped being amusing.

It has become apparent that not only the untalented but also the gifted students with uncertain futures are being hauled down a rosy path that can never lead to art or culture. And so only the strongest possible protests are in order to describe the fiasco of Monday evening.

And that was just the beginning. In the twenty-five years to follow, Alban Berg would become increasingly innovative, influential, and notorious.

September 10th

A Polite Reply

Although Hector Berlioz was capable of stinging irony, when he received a pointed letter from Richard Wagner, his reply was the essence of graciousness. On September 10, 1855, he wrote from Paris to Wagner in Switzerland:

Your letter gave me great pleasure. You're quite right to deplore my ignorance of the German language, and as to what you said about the impossibility of my understanding your works, I've struggled with it many a time. The flower of expression almost always withers under the weight of translation, however delicate the translation may be. There are accents in true music that demand just the right word, and there are words that require their particular accent. To separate the one from the other or to give them approximations is like trying to suckle a puppy on a goat.

But what can I do? Learning languages is devilishly difficult for me. I know only a few words of English or Italian.

So you're melting glaciers with your Niebelungen. How marvelous it must be to write in the presence of grand nature! Another pleasure denied me. The beautiful countryside, the lofty peaks, broad vistas of the sea. Instead of provoking thought, they absorb me completely. I feel, but I'm unable to express anything. I can only draw the moon by looking at its reflection in the bottom of a well.

I wish I were able to send you the parts you gave me the pleasure of requesting. Unfortunately my editors haven't given them to me for a long time. I do have two or three—the Te Deum, L'enfance du Christ, and Lélio, a lyric melodrama, which will appear in a few weeks, which I can send you.

I have your Lohengrin. If you could have Tannhäuser sent to me it would give me great pleasure.

September 11th
When It Mattered Most

Rick Rescorla was a soldier, not a musician. But he knew the power of music and he put it to work when it mattered most.

He was born in Cornwall in 1939. Some of his earliest memories were of Cornish songs, but American culture was also in the air as American troops stationed in England prepared for the invasion of German-occupied Europe.

As he grew up, Rescorla was less than a model student, mediocre in literature, undistinguished in music.

He was supposed to have a music lesson each week, a bout with a recorder still damp from use in the previous class, but an errant note from a fellow student led an angry teacher to confiscate the instruments.

Rescorla auditioned for the school choir and failed.

At seventeen he joined the British Army and served with distinction before moving to New York and enlisting in the US Army, which sent him to Vietnam in 1965, where his bravery led the men in his platoon to nickname him "Hard Corps." One night near Plei Me in the Central Highlands, as they anticipated an enemy attack, he calmed his men with his baritone renditions of "Wild Colonial Boy" and "Going up Camborne Hill."

In the thirty-five years to follow, Rescorla returned to the United States, married, raised a family, held a variety of jobs, and survived cancer. He became director of security for Morgan Stanley, headquartered in the World Trade Center.

He insisted that all employees practice emergency evacuation every three months.

On September 11, 2001, when American Airlines Flight 11 struck Tower 1, Rescorla began evacuating 3,700 employees on 20 floors of Tower 2 and WTC 5. Bullhorn in hand, he kept them calm by singing "God Bless America" and the Cornish songs he had learned as a boy.

Of the 3,700 only six perished.

Among them was Rick Rescorla, who was last seen heading up the stairs on the tenth floor of Tower 2.

September 12th
Versatile Enough

The string quartet is a curiosity, a series of short dances for three violins and cello to be played on open strings. It's attributed to Benjamin Franklin, and since he was so versatile, it's tempting to assume that Franklin would also turn his attention to composing music.

Franklin played the harp, the guitar, and something called the glass dulcimer, but his best known contribution to music was his improvement of the so-called musical glasses. The instrument had become popular in Europe by 1746, when Christoph Willibald Gluck performed in London a "concerto on 26 drinking glasses tuned with spring water," accompanied by an entire orchestra.

In 1762, during a sojourn in London, Franklin described in a letter his improvement of the musical glasses by fitting glass bowls concentrically on a horizontal rod, which was turned by a crank attached to a pedal. The turning of the bowls kept them moist by passing them through water, and enabled the performer to stroke their rims with a minimum of motion. Franklin's new instrument, which he called the *armonica*, was fairly popular in America, but quite the rage in Europe.

A few years later, in a letter to a friend in Edinburgh, Franklin wrote a short treatise on music theory, setting down his ideas about the nature of melody and harmony, and in a letter to his brother Peter he favored clarity and simplicity in vocal music and took issue with the relatively intricate arias of recent operas and oratorios in the Italian style.

The intriguing string quartet attributed to Franklin probably says a lot less about his musical tastes. The manuscript, with Franklin's name on it, was discovered in Paris in the 1940s, but, since then, copies have turned up in Prague, Vienna, and elsewhere, each attributed to a different prominent composer of the time. It's quite possible that the scientist, statesman, and inventor was simply too busy to write music.

September 13th

A Good Catch

In 1764 Leopold Mozart was in London with his family, including his nine-year-old son, Wolfgang Amadeus. Money worries were never far from his mind. On September 13 he wrote to his landlord and banker back in Salzburg:

You've probably deduced that I'll spend the entire winter here at least, and that, God willing, I'll make my major profits of several thousand gulden. I'm now in a city that no one at our Salzburg court has ever yet dared to visit, and which, perhaps, no one will ever again visit. All or nothing.

We have come to our long journey's end. Once I leave England I'll never see guineas again. So we have to make the most of the opportunity. If only God in his graciousness grants us good health, we won't need to worry about the guineas. I'm only sorry that I've had to spend what I might have saved.

But it was God's will. Both in Salzburg and in London we are in His hands. He knows how good my intentions are. During the months to come I'll have to make every effort to win the good will of the aristocracy, which will take plenty of galloping around and hard work. But if I achieve my objective I'll haul in a fine fish—or rather a good catch of guineas.

In a later letter, father Mozart apologized for not being a better correspondent, explaining that providing for the family was keeping him busy in London:

How much a man has to do, who is keeping his whole family in a town where, even with the strictest economy, it costs him £300 sterling a year to do so, and when, in addition, he ought to be saving a little!

September 14th

A Slight Breach of Decorum

By the 1950s Ralph Vaughan Williams was a heavyset, craggy-faced monument to solid British music and decorum, so he must have presented quite a contrast with the guest conductor at a choral competition that took place at the base of the 2nd Battalion Welsh Guards. Vaughan Williams had been invited to judge the event and had carefully rehearsed the choirs.

Presiding over the event was Dame Clara Novello Davies, who had composed a song for the occasion. For the performance of it, she had gone all out.

The commanding officer, Colonel Price, recalled that as the curtains parted, Madame Clara appeared sheathed from head to toe in tight gold lamé topped by a wreath of gold leaves in her hair. She carried a baton of gold leaves that had been presented to her by some long-forgotten president of France. As she came forward to conduct her song, the ranks of assembled choirs in battle dress "parted in amazement."

Just then, things began to go awry. The train of her golden dress caught on a nail in the floor. The music for her song had been placed upside down on the stand, and as she leaned on the stand for support, a loose wing-nut caused the whole thing to fall over, and down she went with it, sprawling before the startled audience.

She recovered, gave a long eulogy for her late son, songwriter Ivor Novello, and then began conducting her song, which went badly. Ignoring Vaughan Williams down in the orchestra pit and forgetting both the audience and the occasion, she began berating the singers.

"You don't know it!" she barked. "Stand up!"

She went on to browbeat the choirs until the regimental Sergeant-Major averted a complete disaster by calling for the men to give "three cheers for Madame Clara."

For the sake of moving on as quickly as possible, Ralph Vaughan Williams no doubt cheered as lustily as any of them.

September 15th

And There Was Music

After graduating from Oxford, Hubert Parry was bound for a business career in London, although money-making was not as interesting to him as music-making. In September of 1870 he couldn't resist a final burst of freedom. He wrote about it in his diary:

I spent a quiet time studying manuscript music, practicing, and shooting till the end of September. The time was specially noticeable for an adventurous trip which Ernest and I took in two canoes from Over Bridge to Sharpness Point on the Severn, wherein we met with various fortune; being cast upon banks and quicksands, narrowly escaping destruction in the rapids by Westbury Cliff, where we avoided a rock by only about one yard; then being benighted, we were cast upon a reef opposite Broad Oak near Newnham by the rapids; and were only relieved of mud, cold and vexation by the kindness of a neighboring gentleman, who at length, having solaced us with beer, sent us on our way to a friendly hostel, where we found food and shelter. Next morning we pursued a more prosperous journey on the glorious broad river.

We had a fine breeze when past the "Nooze" and in the broad part opposite Frampton, and had to wait for a more quiet passage to the Point in the hospitable creek of Gatcombe, where we spent a pleasant hour in the company of the sociable pilots, and enjoyed a simple luncheon and also the beauty of that little cluster of houses nestled in a division of the red cliffs, and afterward, passed across to the Point in safety. There we carried our canoes over the side of the huge locks, and went up the canal to Frampton, where we rested the night and arrived at Gloucester, after a journey of 80 miles, on the following morning.

Within ten years, Hubert Parry would apply equal vigor to the rejuvenation of English music.

September 16th
Falling Star

The thirty-three-year-old pianist was as brilliant as ever. He treated his audience in Besançon to unequaled performances of Bach's B-flat major Partita, Mozart's *Sonata in A minor*, Schubert's G-flat major and E-flat major impromptus, and thirteen of Chopin's fourteen waltzes.

He left out the second Chopin waltz because he was too exhausted to play it. He substituted a transcription of Bach's "Jesu, Joy of Man's Desiring." The young pianist and his audience were aware that this would likely be his last concert.

His name was Dinu Lipatti, and he had been thrilling listeners for thirty years. Music was in his blood. The Romanian virtuoso's mother was a pianist and his father a violinist. His godfather was the great composer Georges Enesco. The disruption of World War I postponed his baptism until he was four years old. For the occasion he played a recital on both the piano and the violin.

At the age of seventeen, he competed in the 1934 Vienna International Piano Competition, which included the distinguished pianist Alfred Cortot as one of the judges. Cortot deemed him the winner, and when Lipatti came in second, Cortot resigned from the jury in protest.

Lipatti went to Paris to study with Cortot and other renowned figures of the day—conductor Charles Munch, composer Paul Dukas, and celebrated music educator Nadia Boulanger, with whom he made a recording of Brahms waltzes.

World War II interrupted his French idyll, but he continued to give concerts, including some in German-occupied areas, before fleeing to Romania in 1943 and making his way to Switzerland with his wife.

He was teaching at the conservatory in Geneva when the first signs of illness appeared, but three or four years passed before doctors were able to diagnose it as Hodgkin's disease.

Although he had just three months to live, when Dinu Lipatti gave his final concert on September 16, 1950, it was such a show of virtuosity that it secured his place as one of the great pianists of the twentieth century.

September 17th
Prime Minister of Opera

"The only Italians here that merit attention are two musicians." So wrote the French Ambassador to Spain in 1746. He went on to say that one of the two was harpsichordist Domenico Scarlatti and the other was a singer named Farinelli.

Farinelli had been born Carlo Broschi in Naples in 1705. When he was a boy, an errant blow from a horse's hoof had caused him to be castrated for medical reasons. In a time when the voices of castrati were considered especially beautiful, young Carlo appropriated the name of a prosperous Italian family and took to the stage.

He was a celebrity of the London opera stage in 1737 when he received a summons from the Italian-born Queen of Spain to come to Madrid to lift King Philip V out of a long debilitating depression. What began as nightly serenades in the room adjoining the king's apartment developed into a Spanish sojourn that lasted more than twenty years.

In 1746, when Ferdinand and his wife, Maria Barbara of Portugal, became King and Queen, Farinelli became such a royal favorite that he was said to have the influence of a prime minister. Many foreign ministers and King Louis XV of France offered him bribes, all of which he turned down. The Queen Mother echoed the sentiments of many Spaniards when she grumbled that the country had been taken over by Portuguese and musicians.

Despite his ascent, Farinelli was a loyal friend of Scarlatti's and helped him out when he ran into financial difficulties. English music historian Charles Burney, who was a generation younger than Farinelli, suggested that the singer was so gracious to those above and below him in rank at court that he was almost incapable of arousing jealousy.

If he had ambition, it lay in the realm of music. Under the new monarch, Farinelli took over the direction of all court operas, and the productions were so lavish that they merit a story in their own right. We'll hear it in November.

261

September 18th

Master or Student?

In the fall of 1824 pianist and composer Ignaz Moscheles was in Berlin, where he became acquainted with the family of fifteen-year-old Felix Mendelssohn. Mendelssohn's parents were concerned about the boy's future, fearful that he would suddenly pass into obscurity, as many other talented children had done. Moscheles had no doubts about Felix's future, but the boy's parents required repeated reassurances.

Time and again, Mendelssohn's parents asked Moscheles to give piano lessons to the boy, but Moscheles was evasive, confiding in his diary, "He doesn't need lessons, and if he wants to pick up something new from me, he can easily do so."

After two cajoling letters from Mendelssohn's mother, Moscheles finally gave in, noting, "From two to three this afternoon, I gave Felix Mendelssohn his first lesson, never forgetting for a moment that I was sitting next to a master and not a student. I'm proud that his excellent parents have entrusted their son to me after knowing me for such a short time, and I am happy to be allowed to pass on a few pointers to him which, given his genius, he picks up and absorbs easily."

Six days later, Moscheles wrote: "Felix Mendelssohn's lessons take place every two days, and I find them increasingly fascinating. By now he has already played my *Allegro di Bravura*, my concerti, and other works, and how he played them! He interprets my most subtle ideas correctly."

In the weeks to follow, Moscheles attended several of the Mendelssohn family's private concerts and a theatrical entertainment of which he wrote that Mendelssohn "distinguished himself" every bit as much as a great actor of the day.

Toward the end of his stay with the Mendelssohn family, Moscheles wrote an impromptu in the family's visitors' book and noted that Felix "played it magnificently at sight."

September 19th

Maggots

Charles Jennens assembled the texts for five of Handel's oratorios, including *Messiah*, but a letter that turned up more than two hundred years after he wrote it shows that he did not hesitate to make fun of the great composer.

In 1738 Jennens and Handel were working on the oratorio *Saul*. Jennens wrote to the Earl of Guernsey on September 19, after a visit to the composer.

"Mr. Handel's head is more full of maggots than ever," he reported.

The first "maggot," he said, was a "very queer" keyboard instrument that made the sound of hammers hitting anvils, with which Handel intended "to make poor Saul stark mad."

The second maggot, Jennens remarked with sarcasm, was an expensive organ that Handel had bought because he was "overstocked with money." Handel was enthusiastic about the organ, Jennens said, because it was to make it easier for him to direct his performers during presentations of *Saul* because, instead of just beating time to the music, he could see the performers while sitting at the organ with his back to the audience.

According to Jennens, the third maggot in Handel's head was a Halleluja he had "trump'd up at the end of his oratorio" to make the finale more powerful. Any lack of power, Jennens declared, was Handel's fault since the words Jennens had provided would've supported the grandest music Handel could write. "But this Hallelujah, grand as it is," he protested, "comes in very nonsensically, having no manner of relation to what goes before."

"I could tell you more of his maggots," Jennens promised, "but it grows late, and I must defer the rest till I write next, by which time, I doubt not, more new ones will breed in his brain."

It seems that Handel was not above taking some of the criticism to heart. His handwritten score of *Saul* suggests that he followed Jennens' advice and moved the Hallelujah in question from the finale of the oratorio to the end of the first chorus.

September 20th
That's All I Ask

On September 20, 1850, Richard Wagner shared his aspirations with critic Theodor Uhlig, writing from Zurich about the key to achieving his latest artistic goal:

What's needed to accomplish the best, most decisive and important project that I can take on in the current circumstances, and to bring to fruition what I consider my life work, is a sum of perhaps 10,000 Thalers.

If I had that kind of money to work with, this is what I would do. Here, where I have a position and where the situation isn't too bad, I'd have a makeshift theater of planks and beams set up, according to my own design, in a beautiful meadow just outside the town, and equipped with the bare essentials of scenery and the machinery necessary for a performance of Siegfried. *Then I'd pick the most suitable singers, wherever they are, and invite them to Zurich for six weeks. I'd try to put the chorus together locally with amateurs (there are outstanding voices and strong, healthy people here).*

I'd assemble the orchestra by invitation the same way. In the New Year I'd place advertisements in all the German newspapers, inviting all lovers of musical drama to attend the proposed music festival...I'd give three performances of Siegfried *in a week, and after three performances the theater would be pulled down and my score burned.*

To everyone who had enjoyed it, I would say, "Now go and do likewise!" But if they wanted to hear something new from me, I'd say, "Now you get the money together!"

Do you think I'm completely crazy? Maybe I am, but I assure you that achieving this is the great hope of my life, the only promise that can spur me to take up any creative work. So find me 10,000 Thalers. That's all I ask.

September 21st
First, the Money

In memoirs he wrote in 1896, conductor Luigi Arditi recalls a situation in which a stubborn baritone named Novara pursued his demand for money all the way into a performance.

Novara had agreed to sing the part of Rocco for three performances of Beethoven's opera *Fidelio* with the understanding that, like everyone else in the company, he would be paid in advance.

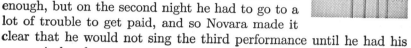

His payment for the first performance went well enough, but on the second night he had to go to a lot of trouble to get paid, and so Novara made it clear that he would not sing the third performance until he had his money in hand.

He arrived at the theater, put on his costume, and asked the impresario's agent for his money, only to be told that impresario James Henry Mapleson was dining out and had forgotten to sign a check for him.

Novara told the agent, Levelly by name, that he wasn't going to sing until he was paid. Find Mapleson and get the money, he demanded.

"I don't know where he is," Levelly said, all too aware that curtain time was approaching. "Here, take my watch as a guarantee, Novara, and, for God's sake, get into your clothes."

The baritone stood his ground. "I don't require your watch, man. I want my money, and unless I get it before the curtain rises, I shall take off this damned wig, and the stage carpenter can sing the role of Rocco."

Levelly ran from the theater and hailed a cab for parts unknown in search of Mapleson.

When the curtain rose and Rocco sang his first aria offstage, conductor Arditi was startled to hear a voice that sounded strangely like that of the stage manager. About then, Levelly ran back into the theater, dripping with sweat, having come up with the necessary cash somewhere. He stuffed it into Novara's hand, and the stubborn baritone rushed onto the stage just in time to save the performance.

September 22nd
Money Sings

In the fall of 1974 soprano Kiri Te Kanawa was cast in the role of Marguerite in a Covent Garden production of Charles Gounod's opera *Faust*. An American philanthropist had offered £500,000 for the staging of his favorite work.

The money came with a string attached. The part of Mephistopheles had to be performed by the donor's favorite bass, American Norman Treigle. Treigle arrived in London late, looking pale and malnourished, and called in sick before his first rehearsal, saying that he had hurt his foot while getting out of bed in his hotel room.

Te Kanawa was not exactly in fine fettle either. Because the rehearsals took place at the Opera Center, she had to endure nerve-wracking drives across London, and she had to learn the opera on short notice while having to cope with last-minute changes made by conductor John Matheson.

Matheson, in the meantime, had his hands full trying to work with Treigle, who was living on a diet of whiskey and water and seemed to be wasting away, voice included, yet challenged Matheson's authority. When Treigle was warned that failure to show up for the dress rehearsal would result in his replacement, the American appeared in full costume—on crutches.

"No one could resist this millionaire who thought he was terrific and that Covent Garden should see him," Matheson said later. "It was a shambles. He was crazy."

Te Kanawa sang beautifully, but the Covent Garden *Faust* won faint praise from the critics, who ultimately blamed Matheson for the lackluster performances. "There was a cabal against me," Matheson recalled, all the more depressed because his friend Kiri seemed to be involved in it.

Matheson quit and was replaced by Charles Mackerras, who conducted the rest of the run without great joy.

Six weeks after *Faust* closed, Norman Treigle, having stuck to his liquid diet, died in his hotel room.

Kiri Te Kanawa left for New York, where she achieved a triumph as Elvira in Mozart's *Don Giovanni*.

September 23rd
Turnabout

The celebrated conductor Sir Thomas Beecham was known for the practical jokes he played on performers. How well would he take it when a performer put one over on him?

In the fall of 1935 Beecham was holding auditions for a season at London's Covent Garden and a long tour through the country, which would include a revival of Puccini's *La Boheme.* A few years earlier, soprano Dora Labbette had won Beecham's admiration singing in Handel's *Messiah* under his direction, and now she wanted to have her operatic debut.

She decided to audition in disguise.

She put on a bright blond wig and a simple black dress and pretended to be a foreigner who couldn't speak a word of English. To avoid having to speak, she wrote "Audition" on an envelope and was admitted backstage, where she waited with six other hopefuls aspiring to win the part of Mimi or Musetta.

Identified only as Number Three, she walked on stage in her disguise, unusually nervous, barely able to make out Beecham in a distant seat as she peered out through her false curls. Despite her nerves, she thought that her voice carried particularly well as she sang Mimi's big arias.

As it turned out, so did Percy Heming, a baritone who helped Beecham with management. He hurried in from the amphitheater to tell Beecham that Number Three was the best of the lot. Beecham told him to talk to the mystery soprano, make her acquaintance, and consider offering her the role.

But backstage, Number Three was nowhere to be found.

The next day, her agent invited Beecham to lunch to meet "a promising young Italian soprano."

Still in disguise and using the name Lisa Perli, Dora Labbette let slip one reference after another to oratorios they had worked on together until Beecham recognized her. With a cry of delight, he ordered champagne and offered her the role of Mimi.

September 24th
American Reverses

On September 24, 1902, Pietro Mascagni sailed for New York with an opera company that he had assembled hastily for an American tour. He would discover some old truths in the New World.

When Mascagni and his wife arrived in New York they received a warm welcome from thousands of cheering Italians who accompanied them up Broadway. The next day, reality set in.

Arriving at the Metropolitan Opera House, Mascagni found two orchestras waiting for him—the one he had brought from Italy and an American orchestra that had been rounded up by the Musical Union, which demanded that Mascagni's orchestra be deported. Pressing on with his own musicians, Mascagni had only two days to rehearse for the debut of his celebrated opera *Cavalleria Rusticana* and a novelty called *Zanetto*.

The audience reaction was enthusiastic and the reviews generally sympathetic. But New Yorkers who struggled through a rainstorm to hear Mascagni's opera *Iris*, only to find that the unprepared composer had rescheduled it, left wet and angry as Mascagni stayed behind locked doors continuing to rehearse the orchestra.

A road tour played to rather small audiences because most wanted to hear the famous *Cavalleria Rusticana* rather than Mascagni's newer operas. In Boston the reviews were favorable, but minutes before the long-awaited debut of the opera *Ratcliff*, the long unpaid musicians walked out. Claiming that Mascagni owed him a small fortune, the American organizer of the tour had the composer confined to his hotel suite until his attorney came up with $4,000 bail.

For the next five months Mascagni pieced and patched his way to San Francisco, where he managed to end his American tour with modest success, and when the Massachusetts Supreme Court threw out the suit against him, Pietro Mascagni took the fastest train and the fastest boats back to Italy.

September 25th
The Split

In the fall of 1931 a Berlin producer thought that a theater version of the opera *The Rise and Fall of the City of Mahagonny* could bring in good money during hard times.

Composer Kurt Weill and playwright Bertolt Brecht made the going rough. During rehearsals, as they made cuts in the opera, Weill argued on behalf of his music, Brecht on behalf of his words. Their quarrels got so hot that their attorneys came into the theater and threatened each other. When a press photographer took a picture of Brecht standing next to Weill, Brecht knocked the camera out of his hands.

Weill stalked out of the theater with Brecht yelling after him: "I'm going to put on full war-paint and throw that bogus Richard Strauss down the stairs!"

Despite the sparring, *The Rise and Fall of the City of Mahagonny* enjoyed a modestly successful run of more than fifty performances.

But the split between Weill and Brecht would grow wider for reasons having nothing to do with artistic temperament. Within a year, Adolf Hitler had strong-armed his way into the German chancellorship, and Nazi demonstrators were threatening Jewish artists and closing down plays given to political satire. A day after the burning of the Reichstag building, which gave Hitler even greater power, Brecht drove to Prague, where he and his family began what would stretch into fifteen years of exile.

Despite the growing danger, Weill remained in Berlin, working on a symphony and music for a film, until one day in 1933, when a friend tipped him off that he was about to be arrested by the Gestapo. He packed a few things into his car, drove to the French border, and slipped past the German border guards on foot. He made his way to Paris. There he and Brecht collaborated one last time on the sung ballet *The Seven Deadly Sins*, after which he went to the United States, where he became a composer of successful Broadway musicals.

Not to Be

When celebrated Czech composer Antonín Dvořák stepped onto the pier in New York on September 26, 1892, he was welcomed as the future discoverer of American music. During his two-and-a-half-year tenure as the director of the National Conservatory of Music in New York, Americans got to hear a variety of his works and he wrote some of his most important music.

But during his lifetime, an important part of his music never got a hearing in America—opera.

Dvořák did what he could. The founder of the National Conservatory, Mrs. Jeanette Thurber, was so ardent in her appreciation of opera that in 1886 she had founded the American Opera Company for the purpose of producing operas in English. After its second season the company folded, but she pressed on with a composition contest that would award its grand prize to an outstanding opera.

No worthy opera emerged, so the irrepressible Mrs. Thurber suggested to Dvořák that he compose an opera on an American theme.

He liked the idea of writing an opera based on Longfellow's poetic narrative *The Song of Hiawatha*, which he had read in a Czech translation. He was going to begin as soon as he found a libretto, but no one ever came up with a prose version of Longfellow's dactylic hexameter, and nothing ever came of the project except for a few sketches that apparently wound up in his New World Symphony.

In 1894 and '95, in New York, after putting the finishing touches to his grand opera *Dmitirj*, begun back in 1881, he returned to Europe.

So America had no opera from him, and, although he devoted the last several years of his life to writing operatic works, not until long after Dvořák's time, in 1935, would America see its first Dvořák opera, when a suburban Chicago Czech-American civic organization put on a performance of his 1900 opera *Rusalka*.

September 27th

A Minor Detail

Franz Lehár was enthusiastic again. Having made his fortune at the age of thirty-five with his 1905 operetta *The Merry Widow*, the Hungarian composer had gone through a fallow stretch during World War I and the collapse of the Austro-Hungarian Empire. But in 1925 he discovered a tenor, Richard Tauber, who inspired him, and found a libretto that seemed just right for a Lehár operetta.

The libretto was based on a book called *Paganini*. It was by an anonymous author and it told of the great violinist's struggle with love and artistry. The manager of Berlin's Künstlertheater was quick to offer the usual royalties to Lehár and a generous fee for Tauber. The contract was all settled.

Except for one minor detail—getting permission from the author to use the libretto.

He turned out to be Paul Knepler, a Viennese book publisher and music-lover. He had used his book as the basis for a libretto called *The Wizard* and shown it to composer Viktor Wögerer, who removed Knepler's name from the title page and took the libretto to an associate of Lehár's.

Lehár was so enthusiastic that he went to work right away and was halfway through the score of an operetta called *Paganini* before he asked Wögerer who had written the book. Wögerer came out with Knepler's name and suggested inviting the author to tea.

When Lehár described his operetta to Knepler, the author was perplexed. "There must be some mistake," he said. "I don't know how the libretto came into your hands, but I wrote it for myself, not for you."

More than a little annoyed, Lehár explained that he was already halfway through composing the score of *Paganini*. He went to the piano and played the first few bars of it. Knepler was impressed and realized that he stood to make good money from such an enjoyable operetta. He gave Lehár permission to use his book, and after the success of *Paganini*, was in great demand to write librettos for other operetta composers.

271

September 28th

The Joker and the Queen

If a story from the 1690s is true, composer Henry Purcell was so self-assured that he dared to play a joke on Queen Mary.

Purcell had been commissioned to compose music for the queen's birthday, the assigned verses being praise of King William's bravery and the queen's virtues. Apparently thinking the poem too long, Purcell left off the last two verses so that the piece ended with a comic twist at the queen's expense. According to Purcell contemporary Sir John Hawkins, the queen may have paid Purcell back with a trick of her own. He wrote:

The tune "Cold and Raw" was greatly admired by Queen Mary.... Having a mind one afternoon to be entertained with music she sent to Mr. Gosling... to Henry Purcell and Mrs. Arabella Hunt, who had a very fine voice, and an admirable hand on the lute, with a request to attend her.... Mr. Gosling and Mrs. Hunt sang several compositions of Purcell, who accompanied them on the harpsichord. At length, the queen beginning to grow tired, asked Mrs. Hunt if she could not sing the old Scots ballad "Cold and Raw." Mrs. Hunt answered yes, and sang it to her lute.

Purcell was all the while sitting at the harpsichord unemployed, and not a little nettled at the queen's preference of a vulgar ballad to his music. But seeing her majesty delighted with the tune, he determined that she should hear it upon another occasion, and accordingly in the next birthday song—that for the year 1692—he composed an air to the words "May her bright example chase Vice in troops out of the land," the bass whereof is the tune "Cold and Raw."

The same kind of imagination and daring no doubt led to Purcell's enduring reputation as one of England's great composers.

September 29th

Second Expedition

During his first sojourn in America, composer Karel Szymanowski had accomplished little more than strengthening his identity as a Polish composer. Nonetheless, in 1921 a friend convinced him that a second visit would be more productive since new contacts there might lead to important performances of Szymanowski's music.

Still jaded from his previous visit, Szymanowski was more inclined to listen to a friend who said that in America he might at least earn enough fame and money to allow him to compose without worrying about his income. Another friend, one more given to bluntness, advised Szymanowski to go over and marry a rich American.

Soon after his arrival in New York at the end of September, Szymanowski did tap a vein or two. He secured a clothing manufacturer as a benefactor and got backing from the daughter of the man who had bankrolled the New England Conservatory and the Boston Opera. Szymanowski rounded up enough money to support his mother for a year.

But, for the most part, the Americans were tight with their dollars because the economic indicators were pointing to a recession.

And the prospecting required such intense socializing that Szymanowski had little time and energy left for more creative pursuits. "It really is a kind of inferno," he wrote to his mother, "in which for entire days it's often impossible to collect one's wits for a single moment!"

Grudgingly, he attended concerts or parts of concerts that involved acquaintances, most of which made him all the more restless to get on with his own work.

Drawing on lessons learned from his first American experience, Szymanowski made a policy of leaving New York only for the Boston performances of his Second Symphony. From time to time, he worked on his opera *King Roger*, but the only work he completed was a set of three short lullabies.

After five months, Szymanowski went back to Europe, less than enthusiastic about his second American expedition.

September 30th

Breaking Through

Seventeen-year-old Johannes Brahms was determined to become a composer, and so in 1850 when Robert Schumann came to Hamburg for a visit, Brahms got up his courage and sent a parcel of his music to Schumann's hotel. The result was discouraging. The parcel came back unopened.

Two years later Brahms traveled to Weimar to meet piano wizard Franz Liszt. Liszt was living in lavish style at the palace of his mistress, surrounded by a throng of students and other admirers. Poverty had forced Brahms to play piano in some of Hamburg's most tawdry entertainment houses. He found the luxurious surroundings intimidating. When Liszt asked him to play some of his pieces, he got nervous and declined.

So Liszt sight-read them, offering constructive commentary as he went through Brahms' E-flat minor scherzo and part of the C major sonata. According to one account, when Liszt played his own *Sonata in B minor*, he looked over and saw Brahms dozing, but took no offense.

Brahms decided to take another chance with Schumann. He took the train to Düsseldorf and turned up on the composer's doorstep at about noon on September 30, 1853. Schumann and his wife Clara weren't home. Their eldest daughter, Marie, told the handsome young man with long blond hair to come back the next morning at eleven o'clock.

When he did, Schumann himself came to the door and asked Brahms to play for him. Much more at ease in the middle-class surroundings of the Schumann household, Brahms launched into his C major sonata. Almost at once, Schumann asked him to stop and ran out of the room to get Clara.

"Now you'll hear music the likes of which you've never heard before," he promised her. Brahms played away the morning and promised to come back every day.

That night Schumann wrote in his diary, "Visit from Brahms, a genius." Soon afterward he wrote to his publishers and recommended that they consider printing whatever music Brahms sent them.

October 1st

Spite and Neglect

In memoirs he began in 1910 and never finished, composer Karl Goldmark looked back six decades to his early experiences as a struggling violinist. After a brief inglorious career as a draftee in a war between Austria and Hungary, the eighteen-year-old musician settled in the town of Ödenburg. His playing wasn't always appreciated.

On October 1, 1848, I joined the orchestra of the Ödenburg Theater as one of the first violins at a monthly salary of eight florins. In order to have the opportunity to play in public, I needed a dress coat. I paid three florins a month for one and another three florins went toward renting a room. That left me two florins to pay all other expenses. I went hungry and cold, but I had a dress coat, and soon enough it made its debut.

The ballet master invited me to play a concerto at his benefit, and I did—Beriot's Concerto in D. It won me a good deal of prestige among my colleagues. But it put the concertmaster (we had just two first violins total) beside whom I sat, in a bad frame of mind, and he got even. At a rehearsal of the opera Zampa, at the singer's request, a difficult violin part was to be transposed one third. My colleague busied himself with his strings and left me to play the part alone. It was my first engagement. I had never played that opera and I made a hash of it.

But it was clear that the breakdown was the product of spite shown a young inexperienced player and the mishap didn't do any further harm.

At the end of the season, the theater company moved to another town, leaving Goldmark and just three other string players to provide overtures and music between acts in the form of string quartets.

"When the curtain rose, I had to stop," Goldmark recalled, "even if we were in the middle of a bar. All in all, the pleasure was limited."

October 2nd

Dear Baroness

The world's greatest composer was feeling giddy when he wrote Baroness von Waldstadten with a special request on October 2, 1782:

I can say truthfully that I am a happy and an unhappy man— unhappy since the night when I saw your ladyship at the ball with your hair so beautifully coiffed—because—gone is my peace of mind! Nothing but sighs and groans! During the rest of the time I spent at the hall I did not dance—I skipped. Dinner was all ordered, but I did not eat, I scarfed. During the night, instead of sleeping gently and sweetly, I slept like a dormouse and snored like a bear and, without being too presumptuous, I might go so far as to wager that your ladyship had the same experience in proportion.

You smile, you blush! Ah, yes—I am indeed happy. My fortune is made!

But alas, who is this tapping me on the shoulder? Who's peeking into my letter? Alas! Alas! Alas! My wife! Well, for heaven's sake, I've taken her and so I have to keep her! What can I do? I have to sing her praises—and pretend that what I say is true!

But now, all joking aside, if your ladyship could send me a jug [of beer] this evening, you would be doing me a big favor because my wife is—is—and has longings—but only for beer brewed in the English way!

Well done, little wife! Finally I see that you are good for something. My wife, who is an angel of a woman, and I, who am a model husband, both kiss your Ladyship's hands a thousand times and are your faithful vassals—Mozart the Great, Small-Bodied and Constanze, most beautiful and prudent of all wives.

One can only hope that the desired beverage was delivered, and only imagine what transpired if it was.

October 3rd

Second Thoughts

Although he had never conducted any of William Walton's music, Thomas Beecham suggested that the young composer write a concerto for violist Lionel Tertis. Walton wrote the concerto and sent it to Tertis, who thought that Walton's music was a little too farfetched, and turned it down.

A friend at the BBC suggested that Walton invite German composer Paul Hindemith to play the first performance of the concerto. With a subsidy from poet Siegfried Sassoon, the cash-strapped Walton went to Baden-Baden to issue the invitation personally. He was delighted when Hindemith agreed to play it as his solo debut in England, with Walton conducting, at a Queen's Hall concert on October 3, 1929.

Hindemith's friend and publisher, Willy Strecker, tried to derail the idea. He wrote to Hindemith's wife, saying that Hindemith should hold out for an English debut in which he would appear as both a composer and a soloist, rather than playing the work of a mediocre English composer.

But Hindemith liked the concerto, which might have reminded him of his own *Kammermusik No. 5* of two years before. He persisted in his plan to play it, even though his first rehearsal convinced him that the orchestra was bad because it consisted mostly of women—and English women at that.

"His technique was marvelous," Walton said of Hindemith's performance after the debut, "but he was rough—no nonsense about it. He just stood up and played."

Among those most impressed by the debut was Lionel Tertis, who reversed his judgment and played the concerto several times during the next three years, most notably at an Edinburgh concert where the audience responded to it with such enthusiasm that conductor Adrian Boult suggested playing the concerto again during the second half of the program.

Equally impressed with Walton's viola concerto was the distinguished musicologist Sir Donald Tovey, who gave it an assessment that would endure when he called it "one of the most important modern concertos for any instrument."

October 4th
Last Laugh

In his autobiography, Karl Ditters von Dittersdorf couldn't resist passing along a story that suggests how seriously eighteenth-century Venetians took their music.

The famous castrato Guadagni had given three fine performances in an opera that was a particular favorite of Venetians. But after an argument with the impresario, he decided to sabotage the opera by pretending to forget his part. After two appeals from audience representatives, Guadagni howled instead of singing and stood stock still instead of acting. Dittersdorf expressed his bewilderment:

Who would not have thought that the audience would run him off the stage with rotten apples and oranges, according to its usual custom? Contrary to all expectation, the performance went on quietly to the end.

The payback would be more frightening.

After the opera Guadagni, still in costume, was about to get into his gondola when four masked abductors blindfolded him and hauled him into a scantly furnished room. Two men brought in a table with a good supper on it. The hungry singer sat down to eat.

"Hands off, sir," said one of the captors. "Unless you sing, you'll get not one bite."

Guadagni refused and the table was carried away. The scene repeated itself for two days until an irresistible soup prompted Guadagni to say, "I would rather sing than starve."

"That is not enough," said the masked man. "If you do not sing—yes, and sing your very best—and act in the bargain, the soup goes out the door!"

Guadagni sang and acted as if impelled by pure love of art.

"Bravo, bravissimo!" exclaimed all the masked critics, clapping their hands. Laughing, they unmasked. The singer found himself face to face with a group of hangmen.

"I am commissioned to warn you to do your duty at all future performances," the spokesman said. "If you do not, you may be sure that the Senate will treat a second insult far more seriously."

There was no second insult.

October 5th

I Am Sick of It All!

After receiving an invitation to write a choral work for the 1898 Leeds Festival, Edward Elgar began work on his cantata *Caractacus*. His inspiration would have to carry him past a series of obstacles, including his own pessimism.

He decided on a story about an ancient British hero, but the man Elgar chose to write the lyrics provided a pompous pastiche that ended with an overblown chorus about the post-Roman rise of British glory.

As he worked on *Caractacus*, Elgar told a friend that parts of it "frightened" him, and as he submitted it to the publisher one scene at a time, he asked that no one say a word about the work, for better or worse, because he already felt tense enough "to die on edge."

When Elgar began orchestrating the first sketch, his friend Augustus Jaeger got a look at it and suggested to Elgar that it was too nationalistic, which elicited a sarcastic defense from the composer.

Elgar started to worry that the chorus would think their part too bland, but as he worked on proofing what he referred to as "correct-a-cuss," and heard it in rehearsal, he wrote to Jaeger that he would alter no more of the cantata, "short of burning the whole thing."

The debut on October 5, 1898, took place before a star-studded audience that included many prominent musicians and Queen Victoria, to whom Elgar had dedicated *Caractacus*. The stage was set for a triumph, but the chorus didn't deliver. It turned out that they had never much cared for Elgar's music.

The reviews were muddled and mixed, and Elgar slid into a funk. "I tell you I am sick of it all!" he wrote to Jaeger. "Why can't I be encouraged to do decent stuff and not hounded into triviality?"

But despite his disgust, he couldn't help composing. Just four days later, he wrote again, saying that he was working on a set of variations on an original theme.

October 6th
Farewell Again

 Adelina Patti was one of the most celebrated sopranos in the history of music, but that didn't put her above the barbs thrown by *New York Evening Post* critic Henry T. Finck.

Finck had several misgivings about Patti, most of them having little to do with her singing, which he described as "so glorious, so incomparable, that while under the spell of her vocal art, the listeners forgot everything else and simply luxuriated in ecstatic bliss."

One of his objections to Patti was her apparent arrogance. It was said that during a rehearsal of a Handel oratorio, she was embellishing the music to show off the beauty and agility of her voice and insisted on doing it her way because she was the prima donna, to which conductor Theodore Thomas replied, "Excuse me, madam, but here I am prima donna."

Finck asserted that Rossini barely recognized one of his own arias when Patti sang it.

Then there was the matter of money. She required $5,000 up front in gold for a performance, so much that any production involving her had to economize in all other areas, making an all-round solid performance impossible. He thought that, at ten dollars a seat, her ticket prices were too high, since even the Berlin Royal Opera House charged as little as a dollar.

"One of the funny things about Patti," he added, "was that each of her visits to America was announced as her farewell." In a review after one such concert, he gave himself over to sarcasm, writing:

It will also be recorded that old men who had as youths heard Madame Patti sing... when her farewell had just been invented, wept with joy on realizing that though she was still "an exile from home" at $4,000 an evening and had not yet succeeded in coming all the way through the rye, she was as delicious to the senses as the last rose of summer, which had become her special property.

October 7th

Praise or Parody?

Russian audiences were cool to Dmitri Shostakovich's Twelfth Symphony during its first performances in October 1961, and according to one account, they had good reason: It was a desperate last-minute substitute for a symphony that was too dangerous.

Shostakovich associate Lev Lebedinsky tells the story this way:

Shostakovich had long chafed under the restrictions of life in the Soviet Union and couldn't resist writing a symphony that made subtle fun of Vladimir Lenin, the revered founder of the Soviet state. Lebedinsky tried to talk Shostakovich out of writing the satire, saying that such a symphony would be too dangerous and that audiences wouldn't pick up on the joke anyway. Shostakovich, he said, replied with a Russian proverb: "He who has ears will hear."

On the eve of the debut a desperate Shostakovich called him and asked him to come to Leningrad to hear the symphony, and, arriving at Shostakovich's hotel, Lebedinsky found the composer pale and haggard.

"I've written an awful symphony," Shostakovich said. "It's a failure, but I've managed to change it."

"Change what?"

"The entire symphony. But we can't talk anymore. My room is full of journalists and all kinds of strange people."

During the ensuing media circus Shostakovich affirmed that his new symphony was indeed about Lenin. When they were alone again, he explained to Lebedinsky that three days before the debut he had gotten cold feet and had dashed off an entirely new symphony.

During the rehearsal Shostakovich held his friend's hand and asked, "Is it really awful?"

For the sake of Shostakovich's mental stability, Lebedinsky lied and assured him that it was perfectly all right.

"No one must know what I told you about the history of this symphony," Shostakovich declared.

"God forbid," Lebedinsky replied.

The evidence neither supports nor contradicts his story of the three-day symphony.

October 8th
Faint Praise

In October 1928 Russian Ballet director Serge Diaghilev wanted the famous Vaslav Nijinsky to endorse dancer Serge Lifar, and he went to great lengths to get a little praise.

An advantage: Diaghilev and Nijinsky had been lovers. A disadvantage: Nijinksky had suffered a nervous breakdown back in 1919 and had been in and out of institutions ever since. But as one of Diaghilev's friends said of him, "He likes people to admire his musicians, his painters, and particularly, his boys and girls of the ballet company. And he doesn't really care if the admirer is the Bey of Tunis or an insane genius."

Diaghilev found Nijinsky in a sanitorium on the outskirts of Paris. The small, bald, grayish little man with expressionless eyes was hardly the image of a heroic dancer. Nijinsky said nothing. When Diaghilev, Nijinksky, and their coterie arrived at the Paris Opéra, a crowd of ballet company members met them at the stage door. When they got inside, Nijinsky resisted walking upstairs to the director's box, so he was carried up in a hand-chair. Stravinsky's *Firebird* had already begun, so the theater was too dark for more than a few to see the arrival of the great dancer.

Diaghilev stood behind Nijinsky's seat, whispering in his ear as the ballet legend took in the dancing, seemingly the first time he had focused on anything all evening. "Tell me, tell me," Diaghilev whispered, "how do you like Lifar? Isn't he magnificent?" He tweaked his ear and poked him in the shoulder without getting any reaction until a pinch prompted Nijinsky to mumble some word of protest.

After the ballet Nijinsky was swallowed up by an admiring crowd, so it wasn't until the drive back to the sanitorium that he had a chance to offer the much-sought endorsement. On the way to the gate the pale dancer, now "limp as an oyster," turned and gave Diaghilev all he was going to get. In a soft, halting voice he said, "Tell him that Lifar jumps well."

October 9th

Awkward Encounters

In the summer of 1907 Spanish pianist and composer Manuel de Falla piled up his meager savings and went to Paris in the hope of breaking into the international music scene. He was in for some setbacks.

The jobs he had arranged fell through, and, after playing piano with a traveling pantomime company, he scraped by in Paris by teaching piano and harmony students. "I'm more and more glad that I decided to leave Madrid," he wrote a friend. "There was no future for me there."

He set about introducing himself to the city's major musical figures, but summer was a bad time for it because many of them were out of town, although Frenchman Paul Dukas went out of his way to be helpful and introduced him to the influential Spanish composer Isaac Albéniz.

Getting to know the celebrated Claude Debussy would not go so smoothly.

Falla finally met him in October, played the piano score of his opera *La vida breve* for him, and found the Frenchman's sarcasm a little intimidating.

A little later, Falla's shyness made for an even more awkward encounter.

Falla came to visit Debussy, was told that he was out, and was ushered by a servant into a dark alcove off the dining room, a storage space filled with grotesque Chinese masks. After a while Falla heard Debussy, his wife Emma, and composer Erik Satie come into the dining room and begin lunch. Falla was too timid to enter the dining room unannounced and sat there in the dark alcove, faint from hunger, staring at the weird and ghoulish faces of the masks.

When the chatting and clatter of lunch seemed loud enough to cover his retreat, he slipped into a dim hallway and hastened toward the egress, only to bump headfirst into Debussy's wife, who screamed.

Even though everybody encouraged Falla to join them for lunch, he was so rattled by the encounter that he made his apologies and departed.

283

October 10th

A Force for Change

Allegro, Andante, Adagio, Presto. We take the venerable tempo indications for granted today. Beethoven did not, as becomes apparent in a letter he wrote to a fellow composer and conductor in 1817:

I am ecstatic that you share my opinions about our tempo indications, which originated in the barbarous age of music. For example, what can be more ridiculous than Allegro, which means "cheerful," and how far we often are from the sense of that tempo, to the extent that the actual piece means the opposite of the indication.... For my part, I've been considering giving up those silly descriptive terms—Allegro, Andante, Adagio, Presto. And Maelzel's metronome gives the best chance to do so. I now give you my word that I shall never use them again in any of my new works.

But there is another issue, namely, whether by doing so we are encouraging the general use of the metronome as a necessary thing? I say, not at all. But I'm sure that we shall be shouted down for being tyrants anyway. If only the cause itself were to be served, it would still be better than to be accused of feudalism. So I imagine that the best solution would be, especially for our countries where music has become a national need and where every village schoolmaster will be expected to use the metronome, that Maelzel should try to sell a certain number of metronomes at a very high price. Then, as soon as he's covered his expenses, he'll be able to sell them so cheaply to the rest of the nation that they'll spread all over the country.

It goes without saying, of course, that some people have to lead the movement in order to drum up enthusiasm. You can certainly rely upon me to do whatever I can, and I look forward to whatever task you're going to assign me.

October 11th

I Quit!

The job was good, the pay quite nice, and the employer friendly, so in 1717 Johann Sebastian Bach accepted the position of conductor of the music staff for Prince Leopold of Anhalt-Cöthen. The only catch: Bach already had a job and he needed to get out of it.

For nine years Bach had put up with the tension and irritations of the court at Weimar, where two quarrelsome noblemen, Duke Wilhelm Ernst and his nephew and heir, Ernst August, made life difficult. When Bach had defied the uncle by arranging a performance at the castle of the nephew, the old prince got back at him by appointing someone else to the position of Kapellmeister when that important job became available.

Then Prince Leopold of Anhalt-Cöthen offered Bach an innovative job, one that required no organ playing, no composing of church music, and the chance to write plenty of instrumental music. Bach was attracted and intrigued. He accepted.

But Wilhelm Ernst liked stability at his court, and he didn't like the idea of giving up such a renowned organist as Sebastian Bach, particularly because he considered Prince Leopold a rival. He refused to let Bach go, and figured that the fiery-tempered musician would eventually get over the flap and settle down.

He was quite wrong.

Bach refused to let the matter drop. Defying the duke's decision, he became so outspoken about wanting to leave that the duke had him arrested. For four weeks he sat in jail, apparently using the time to work on a book of keyboard pieces.

When he showed no sign of relenting or repenting, Wilhelm Ernst became wary of getting into a public argument with the Cöthen court. He let Bach go with a notice of his "unfavorable discharge."

The victory was particularly sweet for Bach, whose father Ambrosius, a generation earlier, had been forced to stay at a position at Eisenach.

October 12th

The New World

On October 12, 1892, newly arrived in the New World, Czech composer Antonín Dvořák wrote from New York to a friend in Moravia about his first impressions of America:

After being in quarantine for just a little while we arrived safely in the promised land. The view from Sandy Hook, the harbor town for New York, with the splendid Statue of Liberty (who has room in her head alone for 60 people and where banquets are often held) is very impressive! Add to that all the shipping from the four corners of the world! As I say, it's astounding.

On Tuesday the 27th we arrived at the town (Hoboken) where all ships dock, and waiting for us was the Secretary of the National Conservatory, Mr. Santon—and what pleased me most—a delegation of Czechs. After we exchanged greetings and said a few words, a carriage awaited us and soon we were in New York, and are still in the same hotel.

The city itself is splendid, attractive buildings and beautiful streets and, everywhere, absolute cleanliness.

Things are expensive here. Our gulden is like a dollar. At the hotel we pay 55 dollars a week for three rooms, admittedly in the most central part of the city, Union Square. But that makes no difference because we will not spend more than 5000 and so, I'm grateful to say, we'll be able to leave the rest untouched.

On Sunday the 9th there was a big Czech concert in my honor. There were 3000 people in the hall, clapping and cheering continuously. There were speeches in Czech and English and I, poor thing, had to give a thank you speech from the platform while holding a silver wreath in my hands.

You can imagine how I felt! And you'll find out about it later from the newspapers. What the American papers write about me is awful. They see in me, they say, the savior of music and who knows what else!

October 13th
Collision Course

In the early days of radio someone decided that it would be a good idea to time orchestral performances. The results were surprising to most conductors, and put two of the greatest on a collision course.

In 1949 Leonard Bernstein was a young up-and-coming conductor and an avid listener to records. Bernstein listened to Arturo Toscanini's NBC broadcast of the Love Scene from Berlioz' *Romeo and Juliet* and found it much slower than the venerable conductor's recording of it for an RCA record. Bernstein was about to conduct the same work and asked Toscanini if they could discuss tempo and other aspects of the work. The hot-tempered Toscanini replied with a cordial invitation for the young conductor to visit him.

"Toscanini" by Enrico Caruso

At Villa Pauline, Toscanini's Riverdale house overlooking the Hudson River, Bernstein found his octogenarian host full of energy, bounding up the stairs two at a time and "bouncing all over the place." Then the two compared their ideas about the Berlioz scores. Toscanini answered most of Bernstein's questions, but when the young American worked up the nerve to ask about the differences in tempo between Toscanini's two performances, the temperamental Italian was hard-pressed for an explanation. He promised to compare the broadcast transcription with the RCA recording.

A few days later Bernstein received a note from Toscanini dated October 13, 1949, in bold red ink. After a comparison of the two performances, Toscanini wrote, he confronted the fact that the version on the record was much faster. He went on to say that he had confronted another fact— "that every man, no matter the importance of his intelligence, can be from time to time a little stupid." He added, "So is the case of the old Toscanini."

Far from taking offence at Bernstein's inquiry about the tempo discrepancies, Toscanini closed by saying that during the visit, "I felt myself forty years younger."

October 14th

I Feel Lost Already

The Guns of Navarone, The Thing from Another World, Friendly Persuasion, Mr. Smith Goes to Washington, High Noon—those classics and more than a hundred other Hollywood movies bear the stamp of composer Dimitri Tiomkin, a Russian émigré who developed a flair for writing American music. He was thirty-one years old before he first set foot in the United States. The year was 1925. Tiomkin was a concert pianist who had been lured to New York by an impresario promising great wealth. There was just one catch.

When he arrived in New York, Tiomkin and a fellow pianist named Raskov discovered that they were to be part of a vaudeville act that would include a ballet troupe dancing to a pastiche of Chopin and Liszt that struck Tiomkin as musical "butchery."

Then there was the matter of performance style. To the unpretentious pianist it was made clear that in vaudeville visual tricks were all-important. A rapid upward treble scale was to end with a flourish of the hand. Fortissimo chords were to be attacked by hands held high. He was to bend his head in concentration for certain expressive but easy passages and to throw back his head or slump down limp to express great emotion.

"You must lose yourself," advised one person in the know, to which Tiomkin said to himself, "I feel lost already."

On opening night at the Palace Theater, just north of Times Square, Tiomkin felt that he was playing well enough, but failing at the flashiness, while Raskov got so carried away with it that the pianos edged dangerously close to the orchestra pit.

The performance was a great hit, largely because of the flamboyant Raskov, Tiomkin figured. Their tour took them across the country to the Pacific coast, the money proved every bit as good as promised, and within a few years, the Americanization of Dimitri Tiomkin was complete when he took his talent to Hollywood and became a citizen of the United States.

October 15th

Red Spin

In 1927 Joseph Schillinger organized and directed the first jazz orchestra in Russia. Schillinger was an academician and a scientist, and so it's not surprising that the Russian debut of symphonic jazz took place not in a theater or a dance hall, but in the State Academic Choir Hall in Moscow.

Schillinger prefaced the concert with a scholarly lecture entitled "The Jazz Band and Music of the Future." At a time when the new Stalinist regime was quick to crack down on any art that smacked of privilege, Schillinger was careful to put the right spin on the program notes for the concert. He referred to jazz as "the music of the masses" and spoke of its "revolutionary role in rejuvenating music."

It turned out that the concert included no real jazz. The program consisted mostly of songs popular in the '20s. Otherwise, the so-called "jazz" was nothing more than syncopated arrangements of well-known classical works in the style of Paul Whiteman. The opening and closing selections were symphonic jazz renderings by Philadelphia Fox Theater conductor Frank Black. The music of Irving Berlin and George Gershwin was also well represented.

Schillinger's jazz band was a hybrid that included three saxophones, three brass, four rhythm instruments, plus two violins and oboe.

Apparently the concert made an impression. A few years later, the chief of the Associated Press Bureau in Moscow remarked that the most powerful pieces of foreign propaganda in Russia were the Sears, Roebuck catalogue and American jazz records.

As for Joseph Schillinger, he would soon have a much bigger impact on jazz, from the inside out. Within a year he had moved to America, where his students would include George Gershwin, Benny Goodman, Glenn Miller, and Tommy Dorsey.

The composer's wife Frances tells the story in her 1949 biography *Joseph Schillinger: A Memoir.*

October 16th

The Cherokee and the Bantu

At the age of twenty-six, Felix Mendelssohn was already well known throughout Europe. In 1835, during a visit to Leipzig, he became acquainted with a young Polish émigré who was rapidly making a name for himself. Mendelssohn wrote to his sister in Berlin on October 16, full of enthusiasm after a day spent with Frédéric Chopin:

He intended to stay for just one day so we spent it together in music. I cannot deny that lately I have found that you by no means do him justice in your judgment of his talents. Maybe he wasn't in the mood to play when you heard him, which may often be the case with him. But his playing enchanted me afresh, and I'm convinced that if you and my father also had heard some of his better pieces as he played them to me, you would say the same. There is something thoroughly original in his pianoforte playing, and at the same time so masterly that he may be called a most perfect virtuoso.

It was a pleasure for me to be with a thorough musician again, and not with those half virtuosos and half classics, and however far apart we may be in our different spheres, still I can get on wonderfully with such a person.

Sunday evening was really remarkable when Chopin made me play through my oratorio for him, while curious Leipzigers stole into the room to see him, and, between the first and second part of it, when he dashed into his new etudes and a new concerto—to the amazement of the Leipzigers. And then I resumed my St. Paul. It was just as if a Cherokee and a Bantu had met to converse. He has also such a lovely new notturno, a considerable part of which I learned by ear for the sake of playing it for our brother's entertainment.

October 17th
Starting Over

By 1770 Charles Burney had come a long way from his exploitive apprenticeship working for composer Thomas Arne. He had become a distinguished and discriminating music critic and historian. During his travels on the Continent, he collected stories from the lives of celebrated composers and performers. Among them was the account of a gifted young singer named František Benda whose voice changed, requiring him to strike out in search of a new musical career:

František Benda

Being now deprived of all hope of gaining a livelihood by singing, and unable to bear the thought of becoming a burden to his relations, he applied himself seriously to the violin, upon which he had made a beginning, but he knows not when, nor under what master. It must, however, have been early in his life, as he was remembered to play the tenor in the concerts performed by the singing boys at Dresden, and to work hard on the violin at Vivaldi's concertos.

After losing his voice, he had no other means of turning his musical talents to account, than by playing dances about the country with a company of strolling Jews, in which, however, there was a blind Hebrew of the name of Löbel, who, in his way, was an extraordinary player. He drew a good tune from his instrument and composed his own pieces, which were wild, but pretty. Some of his dances went up to an A in altissimo, however he played them with the utmost purity and neatness.

The performance of this man excited in Benda so much jealousy that he redoubled his diligence in trying to equal him, and not to be inferior in any part of his trade, he composed dances for his own band, which were far from easy. He often speaks of his obligations to the old Jew for stimulating him to excel on the violin.

After several more years as a traveling virtuoso, František Benda entered the service of King Frederick the Great and became a major violinist and composer of the eighteenth century.

October 18th

Stars That Entertain Unseen Audiences

"Some people grow; others just swell." It was a popular saying in the 1920s when radio was becoming all the rage, making stars overnight. Some of them, already established on stage, brought their egos with them to the airwaves. In 1923 Thomas Cowan, an announcer at New York radio station WJZ, described an encounter with Madame Margaret Namara of the Chicago Grand Opera Company.

After her success as Thais at the Manhattan Opera House in New York, Namara offered to broadcast a repeat performance on WJZ. She came over to the studio three days beforehand because she wanted her "movie man" to film her as she sang. She was not impressed by the plain whitewashed walls, and Cowan spent three days rushing in hangings and paintings from his own apartment and ordering palms and loads of cut flowers, plus a large rose floor lamp to stand behind the piano.

On the night of the big broadcast Madame Namara and her maid commandeered the manager's office for a dressing room, from which the singer emerged in full costume so laden with jewels that Cowan was reminded of the popular song "Rings on her fingers and bells on her toes."

When she beheld the redecorated studio she was so stunned that she threw her arms around Cowan and kissed him, smothering him in face powder.

She sang something called "The Mirror Song" and was photographed "in action" and then got into an argument with her cameraman about close-ups.

When it was all over, Cowan showed her to her car, filled her arms with flowers, and wished her a good trip all the way back to Bayshore, Long Island.

Cowan and the radio station were slow to recover. In the former greenroom he found powder so thick that it showed the singer's footprints, and a squadron of announcers set about cleaning it up in order to avoid a dressing-down from the manager.

October 19th

Win a Prize, Lose a Treasure

Itzhak Perlman had just won a spot in the finals of the 1964 Leav-entritt Contest, and his teachers at Juilliard wanted him to go into the final round of the competition with the best violin available. He couldn't afford to buy a first-rate instrument, so they arranged for him to borrow a valuable 200-year-old Guarnerius from Juilliard's rare instrument collection. With it Perlman nearly turned a monumental win into a crushing loss.

After a brilliant performance in Carnegie Hall, Perlman left the stage and joined his mother Shoshana in a large area called the Orchestra Room to wait for the judges' decision. They placed the Guarnerius on a chair and covered it with Mrs. Perlman's coat. As the judges were about to announce their decision, Perlman left his mother to guard the violin and went into the hall to hear better from backstage.

The judges announced their verdict—Perlman had won! A crowd of well-wishers rushed backstage to congratulate him. In her excitement, his mother hurried out to join them.

A few minutes later, when Perlman and his mother returned to the Orchestra Room to retrieve the Guarnerius, they were horror-stricken to find that it had been stolen.

The headline in the *New York Times* said it all: *Violinist Wins Prize, Loses a Guarnerius.*

A day later, searchers found the precious instrument in a Times Square hock shop, where the thief had pawned it for a paltry fifteen dollars.

When it was returned, Perlman allowed himself the luxury of a typically wry remark, noting that "the thief obviously was not a musician."

A few weeks later, Perlman borrowed the now-notorious instrument again for a concert with the National Symphony Orchestra in Washington. This time, with sheer musicianship, he threw off the shadow of the theft and won a standing ovation.

October 20th

A Marvel of Modern Technology

The grand new theater was one of New York's proudest buildings. The Hippodrome was the work of Frederick Thompson and Elmer Dundy, who had created the Luna Park amusement area at Coney Island. It stood on Sixth Avenue between Forty-Third and Forty-Fourth streets. Its auditorium had 5,300 seats, and it was fitted out with state of the art theatrical technology, including a stage that was twelve times larger than that of any venue on Broadway and could hold a thousand performers or a full-sized circus, including elephants and horses. It also boasted an 8,000-gallon glass water tank that could be raised from below stage by hydraulic pistons for aquatic spectaculars.

It was a marvel of modern technology, but it was not without its imperfections.

The year was 1906, and Victor Herbert, fresh from the triumph of his latest operetta, *Mlle. Modeste*, signed on to conduct his orchestra in a series of Sunday concerts at the Hippodrome. During one of the afternoon rehearsals, a valve supplying water to the giant aquarium malfunctioned, and when the center of the stage suddenly sank several feet into the deluge, the musicians had to scramble to safety.

Both the Victor Herbert orchestra and the Hippodrome survived the mishap, but the entertainment palace soon began a long slide into oblivion. For close to twenty years, the 100- by 200-foot stage of the building billed as the largest theater in the world hosted lavish musical productions with choruses of five hundred and shows with opulent sets and diving horses. In 1918, during his show at the Hippodrome, Harry Houdini made Jenny the elephant disappear.

His magic couldn't save the Hippodrome though. It was an expensive place to maintain, and with a cut-down stage it was leased out for Vaudeville productions and budget operas, and then turned into a sports arena, before the escalating value of the site caused the once-opulent palace to be demolished to make way, eventually, for an office building and a parking garage.

October 21st

Very Original Instruments

After performing a concert together in the 1990s, violinist Nadja Salerno-Sonnenberg and guitarists Sérgio and Odair Assad were eager to collaborate again, and when Sérgio expressed an interest in recording a CD of Gypsy music, Salerno-Sonnenberg jumped at the chance.

Little did she know that playing two of the instruments would be so painful.

The recording session in Aspen in July 1998 covered demanding works by familiar composers—Brahms, Liszt, Saint-Saëns, and Ravel—and Salerno-Sonnenberg skillfully integrated her violin, a much louder instrument than the guitar, in a way that achieved the right balance.

But Sérgio Assad's setting of the Spanish folk tune "Andalucía" presented a special challenge.

In the middle of the tune a flamenco section requires percussion, and the three performers had been limited in what they could do with it in concert, but thought that the recording session would enable them to do something special. They wanted to overdub the percussion, but they couldn't get the right sound. What they tried sounded too tinny.

Studio time was limited, so they had to come up with something on the spur of the moment or leave the percussion out.

Salerno-Sonnenberg made a suggestion.

"If I cupped my hands and slapped them onto the inside of my thighs," she said, "this might create the right sound because we wanted it to sound flamenco but not tinny. The problem was—thankfully we were all friends—I had to pull my pants down, and here we are in the studio and I literally started doing this *takketa-takketa-takketa* with my hands onto the inside of my thighs and the producer said, 'Could you move your right hand down and your left hand up?'"

They kept experimenting until they got the sound they wanted.

"I wound up bruising myself horribly," Salerno-Sonnenberg said. "I mean, the next day it was just black because I spent a good forty minutes just doing that."

October 22nd

A Dream Come True

It's not unusual for musicians to have nightmares about things going wrong during performances. It is unusual for one of those nightmares to come true, but it happened to an organist named Elizabeth Harbison David.

In 1907 David was to accompany a performance by soprano Ernestine Schumann-Heink in a performance of songs and arias from Frederick Converse's new oratorio *Job* in a big auditorium in Ocean Grove, New Jersey. On the night before the performance, David dreamed that the organ was "a strange affair with pipes reaching to the ceiling and consoles on either side." In her dream she cried out, "Oh, what am I to do—how can I play both?" And a voice replied, "Why, you just run back and forth."

The next day, when the usual organist showed her the instrument, she gasped because it was much like the one in her dream. Seeing the two separate consoles, she blurted out the very words from her sleep, "What does one do—run back and forth?"

The man graciously offered to pull the stops out for the performance, and the arrangement worked well during the rehearsal, but when the performance time came, David was so nervous that her hands and knees were shaking. The soprano closed her eyes and made the sign of the cross on her throat, and the two of them walked on stage. David had no idea how she got through the first song, but by the end of it she felt at home, and at the end of the concert the soprano led her to the front of the stage to share the applause.

On the night after the performance Elizabeth David had no nightmares, possibly because she was too excited to sleep. In her mind, she replayed the concert and blessed the man who had helped her to get though it.

October 23rd

Robbed

In his memoirs Nikolai Rimsky-Korsakov gives us a close and colorful look at his fellow composer, Alexander Borodin:

I always thought it strange that certain ladies... who apparently were admirers of Borodin's talent as a composer, relentlessly hauled him to all kinds of charitable committees, harnessed him to the office of treasurer and so on, and in so doing, robbed him of the time which he could have used for creating wonderful, artistic musical works. Thanks to the charitable folderol, his time was frittered away on minutiae that could have been taken care of by those who were not a Borodin.

On top of that, knowing perfectly well how kind and easy-going he was, medical students and all kinds of youthful types of the fair sex hounded him with myriad solicitations and requests, all of which he tried to fulfill with characteristic self-denial. His corridor-like apartment never enabled him to lock himself in or pretend that he wasn't home. Anybody entered his home at any time whatsoever and pulled him away from his dinner or his tea. Dear old Borodin would get up with his meal or his drink half-tasted, would listen to all kinds of requests and complaints and would promise to "look into it."

People would cling to him with unintelligible explanations of their business, chattering away by the hour while Borodin constantly wore a hurried look, having one thing or another to do. It broke my heart to see his life completely filled with self-denial stemming from his own inertia....

In the four rooms of his apartment there often slept several strange persons; sofas and floors were turned into beds. Often it was impossible for him to play the piano because someone lay asleep in the next room.

Given Rimsky-Korsakov's description, it's surprising that Alexander Borodin had time to become one of Russia's great composers.

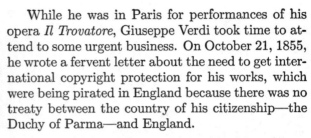

While he was in Paris for performances of his opera *Il Trovatore*, Giuseppe Verdi took time to attend to some urgent business. On October 21, 1855, he wrote a fervent letter about the need to get international copyright protection for his works, which were being pirated in England because there was no treaty between the country of his citizenship—the Duchy of Parma—and England.

He had been advised to change his citizenship to English, French, or Piedmontese in order to gain copyright protection, but instead he appealed to the government of Parma to enter into a copyright treaty with the English.

Three days later, he wrote to publisher Tito Ricordi about an equally pressing matter:

I want to lodge a bitter complaint about the printed edition of my most recent operas, which were very carelessly prepared and loaded with mistakes, and most of all because the first edition of Traviata *was not withdrawn. That is unforgivable negligence!*

If I had not, by pure chance, gone into the shop of the Escudiers, that edition would have circulated all over France. Who knows whether it isn't now going through Germany, Spain, and other countries in the same form!

You know full well that this edition should've been off the market two years ago! It was on that condition only (a condition in my contract, I asked no money for it!) that I made the arrangement for Coletti.

But who has ever cared about the reputation of an artist? I can't help coming to a conclusion that I find very discouraging: In the course of my already long career, I have invariably found all impresarios, publishers, etc., hard-nosed, inflexible, and implacable, with law books at hand if they found it necessary. Fine words and very bad deeds. I've never been considered anything more than an object, a tool, to be used as long as it earns something. That's very sad, but it's true.

October 25th

We Are Barbarians Up Here

At the end of October 1897 English composer Frederick Delius was nervous. He was in Norway to conduct music he had written for Gunnar Heiberg's play, *The Council of the People.* The play satirized the Norwegian parliament and Norwegian pomp in general, and Delius had made his music suitably caustic, but he was jittery about conducting. He spent several days practicing in front of the mirror in his hotel room.

On opening night, he peeked through the heavy velvet curtains and was startled to discover that most in the audience were apparently university students, known for their fervent patriotism.

With a smile, the playwright said, "It may be a lively reception."

After an announcement that he was the composer, Delius descended into the orchestra pit to polite applause.

As the satire progressed, Delius became aware of restlessness in the audience. Talking turned to hissing and heckling, then swearing at Heiberg for disrespecting the Norwegian state. Delius got the orchestra to play louder—just as they got to his minor key parody of the Norwegian national anthem.

Punctuating a collective gasp of disbelief and the stamping of feet were cries of "Traitor!" The startled novice conductor turned in time to see the students rushing the stage. In the gaslight he saw the flash of a silver pistol. A shot rang out.

Delius threw down his baton and made a dash for the rear exit with Heiberg at his heels, to the sound of more shots and shouting. They ran through freezing weather to the nearby Grand Hotel, where they encountered an elderly man nursing his evening drink.

On behalf of his countrymen, he apologized to Delius for the commotion. "You must remember we are barbarians up here," he said. "Allow me to apologize. I am Henrik Ibsen."

After a day or so the students calmed down and explained that the pistol had been firing blanks.

October 26th

Why the Music Stopped

John Ireland wrote plenty of music before and after, but in the chronology of his works, the year 1928 was fallow, and with good reason. He was recovering from his marriage.

For some time, one of Ireland's more talented piano students was not up to her usual standard. Her name was Dorothy Phillips. Ireland asked her what was wrong.

She burst into tears and vented an overwrought complaint against her overbearing father. She asked if Ireland could do something to help her.

He told her that he wouldn't want to interfere in a family matter. After all, I'm only your music teacher, he told her.

"You're my master!" She sobbed, unafraid of sounding melodramatic.

She was about seventeen years old, pretty, high-spirited, and, until now, a fine pianist.

Ireland was forty-eight, lonely, and obsessed with Dorothy. They had spent more and more time together. She had often asked him for advice and he was glad to give it.

After she left, he gave more thought to her problem. As he recalled later, "Then the Devil told me what I could do. That is, to give her my name, as Mrs. Ireland. I'd be her legal protector. No one would have any legal control over her."

The next time she came over, he told her his idea. She was quick to agree.

The famous composer and his young student were married.

The next morning, a haggard, crestfallen Ireland admitted to his friends that the whole idea had been a disaster. He and the bride had separated on the wedding night, their union unconsummated.

The new Mrs. Ireland became demanding, hostile, and extravagant, and made no secret about her disappointment with the arrangement.

The marriage was annulled.

When a friend asked, "Why did you get married?" Ireland said, "I must have been mad!"

He insisted that in any biography he should be described as a bachelor.

October 27th
The Reluctant Conductor

Aram Khachaturian was nervous. In the 1930s and '40s he had made a name for himself as one of the Soviet Union's foremost composers. He had long wanted to conduct, but in 1950, when he was invited to conduct a performance of some of his music, he hesitated.

"At least come to the rehearsals," he was urged. "The orchestra has already rehearsed and everything is ready. The orchestra will play correctly even if you conduct backwards."

Khachaturian consented to conduct the rehearsal. Everything went well and he agreed to conduct the actual performance, scheduled for that evening. Then he got nervous all over again. "I didn't know what to do with my hands," he said later, "or how to stand."

The concert came out all right, and Khachaturian began to take to the idea of becoming a conductor, but not a professional. He just wanted to conduct his own music.

First he conducted close to home, in Armenia. When he got farther away, his self-confidence began to waver.

Fellow composer Dmitri Kabalevsky described a particularly challenging concert at a collective farm in the far-off Altai region in 1958.

The orchestra was squeezed onto a primitive stage in a huge barn-like building in which an audience of about six hundred sat on benches. In the front row, a young man in uniform sat next to his wife, who was breast-feeding their baby. The first part of the program, selections from Khachaturian's ballet *Gayneh*, puzzled the crowd. They exchanged opinions openly during the performance.

Then came Khachaturian's *Violin Concerto*, also puzzling, until the lyrical second movement, during which the audience fell silent. Khachaturian heard later that the young Russian in uniform became captivated by the music and his wife had tears in her eyes.

As he conducted, Khachaturian could see none of the reaction and was more nervous than ever. But at the end, when it was clear that he had won over his listeners, he said that he had never experienced such complete satisfaction.

October 28th

The Status Symbol

Over the course of more than thirty years, Joseph Haydn had worked for three princes of the Esterházy family. The fourth one was a force to be reckoned with—and so was Haydn.

Prince Nikolaus II said that he liked music, but many musicians claimed that he didn't know much about it. By 1794, when Nikolaus became the head of the powerful Esterházy family, Haydn had become one of the most famous and respected composers in Europe.

The prince was not impressed though.

It wasn't that Nikolaus didn't care for the arts; far from it. He commissioned famous painters and sculptors to redecorate his castle, and he brought in first-rate troupes of actors to entertain his guests. It was said that during a visit to Paris he had given composer Luigi Cherubini a ring worth four thousand silver dollars.

He was not so generous when it came to Haydn. The bottom line was that he didn't much care for the venerable composer's works. Although he was hardly straight-laced and had what one observer described as "a temple of debauchery," when it came to music, the playboy prince confined his musical interests almost entirely to works written for use in church. So he preferred the writings of Joseph's Haydn's less gifted younger brother Michael.

In all likelihood he kept Haydn around as a status symbol, one upon whom he could force his musical tastes. But after enough goading, Haydn balked. On one occasion, when the prince voiced an unfounded criticism during a rehearsal, Haydn blurted out, "Your Highness, it is my job to decide this," to which the prince responded by stalking out of the room, much to the horror of his more subservient musicians.

When the husband of Haydn's niece ran up debts and the prince's administrator sent Haydn a letter expecting him to pay them, the beleaguered composer was in no mood to be subservient. That story follows....

October 29th
The Offensive

Joseph Haydn had suffered long enough while employed by Prince Nikolaus II of Esterháza, a musical poseur said to have the disposition of "an Asian despot." He put up with lack of respect and low pay, but in 1796, when the prince's administrator sent Haydn a letter expecting him to pay the debts of his niece's wasteful husband, Haydn went on the offensive:

By the letter sent to me and the enclosure of the worthy Economic Administrator of his Serene Highness Prince Esterházy, I discern that because Luegmayer is unable to pay his debt, I am condemned to pay it for him. Whatever for? Because it's assumed that I am able to? Would to God that it were true! But I swear by the Kyrie eléison that I'm supposed to be writing for my fourth Prince, that since the death of my second Prince—may God rest his soul—I have fallen into the same state of insolvency that Luegmayer has, with just this difference—that he has fallen from his horse to the back of an ass, whereas I have managed to stay on the horse, but without benefit of saddle or bridle.

Therefore, I beg the worthy Economic Administrator of his Highness to be patient at least until I have finished the Dona nobis pacem, and until the prince's housemaster Luegmayer shall begin to receive the just salary due him from his most gracious Prince, instead of drawing it, as he has so far, from the small salary of Kapellmeister Haydn (who has been 36 years in the princely service).

For nothing is more dissonant than one servant paying another servant, in this case the Kapellmeister having to pay the housemaster. If I should, perhaps today or tomorrow, be placed in a better position, either by my own efforts or by the initiative of my gracious Prince, (because I will neither flatter nor beg), of course, I will not fail to comply with the aforementioned demand.

October 30th

Surprise!

October 31 was Mozart's name-day—the feast day of Saint Wolfgang, for whom Mozart was named—and when the day came around in 1781, the twenty-five-year-old composer was in for a surprise. A few days afterward he wrote from Vienna to his father Leopold in Salzburg:

Just as I was going to write to you, a mob of celebrating friends overwhelmed me. At twelve o'clock I drove out to Baroness Waldstadten at Leopoldstadt, where I spent my name day. At eleven o'clock at night I was treated to a performance of my serenade for two clarinets, two horns, and two bassoons that I wrote for St. Theresa's Day.... The six gentlemen who carried it out are miserable clods who nevertheless play quite well together, particularly the first clarinet and the two horns.

But the main reason I wrote it was to let Herr von Strack, who goes over there every day, hear some of my work, so I wrote it rather carefully. It's gotten plenty of applause, too, and on St. Theresa's Night it was performed in three different places because as soon as they had played it in one place, they were hauled off and paid to play it somewhere else.

These musicians asked for the street door to be opened and, taking up positions in the center of the courtyard, surprised me just as I was about to undress, in the most pleasant possible way, with the first chord in E-flat....

It would be very helpful if my opera were ready because Umlauf can't produce his at present as both Mme. Weiss and Mlle. Schindler are ill. I have to rush off to [Gottlieb] Stephanie because he's finally sent word that he has some of the libretto ready for me.

October 31st

The Séance

One night in 1887 William James, the celebrated psychologist, and George Henschel, the English composer and conductor, arrived at a rundown house on Rutland Street in Boston. With them was singer Nettie Huxley, whose mischievous expression was at odds with the somber purpose of the visit—to communicate with the dead.

An elderly man in a black frock coat led them into a dim, musty, gas-lit room where a few others waited. An emaciated, humpbacked girl of about sixteen wrung hymn tunes out of a wheezing parlor organ.

The man in black lectured the group on the necessity of seriousness, saying that the spirits were wary of skeptics. Then he took out a key and turned the gas down so low that the room was almost pitch black.

He asked the spirits, "Are you there?"

No response.

Henschel described what happened next:

Then, to encourage the humble spirits, some more hiccups and more silence, after which there came at last a feeble knock from behind the curtain, and then another, and in quick succession, some stronger ones, and then—will you believe it?—several spirits in white phosphorescent robes rose suddenly from behind chairs, noiselessly flitting across the floor as if in the happy possession of mortal feet, and disappearing in the direction of the curtain.

If only the key had not been in the man's pocket, what fun it would have been to turn on the light during these apparitions! As it was, suppressed exclamations of awe on the part of devout believers could be heard in some portions of the room, whilst there was a distinct sound of something like, I am afraid, suppressed giggling coming from where we sat.

That settled it. Some of the spirits must have communicated the outrage to their still immaterialized brethren, for in spite of the redoubled efforts of the girl at the harmonium to appease the wrath of the offended spirits, there was no sign of willingness on their part to honor us again.

November 1st

The Latest from Paris

At the beginning of November 1853, Franz Liszt wrote from Weimar to violinist Joseph Joachim in Hanover about musical discoveries he had made during a recent visit to Paris:

As for news from Paris, I have none except for the vigorous rehearsing of Meyerbeer's new opera L'Étoile du Nord *at the* Opéra Comique, *for which he tells me he has re-used only four or five pieces from his* Feldlager in Schliesen, *all the rest of the three acts being entirely new.*

Then there's the complete success of the instrument that I've often mentioned to you, which they insist upon naming Piano-Liszt. It has three keyboards—plus a keyboard of two staves with attached pedal—and without being too loud or complicated, it produces a harmonious and well-proportioned combination of piano and organ. Berlioz heard it and liked it, and in a month the instrument will be here at Weimar, where I'll stay put for the whole winter.

We also heard in Paris, Wagner and I, two of Beethoven's last quartets, the E-flat and C-sharp minor, played by Mr. Maurin, Mr. Chevillard and company. These gentlemen earned a special reputation last winter with their performance of B.'s last quartets, which seems well deserved to me.

The next day [Charles Joseph] Sax produced for our benefit his large family of Saxophones, Sax horns, Sax Tubas, etc., etc. Several of them, especially the Tenor Saxophone and the Alto Saxophone, will be extremely useful, even in our ordinary orchestras, and the ensemble has a truly magnificent effect....

Remény has your room at Altenburg and had a very successful debut in the Weimar orchestra as the leader of the first violins the day before yesterday at the performance of The Flying Dutchman, *which I conducted. The hall was packed, the performance better than the previous ones, and the audience more sympathetic.*

In ten days I'll return to my desk to conduct William Tell *and then* Tannhäuser....

November 2nd

Great Battle, Great Victory

Composer Hector Berlioz thought big and fought big, as becomes apparent in this letter he wrote to his sister on November 2, 1840:

I've just put on a festival at the Paris Opéra. I conducted 450 instrumentalists and singers in selections from my Requiem....

A couple of weeks earlier there had been plots to prevent the Opéra orchestra from playing for me, slurs in the newspapers, threats, and so on. The rehearsal the day before yesterday was awfully tiring and muddled, so you can imagine how worried I was.

But when I made my entrance yesterday evening on that vast Opéra stage, made even more vast by a ramp sloping down to the audience, when I saw my attentive troops and the entire auditorium bathed in light, when I heard the audience tremble at the first chorus sung by the priestesses of Diana during the storm, and when I heard the applause after the chorus of the Scythians, I knew that everything was all right.

So I started my Dies Irae confidently, despite two or three pests I knew to be in the stalls. The mass of sound was awesome. The place was shaking from the force of the voices, the thundering, and the trumpets. This rendition of the Last Judgment overwhelmed them, and three times in the middle of the piece, applause and shouts from the audience drowned out my army of singers.

At the end of the piece some helpful foe was dumb enough to let out a blast on a whistle, and the entire audience stood up and yelled at him. My performers added their own applause. The women were clapping with their music, the violins and double basses with their bows, the timpanists with their sticks. So you might call the whole thing a furious success.

Picaresque

Soldier, gambler, churchman, womanizer—Giacomo Casanova was all of them, and a musician whose misadventures matched his headlong lifestyle.

At twenty-one he was a mediocre violinist in Venice's San Samuele theater, later describing himself as "a menial journeyman of a sublime art in which, if he who excels is admired, the mediocrity is rightly despised," adding, "I soon acquired all the habits of my degraded fellow musicians."

The next twenty years of his life consisted of various hare-brained schemes and hair-breadth escapes, amorous intrigues, and banishment from one city after another.

He became so notorious in most of Europe that in 1767 he headed to Spain, where his escapades were little known. He was an avid dancer, learned the fandango, and attended the Italian Opera in Madrid, where his abilities as a librettist led to some commissions.

"An Italian conductor wanted to have a play set to music," he recalled. "The time was too short to send to Italy, and so I declared myself ready to compose a play on the spot." He summarized the creative process by saying, "The music was highly praised, and in a fortnight the whole opera was produced."

But whatever success he had in Spain went bad because of his involvement with a dancer named Nina in Barcelona. Her specialty was a maneuver called the rebaltalde, a kind of back-flip with pirouettes, and one memorable night, while executing it, she "exposed her drawers to the belt."

In Spain there was a fine of one dollar for revealing that particular undergarment in public, and so for her next performance Nina avoided the fine on a technicality by dispensing with the offending part of her costume entirely, causing an uproar that was a mix of indignation and enthusiasm.

After an attempt on his life and six weeks imprisonment in the local Citadel, Casanova beat it back to Venice, where he got into the good graces of the authorities for a time by working for them as a commercial spy.

November 4th

American Enlightenment

Pianist Henri Herz was dismissed by Robert Schumann as a mere "stenographer," but in the 1830s he was the most fashionable and sensational keyboard player in Paris. In 1845, when he wanted big money to bankroll his new piano manufacturing firm, Herz headed for America.

In his book *My Trips to America*, Herz describes the eccentricities of concertizing in the New World. P. T. Barnum, who was Jenny Lind's manager at the time, approached Herz in New York and suggested that he play in a concert during which the famed Swedish soprano would appear as an angel descending from heaven. Although Herz was such a flamboyant player that his gesticulations were known to make audiences burst into laughter, in the interest of dignity, Herz declined Barnum's offer, not knowing that even more farfetched proposals would come his way.

Herz arrived in Philadelphia to find that arrangements had already been made for him to perform "illuminated by one thousand candles." The promised novelty had made the concert sell out in less than a day. But the full house was not necessarily a blessing. When Herz finished playing the first piece on the program, an audience member shouted out that the stage was eight candles short of the advertised number, demanded his money back, and strode from the hall.

Herz's manager, Bernard Ullmann, was a Barnum-in-training. He arranged for Herz to play in a grand patriotic concert that would involve five orchestras, chorus, and soloists, a patriotic speech, and a grand triumphal march for forty pianos. Herz balked, but agreed to perform with a mere sixteen pianos. His own chorus *Le Capitole* was to follow, and the finale would be a grand military rendition of *Hail, Columbia*.

If anyone laughed at the performance, Herz would have shared in the merriment. He returned to Paris a wealthy man.

November 5th
Viva L'America!

Ruggiero Leoncavallo was hoping to revive his career with a conducting contract or a commission for an opera when he agreed to undertake an American tour in the fall of 1906. He traveled with plenty of company—seven singers and the 75-piece La Scala orchestra—and all of them were in for a tough time.

The indignities began while Leoncavallo was still aboard the *Kaiser Wilhelm* on his way from Bremen to New York. *The Minneapolis Tribune* printed the remark of a shipboard acquaintance who reported that Leoncavallo was "short, fat, and round-about."

Leoncavallo had written a short piano piece called "Viva L'America" based on "Yankee Doodle" and "Dixie," which he had dedicated to President Theodore Roosevelt and planned to present personally.

Upon his arrival in New York, Leoncavallo pointed to the sky and the Staten Island shore and proclaimed hopefully, "Splendide! Magnifique! Perhaps I shall find a theme over here for an opera!"

The reviews of his Carnegie Hall concerts were mostly bad. One said that Leoncavallo seemed "strangely out of place" conducting an orchestra that played his music out of tune while his countrymen in the audience voiced their enthusiasm.

As the tour progressed, even "Viva L'America" took some knocks, being described by *The New York Tribune* as "as sorry a tribute to the nation and its head as it is to the talents of the author."

The tour had worse problems on the road. When the troupe advertised as "the largest operatic concert company that ever toured America" pulled into Springfield, Ohio, the "Leoncavallo Opera" train killed two railway workers.

The tour gathered momentum nonetheless, enough to be extended, which made it impossible for Leoncavallo to deliver the elaborately etched "Viva L'America" to Theodore Roosevelt.

After traveling 27,000 miles in eight weeks, Leoncavallo had failed to get a contract or win a commission for an American opera, but at least he had managed to lodge some of his works in the international repertory.

310

November 6th
Saved!

On November 6, 1891, Peter Tchaikovsky had just conducted his new symphonic poem *Voyevode* in a Moscow concert arranged by his young editor Alexander Siloti. The applause seemed restrained, and when Tchaikovsky came back into the artists' greenroom, he destroyed the manuscript and told the attendant to gather all of the orchestral parts and bring them to him.

Siloti intervened, saying, "Excuse me, Pyotr Ilyich, but I am the master here, and I alone can give orders." He ordered that all of the orchestral parts be taken to his house.

Tchaikovsky, who was already depressed, protested, "How dare you talk to me like that!"

Siloti answered, "We'll talk about it some other time."

The next night, a gathering was arranged at which friends of Tchaikovsky would try to dispel the gloom he felt about *Voyevode*. His brother Modest was first to arrive, and he reported that Tchaikovsky had been feeling very low all day and inclined to stay holed up in his hotel room.

At the gathering, Tchaikovsky's friends were discussing the new piece without enthusiasm when Tchaikovsky arrived. The first thing he said was, "Well, what do you think of my *Voyevode*? Bad, isn't it?"

An awkward silence ensued, broken only when Tchaikovsky asked the outspoken composer Sergei Taneyev his opinion.

"Well," Taneyev said, "it is rather poor. I mean, your love scenes—*Romeo*, for example, and *Francesca*, are fine, but here—"

"Yes, you are quite right," Tchaikovsky said, "it's a lousy piece."

All efforts to cheer him up failed until inventor Julius H. Block played some phonograph recordings, including a performance of Tchaikovsky's *Piano Trio in A minor*, which kept him entranced until 1:30 in the morning.

As he left, Tchaikovsky told Block, "I came here feeling sick and worn out, but I leave you completely cured and happy. Allow me to repeat the cure whenever I feel depressed."

Julius Block tells the story in a reminiscence of his friendship with Tchaikovsky.

311

November 7th

The Congressman and the Conductor

In 1938 twenty-six-year-old Erich Leinsdorf was in New York building a career as a conductor for the Metropolitan Opera when his visa expired, requiring him to return to Austria.

For professional and personal reasons, it was a bad time to go home. Young Leinsdorf had risen quickly in the ranks of the musical establishment, and to leave the Met as opportunities were opening up would be to lose important momentum. At the same time, Austria had just been annexed by Germany, and since Hitler's rise to power in 1933, Leinsdorf had seen enough of the dark side of his German colleagues. He had no wish to be a citizen of the Third Reich.

Leinsdorf applied for an extension of his six-month visitors' visa, but received no answer, and with just a few days remaining on it, his American friends Charles and Alice Marsh suggested a trip to Washington to talk with a young Congressman about Leinsdorf's situation. Charles owned several newspapers in Texas and Alice had been a secretary to a state senator in Austin. The Congressman they had in mind was a lanky thirty-year-old named Lyndon Johnson.

Johnson arranged for Leinsdorf to leave the country and re-enter via Havana, this time as an immigrant, and within a month Leinsdorf was back in the United States, filling out papers declaring his "intention to become a citizen."

For the next thirty years Leinsdorf kept in touch with Johnson, and when Johnson ran for the U.S. Senate, Leinsdorf sent him a contribution. But when Senator Johnson's politics proved at odds with his own, Leinsdorf wrote to him of his disagreement. Johnson's cordial reply was, "Your letter makes me proud that I could have a hand in making a new citizen, who would so well use his citizenship."

Leinsdorf tells the story in his 1976 autobiography *Cadenza*.

November 8th

More Than They Bargained For

As a child pianist, Erich Wolfgang Korngold had impressed Gustav Mahler and Richard Strauss. By 1934, when the composer came to Hollywood, he wasn't about to let a movie producer tell him how to do his job.

Hal Wallis had brought Korngold to town for Warner Brothers, to tailor the music of Felix Mendelssohn for a film version of *A Midsummer Night's Dream*. When Korngold arrived, he saw to it that the Warner Brothers orchestra was transformed from a savvy dance band into a full-fledged symphony orchestra capable of playing classical music.

On his first visit to the studio, Korngold asked how long a foot of film would last on screen and determined that it was exactly the length of the first two bars of Mendelssohn's Scherzo from *A Midsummer Night's Dream*. He could tell that Mendelssohn's original incidental music wouldn't be enough to accompany the film, so he adapted music from Mendelssohn's Scottish Symphony and *Songs without Words*. In order to make quick transitions from one section of the film to the next, he wrote short linking passages in the style of Mendelssohn.

He recorded music to play back for the dancers during the filming of ballet sequences, conducted the orchestra on stage for more complicated scenes, and, after the filming, conducted pieces to insert as background music. He used a combination of all three techniques for music to accompany dialogue.

He directed the actors on stage to get them to speak their lines in time to the music.

Hal Wallis became concerned that Korngold was overstepping his authority by telling the actors how to say their lines. He wrote a memo to his bosses saying, "I would rather not have him on the set at all if this is going to be the case."

Korngold not only stayed on the set, but also began exerting an influence on how the film was edited, and he won enough respect that he got his way on every other film that employed him.

November 9th
Jubilee

Fifty years after the publication of Giuseppe Verdi's opera *Oberto*, an Italian newspaper proposed a Verdi Jubilee. The seventy-five-year-old composer responded to the idea in a letter to publisher Giulio Ricordi on November 9, 1888, thinking for a moment that the superstar of the age, soprano Adelina Patti, might participate. Then he settled back into his doubts and closed with a self-deprecating quotation from *Hamlet:*

I see that the papers are talking about a jubilee! Take pity on me! Of all the useless things in the world, that is the worst, and I, who have done so many useless things, hate them wholeheartedly. Anyway, it can't be done, and it's an imitation of foreign customs that opens the door to assumptions that are untrue, and cannot be true, and must not be true.

In repertory theaters this jubilee would be, although still useless, nevertheless possible. But in that case the inevitable result would be a wretched, ridiculous folderol. They are even talking about artist celebrities. Ugh! Patti, who is a genuine artist, might in a moment of madness, say yes. But others, while not outright refusing, would later conveniently recall "obligations"—outside the known world if necessary.

You, who can be reasonable when you want to, must write a couple of lines opposing this idea as useless and impossible. You, who are an authority in matters like this, will no doubt be believed. And if you find that there has to be some kind of accommodation, suggest that the jubilee be scheduled for fifty days after my death. Three days are sufficient to consign men and objects to oblivion!

"Oh, heavens!" says the poet of all poets. "Died two months ago and not forgotten yet?"

I am depending on the three days. Farewell!

Neither three days nor two months was enough to make people forget Verdi, and his funeral in Milan in 1901 is said to have been the largest public assembly in the history of Italy.

314

November 10th
Making Do

By the late 1940s Georges Enesco had long since established a world reputation as a composer and conductor. As he entered his mid-sixties, he would have to fall back on a third ability, and the going would not be easy.

World War II had taken its toll on Enesco's sizeable nest egg. As a patriotic Romanian, he had put his earnings in Romanian banks, but at war's end, the Communist regime denied him access to the money, and his best hope for making a living was in the concert halls of Europe and the United States.

A plan to make him deputy conductor of the Philadelphia Orchestra fell through, perhaps because conductor Eugene Ormandy didn't want to be overshadowed by a world-class composer.

Enesco's best chance to achieve security was to build on his fame as a great violinist.

Then a big problem arose.

Just before Enesco had left Romania, a doctor had used a syringe to remove wax from his ears. Whether the procedure created a situation or merely brought it to the fore, not long afterward, Enesco was listening to a string quartet on the radio and found the players terribly out of tune.

When he took them to task for it, the performers reacted with surprise and asked him what he meant.

Suddenly Enesco realized that his hearing was impaired. Certain notes were coming across off-pitch so that basic chords sounded like a jumble of noise.

How was he supposed to make a living as a concert violinist?

At some of his recitals he arranged for student Helen Dowling to sit in the front row and let him know via subtle sign language whether he was playing too flat or too sharp, a difficult compromise for a violinist once renowned for the purity of his intonation.

Relying on that system and his sheer technique and determination, Enesco managed to piece together a concert career for the next several years.

November 11th

A Simple Twist of Fate

In 1916 Spanish composer Enrique Granados was in New York for the world premiere of his opera *Goyescas*. The opera ends with a tragic duel in which the protagonist dies in the arms of his beloved. By a simple twist of fate, Granados would soon experience a real-life tragedy every bit as poignant.

The piano suite *Goyescas* consisted of two books of three pieces each, representing eighteenth- century Madrid as evoked in the paintings of Francisco Goya. When Granados played it in Barcelona in 1911 it caused a sensation, and three years later, after a Paris performance, Granados was encouraged to adapt parts of *Goyescas* for the Paris Opéra.

Then World War I broke out and Granados retrieved *Goyescas* from the Paris Opéra and offered it to the New York Metropolitan Opera, where it had its debut in January 1916. Although one account suggests that Granados was less than pleased with the performance, the opera was a hit with audiences, and the composer wrote to a friend, "I have a world of ideas.... I am only now starting my work."

He planned to take a boat directly back to Spain, but President Woodrow Wilson requested a White House recital, causing Granados and his wife to delay their departure for a week and to return via England. In Liverpool they boarded the *Sussex* bound for Dieppe, and when the ship was in the middle of the English Channel a German U-boat torpedoed it.

According to one account, Granados sank to the bottom because he was weighed down by a money belt full of gold from his American performances. But the prevailing story has it that the composer had already been picked up by a lifeboat when he saw his wife struggling in the water, dove in to save her, and perished with her.

316

November 12th

Keep Your Day Job

Thomas Gainsborough was one of England's great painters. He thought that he could become a fine musician too. One friend had grave doubts.

In the 1770s Henry Angelo and his wife hosted gatherings that brought together various kinds of artists. In memoirs he wrote in 1830, he recalled that Gainsborough tried to buy Felice de Giardini's violin and composer Karl Friedrich Abel's viola, thinking that some of their skill would rub off on him. When he attempted to play Johann Christian Fischer's bassoon, Johann Christian Bach had to break the bad news to him.

Bach stopped by Gainsborough's lodgings one day and found the painter blaring away puffy-cheeked and red-faced. Bach, who had lived in London for close to twenty years, still had a thick German accent, which Angelo captured in his account of what happened next.

"Pote it away, man, pote it away!" Bach bellowed above the racket of the bassoon. "Do you vant to burst yourself like the frog in the fable? De defil! It is only fit for the lungs of a country blacksmith!"

"No, no," Gainsborough said. "It is the richest bass in the world. Now, do listen again."

"Listen!" Bach shouted, "I did listen at your door, and py all the powers above, as I hobe to be saved, it is just for all the world as the veritable praying of a jackass."

"Damn it," snapped Gainsborough, "you have no ear, man, no more than an adder."

"Baw, baw!" Bach yelled, plugging his ears, "Vorse and vorse! No more of your canarding!—Tis as a duck, by Gar! Tis vorse as a goose!"

At Angelo's house Gainsborough tried his hand at the harpsichord, playing tunes by Henry Purcell and William Byrd. Pushing him away from the keyboard, Bach cried, "Now dat is too pad! Dere is no law, by goles! Why the gompany is to listen to you murder all these ancient gomposers."

November 13th

The Assistant

As assistant conductor of the New York Philharmonic twenty-five-year-old Leonard Bernstein was to sit in on all rehearsals and learn the scores well enough to be able to conduct them in place of Artur Rodzinski or any guest conductor.

On November 13, 1943, as he attended the Town Hall recital of a friend, Bernstein had a secret. Philharmonic business manager Bruno Zirato had called him to say that the eminent Bruno Walter had come down with the flu and might not be able to conduct the next afternoon's Carnegie Hall performance.

The concert would be broadcast on CBS radio, making it a national event.

At nine o'clock the next morning Zirato called Bernstein again.

"Well, this is it. You have to conduct at three o'clock in the afternoon. No chance of a rehearsal. Bruno Walter... is all wrapped up in blankets at the hotel and says he will be happy to go over the scores with you."

The broadcast part of the concert consisted of Schumann's *Manfred Overture, Theme, Variations, and Finale* by Miklós Rózsa, and the massive, complex *Don Quixote* of Richard Strauss—none of which Bernstein had ever conducted. After the broadcast, the concert would continue with Wagner's *Meistersinger* Prelude, the only piece that the orchestra had not performed recently, but which Bernstein had conducted three years previously at a Boston Pops Esplanade concert.

When Bernstein stopped by the Carnegie drugstore for a cup of coffee, a sympathetic druggist gave him two pills. "Look," he said, "before you go on, just pop these into your mouth. One will calm you down, the other will give you energy."

Backstage before the concert, Bruno Zirato gave him a hug and said, "Hey, Lenny, good luck, baby."

Bernstein took the pills from his pocket and threw them as far as he could, saying "I'm going to do this on my own."

And he did. The concert propelled Leonard Bernstein into the ranks of world-class conductors.

November 14th

A Natural Solution

Although American pianist and composer Edward MacDowell would soon come to grief in his dealings with administrators at Columbia University, he had a strong rapport with his students, in part because he broke down the barriers of formality.

Perhaps the same shyness that made MacDowell a reluctant performer was behind the informal approach to lecturing that caused many at Columbia to view him with suspicion. At the close of the nineteenth century, one of his students was John Erskine, who went on to become an influential educator and author. He recalled that MacDowell was likely to start an hour's lecture not by reading at a lectern, but by leaning against the piano and speaking without notes.

Sometimes a class would begin not where the previous one left off, but with some musical problem that he had just come across, and yet, like his piano pieces, the lectures seemed spontaneous, but were actually planned out in such detail that he later published many of them.

Another student was Upton Sinclair, who would soon become famous not as a musician but as an investigative journalist and advocate of social reform. He remembered that in his general music culture lectures MacDowell sometimes had trouble coming up with the right words, that the ideas would come out jumbled and end with a gesture of futility.

Sinclair made a habit of staying after class to dig out the meaning of what MacDowell had in mind. One day he dared to suggest a natural solution to MacDowell's communication problem, "You are not a man of words," he said. "So why do you try to lecture in words? You ought to play us the music and talk about it before and after."

MacDowell took him up on the suggestion, and before long the class consisted of the students listening to MacDowell play the piano and then asking him questions about the music.

November 15th

Festival or Funeral?

Charles Villiers Stanford was described by a contemporary as "vibrant, untiring, and humorous," traits that put him at odds with the organizers of the Leeds Festivals in the first years of the twentieth century.

Stanford became the conductor of the Leeds Philharmonic in 1898, but had his conflicts with the secretary of the Leeds Festival, conflicts that spilled over into the music played during the festival. Stanford's main beef was that he was not consulted when the programs were put together. He wrote to a friend about the situation in a letter of November 15, 1903:

The whole situation is ludicrous and unprecedented in any festival. The result of the program is a long series of solemn funeral music, without a single point of relief. The mornings would have been excellent, with the substitution of Israel *for* Elijah, *and if the evenings had had one brilliant or lively pièce de résistance in each. But you have got* Everyman *(the deepest of tragedies),* The Burial March of Dundee *(another tragedy) and* The Witch's Daughter, *which sounds like a third. It is all Black-edged, and it will be damnably depressing. Death without Transfiguration, and ending with* The Golden Legend, *which is dead played out.*

A little timely consultation would have prevented it; but as they made their own program, I said nothing beyond suggesting alterations when they wanted them: and I must be content to take, and I shall have to, whether the Committee think so or not, the severe criticisms which will be most certainly made, on my own shoulders. . . .

The report will probably say that the program has been arranged "after consultation with me." This must not be allowed to pass uncorrected. In no important particular was I consulted at all.

Charles Villiers Stanford's festival woes would continue. Next we'll hear about the black eye.

November 16th

The Black Eye

During the early years of the twentieth century, Charles Villiers Stanford had his hands full as the conductor of the Leeds Festival. He was not consulted about the music to be played, and so had to put up with a dreary procession of pieces by composers known as "funeralists." He was also unsuccessful in getting more than one work by personal favorite Edward Elgar into the program. On top of that, the 1904 festival nearly began with a disaster because of a black eye. But a tenor came to the rescue without singing a single note.

The opening work of the festival was to be Mendelssohn's *Elijah*, with a prominent singer, the Scottish baritone Andrew Black, in the title role. The concert was to begin at eleven in the morning, and at nine o'clock, tenor Ben Davies went to Black's room to see if he was ready for breakfast. He was greeted by Black's "hollow voice" coming out of the pitch darkness, saying that he was not going to sing and was returning to London immediately.

During the night, the baritone had forgotten where the light in his bedroom was, and going up to bed the night before, he had walked into the wardrobe and gotten a black eye "of such gigantic proportions that he could not face the music," figuratively or literally.

Davies declared that he would "jolly well" see to it that Black would perform. He locked him into his room, rushed off to a theater, stole some grease-paint, and painted out Black's black eye so skillfully that not even those in the front row at the performance could tell that Elijah's eye had been doctored. As to the performance, an audience member familiar with the singer remarked that Black "never sang Elijah better in his life."

November 17th

The Ampersand Goes

Librettist William S. Gilbert and composer Arthur Sullivan had collaborated off and on since 1871, but, after twenty-five years, the magic had begun to wear off, and they went their separate ways.

The separation had been in the making for a long time. Changes to Gilbert's words had begun to unravel the partnership, but a quarrel over a carpet split it apart.

In April 1890 Gilbert refused to pay a share of expenses for new carpet in the lobby of the Savoy Theatre. He and theater manager Richard D'Oyly Carte got into a red-faced argument that ended when Gilbert stormed from the theater, saying that Carte was "kicking down the ladder by which he had risen."

A flurry of angry letters followed. Gilbert wrote to Sullivan, who was not entirely sympathetic, but suggested a calm reassessment of their arrangement with the theater.

Further inflamed by a failure to get a meeting with Carte to discuss the matter, Gilbert sent a letter to Carte and Sullivan, withdrawing the rights to his librettos and saying that after the retirement of their current production, *The Gondoliers*, "our united work will be heard in public no more."

In his diary, Sullivan wrote, "Felt ill all day; received letter from Gilbert... breaking off finally our collaboration—nothing would induce me to write again with him. How have I stood him so long!! I can't understand."

And yet, grudgingly, they collaborated twice more, in 1893 for *Utopia Limited*, and three years later for the disappointment of *The Grand Duke*.

When Sullivan's musical drama *The Beauty Stone* opened, for unknown reasons, Gilbert was not invited to attend.

The postscript came on November 17, 1898, after a twenty-first anniversary revival of their comic opera *The Sorcerer*. "Call for Gilbert & Self," Sullivan wrote in his diary description of the enthusiastic audience response. "We went on together, but did not speak to each other."

It was the last time they appeared as partners.

322

November 18th

Too Lonely!

In the fall of 1886 Gustav Mahler was the director of the Leipzig Opera house. In a letter that he wrote to his friend Friedrich Löhr, he spoke of positive experiences with composer Karl Reinecke and pianist Anton Rubinstein. He spoke in less positive terms of his relationship with Leipzig Opera principal conductor Arthur Nikisch:

My dear Fritz, First of all, thanks for what you have done for my father. You can imagine how painful all of this has been for me. I'm not in a position to have a relationship with my own people and have to watch them going down without lifting a finger. How alienated and lonely I feel sometimes. My whole life is one long case of homesickness.

You'd like to know how I'm getting along with Nikisch! I'm often quite happy about him and can look forward to a performance directed by him as much as if I were conducting it myself, even though the heights and the depths are beyond him. But how seldom I have a chance to bring them out myself. Mostly I have to content myself with preventing outright cruelties.

I really have little to do with him. He is cold and distant, whether from vanity or mistrust—I simply don't know! In short, we pass each other by without saying a word! Other than that I get plenty of recognition, often from those who are quite dear to me. Right now I'm rehearsing Armida. Not long ago Reinecke invited me to meet Rubinstein (just me). Unfortunately, he had never heard of me, so that I could only "look and not create." On such occasions it's always painful just to be an unknown quantity. I say nothing so as not to be a bore because I know how annoyed I get by admiring nobodies and how ridiculous they are.

Mahler closed his letter with the words, "Too lonely! Too lonely!"

November 19th

A Voice from the Crowd

On November 19, 1916, celebrated conductor Arturo Toscanini was at the Augusteo Theater in Rome to conduct the first of three concerts. The program included two pieces by Wagner—*Forest Murmurs* from *Siegfried* and the funeral music from *Götterdämmerung*. On previous occasions, the orchestra had performed music by major German and Austrian composers without incident, but this night would be different.

Three months earlier, Italy had declared war on Germany, and, just a few days previously, a German air raid had killed more than a hundred Italians, most of them old people, women, and children. To Italians, Wagner represented imperial Germany. When Toscanini arrived at the hall, he was greeted with a shower of leaflets protesting German music in general and Wagner in specific.

After the hall had settled down, *Forest Murmurs* went smoothly enough, but during a quiet moment at the beginning of the funeral music, a voice from the balcony called out, "This is for the dead of Padua!"

Toscanini tried to quell the resulting uproar by playing the Royal March. When he realized that the crowd was not to be quieted, he threw down his baton, stalked out of the hall, and left the city.

Some years later, the man who had uttered the inflammatory words was identified. At the time of the uproar he was a soldier on leave, and had not intended to cause a commotion, had intended only to say that the music was the homage given by the enemy to the dead.

The incident would not be Toscanini's last clash with politics. Fifteen years later he would be battered by young fascists after he refused to play their signature song before a concert in Naples.

Composer Alfred Casella tells the story in his 1924 autobiography *Music in My Time*.

November 20th

Incognito!

Back in 1910 Darius Milhaud had written an opera called *La Brebis égarée*, and although he was aware of its youthful flaws, he did not object in November 1923 when the Paris Opéra-Comique decided to produce it. The experience would give him some of his most sincere audience response.

The opera was put on with great planning and care, including clever set changes for the twenty scenes. Milhaud saw to it that the opera's narrators—there were three of them—were dressed in 1910-vintage costumes in keeping with the period in which he had written the opera, even though he thought that the period in question was one of "excruciatingly bad taste."

To his way of thinking, the opera was flawlessly produced.

The audience reacted to it with "violent demonstrations of feeling."

Milhaud blamed the protests on the opera's colloquial language and little realistic details in the action that occasionally prompted laughter. Whistles and catcalls and "untimely applause" came one after the other until a backlash arose in Milhaud's defense.

Following his custom of mingling with the people in the cheaper seats during performances of his works, Milhaud was in the gallery, where students were shouting "dirty bourgeois" at the detractors in the boxes and orchestra seats. A young man next to him, applauding vigorously, became impatient with Milhaud's lack of demonstration, turned to him and said, "Why don't you clap—shout—cheer? You ought to come back every time they play this opera! I'm here every time to defend it!"

During intermission Milhaud introduced himself to his ardent young supporter and made a point of inviting him to all of his opening nights from then on.

In response to the protests, Opéra Comique director Albert Carré placed on every seat a copy of sarcastic reviews that, early on, had attacked Claude Debussy's masterpiece *Pelléas and Mélisande*. The text of the leaflets ended with the caution *Be careful*.

But it was not enough to save *La Brebis égarée*, which folded after four nights.

November 21st

Lavish in the Extreme

At the court of Spain's King Ferdinand V and Queen Maria Barbara, the famed Italian castrato Farinelli was such a royal favorite that he could have influenced Spain's politics, but he preferred to make his mark on the country's musical life—and that he did with a vengeance.

As the director of court operas, Farinelli brought in Europe's best singers and commissioned new music and new librettos. But when it came to the scenery and special effects, he went all out.

In 1750 he outdid himself.

For an opera by Giovanni Battista Mele two hundred chandeliers illuminated a 41-piece orchestra tricked out in new scarlet and silver uniforms. The first act of the opera had a pastoral landscape, songbirds in cages, and eight fountains, two of which shot water so high that it put out the candles on a chandelier hanging sixty feet overhead.

The last scene of the opera took place in the temple of the Sun, in which tall columns of red and white crystal sported transparent silver and gold figures that stood out against a rosy glow. Various colors of crystal globes hung upstage, as did two hundred rotating stars. Prominent above all were the transparent signs of the zodiac.

At center stage stood the octagonal house of the Sun supported by columns of green and white crystal. Inside it waited the chariot of the Sun in gold and crystal, to be driven by Apollo with the Sciences personified at his side. The horses moved in globes of cloud. The Sun, five feet in diameter, was made of crystal, and from it radiated two sets of spiral crystal rays spinning in opposite directions, extending the orb's diameter to twenty-one feet. As backstage machinery raised the house and the Sun chariot, the park of Buen Retiro appeared, illuminated by fireworks and many-colored lights.

The set and special effects impressed the king and queen so much that Farinelli received one of the highest orders of knighthood in Spain.

November 22nd
Caught in the Muddle

He would later become known as one of the twentieth century's great pianists and composers, but in 1897, at the age of twenty-four, Sergei Rachmaninoff jumped at the chance to be the assistant conductor to one Eugene Esposito in a new private opera company opened in Moscow by a tycoon named Mamontov. He soon found that he had jumped into a maelstrom, as he wrote to a friend on November 22:

In our theater chaos reigns supreme. Nobody knows what's supposed to happen the day after tomorrow, tomorrow, or today for that matter. There's nobody to sing, not because we have no singers, but because in our big company of 30 or so, about 25 should be fired for incompetence. There is also nothing to perform. The repertory is huge, but everything is produced so badly, with such sloppiness (except for Khovantshchina*) that 95 percent of the repertory should be chucked out or completely reworked.*

Mamontov can't make his mind up and gives in to everyone's opinion. For example, I got him so interested in the idea of producing Schumann's Manfred *that he immediately gave the word to begin production on it.... About five minutes later his friend Korovin, who understands nothing about music (but is a very nice person, just like Mamontov) had talked him out of it....*

Nonetheless, I am still employed at the theater and hope to stick it out with this job until the end of the season...because I now need the complete attention and cooperation of the musicians, which as an assistant conductor elsewhere I would never get from them. By the way, one of these gentlemen, right in front of the orchestra and a full audience, slapped Esposito for some supposed slight. What if that should happen to me? God forbid!

November 23rd

Hard Fall

Handel was having enough trouble as it was. When a competitor came to town, his situation could only get worse. In November 1721 his opera *Arsace* failed to attract London audiences, and its successor met a worse fate. After *Floridante* flopped, two operas by Handel's new rival, Giovanni Battista Bononcini, played to packed houses.

Bononcini had been brought in from Rome by Lord Burlington, who disliked the court of German-born King George I, and, by association, the music of the German-born Handel. With his tuneful operas and warm Italian songs, Bononcini became the darling of London.

Some said that Handel was on the way out.

But Bononcini had a fatal flaw.

While Handel took a hard look at his failures, imported a spectacular if quarrelsome soprano, and wrote better and better operas, Bononcini turned to plagiarism.

He supplied an amateur musical club with a composition that was revealed to be by a composer living in Vienna. He presented the Academy of Ancient Music with a madrigal in five voices. Three years later it was proved to have been written by Antonio Lotti twenty-three years earlier.

He enjoyed the protection of the Duchess of Marlboro, who had hired him to be her house composer. Under her roof, he continued to weather the storm of his plagiarisms.

Then she died.

By the end of the opera season in 1732, he had long since run out of ideas. Fifteen years later he died in poverty in Vienna. Handel started the new season with the opera Orlando, and scored a rousing success.

Poet John Byrom parodied both composers in an epigram that ended with the first appearance in print of another famous duo:

> *Some say, compar'd to Bononcini*
>
> *That Mynheer Handel's but a Ninny.*
>
> *Others aver, that he to Handel*
>
> *Is scarcely fit to hold a Candle.*
>
> *Strange all this Difference should be*
>
> *'Twixt Tweedle-dum and Tweedle-dee!*

November 24th

Home in Rome

As a winner of the prestigious Prix de Rome, young Claude Debussy earned the opportunity to further his musical development at the Villa Medici, but the honor was in some ways a setback.

Before he even got to Rome, Debussy was homesick for Paris, and the villa's vast view of the city did little to lighten his spirits. His assigned room was so austere that it was known as "the Etruscan

Claude Debussy (top center) at Villa Médici, 1885

Tomb," and the work also left him cold because he was expected to compose in a style not his own.

Debussy's prime objective was to get back to Paris as soon as possible.

And yet he did find kindred spirits in Rome—two sixteenth-century composers. On November 24, 1885, he wrote of them to a friend:

I have to tell you about the one time I went out this month. I went to hear two masses, one by Palestrina, the other by Orlando di Lasso at a church called S. Mari dell'Anima. I don't know if you're familiar with it. It's tucked away in a maze of wretched little streets....The Anima is the only place to hear that kind of music, which is the only church music I can tolerate. That of Gounod and company seems to me to come from a hysterical mysticism and comes across like a sinister farce.

The two aforementioned people are masters, especially Orlando, who is more decorative and more human than Palestrina. The effects they produce entirely from their extensive knowledge of counterpoint are spectacular accomplishments. You probably aren't aware that counterpoint is the most formidable aspect of music. In their work, though, it's wonderful because it's made to underline the significance of the words and brings out their incredible depths; and sometimes there are winding melodic lines evocative of illuminated manuscripts and ancient missives.

Debussy referred to the discovery of Palestrina and di Lasso as the only time when "the lord of musical feeling came to life in me again."

November 25th

Tug of War

The celebrated Austrian cellist Emanuel Feuermann didn't care for recording, so he probably came into the Columbia session with a bad attitude, and the effort to make a record of Haydn's *Concerto in D* went awry from the start.

It was November 1935. The conductor was Malcolm Sargent who was businesslike and accustomed to being in control. There would be a rehearsal, a break, and then the recording session.

At the end of the introduction Sargent cued Feuermann, but the cellist just sat there. Sargent gave him an inquiring look, went back several phrases, and took another pass at the entrance for the solo. Again the cellist declined to play.

This time Sargent had to ask what was going on. "Anything wrong, Mr. Feuermann?"

The cellist replied, "Aren't you going to tune the orchestra?"

The oboist gave the A and the orchestra joined in with a token tuning.

Sargent began again. Again Feuermann declined to enter. "They are not in tune," he insisted. He played a loud A on his cello. The oboe joined in and the rest followed. They began the concerto yet again and yet again Feuermann refused to enter.

"Have the violins play a D major scale," he said.

This time it was Sargent who declined to respond. Feuermann started playing the scale himself.

Columbia producers motioned to Sargent that they were eager to get on with it. He relented, said "Everyone," and made a motion with his baton. Now the musicians held back, feeling that they had been insulted.

Then a single flutist began the scale. The concertmaster joined in and a few others, then the rest, perhaps realizing that no recording meant no pay and no more work for Columbia.

They got through it. But the orchestra's playing suffered, and the recording became a memento of the tug of war between a proud soloist and a proud conductor.

330

November 26th

Passed By

With the help of publisher John Stark, Scott Joplin made his name with a succession of genteel, lilting ragtime piano pieces, beginning with the million-seller *Maple Leaf Rag* in 1899.

By 1911 he felt that he was in a position to create an entirely new kind of music, an American opera dealing with an American subject—free from outside influences.

He sent his first opera, *A Guest of Honor*, to the copyright office. It disappeared in the mail, never to be seen again.

He pinned all of his hopes on his second effort, *Treemonisha*, which was set on a plantation and told of a young woman who wanted to free her people from poverty, ignorance, and superstition.

Joplin had been looking for a backer for two years by the time the manager of New York's newly-integrated Lafayette Theatre agreed to put on the opera. Joplin sent out an urgent call for performers, hoping to put on *Treemonisha* by the fall of 1913. But while he worked frantically to line up a cast, the theater changed management and switched to musical comedy.

In the meantime, black music was passing Joplin by. Ragtime songs, many of which he considered vulgar, superseded instrumentals. And at the piano, the genteel lilt gave way to speed.

By 1915, when *Treemonisha* finally was staged at the Lincoln Theatre in Harlem, it was a shadow of what Joplin had envisioned. Instead of hiring a forty-piece orchestra, Joplin played the accompaniment on the piano. Props and costumes were few.

A friend of Joplin's described the resulting performance as "thin and unconvincing," and pointed out that its Harlem audience had no interest in re-establishing connections with a plantation past that too many of them had worked hard to forget.

Treemonisha was performed in full for the first time in 1972, more than half a century after Joplin's death. Four years later, he was awarded a posthumous Pulitzer Prize for his contribution to American music.

November 27th
A Visitor Incognito

In 1822 the most famous touring pianist in Europe was Johann Nepomuk Hummel, who had been a child prodigy so impressive that at the age of seven he became a live-in student of Mozart's.

Hummel's closest rival was Irish-born pianist John Field, who had been living in Russia for nearly twenty years by the time he and Hummel came face to face.

According to a story popular at the time, Hummel arrived in St. Petersburg, eager to see Field perform, but was disappointed to find that Field had no concert scheduled. Apparently someone had told him that the Irishman didn't like giving one-on-one recitals. So one morning Hummel showed up at Field's apartment posing as a German businessman who loved music so much that he couldn't bear to leave Russia without hearing the great John Field play.

At the time of Hummel's arrival Field was teaching a lesson, but as soon as he had finished, he sat down at the piano and launched into one of his most impressive pieces. Hummel was touched and thanked him for being so obliging.

Perhaps thinking to put his presumptuous visitor on the spot, Field asked his guest, "Since you're so fond of music, won't you play something yourself?"

After polite protests and disclaimers, Hummel finally allowed himself to be persuaded and responded with an improvisation—on themes from the piece Field had just played.

At first, the stunned Irishman was at a loss for words, and then suddenly he cried out, "Either you're the Devil or you are Hummel! Only he could play like that!"

The story has it that the two great pianists embraced and expressed their mutual admiration.

One thing is certain. A few days after the encounter, Field and Hummel gave a concert together and remained friends for the rest of their lives.

November 28th

The Elusive Tune

Composer Jacques Offenbach had eight bars of a tune running through his head—a waltz that his mother had sung to him as a lullaby.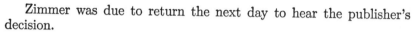

Offenbach's father overheard him humming it and told him that it was by a once-promising young composer named Zimmer, who had suddenly dropped out of sight.

Sometime later, Offenbach's publisher mentioned a poor old composer named Zimmer who had brought by a score that the publisher intended to reject because the composer was an unknown.

Zimmer was due to return the next day to hear the publisher's decision.

Offenbach became excited. "Do me a big favor," he said. "Publish his piece, pay him ten times what it's worth, put it on my account, and send him to see me. I've got to meet him."

Zimmer never showed.

Some years later, in Vienna, Offenbach came across a crowd gathered outside a low-class dance hall where an emaciated old man lay unconscious on the pavement. The man worked at the dance-hall doing odd jobs, but he had once been a music teacher. His name was Rudolph Zimmer.

Offenbach saw to it that he was cared for, and eight days later Zimmer called on him at his hotel room to thank him. Offenbach played the eight bars of the haunting waltz and asked Zimmer to play the rest, but he, too, got stuck after eight bars.

A month later, when Offenbach returned to Vienna, Zimmer was dead. But he had left Offenbach four things—the waltz, a sapphire ring, a faded envelope, and a letter explaining that he had never recovered from the death of his beloved just before their wedding day. He asked Offenbach to keep the sapphire ring, which he had given to the girl as an engagement ring, and to burn the faded envelope, which contained a lock of her hair.

After complying with the requests, Offenbach had the waltz published.

November 29th
What Else Did He Know?

Arthur Rubinstein was one of the twentieth century's greatest pi-anists.He didn't begin speaking until he was three, but began playing the piano at age two, and so it's reasonable to assume that the piano was his whole life.

But an appearance on radio's popular quiz show *Information Please* on November 29, 1943, demonstrated that Rubinstein's knowledge was by no means limited to the piano.

Former Simon and Schuster editor Clifton Fadiman was the knowl-edgeable emcee of the show. The panelists were the urbane New York columnist Franklin P. Adams, John Kiernan, a sports columnist who could quote Shakespeare and speak Latin, and Oscar Levant, the witty Pittsburgh piano prodigy who had been a crony of George Gershwin.

The first question for the panelists: Identify a painter who was also a bullfighter. Rubinstein was quick to answer, "Goya" and provided some details.

When the questions turned to a Russian poet who died in a duel, Rubinstein identified Mikhail Lermontov, which was correct, but quiz-master Fadiman clearly had another Russian poet in mind, so Rubin-stein added Alexander Pushkin, and identified the slayer as Pushkin's brother-in-law, a Russian with a French name.

Another question required the panelists to define the family rela-tionships among a group of monarchs who ruled at the beginning of World War I—George V, Nicholas II, Haakon VII, Wilhelm II, and Christian X.

"I know them all," Rubinstein said, "I can tell you exactly their families—much better than my own." He went on in such detail that an overwhelmed Fadiman quipped, "I'm not more than a mile behind you."

There were music questions, too. When asked to identify the source of a French horn solo, Rubinstein and Levant named Brahms' *Piano Concerto in B-flat*, and Rubinstein added, "I don't like to talk about that concerto. I'm going to play it the day after tomorrow in Cleveland and it frightens me to hear it."

334

November 30th

Parting Gift

Ástor Piazzolla had gone a long way toward bringing the tango into the classical repertory and had written innovative classical music for the bandoneón, the concertina-like instrument popular in Argentine dance bands.

It was 1959. Piazzolla was in San Juan, Puerto Rico, playing at the Club Flamboyan when he received a telegram from back home in Mar del Plata, Argentina, informing him that his father had been injured in a bicycle accident. Between the night's two shows, his fellow performers—dancers Juan Carlos Copes and Maria Nieves— urged him to phone home for an update. He called and talked to his cousin, who informed him that his father, Vincente Nonino Piazzolla, had died from complications of a leg injury.

"We plucked up courage and went on working," recalled Copes, but for the first time ever, as they went onstage for their final bow, Piazzolla gripped the hands of his fellow performers.

Piazzolla had been working in New York as an arranger, and his return became dangerous when the plane skidded on the runway, giving Piazzolla a strange reminder of the time in his boyhood when his father had forbidden him to tour with a tango band that later perished in a plane crash.

A day after his return, he asked his wife and her sister for some time alone, and from the kitchen they could hear him behind the closed door of an adjoining room as he played the bandoneón. He began with "Nonino," a cheerful tango he had dedicated to his father a few years previously. He paused and then, sighing and weeping, went into an unfamiliar tune, haunting and elegiac.

The new tune was "Adios, Nonino," which became one of Piazzolla's best known pieces. "Perhaps I was surrounded by angels," Piazzolla said years later of its inception. "I was able to write the finest tune I have written. I don't know if I shall ever do better. I doubt it."

It was his father's parting gift.

The Unlikely Soldier

Anton Webern had chafed against the restraints of the conducting jobs he'd had, and yet, at the outbreak of World War I, the Austrian composer decided to work under even greater constraints—in the army. Yielding to family concerns about his poor eyesight, he trained to be a male nurse, and then, in February 1915, he volunteered for non-combatant infantry service, was accepted, and stationed near Trieste.

He took to life in the army, was transferred to various places in southeastern Europe, was quickly promoted to a rank equivalent to sergeant and put in charge of training a group of older recruits. He liked the work, which he said was not much different from conducting a chorus. He played cello in a string quartet of fellow soldiers.

As the war dragged on, Webern got fellow composer Alexander Zemlinsky to secure his release from the army and moved to Prague, where he threw his energies into a production of Mozart's opera *Così fan tutte* and Schumann's *Scenes from Goethe's Faust*.

When he found out that his mentor Arnold Schoenberg was in the army, the guilt-stricken Webern did an about-face and roused Zemlinsky's wrath by re-enlisting. This time he was sent to train younger recruits for the battlefield, an assignment that involved strenuous treks into the surrounding mountains, no great strain for a man accustomed to climbing.

Just as a transfer to the front looked likely, an eye exam relegated Webern to the reserves, where he played cello with a chamber ensemble.

During his time in uniform, Webern had made a personal cause of trying to get Schoenberg out of the army, and, in 1916, when he found out that Schoenberg had been discharged, his enthusiasm for military life ebbed again. In December the issue was settled once and for all when Webern's eyesight caused him to be declared unfit for further service.

Again a civilian, he settled in Vienna and, for the first time in three years, settled down to compose.

December 2nd

Offended

In 1943, at Lindy's Restaurant in Manhattan, Marc Blitzstein introduced twenty-five-year-old Leonard Bernstein to twenty-nine-year-old Morton Gould. The two composers had plenty in common. For a time, their careers ran parallel courses and then they collided.

Gould was well known in musical circles. His music was being played on the radio. He was well connected in New York musical life, but lacked self-confidence and didn't mix easily. He thought that if he worked hard his talent would be discovered. His big dream was to conduct the New York Philharmonic in Carnegie Hall.

Bernstein's fame hadn't spread so far yet, although those who knew him knew how brilliant he was as a conductor and composer. He was an aggressive self-promoter. In September he became the assistant conductor of the New York Philharmonic. On November 14, as a last-minute stand-in for Bruno Walter, he became famous overnight by conducting a Sunday matinee concert that was broadcast nationwide.

By the mid-1940s the younger composer was in a position to help the elder. Gould brought over some records and scores of his music, and as he played them, Bernstein began to call out the names of composers who supposedly had influenced what he was hearing.

"I listened. I heard. I was getting a little restless," Gould recalled half a century later. "And then he said—*Bernstein!*"

But Gould had written the piece in question three or four years before Bernstein had composed the music that allegedly had influenced it. Gould said something about Bernstein's ability to write history backwards, closed the score, and stopped the record.

"What are you doing?" Bernstein asked.

"Forget it," Gould said. He left and told his publisher never to send Bernstein another score.

Apparently name-that-influence was a game that Bernstein liked to play occasionally. He did the same thing with composer Vincent Persichetti and he did it with Aaron Copland, who just laughed it off.

December 3rd

Uh-oh!

In his 1952 memoir *My Life*, Russian émigré composer Alexander Gretchaninoff tells how simple carelessness nearly resulted in disaster.

In 1925 the composer and his wife were living in Paris. He went to Rome to conduct two concerts, the second of which was to include his Third Symphony and excerpts from his opera *Dobrinya Nikititch.* During the night before the first rehearsal, Gretchaninoff began to feel nervous. He slipped away from a reception to go back to his hotel for a last-minute look at the wind instrument parts. He was shocked to find that he had brought the wrong music.

He came up with the idea of sending a telegram to a neighbor, who could give the missing wind parts to a friend leaving for Rome the next day. In the meantime, the nervous composer devoted two full Monday rehearsals to the finale of the second act of his opera.

On Tuesday morning neither the friend nor the missing parts showed up at the train station in Rome. What was he supposed to do now, Gretchaninoff wondered, devote another two rehearsals to the same section of the opera? Before Wednesday's rehearsals the friend arrived at last—but empty-handed. Gretchaninoff's neighbor had been unable to find her before she left for Rome.

Gretchaninoff tried to think of an excuse—illness, a sudden need to skip town? "What other alternative is open to me?" he asked himself. "Put a bullet through my brain?"

For the Wednesday morning rehearsal he worked on just the string parts of the symphony and gave some inaudible excuse for dismissing the wind players. By the time of the evening rehearsal he was beginning to feel ill in earnest.

Finally his wife arrived with a telegram from the neighbor. He had persuaded a Rome-bound passenger to take the wind parts. The next morning a joyful Alexander Gretchaninoff had the missing parts in hand, and the two concerts proved profitable enough to support him for the year to come.

December 4th

Out of the Body

Some people are said to have the ability to see themselves as if from a distance. Richard Wagner was one of them. He delivered an address at a ceremony marking the relocation of the remains of composer Carl Maria von Weber from London to Dresden in December 1844. In his autobiography, he wrote of a strange sensation that overcame him.

On the occasion I had a strange experience when for the first time in my life I had to deliver a solemn public speech. Since then I have always spoken extemporaneously, but since this was my first appearance as an orator, I had written out the speech and carefully memorized it.

Since I was completely under the influence of my subject, I had such confidence in my memory that it never occurred to me to make any notes....

I began my speech in a clear and full voice, but suddenly the sound of my own words and their particular intonation had such an effect upon me that, carried away as I was by my own thoughts, I imagined I was seeing as well as hearing myself speaking before the breathless multitude.

While I appeared that way to myself, I remained in a sort of trance, during which I seemed to be waiting for something to happen, and I felt like quite a different person from the man who was supposed to be standing there speaking.

It was neither nervousness nor absent-mindedness on my part. Only at the end of one sentence there was such a long pause that those who saw me standing there must have wondered what in the world to think of me.

Finally my own silence and the stillness around me reminded me that I was not there to listen, but to speak. I continued my remarks and spoke with such fluency that the celebrated actor, Emil Devrient, assured me that, apart from the solemnity of the occasion, he had been quite impressed just from the standpoint of a dramatic orator.

December 5th

The Pianist

In December 1815 composer Giacomo Meyerbeer was in London visiting celebrated composers and performers. When it came to pianists, he was most impressed by a fellow German who had settled in London, Johann Baptiste Cramer. In his journal Meyerbeer wrote:

Cramer is in his forties, a big, sturdy man with an impressive face. His fingers are long and slender but powerful. He left Germany when he was so young that he can barely understand German anymore. We spoke in French, in which he's fluent. We talked for about a half-hour, mostly about the Philharmonic Society, of which he's a member—a little strange because he formed a competing organization.

He was kind enough, of his own volition, to play us twelve pieces of his that go by the title Sweet and Useful. *I don't think that I'm exaggerating when I say that even on the heaviest Broadwood instrument his touch is lighter than Hummel's celebrated touch on the Viennese piano.*

The evenness of his playing, the lightness and diminuendo are beyond praise. With those three abilities he gives a new quality and elegance even to the most commonplace things. Even in the most difficult passages his light touch and delicacy don't change, which gives his playing a color and force all its own.

At the same time, though, that amazing evenness lends itself to a kind of monotony because the arching of his fingers, appropriate for the style, hinders powerful playing in the passages that call for it. Cramer does tend to bang and hammer occasionally, but that's only a fleeting shadow that hardly diminishes his reputation. Anybody who can match Cramer in this genre is by definition the number one pianist in the world, regardless of one's opinion of the genre itself.

Meyerbeer's youthful enthusiasm had its limits though. Later in the same journal entry, he criticized Cramer's playing of Bach as "affected" and "inappropriate to the style required by the music."

December 6th

This Other World

Twenty-one-year-old Frédéric Chopin was dis-
covering a galaxy of famous musicians of the day
when he wrote to a friend back in Poland in December 1831:

*Paris is whatever you want it to be. You can
entertain yourself, be bored, laugh, cry, do whatever
you want and nobody notices you because thousands
of others are doing the same thing you are, and everyone follows his own inclinations. I don't know
where else you can find so many pianists— so many dolts and so many
virtuosi.*

*I came here with very few introductions...but in Stuttgart, when I
received the news about the taking of Warsaw, I made up my mind to
migrate to this other world. Through Paër, who is court composer here,
I have met Rossini, Cherubini, Baillot, etc.—and also Kalkbrenner.
You can't imagine how curious I was about Herz, Liszt, Hiller, etc.
They are all zero compared to Kalkbrenner. I admit that I have played
like Herz, but aspire to play like Kalkbrenner.*

*If Paganini is perfection, Kalkbrenner is his equal, but in a very
different style. It would be hard to describe his calm, charming touch,
his incomparable evenness, and the confidence that he showed in every
note. He's a giant walking over Herz and Czerny and all—and over
me.*

*What can I do about it? When I was introduced, he asked me to
play something. I would've preferred to hear him first, but, aware of
how Herz plays, I put my pride in my pocket and sat down. I played
my E minor...I amazed Kalkbrenner, who asked me at once if I was not
a student of John Field, because I have Cramer's method and Field's
touch. That delighted me. I was even more pleased when Kalkbrenner,
sitting down at the piano and wanting to do his best, made a mistake
and had to stop! But you should have heard it when he started again.
I had never dreamed of anything like it.*

December 7th
Faking It

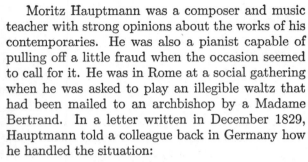

Moritz Hauptmann was a composer and music teacher with strong opinions about the works of his contemporaries. He was also a pianist capable of pulling off a little fraud when the occasion seemed to call for it. He was in Rome at a social gathering when he was asked to play an illegible waltz that had been mailed to an archbishop by a Madame Bertrand. In a letter written in December 1829, Hauptmann told a colleague back in Germany how he handled the situation:

I couldn't help chuckling when I saw them all under the delusion that they were going to listen to Madame Bertrand's waltz, knowing the whole time that it wouldn't be anything of the kind. However, something had to be played, if only to make the people get up again. I looked carefully at the cramped notes of the music and began to extemporize a waltz of some sort in 3/4 time, imitating as best I could the principal features of the manuscript.

The Archbishop was at my side, looking over the music; so where the notes went up, I went up; where there were eighth notes I played eighth notes, and once or twice I shifted my hands across where the passage seemed to require it. My only object was to get through a rhythmical something or other without breaking down; the rest was not my affair, but Madame Bertrand's.

No waltz lasts longer than three or four minutes, and I was careful not to make mine an exception. Then came the compliments and discussions; they thought it charming, only some of them doubted whether it was quite suitable for a dance, on account of its elegiac character and so forth. I know I was glad enough to get out into the open air, and very glad indeed that it was dark; the more I thought over what had passed, the more ludicrous it seemed to me, and I laughed till I cried.

December 8th

Cardboard Rocks

When it came to judging fellow composers Peter Tchaikovsky had strong opinions. He wrote to his patroness, Nadezhda von Meck, on December 8, 1877:

I attended Wagner's Die Valkürye. *It was a wonderful production. The orchestra was excellent. The singers did everything they could to make the best of the work...all the same, it was boring. What a Don Quixote Wagner is! Why does he throw all of his strength into chasing after the unattainable when he holds in his hands the ability to draw out an ocean of musical beauty? In my opinion Wagner is a born symphonist. The man has enormous talent, but that talent is thrown aside for the sake of proving a theory he has invented.*

In his quest for reality, truth, and the rational in opera he has completely abandoned music. It's noticeably absent from his last four operas, because I can't apply the word music to the kaleidoscopic grab-bag of musical tidbits that follow one after the other without going anywhere and never give you a chance to relax in any worthwhile musical form. There's not a single ongoing melody that enables a singer to blossom. He has to chase the orchestra all the time and worry about how to thrust in his own part, which is about as important as the fourth horn part.

You've probably heard in a concert his wonderful "Ride of the Valkyries." What grandeur in a musical picture! One can really imagine those giantesses thundering and crackling through the clouds on their magnificent steeds. In the concert hall the piece always makes a great impression. In the theater, seeing cardboard rocks and rag clouds, and the warriors blundering across the stage in the background, and, the ridiculous theatrical sky, supposedly representing the vast firmament on high, the music loses all of its pictorial power. So the theater doesn't tweak the impression, but dampens it like a glass of cold water.

343

The Rebellious Prince

King Frederick the Great of Prussia was one of the great patrons of music, but in his early years he suffered for his art—and so did others.

His father, Friedrich the First, was so steeped in military matters that he tried to squelch young Frederick's fondness for the fine arts. The prince was supervised constantly, and when he dared to stray from his father's prescribed routine, the punishment was both verbal and physical.

Despite the dangers, and with the help of his mother and sister, Frederick read forbidden books and played flute duets with a servant. In 1730, at the age of eighteen, Frederick tried to escape to England, but was caught and imprisoned; and in his presence one of his alleged accomplices was beheaded. From then on, Frederick took his military studies seriously, but continued to nurture his interest in music.

In 1740, when his father died, the new king, soon to be known as Frederick the Great, wasted no time in expanding Prussia culturally as well as geographically. He composed flute sonatas and concertos by writing out the melody and the bass line and leaving the details to others. By all accounts, his abilities as a flutist were far above average. He wrote 122 flute sonatas, four flute concertos, and four symphonies, which—like his army and his government—were efficient and regimented.

He brought some of the best composers and performers of the day into his court and paid them royally. His boyhood flute teacher, Johann Joachim Quantz, came from a position in Dresden—at eight times the salary. One singer received higher pay than that of a cabinet minister. And while Frederick's musical tastes became increasingly conservative and restrictive, he made a lasting contribution to music by supporting some of its best practitioners.

December 10th
A Different Kind of Virtuoso

In the 1920s the Berlin home of operetta composer Oscar Straus became the gathering place of the brightest people in Europe. Entrepreneurs, theatrical managers, actors, statesmen, scientists, and musicians mingled—sometimes with amusing results.

A regular visitor to the Straus home was Albert Einstein. The great physicist and Straus sometimes talked for hours, and when asked what they were discussing, Straus quipped that the conversation was *relatively* difficult, "I want to talk about mathematics and astronomy all the time," Straus said, "and he wants to talk about music, but somehow we always bring our parallel lines together in the end."

As an amateur violinist, Einstein was not above being the butt of a good-natured joke. One day he asked Straus, "Do you think I could try to give a little concert of my own at the Philharmonic?"

"Of course, Professor," Straus said. "You'll have a tremendous success and you can make a lot of money too."

Einstein was encouraged. "Oh, do you really think so?"

"Indeed I do," Straus told him. "Just advertise the concert and put on all the posters: *Entrance free.* Then, after a few items, if people want to leave the Philharmonic, they find a poster on all the doors saying: *Exit, ten marks.*"

When it came to his music, though, Einstein would take only so much abuse, and one incident showed that he was a virtuoso of the comeback. He enjoyed playing the violin and liked to take part in drawing-room concerts. One evening he and Straus were playing a Mozart violin sonata. The Hungarian playwright Ferenc Molnár was in the front row laughing and talking to the lady next to him. When he had finished playing, Einstein said to Molnár, "It's not very nice of you to keep on laughing while I play the violin. Have you ever seen me laugh during one of your comedies?"

December 11th
It Sounds All Right

Gaspare Spontini

Composer Hector Berlioz was born December 11, 1803, and cut a wide swath through music from the 1830s to the 1860s. In 1853 he became a best-selling author with *Musical Evenings,* a collection of reminiscences and anecdotes that reveal a good deal of Berlioz' forceful personality and caustic sense of humor.

Berlioz tells the story of opera composer Gaspare Spontini, who had experienced some setbacks in Paris beginning in 1805, most notably the utter failure of a comic opera called *The Little House,* which had culminated with a celebrated singer responding to hisses with "a gesture of scorn" that sparked a fracas between audience and orchestra.

In December 1807 Spontini was ready to try again with an opera called *La Vestale,* but professors and students at the Paris Conservatoire set about lampooning Spontini, saying that his melody lay on his accompaniment "like a handful of hair on a bowl of soup." Berlioz relates that "all these young note-spinners , who were about as capable of grasping and feeling greatness in music as the janitors, their fathers, were of judging literature and philosophy, banded together to bring about the downfall of *La Vestale.*"

During the opera, they intended to laugh and yawn, and at the end of the second act, to put on nightcaps and pretend to go to sleep. They were in for a surprise.

Although they later declared the first act very badly written, the conspirators were heard to say with astonishment, "It sounds all right." With a particularly compelling temple scene, the second act kept them from bringing out the nightcaps, and the finale elicited their whole-hearted applause.

Berlioz concludes the story by saying that the upstarts probably had to do penance the next day "by continuing to denigrate in their classes the ignorant Italian who had all the same moved them so deeply."

346

December 12th

The Infernal Machine

On the night of December 12, 1800, Napoleon Bonaparte was on his way to attend the first French performance of Haydn's oratorio *The Creation.* He showed up late, but he had a good excuse. Someone had tried to kill him.

Seven Breton royalist insurrectionists were in on the plot to assassinate Napoleon. They attached a large wine cask to a cart and filled the cask with gunpowder, flammable materials, and bullets, which would be ignited with a long fuse. A similar arrangement had been designed and used more than two centuries earlier by an Italian engineer who called the device a *machine infernale.*

Conspirator Pierre Robinault de Saint-Régeant drove to the Place du Carousel looking for the right place for the infernal machine. He chose a place north of the Tuileries Palace, not far from where Napoleon's troops had slaughtered royalist rebels in 1795.

They positioned a lookout at the Hotel Longuevieu, who would be able to see Napoleon's carriage as it left the Tuileries Palace, and would signal Saint-Régeant, who would ignite the barrel of explosives by lighting the fuse.

At eight o'clock Napoleon rode in his carriage toward the Paris Opéra to attend *The Creation.* Preceding him was a cavalry escort. At the critical moment, the lookout lost his nerve and failed to signal Saint-Régeant to light the fuse. As the cavalry escort approached, Saint-Régeant lit the fuse and ran.

The infernal machine exploded, killing and injuring a number of bystanders. Napoleon continued on to the Opéra, where he received a standing ovation. He used the attempt to justify cracking down on all presumed plotters. Most of the conspirators and some innocent people were rounded up and executed.

A delegation from various Parisian societies visited Napoleon to congratulate him on his escape. Among them, representing the Paris Conservatory, was composer Luigi Cherubini, whose barbed responses to Napoleon's music criticisms would not go unnoticed. That story on December 26.

December 13th
The Right Audience

At the close of the American Civil War, after a perilous concert tour of the Northern states, New Orleans-born composer Louis Moreau Gottschalk left the country for Latin America. He soon found himself in circumstances as difficult as those he had encountered at home, and he had to resort to an unusual trick in order to salvage a concert. He wrote in his journal in Lima, Peru, on December 13, 1865:

My fears are realized on the subject of the locality, which the partial giving way of the theater has forced me to choose, in order to continue the series of my concerts which have been interrupted. It was in fact doubtful that the society of Lima would not be frightened at the idea of entering into the hall and gardens where every Sunday the veiled women and their friends had their rendezvous to give themselves up to the stormy Zamaenecas and other indigenous dances, which although very picturesque, are not such as prudent mothers permit their daughters to indulge in.

In the face of this difficulty there was only one means of overcoming it—raise the price of the tickets so high as to be only within the reach of those privileged by fortune. I put them up to two dollars....

One of my friends persuaded his sisters to sacrifice themselves. The rumor spread that the general and his family had taken twenty seats. In four hours the hall was full. The first concert was not finished before the seats were already taken for a second....

At each of my concerts "Banjo," "Murmurs eoliens," "Charmes du foyer," "Ojos criollos." (The last has been encored three times) were called for again.

This evening I gave a seventh concert. I play for the first time an important arrangement which I have just written on Un Ballo in Maschera.

We are literally on the eve of a war with Spain, for the decree, the people say, is to be published tomorrow. The conflict between the latter and Chile renders imminent the hostile participation of Peru, the Spanish American republics being so strongly connected with each other by their common origin and their political institutions.

December 14th

An Easy Act to Follow

As the new court pianist of Empress Eugénie, wife of Napoleon III of France, Emil Waldteufel was expected to play dance music for the autumn house parties of the imperial family. The social occasions at the castle of Compiègne, fifty miles north of Paris, included not just the aristocracy, but also important personages in the arts, and enabled the royalty to enjoy the pleasure of their guests in relatively informal surroundings.

After the hunting, the woodland excursions, the procession to the dining room, dinner, and a variety of parlor games and entertainments, came dancing.

But amid the splendor and merriment, the dancing was strangely austere.

Napoleon III insisted upon privacy, and he felt that the presence of an orchestra at Compiègne would compromise the pleasure of his gatherings. His solution—instead of dancing to an orchestra, his guests cut the rug to a mechanical piano.

The Debain "Antiphonel" piano played pieces reproduced by a board studded with pins. As a chamberlain or one of the guests turned a handle in the front of the piano, the board moved over a plate that had a series of openings in it. The pins forced down metal points projecting through the metal plate, and operated a series of levers that depressed the pads of the piano keys.

It seemed to work all right, but, for some guests, the mechanical piano was less than inspiring. In 1857 the British Ambassador wrote to Lord Clarendon, Minister of Foreign Affairs, from Compiègne about dancing to a "hand organ" that was "a dreadful trial to one's nerves," and referred to "a wretched chamberlain" who had to grind away at it all evening.

Enter a live pianist—Emil Waldteufel, who soon became "the life and soul of the informal dances."

The honor applied regardless of the hour, so that one night a chamberlain hauled Waldteufel out of bed and dressed him so that he could go to the ballroom and play waltzes.

December 15th
Professionals

Robert Schumann did more than anyone else to make the music of Johannes Brahms known to the world. After Schumann's death in 1856, his widow Clara continued to promote the piano music of Brahms by performing it in and around Leipzig. On December 15, 1861, just before the publication of his *Variations and Fugue on a Theme by Handel*, she wrote to violinist Joseph Joachim about her most recent performances:

Dear Joachim, I must write to you today. I know you'll rejoice with me. I was quite successful with Johannes' Variations, and they received hearty applause, recalls, etc. The people I spoke with had to concede that they are "interesting," although I found, as I always do, that the professional musicians are the hardest to talk to. They can't rejoice without misgivings at the thought that someone else is writing good things again. They can hardly bring themselves to admit that there is anything worthwhile in it!

The recent Mozart concerto went over much better than I expected, except that Reinecke was unfortunate enough not to come in with the orchestra after the cadenza, which resulted in a rough landing for me. The rest went quite well, but I couldn't feel happy anymore. I had the great pleasure of hearing Robert's songs for mixed voices, which Reinecke has rehearsed with great charm, and which the audience found delightful. The Zigeunerleben with Grädener's instrumentation sounded wonderful. I could hardly believe it was the same thing I had heard in Cologne, when all of it sounded just as tedious as it could be.

I saw those dear artistic people the Röntgens today, and I'm expecting them this evening, when we're planning to have some music. Unfortunately, his health is really poor right now, but he played so beautifully at the Gewandhaus the other day that everyone still speaks of it in glowing terms, I'm happy to say.

December 16th
Run Away!

Perhaps it was an omen. Wagner had agreed to accept the dedication of Anton Bruckner's new symphony. They had spent a day together, drinking beer and talking music. It was one of the happiest days of Bruckner's life—until he forgot which symphony he was supposed to dedicate—the second or the third?

After a little maneuvering, Bruckner determined that it was the third, a symphony in D minor, that would become the Wagner Symphony.

Bruckner had conducted his second symphony in Vienna in October 1873, and it was well received by audience and critics alike. But in 1875, Vienna Philharmonic musicians attempting the Wagner Symphony declared it unplayable, and Bruckner revised it thoroughly. Its debut was set for December 16, 1877.

Just before the day of the concert, the conductor died suddenly, forcing Bruckner to take on the job of presenting it to an eager public. Wagner was very sparing with his praise of his fellow composers, but, arriving in Vienna in 1875, he had told Bruckner at the train station, "This symphony must be performed." Then he turned and announced to the crowd, "There's Bruckner. He's my man."

The performance turned out to be one of the worst experiences in Bruckner's life.

For reasons that never became clear, at the end of each movement, large numbers of the audience broke for the exit, "fairly ran away" according to one account, so that during the finale not more than a dozen people remained in the hall.

At the end of the concert, the musicians got away as quickly as possible, leaving Bruckner alone on the podium with his music, casting a pained glance around the empty hall.

A few of his friends and students approached him to offer encouragement, among them a young Gustav Mahler, but Bruckner waved them off. One of the last to go was a publisher who issued the Wagner Symphony at his own expense.

December 17th
Stop the Presses!

At the end of 1784, when Carl Philipp Emanuel Bach found out that his new cantata was going to cost a lot more than expected, he fired off an urgent letter to the printer:

The contents of your last letter all but made me sick. Oh, how beholden I would have been to you if only you had let me know sooner about the size of my cantata in print. In any event, I ask that as soon as you receive this letter, you stop printing my cantata.

People here have made promises that they have not kept. You have not one single subscriber and I have about ten. In all likelihood, I can get at most 50 subscribers. Given these circumstances, I can lose my reputation. If I wanted to raise the subscription price, most would back out. Most of them are poor cantors and that kind of thing. Enough. It is decided: The printing of my cantata in score is not to be continued and will be abandoned. Instead you will be so kind as to print my fifth collection For the Connoisseur and Amateur, *which is waiting here finished. And as soon as I get back my manuscript of the cantata from you I'll make a keyboard reduction of it, and that will be printed.*

I now throw it into your hands, my consolation being that they are the hands of a completely honest man and my dear friend.

But please don't think that I'm expecting you to incur the slightest loss, which would be unreasonable and unfriendly. No! You'll be so kind as to let me know at once how much is printed and what I owe you, and I hope that it will be little. Regardless of what it is, though, I must and will pay it all gladly. It's better to have a small loss than one from which I'll never recover.

Two years would pass before the full cantata would see print.

December 18th

A Remarkable Christmas Present

On December 18th, 1867, violinist Joseph
Joachim was in Vienna and eager to get home to
Hanover. He wrote to his wife Amalie about Christmas plans and a remarkable present for the thirteen-
year-old son of Robert and Clara Schumann:

*I'm getting an early start on the twenty-third,
and God willing, I shall have lunch with you all
on the twenty-fourth. But maybe it would be better to postpone the presents until the twenty-fifth
and then we can decorate the tree together on the
twenty-fourth. How I am looking forward to it! Do what you prefer
about this. It's really unfortunate that the twenty-second was the only
possible day left!*

*They're doing their best here to reorganize the management of the
Conservatory and to make arrangements so that they can offer me
a decent salary as Director. The appointment would give me enough
authority to have considerable influence. I do not think it will amount
to anything and I've said so to people who have asked me, but at the
same time I said that I would consider it my duty to accept a permanent
position that would give me a good handle on musical matters....*

*Something could be done with the talents and the public here. But
then again I have become so very North German that I can't stand these
polite, fawning people, hardly any of whom has the courage to follow
through on his convictions. The North Germans are simpler and more
likely to follow through, although they are less impressionable and don't
have the same joie de vivre. They are faster to get to the root of things.
Well, we'll soon be able to talk about this and many other things....*

*I don't know what to send to Frau Schumann, but take the Guarneri
from my violins, have it carefully packed and insured with expert assistance and send it by way of the Grimms to Felix Schumann. It was
always my intention to give it to my ideal godchild.*

December 19th

The Nettlesome Messiah

For Christmas 1881 the Cincinnati Music Festival Association wanted to top its lackluster performance of the previous year and at the same time to upstage the festival of a rival opera company in the same city. So conductor Theodore Thomas hired the most famous prima donna of the day—Madame Adelina Patti—to perform in Handel's *Messiah*.

Although Patti had built her career as a singer not of English oratorios, but of Italian operas, her voice had never been better. Patti was aware of the competition for her services and raised her fee to a stunning $6,000 at a time when $10,000 was a handsome annual salary for a major conductor. The other *Messiah* soloists were to receive from $200 to $500.

Despite the outlay and star power, the Cincinnati *Messiah* was less than stellar. Patti took offense when Thomas neglected to accompany her to her seat on the platform at the beginning of the oratorio. Once she got up there, she found the $500 soloist sitting in the chair next to the conductor. On top of that, she had her own ideas about how her part was to be sung—and stuck to them regardless of Thomas' conducting. After the performance she told the press that Thomas was full of "vanity and conceit" and that his tempi would destroy the efforts of any soloist because he took everything too fast. As a parting shot she added, "Last night he was drinking brandy and had the audacity to offer a brandy bottle to me," which prompted the newspaper headline *After the Messiah Comes the Day of Wrath.*

Despite the friction, the box office take was good enough to recoup the association's losses from the two previous concerts. Theodore Thomas' competitor went ahead and signed Patti for its 1882 festival, but she pleaded a sore throat and refrained from singing until the festival's closing night, at a cost of $14,000.

December 20th

The Connection

After writing the librettos to operas by Mozart, Salieri, Gluck, and other prominent composers, Lorenzo Da Ponte fell on hard times and sailed for brighter prospects in America. But, after a stint as a grocer in New York led to more financial setbacks, he was again insolvent. By December 1807, without money or friends, he was desperate for a way to support his family.

He determined that New Yorkers had little interest in a teacher of Latin and Italian.

But on a whim, he entered a bookstore and asked the proprietor if he had any Italian books in stock. The store had a few, but nobody ever asked for them.

Just then a Professor Moore walked into the store and joined the conversation. He was well-versed in the Latin classics, but he placed limited value on modern Italian literature. Da Ponte made a convincing case for studying it, though, and within three days the professor had sent twelve students to him to learn Italian.

"I began my career as a teacher in New York," Da Ponte wrote in his memoirs, "under the happiest auspices."

Professor Moore was well-connected to cultural and academic life in the city. He taught Biblical learning at General Theological Seminary; and within a month he had sent twenty-four students to Da Ponte. Before long, Moore had become a zealous proponent of Italian literature.

With Moore's recommendation, Da Ponte became the first professor of Italian at Columbia College, the forerunner of Columbia University. Over the years, he taught more than five hundred students.

As for Professor Clement Clarke Moore, he remained a lifelong friend of Da Ponte and continued to be a major force in New York cultural life. His most important scholarly work was his Hebrew and English Lexicon, but he's best remembered today for writing a poem that drew on none of his erudition—"A Visit from St. Nicholas," popularly known as "'Twas the Night Before Christmas."

December 21st
The Tightrope Walker

Johannes Brahms held his gruffness at bay when writing to thank Elizabet von Herzogenberg for sending some duets her husband Heinz had written, music that Brahms didn't entirely care for. His reply also included some of his own choral songs, plus a copy of a "very special favorite"—Georges Bizet's opera *Carmen*. Brahms wrote from Vienna to Elizabet in Leipzig on December 21, 1883:

Today I'll just write two lines of thanks for your parcel full of interesting things. If I take them to the piano, I am transported to your pleasant comfortable rooms, and can distinctly hear your very sweet singing. But if, like a real German, I start to grumble, an alarm sounds in my head and I think, "You'd better be quiet. All of those misgivings apply equally to you, too, and your own music has such a dreadful bachelor ring as well!"

I'll be able to spill some of the grumbling to Heinz without exposing my thoughts too much....

His music, or his way of writing, often reminds me of his charming rhymes, and, now that I remember, I particularly want you to save up all his Christmas verses this year for me to read.

I have suddenly decided to send you a few songs. I hardly know whether to ask you to forward them to publisher Simrock.

Maybe you will favor me with your candid opinion of them? I am also sending you a beautiful work by Georg Muffat, which you may not know. I now have the original edition, so you don't need to keep a copy.

Beside which I am asking Simrock to send you one of my very special favorites. I can't get it here in its original garb (that is, language), and have never seen it at your house. If you should fail to share my enthusiasm, I shall be happy to tuck it under my arm and carry it off again in February.

December 22nd

King of Kings

"Having just done a picture in which Jesus played a supporting role, I was dumbfounded to learn that the new film was *King of Kings*, in which he was the star."

So said composer Miklós Rózsa in his autobiography about the MGM assignment that followed his Oscar-winning work on the 1959 film *Ben-Hur*. His first challenge was to come up with fresh music for Salome's notorious *Dance of the Seven Veils*, which had been done effectively by Richard Strauss back in 1905 for his opera *Salome*.

When he arrived in Madrid to begin composing, Rózsa tried to talk about the dance with the screenwriter, who ducked his questions and left town in a hurry. Rózsa found out that the choreographer was the director's wife, a veteran of many musicals who had never actually done any choreography, but was deemed ready to give it a try.

For his Salome the producer had chosen a plump Chicago schoolgirl about sixteen years old. She had never acted nor danced.

"I was almost in tears," Rózsa recalled. But he went ahead and put something together, a piece six or seven minutes long that he practiced on a piano in the basement of the Madrid Hilton—to bursts of applause from kitchen staff that came to listen.

The film was an episodic mishmash of badly acted, badly directed biblical scenes glued together with a narration written by science fiction author Ray Bradbury. Instead of dancing, Salome scuttled from pillar to pillar wiggling seductively.

After a catastrophic preview, Rózsa and editor Margaret Booth whittled her scene down to two minutes, removing most of the dance Rózsa had written.

No lover of avant garde music, Rózsa took secret satisfaction from using his one and only twelve-tone piece to represent the Devil during the Temptation of Christ.

Despite the disaster of *King of Kings*, the producer asked him at once to write music for *El Cid*, which would win Miklós Rózsa his next Oscar.

December 23rd
A Gift from the Magi

Back in 1939 NBC producer Samuel Chotzinoff had commissioned Gian Carlo Menotti to write an opera for radio. In 1951 he commissioned a second opera from Menotti, this time for the up-and-coming medium of television.

Although he accepted the commission, Menotti was not fast to fulfill it. The opera was scheduled to be broadcast on December 24, and, as Halloween passed, Menotti still hadn't come up with an idea. During a gloomy ramble through the Metropolitan Museum he caught sight of the painting *The Adoration of the Kings* by Hieronymus Bosch, and, as he studied it, he was reminded of the Three Kings of his childhood Christmases in Italy, in particular what he remembered as "the weird cadence of their song."

"They had come back to me," he said later, "and had brought me a gift."

He was perhaps reminded as well of a childhood leg injury that had healed after a visit to an image of the Madonna.

Menotti suggested a title for his opera about the Three Kings, but nobody else liked it, so the days passed and he wrote nothing. Finally, after Thanksgiving dinner, he decided to go with the title anyway. He called up Chotzinoff and said, "I'm going to call the opera *Amahl and the Night Visitors*."

Later that night he began work on the opera and finished the first three or four pages. Within days he had completed a one-hour children's opera about a crippled boy whose life is transformed when three kings spend a night at his house on their way to Bethlehem.

As he had done when directing his first film, an adaptation of his opera *The Medium*, Menotti didn't pay much attention to the medium he was working in, choosing instead to write the opera for a small stage, and, within twenty years of its live television debut, *Amahl and the Night Visitors* had become the most frequently performed opera in the United States.

December 24th

The Contest

On December 24, 1781, Austrian Emperor Joseph II had two celebrated keyboard players in his Vienna palace and he couldn't resist setting them against each other in an unusual competition. This is what Mozart wrote to his father about the contest that pitted him against Muzio Clementi:

A word about Clementi. He's a first-rate harpsichord player, period. He has a very nimble right hand. His strong suit is thirds. But aside from that he doesn't have a penny's worth of taste or sensitivity. He's a mere mechanic.

After we had spent enough time on the formalities, the emperor declared that Clementi should begin. "La Santa Chiesa Catolica," he said since Clementi is a Roman. He improvised and then played a sonata. Then the emperor turned to me. "All right, have at it." I improvised and played variations. The Grand Duchess came up with some sonatas by Paisiello, scribbled out in his own handwriting, of which I had to play the Allegros and Clementi the Andantes and Rondos. Then we picked out a theme from them and developed it on two pianofortes.

Strange to say, even though I had borrowed Countess Thun's pianoforte, I played it only when I played alone. That's what the emperor wanted, and by the way, the other instrument was out of tune and three keys were stuck. "That doesn't matter," said the emperor. Well, I made the most of the situation, assuming that the emperor knew my skill and my knowledge of music and just wanted to show a special courtesy to a foreigner. Anyway, I have it on good authority that he was quite pleased with me. He was very gracious and said a good deal to me in private, and even mentioned my marriage.

The Christmas Eve keyboard contest between Mozart and Clementi is the first two-piano performance on record.

December 25th

Christmas 1818

December 25th, 1818, was a red-letter day for Christmas music large and small.

According to legend, mice had damaged the organ in St. Nicholas' church in the Bavarian village of Oberndorf, causing it to break down on Christmas Eve. The setback forced the organist and the parish priest to scrap the music they had planned for Midnight Mass.

The organist, Franz Gruber, had come by his church position the hard way. He had grown up to a life of manual labor, managing to study music on the side, and had finally gotten a job as organist at the church in Oberndorf.

Joseph Mohr was the assistant priest at St. Nicholas. He and Gruber had to come up with something that could be performed by the musical forces available—two solo voices to be provided by Gruber and Mohr, plus choir, and guitar, which would be played by Mohr.

Mohr provided a poem about peace and radiance and redemption. Gruber dashed off a tune for it, and they performed the song in church almost immediately.

Their eleventh-hour effort proved immediately popular, and over the next dozen or so Christmases, in various forms, it made the rounds of Austria, Bavaria, and the Tyrol. In 1838, it was published. But by then it was so well known that it was generally considered to be a folk song. In 1854, in an effort to set the record—and the tune—straight, Gruber wrote an account of the supposed folk song's composition. Eventually he arranged it for voice and organ, and that version is the closest approximation to the long-lost original guitar version of "Silent Night."

Christmas Day 1818 was musically significant in another way. As Gruber's Christmas miniature was being performed for the first time in Bavaria, the Handel and Haydn Society of Boston was giving the first complete American performance of Handel's *Messiah*.

December 26th

The Price of a Comeback

On December 12, 1800, Napoleon had survived an assassination attempt in Paris, and although a number of bystanders were killed by the explosive device known as "the infernal machine," a deputation from Paris societies and corporations waited to congratulate the First Consul on his escape. Representing the Paris Conservatory was composer Luigi Cherubini, who wisely stayed in the background because he had a history of crossing words with Napoleon.

But Napoleon couldn't resist drawing out the composer. "I do not see Monsieur Cherubini," he said, pronouncing the name in the French way, implying that Cherubini wasn't worthy of being called an Italian composer. When Cherubini came forward, the two of them just stood there in stony silence.

At a banquet soon afterward, though, Cherubini would say more than enough.

"Well," said Napoleon, "the French are in Italy."

Cherubini replied, "Where would they not go led by such a hero as you?"

Napoleon seemed pleased, but switched from French to Italian so much that Cherubini became confused. Then Napoleon said something that was all too clear.

"You are very talented, but there's too much accompaniment." He mentioned an aria by Giovanni Paisiello as an example of the sort of thing he liked.

Cherubini had heard it before. He remained calm. "Citizen Consul, I write to French tastes. In the words of the proverb, when in Rome do as the Romans do."

"Your music makes too much noise," Napoleon declared. "Speak to me like Paisiello does. Lull me gently."

Cherubini couldn't resist a comeback that would cost him dearly. "I understand," he said. "You like music that doesn't keep you from thinking about state affairs."

When a lucrative position came up, Paisiello got it, and for the next two years the downcast Luigi Cherubini wrote little music, choosing instead to devote himself to his botanical pursuits.

December 27th

Summation

As the year 1842 ended, Gaetano Donizetti was nominated to become a corresponding member of the prestigious French Academy. Coming at the twilight of his career, his acceptance speech was an opportunity for the composer to sum up his philosophy of music.

He devoted a significant part of his remarks to explaining how a contemporary, a fellow Italian composer, had been able to accomplish great things:

The intellect is a rough stone that becomes polished with effort, but not in every part. For example, a painter practices his art but is nothing as a musician. Only rarely does a Michelangelo appear. A person can have musical science and no taste; a person can have practical taste but no science; a person can have both—and be a genius.

Anyone who applies himself can learn musical science. It comes with opportunity and work. Taste and genius have to be innate in a composer. For example, Rossini is a genius, and as such has opened up the imaginations of his contemporaries. After him—I am speaking here of Italy—every other composer lived or lives with the science and with the taste and with the practice that emerge from the style invented by his genius.

Rossini appeared and achieved something that only a genius had the gifts to accomplish. Even though he was young and almost ignorant of art, he sensed the effects of Mozart in Don Giovanni, *of Beethoven in the symphonies.... The public, roused from a kind of musical indifference, encouraged the new composer and, greatly encouraged by his successes, he strove and succeeded.... Not through study, but by ongoing opportunities to write, he improved and made himself rigidly correct in his art. From all of that genius, all of that practice, and—despite himself—from musical science—sprang Rossini's* William Tell....

German composers should sing a little more, Italians a little less. The French don't get that criticism because they send their students to Italy, making them perfect their taste for vocal melody.

December 28th

The Magic Touch

Canadian pianist Glenn Gould had enough quirks as it was, but a concert tour of Israel brought out even more.

He was scheduled to play Beethoven's Second Piano Concerto in Jerusalem on a cold December day, but let it be known that he had changed his mind. He and his manager had been to the hall, he said, and there was no heating in the place.

When informed that the concert had been sold out and that thousands of ticket-holders were planning to sit in the frigid hall to hear him, he replied that he was susceptible to colds. "I see no point in being heroic about it," he said. "If I get sick, I won't be able to go through with the rest of my concerts here."

The management had eight space heaters placed on the stage in the hope that Gould would reconsider, without any reassurance that he would.

Gould had a second problem that he hadn't mentioned. The piano was, in his opinion, "absolutely rotten," and during a rehearsal, he had "played like a pig," unable even to get through a C major scale to his own satisfaction.

He hit upon an unusual approach in order to come to terms with the instrument. He drove into the desert and imagined himself playing the entire Beethoven concerto on one of his favorite pianos, a Chickering, and "tried desperately to live with that tactile image throughout the balance of the day."

On the night of the concert, just as a member of the orchestra was announcing that Gould would be unable to perform, in bounded the pianist bundled in a long overcoat and muffler.

He was shocked at first by the lack of sound and the difference between the touch of the Israeli piano and the Chickering of his memory, but he adjusted to the instrument at hand and played what turned out to be an extraordinary and unforgettable rendition of Beethoven's Second Piano Concerto.

December 29th

The Humpty-Dumpty Concerto

The two sisters from Baltimore so impressed Max Bruch with their performance of his *Fantasy for Two Pianos* that he agreed to write a two-piano concerto for them. Writing it would be relatively easy. Putting it back together would be the hard part.

When Ottilie and Rose Sutro asked Bruch to write the concerto for them, he was in need of some cash because the outbreak of World War I had cut off his royalties from performances of his works abroad. He reworked the unpublished Third Suite for organ and orchestra that he had begun while vacationing in Capri in 1904, and the sisters gave the first public performance of the two-piano concerto in Philadelphia on December 29, 1916, with the Philadelphia Orchestra conducted by Leopold Stokowski.

But the work the sisters played was not what Bruch had sent them. Without telling anyone, they had re-orchestrated the concerto and simplified the piano parts. A reviewer pointed out that the solos were often so submerged in the orchestra that it was hard to tell how good the soloists were.

The sisters copyrighted their version of the concerto and sent it to the Library of Congress, although they seem to have sneaked it back out for the sake of further revisions.

Ottilie died in 1970 at the age of ninety-eight, Rose having predeceased her by thirteen years. After the auction of her belongings, one item remained—a trunk full of scraps of music that pianist Nathan Twining bought for $11. He and pianist Martin Berkofsky played through the fragments of the reworked concerto and discovered that the sisters had continued to write revisions to it over the course of forty years, although they hadn't performed it since 1917.

After a painstaking reconstruction, Bruch's concerto nearly slipped from sight again because Twining and Berkofsky argued over the possession of its copyright. But after most of a century, Bruch's *Concerto for Two Pianos* finally saw the light of day.

December 30th
The Right Season

"I think they're very interesting. You should learn them." So said conductor Alfredo Antonini to violinist Louis Kaufman in the autumn of 1947. The Columbia Broadcasting System's music director had just said much the same thing in the hope that Kaufman would perform the distinctive 200-year-old Vivaldi concertos in an upcoming concert. Kaufman was reluctant. He had never heard of the four concertos known collectively as *The Four Seasons*.

Two days later Kaufman got a call from Samuel Josefowitz, the co-owner of Concert Hall Records, wondering if Kaufman could record some concertos for solo instrument and small orchestra during a visit to New York. Kaufman mentioned the Vivaldi concertos and Josefowitz snapped up the idea because Vivaldi was all but unknown to performers and concert goers.

Josefowitz had another reason to be eager. The president of the American Federation of Musicians had banned all recordings after December 31, 1947, unless record companies accepted his terms requiring the payment of domestic royalties to the Federation rather than to the musicians. The big companies—RCA, Columbia, and Decca—had big stockpiles of unreleased discs that they could use to skirt the ultimatum. Smaller companies like Concert Hall Records were working hard to stockpile recordings before the deadline.

Josefowitz hired string players from the New York Philharmonic and conductor Henry Swoboda and rented Carnegie Hall for the last four nights of the year, with the sessions in the tightly-booked hall to begin at midnight. Kaufman received the Vivaldi scores from CBS the day before he boarded the train from Los Angeles. He studied them en route and found them enchanting.

The musicians were charmed too. Despite the late hour and their fatigue from being overbooked, they worked with enthusiasm and completed the very first recording of *The Four Seasons* just hours before the deadline, at four o'clock in the morning of December 31, 1947.

December 31st

A New Year's Eve Ball

London diarist Samuel Pepys was twenty-eight before he tried dancing for the first time, and he wrote that it was something "I did wonder to see myself to do."

Not long afterward, on New Year's Eve 1662, he attended a royal ball, after which he wrote of his enthusiasm about the lively dances of the day and the elegant skill of King Charles II and his fellow revelers:

First to the Duke's chamber, where I saw him and the Duchess at supper, and thence into the room where the Ball was to be, crammed with fine ladies, the greatest of the Court. By and by comes the King and Queen, the Duke and Duchess, and all the great ones; and after seating themselves, the King takes out the Duchess of York, and the Duke and Duchess of Buckingham, the Duke of Monmouth, my Lady Castlemayne, and so other lords other ladies; and they danced the Bransle. After that, the King led a lady in a single Coranto, and then the rest of the lords, one after another, other ladies.

Very noble it was, and great pleasure to see. Then to Country dances; the King leading the first which he called for; which was—says he—Cuckolds all a-row, the old dance of England.

Of the ladies that danced, the Duke of Monmouth's mistress and my Lady Castlemayne and a daughter of Sir Harry De Vickes were the best. The manner was, when the King dances, all the ladies in the room, and the Queen herself, stands up; and indeed he dances rarely and much better than the Duke of York.

Having stayed here as long as I thought fit, to my infinite content, it being the greatest pleasure I could wish now to see at Court, I went out, leaving them dancing. . . .

Thus ended this year with great mirth to me and my wife.

Bibliography

X Ainger, Michael: *Gilbert and Sullivan: A Dual Biography.* Oxford; New York: Oxford University Press, 2002.

Allitt, John: *Donizetti: In the Light of Romanticism and the Teaching of Johann Simon Mayr.* Shaftesbury; Dorset, England; Rockport, Mass., Element, 1991.

X Anderson, Robert: *Elgar.* New York: Schirmer Books; Maxwell Macmillan International, 1993.

Antheil, George: *Bad Boy of Music.* Garden City, N.Y.: Doubleday, Doran & Company, Inc., 1945.

Appleby, David P.: *Heitor Villa-Lobos: A Life.* Lanham, Md.: Scarecrow Press, 2002.

Arditi, Luigi: *My Reminiscences.* Edited and compiled by Baroness von Zedlitz. New York: Dodd, Mead and Company, 1896.

Ashbrook, William: *Donizetti.* London, Cassell, 1965.

Auer, Leopold: *My Long Life in Music.* New York: Frederick A. Stokes Company, 1923.

Azzi, María Susana and Simon Collier: *Le Grand Tango: The Life and Music of Astor Piazzolla.* New York: Oxford University Press, 2000.

Bach, Carl Philipp Emanuel: *The Letters of C.P.E. Bach.* Translated and edited by Stephen L. Clark. Oxford: Clarendon Press; New York: Oxford University Press, 1997.

Bantock, Myrrha: *Granville Bantock: A Personal Portrait.* London: Dent, 1972.

X Banfield, Stephen: *Gerald Finzi: An English Composer.* London; Boston: Faber and Faber, 1998.

Barenboim, Daniel: *Daniel Barenboim: A Life in Music.* Edited by Michael Lewin; New York: C. Scribner's Sons; Maxwell Macmillan International, 1992.

Bargren, Melinda: "Sometimes an Orchestra Can Be a Bit Too Festive"; *Seattle Times*, December 27, 1998, p. G 3.

Barrett, William Alexander: *Balfe, His Life and Work.* London: W. Reeves, 1890?

Bauer, Harold: *Harold Bauer, His Book.* New York, W. W. Norton, 1948.

Beethoven, Ludwig van: *Beethoven's Letters.* Translated by J. S. Shedlock. Selected and edited by A. Eaglefield-Hull. New York: Dover Publications, 1972.

Beethoven, Ludwig van: *Letters.* Collected, translated and edited by Emily Anderson. New York: St. Martin's Press, 1961.

Behrman, Carol H.: *Fiddler to the World: The Inspiring Life of Itzhak Perlman.* Belvidere, N.J.: Shoe Tree Press, 1992.

Bellasis, Edward: *Cherubini: Memorials Illustrative of His Life.* London: Burns and Oates, 1874.

Benestad, Finn: *Johan Svendsen, The Man, the Maestro, the Music.* Translated by William H. Halverson. Columbus, Oh.: Peer Gynt Press, 1995.

Benham, Hugh: *John Taverner: His Life and Music.* Aldershot, England; Burlington, Vt.: Ashgate, 2003.

Bennett, Joseph: *Forty Years of Music.* London: Methuen & Co., 1908.

Berlioz, Hector: *Evenings with the Orchestra.* Translated by Charles E. Roche; New York: A. A. Knopf, 1929.

Berlioz, Hector: *The Memoirs of Hector Berlioz.* Translated and edited by David Cairns; London: Everyman's Library, 2002.

Berlioz, Hector: *The Memoirs of Hector Berlioz, from 1803 to 1865, Comprising His Travels in Germany, Italy, Russia, and England.* Translated by Rachel and Eleanor Holmes; New York: Dover Publications, 1966.

Berlioz, Hector: *The Selected Letters of Berlioz.* Edited by Hugh Macdonald; translated by Roger Nichols. New York: W.W. Norton, 1997.

Bertensson, Sergei and Leyda, Jay: *Sergei Rachmaninoff: A Lifetime in Music.* Bloomington: Indiana University Press, 2001.

Biancolli, Amy: *Fritz Kreisler: Love's Sorrow, Love's Joy.* Portland, Or.: Amadeus Press, 1998.

X Bird, John: *Percy Grainger.* Oxford; New York: Oxford University Press, 1999.

Bizet, Georges: *Lettres de Georges Bizet; impressions de Rome (1857-1860); la commune (1871).* Paris: Calmann-Leévy 1907.

Bowen, Catherine Drinker: *"Free Artist"; the Story of Anton and Nicholas Rubinstein.* New York: Random House, 1939.

Bowers, Faubion: *Scriabin, a Biography.* New York: Dover, 1996.

Boyden, Matthew: *Richard Strauss.* Boston: Northeastern University Press, 1999.

Britten, Beth: *My Brother Benjamin*. Abbotsbrook, Bourne End, Buckinghamshire: Kensal Press, 1986.

Burk, John N.: *Clara Schumann; a Romantic Biography*. New York, Random House, 1940.

Burney, Charles: *Music, Men, and Manners in France and Italy, 1770*. Edited by H. Edmund Poole. London: Eulenburg Books, 1969.

Burney, Charles: *The Present State of Music in Germany, the Netherlands and United Provinces*. New York: Broude, 1969.

Busoni, Ferruccio: *Selected Letters*. Translated and edited by Anthony Beaumont. New York: Columbia University Press, 1987.

Busoni, Ferruccio: *Letters to His Wife*. Translated by Rosamond Ley. New York: Da Capo Press, 1975.

Calvocoressi, M. D.: *Music and Ballet; Recollection of M. D. Calvocoressi*. London, Faber and Faber Ltd., 1934.

Careri, Enrico: *Francesco Geminiani*. Oxford, England: Clarendon Press; New York: Oxford University Press, 1993.

Carner, Mosco. *Puccini: A Critical Biography*. London: Duckworth, 1974.

Carroll, Brendan G. *The Last Prodigy: A Biography of Erich Wolfgang Korngold*. Portland, Or.: Amadeus Press, 1997.

Casella, Alfredo: *Music in My Time: The Memoirs of Alfredo Casella*. Translated and edited by Spencer Norton; Norman: University of Oklahoma Press, 1955.

Chapin, Schuyler: *Sopranos, Mezzos, Bassos, and Other Friends*. New York: Crown Publishers, Inc., 1995.

Chopin, Frédéric: *Correspondance de Freédeéric Chopin*. Edited, revised, annotated, and translated by Bronislas Eédouard Sydow and Suzanne et Denise Chainaye. Paris: Richard-Masse, 1953-1960.

Chopin, Frédéric: *Friedrich Chopins Gesammelte Briefe, zum erstemal hrsg. und getreu ins deutsch*. Leipzig: Breitkopf und Härtel, 1911.

Chopin, Frédéric: *Letters*. Collected by Henryk Opienski. Translated from the original Polish and French by E. L. Voynich New York, Vienna House, 1971.

Clark, Walter Aaron: *Enrique Granados: Poet of the Piano*. Oxford; New York: Oxford University Press, 2006.

Coveney, Michael: *The Andrew Lloyd Webber Story*. London: Arrow, 2000.

Cummings, William Hayman: *Purcell*. London: S. Low, Marston, Searle & Rivington, 1881.

Curtis, Susan: *Dancing to a Black Man's Tune: A Life of Scott Joplin*. Columbia: University of Missouri Press, 1994.

Curtiss, Mina Kirstein: *Bizet and His World*. New York: Knopf, 1958.

Da Ponte, Lorenzo: *Memoirs of Lorenzo Da Ponte*. Translated from the Italian by Elisabeth Abbott; Edited and annotated by Arthur Livingston; New York: Dover Publications, 1967.

David, Elizabeth Harbison: *I Played Their Accompaniments*. New York; London: D. Appleton-Century Company, Inc., 1940.

Davies, Laurence: *César Franck and His Circle*. London, Barrie & Jenkins, 1970.

Dean, Winton: *Georges Bizet, His Life and Work*. London, J.M. Dent, 1965.

Dickson, Harry Ellis: *Gentlemen, More Dolce, Please! An Irreverent Memoir of Thirty Years in the Boston Symphony Orchestra*. Boston: Beacon Press, 1969.

Dittersdorf, Karl Ditters von: *The Autobiography of Karl von Dittersdorf*. Translated by A.D. Coleridge; London: R. Bentley and son, 1896.

Dohnányi, Ilona von: *Ernst von Dohnányi: A Song of Life*. Edited by James A. Grymes; Bloomington: Indiana University Press, 2002.

Dryden, Konrad Claude: *Leoncavallo: Life and Works*. Lanham, Md.: Scarecrow Press, 2007.

Dunning, John: *On the Air: The Encyclopedia of Old-Time Radio*. New York; Oxford: Oxford University Press, 1998.

Engel, Lehman: *This Bright Day; an Autobiography*. New York: Macmillan, 1974.

Feinstein, A. (Anthony): *Michael Rabin: America's Virtuoso Violinist*. Pompton Plains, N.J.: Amadeus Press, 2005.

Fifield, Christopher: *Max Bruch: His Life and Works*. Woodbridge, Suffolk; Rochester, N.Y.: Boydell Press, 2005.

Finck, Henry Theophilus: *My Adventures in the Golden Age of Music*. New York: Funk & Wagnalls, 1926.

Flower, Newman: *George Frideric Handel, His Personality and His Times*. London: Cassell, 1959.

Forbes, Elliot, ed.: *Thayer's Life of Beethoven.* Princeton: Princeton University Press, 1967.

Friedheim, Arthur: *Life and Liszt; The Recollections of a Concert Pianist.* Edited by Theodore L. Bullock. New York, Taplinger Pub. Co. 1961.

Friedrich, Otto: *Glenn Gould: A Life and Variations.* New York: Random House, 1989.

Gal, Hans, ed.: *The Musician's World.* London: Thames and Hudson, 1965.

Garden, Edward: *Balakirev; a Critical Study of His Life and Music.* New York: St. Martin's Press, 1967.

Gartenberg, Egon: *Johann Strauss; the End of an Era.* University Park: Pennsylvania State University Press, 1974.

Geiringer, Karl: *Brahms, His Life and Work.* New York: Da Capo Press, 1982.

Geiringer, Karl: *Haydn: A Creative Life in Music.* Berkeley: University of California Press, 1982.

Geiringer, Karl: *Johann Sebastian Bach: The Culmination of an Era.* New York; Oxford University Press, 1966.

Gillies, Malcolm: *Bartók Remembered.* London: Norton, 1991.

Goldmark, Karl: *Notes from the Life of a Viennese Composer, Karl Goldmark.* Translated by Alice Goldmark Brandeis; New York: A. and C. Boni, 1927.

Goodman, Peter W.: *Morton Gould: American Salute.* Portland, Or.: Amadeus Press, 2000.

Gorrell, Lorraine: *The Nineteenth-Century German Lied.* Portland, Or.: Amadeus Press, 1993.

Gottschalk, Louis Moreau: *Notes of a Pianist.* London: J. B. Lippincott, 1881.

Gounod; Charles: *Autobiographical Reminiscences,* Translated by W. Hely-Hutchinson; London: W. Heinemann, 1896.

Graves, Charles L.: *Hubert Parry, His Life and Works.* London: Macmillan and Co., Limited, 1926.

Grechaninov, Aleksander *Tikhonovich: My Life.*

New York: Coleman-Ross Co., 1952.

Greene, Harry Plunket: *Charles Villiers Stanford.* London: E. Arnold & Co., 1935.

Grieg: Edvard: *Breve fra Grieg.* Edited by Gunnar Hauch. Copenhagen: Gyldendal, Nordisk Forlag, 1922.

Grieg, Edvard: *Letters to Colleagues and Friends.* Selected and edited by Finn Benestad; Translated by William H. Halverson. Columbus: Peer Gynt Press, 2000.

Gruen, John: *Menotti: A Biography.* New York: Macmillan, 1978.

Grun, Bernard: *Gold and Silver; the Life and Times of Franz Lehár.* New York, D. McKay Co., 1970.

Grun, Bernard: *Prince of Vienna; the Life, the Times, and the Melodies of Oscar Straus.* London, W.H. Allen, 1955.

Hagan, Dorothy Veinus: *Félicien David, 1810-1876: A Composer and a Cause.* Syracuse, N.Y.: Syracuse University Press, 1985.

Harding, James. *Erik Satie.* London: Secker & Warburg, 1975.

Harper, Nancy Lee: *Manuel de Falla: His Life and Music.* Lanham, Md.: Scarecrow Press, 2005.

Hauptmann, Moritz: *The Letters of a Leipzig Cantor; being the Letters of Moritz Hauptmann to Franz Hauser, Ludwig Spohr, and Other Musicians.* Edited by Alfred Schöne and Ferdinand Hiller Translated and arranged by A. D. Coleridge. New York, Vienna House, 1972.

Haydn, Joseph: *The Collected Correspondence and London Notebooks of Joseph Haydn.* Compiled and translated by H.C. Robbins Landon. London: Barrie and Rockliff, 1959.

Haydn, Joseph: *Joseph Haydn; gesammelte Briefe und Aufzeichnungen.* Compiled by H. C. Robbins Landon. Edited and annotated by Deénes Bartha Kassel, New York, Baärenreiter, 1965.

Haydon, Geoffrey: *John Tavener: Glimpses of Paradise.* London: Gollancz, 1995.

Hayes, Malcolm. *Anton von Webern.* London: Phaidon, 1995.

Heath: Louis Jay: "The Stars that Entertain Unseen Audiences" in *The Home* supplement to Woman's Weekly, p. 68; Magazine Circulation Company, Inc., 1922.

Hell, Henri. *Francis Poulenc.* Translated by Edward Lockspeiser. London: J. Calder, 1959.

Henry, Leigh: *Dr. John Bull.* London: H. Joseph, 1937.

Henschel, George: *Musings and memories of a Musician.* New York, The Macmillan Company, 1919.

Herz, Henri: *My Travels in America.* Translated by Henry Bertram Hill. Madison: State Historical Society of Wisconsin, 1963.

Hess, Carol A.: *Sacred Passions: The Life and Music of Manuel de Falla.* New York: Oxford University Press, 2005.

Heyworth, Peter: *Otto Klemperer, His Life and Times.* Cambridge, England; New York: Cambridge University Press, 1996.

Hicks, Michael: *Henry Cowell, Bohemian.* Urbana: University of Illinois Press, 2002.

Hitchcock, H. Wylie, and Sadie, Stanley, eds.: *The New Grove Dictionary of American Music.* Washington, D.C.: Grove's Dictionaries of Music, Inc., 1986.

Holmes, Edward: *A Ramble among the Musicians of Germany.* New York: Da Capo Press, 1969.

Itzkoff, Seymour W.: *Emanuel Feuermann, Virtuoso: A Biography.* University of Ala.: University of Alabama Press, 1979.

Ivry, Benjamin: *Francis Poulenc.* London, Phaidon, 1996.

Jablonski, Edward: *Gershwin.* New York: Doubleday, 1987.

Jackson, Paul R. W.: *The Life and Music of Sir Malcolm Arnold: The Brilliant and the Dark.* Burlington, Vt.: Ashgate, 2003.

Jahoda, Gloria: *The Road to Samarkand: Frederick Delius and His Music.* New York, C. Scribner's Sons, 1969.

Jarman, Douglas: *Kurt Weill, an Illustrated Biography.* Bloomington: Indiana University Press, 1982.

Jenkins, Garry, and d'Antal, Stephen: *Kiri: Her Unknown Story.* Prymble, NSW, Australia: HarperCollins Australia, 1999.

Joachim, Joseph: *Letters from and to Joseph Joachim.* London: Macmillan 1914.

Kalush, William and Sloman, Larry: *The Secret Life of Houdini: The Making of America's First Superhero.* New York: Atria Books, 2007.

Kaufman, Louis and Annette: *A Fiddler's Tale: How Hollywood and Vivaldi Discovered Me.* Madison: University of Wisconsin Press, 2003.

Kendall, Alan: *Gioacchino Rossini, the Reluctant Hero.* London: V. Gollancz, 1992.

Kennedy, Michael: *Adrian Boult.* London: H. Hamilton, 1987.

Kennedy, Michael: *Portrait of Walton.* Oxford; New York: Oxford University Press, 1989.

Kirk, Elise K.: *Musical Highlights from the White House.* Malibar, Fla.: Krieger Publishing Company, n.d.

Kirk, H. L.: *Pablo Casals; a Biography.* New York: Holt, Rinehart and Winston, 1974.

Kirkpatrick, Ralph: *Domenico Scarlatti.* Princeton, N.J.: Princeton University Press, 1955.

Kite, Rebecca: *Keiko Abe: A Virtuosic Life: Her Musical Career and the Evolution of the Concert Marimba.* Leesburg, Va.: GP Percussion, 2007.

Kracauer, Siegfried: *Orpheus in Paris; Offenbach and the Paris of His Time.* Translated from the German by Gwenda David & Eric Mosbacher; New York: Vienna House, 1972.

Kroll, Mark: *Johann Nepomuk Hummel: A Musician's Life and World.* Lanham, Md.: Scarecrow Press, 2007.

Labounsky, Ann: *Jean Langlais: The Man and His Music.* Portland, Or.: Amadeus Press, 2000.

Lamb, Andrew: *Skaters' Waltz: The Story of the Waldteufels.* Croydon: Fullers Wood Press, 1995.

Large, Brian: *Smetana.* London: Duckworth, 1970.

Layton, Robert: *Franz Berwald.* London: A. Blond, 1959.

Leinsdorf, Erich: *Cadenza: A Musical Career.* Boston: Houghton Mifflin, 1976.

Levy, Alan Howard: *Edward MacDowell, an American Master.* Lanham, Md.: Scarecrow Press, 1998.

Liszt, Franz: *Letters of Franz Liszt.* Collected and edited by La Mara [pseud.] Translated by Constance Bache. London: H. Grevel & Co., 1894.

Lloyd, Stephen: *William Walton: Muse of Fire.* Rochester, N.Y.: Boydell Press, 2001.

Lockspeiser, Edward: *Debussy.* New York, E. P. Dutton and Co., 1936.

Lockspeiser, Edward: *Debussy; His Life and Mind.* London: Cassell, 1965.

Longmire, John: *John Ireland: Portrait of a Friend.* London, J. Baker, 1969.

Lonsdale, Roger H.: *Dr. Charles Burney; a Literary Biography.* Oxford: Clarendon Press, 1965.

Luening, Otto: *The Odyssey of an American Composer: The Autobiography of Otto Luening.* New York: Scribner, 1980.

MacDonald, Malcolm: *Brahms.* New York: Schirmer Books, 1990.

Mackenzie-Grieve, Averil: *Clara Novello.* London, Bles, 1955.

Mahler, Gustav: *Briefe.* Wien: Zsolnay, 1982.

Mahler, Gustav: *Selected Letters of Gustav Mahler.* Translated from the German by Eithne Wilkins & Ernst Kaiser and Bill Hopkins. New York: Farrar, Straus, Giroux, 1979.

Malcolm, Noel: *George Enescu: His Life and Music.* London: Toccata Press, 1990.

Mallach, Alan: *Pietro Mascagni and His Operas.* Boston: Northeastern University Press, 2002.

Martin, George: *Verdi at the Golden Gate.* Berkeley, Los Angeles, Oxford: University of California Press, 1993.

Mason, Daniel Gregory: *Music in My Time, and Other Reminiscences.* New York: The Macmillan Company, 1938.

Mason, Lowell: *A Yankee Musician in Europe: The 1837 Journals of Lowell Mason.* Edited by Michael Broyles. Ann Arbor, Mich.: UMI Research Press, 1990.

Massenet, Jules: *My Recollections.* Translated by H. Villiers Barnett; Westport, Conn.: Greenwood Press, 1970.

McKay, David Phares and Crawford, Richard: *William Billings of Boston: Eighteenth-Century Composer.* Princeton, N.J.: Princeton University Press, 1975.

McKenna, Marian C.: *Myra Hess: A Portrait.* London: Hamilton, 1976.

Mendelssohn-Bartholdy, Felix: *Briefe.*

Berlin, de Gruyter, 1968.

Mendelssohn-Bartholdy, Felix: *Letters of Felix Mendelssohn from 1833 to 1847.* Edited by Paul and Carl Mendelssohn-Bartholdy. Compiled by Julius Rietz. Translated by Lady Grace Wallace. London: Longman, Green, Longman, Roberts, and Green, 1863.

Mendelssohn-Bartholdy, Felix: *Letters.* Edited by G. Selden-Goth; New York, Pantheon, 1945.

Meyerbeer, Giacomo: *The Diaries of Giacomo Meyerbeer.* Translated, edited, and annotated by Robert Ignatius Letellier. Madison, N.J.: Fairleigh Dickinson University Press, 2004.

Milstein, Nathan, and Volkov, Solomon: *From Russia to the West: The Musical Memoirs and Reminiscences of Nathan Milstein.* Translated from the Russian by Antonina M. Bouis. New York: H. Holt, 1990.

Mollenhoff, David: Madison: *A History of the Formative Years.* Kendall/Hunt Pub. Co., 1982

Monson, Karen: *Alban Berg.* Boston: Houghton Mifflin Co., 1979.

Mozart, Wolfgang Amadeus: *Die Briefe W.A. Mozarts und Seiner Familie.* München und Leipzig: G. Miller, 1914.

Mozart, Wolfgang Amadeus: *Mozart's Letters, Mozart's Life: Selected Letters.* Translated and edited by Robert Spalding. New York: Norton, 2000.

Mozart, Wolfgang Amadeus: *The Letters of Mozart & His Family.* Translated and edited by Emily Anderson; London, Macmillan and Co., Limited, 1938.

Myers, Rollo H.: *Emmanuel Chabrier and His Circle.* London: Dent, 1969.

Nabokov, Nicolas: *Old Friends and New Music.* Boston: Little, Brown and Co., 1951.

Nettel, Reginald: *Havergal Brian and His Music.* London: Dobson, 1976.

Nettl, Paul: *The Other Casanova.* New York: Da Capo Press, 1970.

Newton, Ivor: *At the Piano: Ivor Newton: the World of an Accompanist.* London: H. Hamilton, 1966.

Nice, David: *Prokofiev: from Russia to the West, 1891-1935.* New Haven: Yale University Press, 2003.

Nicholas, Jeremy: *Godowsky, the Pianists' Pianist: A Biography of Leopold Godowsky.* Northumberland, England: Appian Publications & Recordings, 1989.

Noss, Luther: *Paul Hindemith in the United States.* Urbana: University of Illinois Press, 1989.

Olleson, Philip: *Samuel Wesley: The Man and His Music.*

Rochester, NY: Boydell Press, 2003.

Osborne, Richard: *Herbert von Karajan: A Life in Music.* Boston: Northeastern University Press, 2000.

Paderewski, Ignacy Jan and Lawton, Mary: *The Paderewski Memoirs.* New York: C. Scribner's Sons, 1938.

Palmer, Fiona M.: *Domenico Dragonetti in England (1794-1846): The Career of a Double Bass Virtuoso.* Oxford: Clarendon Press; New York: Oxford University Press, 1997.

Paperno, Dmitri: *Notes of a Moscow Pianist.* Portland, Ore.: Amadeus Press, 1998.

Pegolotti, James A.: *Deems Taylor: A Biography.* Boston: Northeastern University Press, 2003.

Pepys, Samuel: *The Diary of Samuel Pepys: A New and Complete Transcription;* Edited by Robert Latham and William Matthews. London, Bell & Hyman, 1970.

Piggott, Patrick: *The Life and Music of John Field, 1782-1837, Creator of the Nocturne.* Berkeley, University of California Press, 1973.

Plantinga, Leon: *Clementi: His Life and Music.* London; New York: Oxford University Press, 1977.

Plaskin, Glenn: *Horowitz: A Biography of Vladimir Horowitz.* New York: Quill, 1983.

Poznansky, Alexander, ed.: *Tchaikovsky Through Others' Eyes.* Translated from Russian by Ralph C. Burr, Jr. & Robert Bird; Bloomington: Indiana University Press, 1999.

Primrose, William: *Walk on the North Side: Memoirs of a Violist.* Provo, Utah: Brigham Young University Press, 1978.

Puccini, Giacomo: *Letters of Giacomo Puccini.* Edited by Giuseppe Adami; translated from the Italian and edited for the English edition by Ena Makin. Philadelphia and London: J.B. Lippincott Co., 1931.

Reid, Charles: *The Music Monster: A Biography of James William Davison, Music Critic of the* Times of London. Publisher: London; New York: Quartet Books, 1984.

Reid, Charles: *Thomas Beecham; an Independent Biography.* New York, Dutton: 1962.

Richter, Sviatoslav: *Richter.* Compiled and edited by Bruno Monsaingeon; Translated by Stewart Spencer. Princeton, N.J.: Princeton University Press, 2001.

Rimsky-Korsakov, Nikolai: *My Musical Life.* Translated by Judah A. Joffee; edited by Carl Van Vechten. New York: Vienna House, 1972.

Rodmell, Paul: *Charles Villiers Stanford.* Aldershot; Burlington, Vt., Ashgate, 2002.

Rossi, Nick: *Domenico Cimarosa: His Life and His Operas.* Westport, Conn.: Greenwood Press, 1999.

Rothschild, Germaine de: *Luigi Boccherini; His Life and Work.* Translated by Andreas Mayor. London; New York: Oxford University Press, 1965.

Rózsa, Miklós: *Double Life.* New York: Wynwood Press, 1989.

Rubinstein, Arthur *My Many Years.* New York: Knopf, 1980.

Sadie, Stanley, ed.: *The New Grove Dictionary of Music and Musicians.* Washington, D.C.: Grove's Dictionaries of Music, Inc., 1980.

Šafrànek, Miloš: *Bohuslav Martinů, His Life and Works.* Translated by Roberta Finlayson-Samsourová; London: A. Wingate, 1962.

Salerno-Sonnenberg, Nadja: Interview on Wisconsin Public Radio, March 11, 2005.

Schabas, Ezra: *Theodore Thomas: America's Conductor and Builder of Orchestras.* Urbana: University of Illinois Press, 1989.

Schillinger, Frances: *Joseph Schillinger, a Memoir by His Wife.* New York: Greenberg, 1949.

Schubert, Franz: *Letters and Other Writings.* Edited by Otto Erich Deutsch; translated by Venetia Savile. New York: A. A. Knopf, 1928.

Schumann, Clara: *Letters of Clara Schumann and Johannes Brahms.* Edited by Berthold Litzmann. New York, Longmans, Green and Co.; London: E. Arnold & Co., 1927.

Schumann, Robert: *The Letters of Robert Schumann.* Selected and edited by Karl Storck; Translated by Hannah Bryant. London: J. Murray, 1907.

Scott, Cyril: *Bone of Contention; Life Story and Confessions.* New York, Arco Pub. Co., 1969.

Searle, Muriel V.: *John Ireland, the Man and His Music.* Tunbridge Wells: Midas Books, 1979.

Semler, Isabel Parker: *Horatio Parker; a Memoir for His Grandchildren, Compiled from Letters and Papers.* New York: G. P. Putnam's Sons, 1942.

Seroff, Victor Ilyitch: *Debussy; Musician of France.* New York: Putnam, 1956.

Seroff, Victor Ilyitch: *Maurice Ravel.* New York, Holt, 1953.

Shead, Richard: *Constant Lambert; with a Memoir by Anthony Powell.* London: Simon Publications, 1973.

Shostakovich, Dmitri: *The Memoirs of Dmitri Shostakovich.* Edited by Solomon Volkov; translated from the Russian by Antonina W. Bouis. Harper Colophon ed. Publisher: New York: Harper Colophon Books, 1980.

Simpson, Anne Key: *The Life and Music of R. Nathaniel Dett.* Metuchen, N.J.: Scarecrow Press, 1993.

Slonimsky, Nicolas: *Perfect Pitch: An Autobiography.* New York: Schirmer Trade Books, 2002.

Smallman, Basil: *Schütz.* Oxford; New York: Oxford University Press, 2000.

Smidak, Emil: *Ignaz Moscheles: The Life of the Composer and His Encounters with Beethoven, Liszt, Chopin, and Mendelssohn.* Hampshire, England: Scholar Press; Brookfield, Vt., Gower Pub. Co., 1989.

Smith, Cyril: *Duet for Three Hands.* As told to Joyce Egginton; London: Angus & Robertson, 1966.

Smith, Moses: *Koussevitzky.* New York: Allen, Towne & Heath, Inc., 1947.

Solti, Georg: *Memoirs.* with assistance from Harvey Sachs; New York: Alfred A. Knopf, 1997.

Sousa, John Philip: *Marching Along: Recollections of Men, Women, and Music.* Edited by Paul E. Bierley; Westerville, Oh: Integrity Press, 1994.

Spalding, Albert: *Rise to Follow, an Autobiography.* New York: H. Holt, 1943.

Spohr, Louis: *Autobiography.* New York, Da Capo Press, 1969.

Starker, Janos: *The World of Music According to Starker.* Bloomington: Indiana University Press, 2004.

Stebbins, Lucy Poate, and Stebbins, Richard Ponte: *Enchanted Wanderer; the Life of Carl Maria von Weber.* New York: G. P. Putnam's Sons, 1940.

Stendhal: *Life of Rossini.* Translated and annotated by Richard N. Coe; New York: Riverrun Press, 1985.

Stern, Isaac: *My first 79 Years.* Written with Chaim Potok; New York: Alfred A. Knopf, 1999.

Stewart, James B.: *Heart of a Soldier: A Story of Love, Heroism, and September 11th.* New York: Simon & Schuster, 2002.

Stravinsky, Igor: *An Autobiography.* New York: Norton, 1962.

Stuckenschmidt, Hans Heinz: *Schoenberg: His Life, World, and Work.* Translated by Humphrey Searle; London: Calder, 1977.

Swafford, Jan: *Charles Ives: A Life with Music.* New York: W.W. Norton, 1996.

Talbot, Michael: *Vivaldi.* New York: Schirmer Books; Maxwell Macmillan International, 1992.

Tammaro, Ferruccio: *Jean Sibelius.* Torino: ERI, 1984.

Tchaikovsky, Modeste: *Life and Letters of Peter Ilich Tchailkovsky.* Edited from the Russian by Rosa Newmarch; New York: Haskell House Publishers, 1970.

Tchaikovsky, Peter Ilich: *"To My Best Friend": Correspondence between Tchaikovsky and Nadezhda von Meck, 1876-1878.* Translated by Galina von Meck; edited by Edward Garden and Nigel Gotteri; Oxford; New York: Oxford University Press, 1993.

Tchaikovsky, Peter Ilich: *Polnoe sobranie sochinenii;* Edited by B. V. Asafiev. Moscow: Government Musical Series, 1959.

Terry, Charles Sanford: *John Christian Bach.* London: Oxford University Press, H. Milford, 1929.

Thayer, Alexander Wheelock: *Thayer's Life of Beethoven.* Princeton, N.J.: Princeton University Press, 1970.

Thomas, Theodore: *Theodore Thomas, a Musical Autobiography.* Edited by George P. Upton; New York: DaCapo Press, 1964.

Thomson, Andrew: *Vincent d'Indy and His World.* New York: Oxford University Press, 1996.

Tibbetts, John C., ed.: *Dvořák in America, 1892-1895.* Portland: Amadeus Press, 1993.

Tiomkin, Dimitri: *Please Don't Hate Me.* Garden City, N.Y.: Doubleday, 1959.

Tommasini, Anthony: *Virgil Thomson: Composer on the Aisle.* New York: W.W. Norton, 1997.

Varèse, Louise: *Varèse: A Looking-Glass Diary.* New York, Norton 1972.

Vaughan Williams, Ursula: R.V.W.: *A Biography of Ralph Vaughan Williams.* London: Oxford University Press, 1964.

Verdi, Giuseppe: *Verdi, the Man in His Letters.* Edited and selected by Franz Werfel and Paul Stefan; Translated by Edward Downes. New York, L.B. Fischer, 1942.

Verdi, Giuseppe: *Letters of Giuseppe Verdi.* Selected, translated and edited by Charles Osborne. London: Gollancz, 1971.

Wagner, Richard: *My Life.* New York: Dodd, Mead and Company, 1911.

Wagner, Richard: *Saämtliche Briefe.* Edited by Gertrud Strobel and Werner Wolf. Leipzig: Deutscher Verlag fuür Musik, 1967.

Wagner, Richard: *Selected Letters of Richard Wagner.* Translated and edited by Stewart Spencer and Barry Millington. New York: W.W. Norton, 1987.

Walker, Alan: *Franz Liszt.* New York: Knopf, 1983.

Waters, Edward N.: *Victor Herbert; a Life in Music.* New York, Macmillan, 1955.

Weinstock, Herbert: *Vincenzo Bellini: His Life and His Operas.* New York, A.A. Knopf, 1971.

Weschler-Vered, Artur: *Jascha Heifetz.* New York: Schirmer Books, 1986.

Wightman, Alistair: *Karol Szymanowski: His Life and Work.* Brookfield, Vt.: Ashgate, 1999.

Wilson, Elizabeth: *Shostakovich: A Life Remembered.* Princeton, N.J.: Princeton University Press, 2006.

Wolf, Hugo: *Briefe an Melanie Köchert.* Fran Grasberger, Tutzing H. Schneider, 1964.

Wolf, Hugo: *Letters to Melanie Köchert.* Edited by Franz Grasberger; Translated by Louise McClelland Urban; Madison, Wis.: University of Wisconsin Press, 2003.

Wolff, Werner: *Anton Bruckner, Rustic Genius.* New York: E. P. Dutton & Co., Inc., 1942.

Wood, Henry Joseph: *My Life of Music.* London: V. Gollancz, Ltd., 1938.

Yuzefovich, Victor: *Aram Khachaturyan.* Translated by Nicholas Kournokoff and Vladimir Bobrov. New York: Sphinx Press, 1985.

Index

Abbot, George, Archbishop of Canterbury 224
Abdul 101
Abe, Keiko 164
Abel, Karl Friedrich 140, 317
Adams, Franklin P. 334
Albéniz, Isaac 283
Albert, Eugen d' 177
Albert, Prince 35
Aldrich, Richard 246
Alexandra Feodorovna, Czarina 111
Alford, Kenneth 195
Allegri, Gregorio 223
Angelo, Henry 317
Antheil, George 228
Antoine, André 18
Antonini, Alfredo 365
Appiani, Giuseppina 179
Arco, Count Georg Anton 95
Arditi, Luigi 265
Arne, Thomas 236, 291
Arnold, Malcolm 129, 195
Arnold, Philip 129
Arnold, Sheila 129
Ashton, Frederick 39
Assad, Odair 295
Assad, Sérgio 295
Auber, Daniel-François 229
Auden, W.H. 171
Auer, Leopold 41, 187, 221
Augusta, Empress of Prussia 159
Augusta of Saxe-Gotha 118
Auric, Georges 85
Aurnhammer, Josephine von 146
Bach, Ambrosius 285
Bach, Carl Philipp Emanuel 81, 352
Bach, Cecelia 82
Bach, Johann Christisan (John) 82, 140, 317
Bach, Johann Gottfried Bernhard 145
Bach, Johann Sebastian 54, 57,

70, 81, 82, 98, 130, 145, 153, 175, 196, 222, 245, 252, 260, 285, 340
Bacon, Pop 210
Baillot, Pierre 341
Balakirev, Mily 58, 134
Baldrige, Letitia 213
Balfe, Michael 229
Banks, Nathaniel 147
Bantock, Granville 141
Barbirolli, John 67
Barenboim, Daniel 48
Barnum, P. T. 131, 309
Bartók, Béla 20, 71, 135, 165
Bauer, Harold 61, 132, 210
Beaumarchais 49, 127
Beauregard, P.G.T. 147
Beckett, Gilbert A' 170
Beecham, Thomas 92, 162, 267, 277
Beethoven, Karl van 59, 94
Beethoven, Kasper Anton Karl 59
Beethoven, Ludwig van 7, 28, 34, 54, 59, 60, 80, 87, 94, 98, 99, 103, 113, 125, 126, 139, 141, 142, 148, 158, 162, 175, 176, 191 208, 218, 220, 222, 265, 284, 306, 362, 363
Belleville, Anna Caroline de 181
Bellini, Vincenzo 76, 239
Benda, František 291
Benedetti, Michele 11
Bennett, Joseph 201
Berg, Alban 91, 253
Berkofsky, Martin 364
Berlin, Irving 289
Berlioz, Adèle 307
Berlioz, Hector 52, 102, 116, 131, 185, 254, 287, 306, 307, 346
Bernstein, Leonard 287, 318, 337
Bertrand, Madame 342
Berwald, Franz 136
Best, W.T. 205
Billings, William 186
Birchall 59
Bizet, Georges 32, 63, 79, 100, 356

384

Björling, Jussi 38
Bjørnson, Bjørnstjerne 2
Black, Andrew 321
Black, Frank 289
Bliss, Arthur 36
Blitzstein, Marc 337
Block, Julius H. 311
Boccherini, Luigi 143
Bockelmann, Rudolf 154
Bonaparte, Louis-Napoleon 32
Bononcini, Giovanni Battista 328
Bontempi, Giovanni Andrea 234
Booth, Edwin 114
Booth, John Wilkes 114
Booth, Margaret 357
Borodin, Alexander 58, 174, 297
Bosch, Hieronymus 358
Botticelli, Bartolommeo 49
Boulanger, Nadia 71, 260
Boult, Adrian 56, 277
Bradbury, Ray 357
Brahms, Johanna 249
Brahms, Johannes 24, 28, 141, 153, 177, 192, 200, 220, 247, 249, 260, 274, 295, 334, 350, 356
Brecht, Bertolt 244, 269
Brian, Havergal 104
Bridgetower, George Augustus Polgreen 60
Brightman, Sarah 219
Britten, Benjamin 171, 219
Britten, Beth 171
Bronfman, Yefim 34
Bruch, Max 157, 203, 364
Bruckner, Anton 248, 351
Brunetti, Antonio 95
Bull, John 150, 224
Bull, Ole 110
Bull, Sara Thorp 110
Bülow, Hans von 25
Burgoyne, John 186
Burlington, Lord 328
Burney, Charles 236, 261, 291
Busoni, Ferruccio 69, 130

Butterworth, George 16, 56
Byelotserkovsky (NKVD agent) 218
Byelyayev, M. P. 174
Byrd, William 317
Byrom, John 328
Byron, George Gordon, Lord 98, 211
Calvocoressi, Michel 18, 232
Cannabich, Christian 8
Carlo (dog) 125
Carré, Albert 105, 325
Carré, Michel 233
Carte, Richard D'Oyly 322
Casals, Pablo 123, 175, 220
Casanova, Giacomo 308
Casella, Alfredo 96, 324
Catherine II "The Great" 163
Catherine of Braganza, Queen of England 366
Chabrier, Emmanuel 226
Chadwick, George Whitefield 247
Chapin, Schuyler 133
Chaplin, Charlie 108
Charles II, King 366
Charles X, King 45
Charles, Prince of Asturias 143
Chateaubriand, François-René de 98
Cherubini, Luigi 28, 52, 64, 229, 302, 341, 347, 361
Chevillard, Pierre 306
Chézy, Helmina von 242
Chopin, Frédéric 26, 35, 47, 100, 130, 132, 142, 144, 190, 260, 288, 290, 341
Chotzinoff, Samuel 358
Cillario, Carlo 133
Cimarosa, Domenico 163
Clementi, Muzio 113, 178, 359
Clinton, Henry 186
Cocteau, Jean 10, 172
Coletti, Antonio Magini 298
Collard, William 113

Colloredo, Count Hieronymus von, Archbishop of Salzburg 95

Constantine, Grand Duke 25

Converse, Frederick 296

Copes, Juan Carlos 335

Copland, Aaron 337

Corelli, Franco 133

Cornwallis, Charles 186

Cortot, Alfred 260

Cowan, Thomas 292

Coward, Noel 15

Cowell, Henry 86, 137

Cramer, Johann Baptiste 340, 341

Crawford, Francis Marion 4

Crosdill, John 178

Curtis, Natalie 69

Czapek, Josef 103

Czerny, Carl 94, 341

Czerny, Joseph 26

Da Ponte, Lorenzo 127-8, 355

David, Elizabeth Harbison 296

David, Félicien 79, 176

David, Ferdinand 28

Davidoff, Charles 25

Davies, Ben 321

Davies, Clara Novello 258

Davison, James William 35

Debussy, Claude 17, 85, 89, 105, 130, 173, 200, 217, 227, 228, 232, 283, 325, 329

de Gaulle, Charles 238

Delibes, Léo 32

Delius, Frederick 3, 299

Derain, André 172

Dett, Nathaniel 112

Devrient, Emil 339

Diaghilev, Serge 96, 282

Dickson, Harry Ellis 106

Disney, Walt 57

Dittersdorf, Karl Ditters von 5, 240, 278

Dohnányi, Ernst von 37, 204

Dohnányi, Ilona 204

Domingo, Placido 219

Donizetti, Gaetano 42, 73, 169, 216, 239, 362

Dorati, Antal 135

Dorati, Sándor 135

Dorsey, Tommy 289

Dowling, Helen 315

Downes, Olin 156

Dragonetti, Domenico 125, 126

Dryden, John 118

Dubois 150

Dukas, Paul 96, 227, 260, 283

Du Maurier, George 199

Duncan, Isadora 132

Dundy, Elmer 294

Duparc, Henri 226

Dvořák, Antonín 141, 270, 286

Dwight, John 201

Einstein, Albert 345

Elgar, Edward 141, 191, 279, 321

Elgar, Henry 191

Elgar, William 191

Elizabeth I, Queen 150, 224

Emmett, Daniel D. 147

Enesco, Georges 93, 220, 260, 315

Engel, Lehman 88

Epstein, Max 151

Erard, Pierre 229

Ernst August, Duke 285

Ernst, Heinrich Wilhelm 185

Erskine, John 319

Esperanza, Paolo 183

Esposito, Eugene 327

Esterházy, Prince Anton 14

Esterházy, Prince Nikolaus I 303

Esterházy, Prince Nikolaus II 241, 302-3

Eugénie, Empress 349

Evans, Warwick 200

Eyer, Harold 153

Fadiman, Clifton 334

Falla, Manuel de 227, 283

Fanelli, Ernest 228

Farinelli 117, 261, 326

Farnese, Elizabeth, Queen of Spain 261
Ferdinand I, Emperor 169
Ferdinand V, King of Spain 261, 326
Ferdinand, King of Romania 93
Feuermann, Emanuel 330
Field, John 332, 341
Finck, Henry T. 280
Finzi, Gerald 189
Fischer, Johann Christian 82, 317
Ford, Henry 67
Franck, César 53
Franklin, Benjamin 256
Frederick II, King of Prussia 291, 344
Frederick, Prince of Wales 117, 118
Friedheim, Arthur 159
Friedrich I, King of Prussia 344
Friedrich Wilhelm III, King of Prussia 68
Fuchs, Eugen 154
Gainsborough, Thomas 82, 317
Gallini, Signor 14
Garcia, Manuel 49, 50
Garden, Mary 105, 108
Gauk, Alexander 166
Gay, John 29
Gedalge, André 17
Geminiani, Francesco 66, 77
Genzinger, Maria von 62
George, King of Hanover 41
George I, King 328
George II, King 29, 117, 118
George III, King 14, 82, 140
George IV, King 82
Gericke, Wilhelm 247
Gershwin, George 184, 289, 334
Giardini, Felice de 317
Giesemann, Adolf 249
Giesemann, Lieschen 249
Gilbert, William S. 177, 322
Gilmore, Patrick 201

Glazunov, Alexander 121, 174
Glière, Reinhold 46
Glinka, Mikhail 25
Glover, William Howard 185
Gluck, Christoph Willibald von 5, 256, 355
Goddard, Arabella 35
Godfrey, Dan 201
Godowsky, Frieda 250-1
Godowsky, Leopold 250-1
Goebbels, Joseph 57
Goethe, Johann Wolfgang von 41, 336
Goldmark, Karl 72, 235, 275
Goodman, Benny 289
Gosling, John 272
Gottschalk, Louis Moreau 84, 114, 115, 147, 168, 348
Goula 150
Gould, Glenn 363
Gould, Morton 337
Gounod, Charles 9, 41, 63, 190, 266, 329
Goya, Francisco José de 316, 334
Grädener, Carl 350
Grainger, Percy 161, 207
Granados, Amparo Gal 316
Granados, Enrique 83, 316
Gretchaninoff, Alexander 338
Gretry, André 65
Greville, Fulke 236
Grieg, Edvard 2, 55, 67, 100, 157, 207
Grieg, Nina 207
Grisi, Giulia 229
Gruber, Franz 360
Guadagni, Gaetano 278
Gütermann, Anna Maria 154
Hadley, Henry 12
Halévy, Ludovic 63
Halvorsen, Johan 55
Hammond, Perry 101
Handel, George Frederick 29, 70, 117, 118, 140, 144, 191, 205, 236,

263, 267, 280, 328, 350, 354, 360
Harding, Ann 171
Hauptmann, Moritz 342
Hauwe, Walter van 164
Hawkins, John 272
Haydn, Joseph 7, 14. 28, 60, 62, 125, 241, 245, 302-3, 330, 347
Haydn, Michael 302
Heiberg, Gunnar 299
Heifetz, Jascha 151
Hellmesberger, Joseph 24
Heming, Percy 267
Henschel, George 4, 192, 305
Henselt, Adolf 185
Herbert, George Augustus, Earl of Pembroke 178
Herbert, Victor 69, 149, 194, 294
Hérold, Ferdinand 275
Herz, Henri 309, 341
Herzogenberg, Elizabet von 356
Hess, Myra 67, 252
Heyward, DuBose 184
Hiller, Ferdinand 144, 196, 341
Hindemith, Paul 57, 277
Hinkley, Isabella 51
Hitler, Adolf 154. 269, 312
Hofmann, Józef 33
Hogarth, George 185
Hohenlohe, Prince 235
Holmes, Edward 230
Homer 98
Hoover, Herbert 112
Horowitz, Vladimir 130
Houdini, Harry 149, 294
Houseman, John 39, 101
Howe, Julia Ward 4
Howe, William 186
Howells, Herbert 15
Hugo, Victor 98
Hummel, Johann Nepomuk 26, 98, 181, 241, 332, 340
Humperdinck, Engelbert 202
Hunt, Arabella 272
Hurok, Saul 34

Huxley, Nettie 305
Ibsen, Henrik 2, 55, 74, 299
Illica, Luigi 199
Indy, Vincent d' 87, 138, 232
Ireland, John 22, 300
Irving, Washington 199
Isherwood, Christopher 171
Ives, Charles 109
Jackson, Thomas "Stonewall" 147
James, William 305
Jarre, Maurice 195
Jennens, Charles 263
Joachim, Joseph 28, 306, 350, 353
Johann Georg, Elector of Saxony 234
Johann Georg II 234
Johnson, Lyndon Baines 312
Joplin, Scott 331
Josefowitz, Samuel 365
Joseph II, Emperor 359
Kabalevsky, Dmitri 301
Kalkbrenner, Friedrich 341
Karajan, Herbert von 154
Kaufman, Louis 365
Kennedy, Jacqueline 213
Kennedy, John F. 213
Khachaturian, Aram 119, 158, 195, 301
Kiernan, John 334
Kilényi, Edward 80
Kinsky, Prince 208
Kirsten, Dorothy 133
Klemperer, Otto 222
Klindworth, Karl 185
Klingemann, Karl 180
Kneisel, Franz 247
Knepler, Paul 271
Köchert, Melanie 202
Kodály, Zoltán 135
Korngold Wolfgang Erich 313
Koussevitzky, Serge 75, 173
Kozeluch, Leopold 169
Kreisler, Fritz 157
Kreutzer, Rudolphe 60

Krommer, Franz 169
Kubrick, Stanley 195
Kurka, Robert 153
Labbette, Dora 267
Labey, Marcel 17
Laloy, Louis 85
Lamartine, Alphonse de 98
Lambert, Constant 209
Lanari, Antonio 21
Langlais, Jean 238
Lanner, Joseph 26, 101
Lasso, Orlando di 329
Lean, David 195
Lebedinsky, Lev 281
Leblanc, Georgette 105
Lee, Robert E. 114
Lefort 54
Lehár, Franz 271
Leinsdorf, Erich 38, 312
Lenin, Vladimir 281
Lenya, Lotte 244
Leoncavallo, Ruggiero 310
Leopold, Prince 285
Lermontov, Mikhail 334
Levant, Oscar 334
Levelly 265
Liadov, Anatol 58
Lichnowsky, Prince Karl von 60, 126
Lifar, Serge 282
Lincoln, Abraham 51, 84, 114, 115
Lincoln, Mary Todd 84
Lind, Jenny 1, 131, 179, 309
Lipatti, Dinu 260
Liszt, Franz 13, 45, 58, 98, 99, 103, 141, 159, 167, 190, 194, 232, 274, 288, 295, 306, 341
Löbel 291
Lloyd Webber, Andrew 219
Locke, John 98
Löhr, Friedrich 323
Long, Kathleen 252
Longfellow, Henry Wadsworth 270
Longland, John 19

Lotti, Antonio 328
Louis XV, King 261
Louis Philippe, King 229
Loyselet, Elisabetta 49
Luegmayer 303
Luening, Eugene 245
Luening, Otto 245
Luegmayer, Joseph Aloys 303
Ma, Yo-Yo 34
MacDonald, Ramsey 112
MacDowell, Edward 194, 319
Mackerras, Charles 266
MacNeice, Louis 171
Maelzel, Johann 284
Maeterlinck, Maurice 105
Magnard, Albéric 96
Mahler, Gustav 91, 246, 313, 323, 351
Malfatti, Therese 139
Mamontov 327
Mardrus, Lucie 27
Marek, George 38
Maria Barbara, Queen of Spain 261, 326
Markes, Charles 22
Marlboro, Duchess of 328
Marsh, Alice 312
Marsh, Charles 312
Marshall, Frank 83
Martini, Giovanni Battista 5
Martinů, Bohuslav 225
Martynov, Alexei 211
Marx, Adolph Bernhard 68
Marxsen, Edward 249
Mary, Queen 272
Mascagni, Pietro 268
Mason, Daniel Gregory 17
Mason, Lowell 193
Massé, Victor 79
Massenet, Jules 233, 237
Matheson, John 266
Maurin, Jean Pierre 306
Mele, Giovanni Battista 326
Mendelssohn, Abraham 64, 70

Mendelssohn, Fanny 290
Mendelssohn, Felix 1, 22, 35, 64, 70, 103, 111, 116, 136, 144, 175, 180, 196, 203, 245, 262, 290, 313, 321
Mendelssohn, Francesco von 175
Mendelssohn, Lea Salomon 262
Mendelssohn, Rebecca 196
Menotti, Gian Carlo 231, 358
Mercadante, Saverio 239
Meshchersky, Nina 124
Meshchersky, Talya 124
Messager, André 105
Meyerbeer, Giacomo 69, 185, 229, 306, 340
Miaskovsky, Nikolai 119
Michelangelo 98, 362
Milanov, Zinka 38
Miles-Kingston, Paul 219
Milhaud, Darius 325
Miller, Glenn 289
Milstein, Nathan 152
Mintz, Schlomo 34
Mitropoulos, Dimitri 7
Moffo, Anna 38
Mohr, Joseph 360
Molnár, Ferenc 345
Monteux, Pierre 34
Moore, Clement Clarke 355
Moscheles, Charlotte Emden 116
Moscheles, Ignaz 116, 262
Mottl, Felix 159, 221
Mozart, Constanze Weber 44, 120, 146, 243, 276
Mozart, Leopold 8, 44, 128, 140, 146, 243, 257, 304, 359
Mozart, Nannerl 44, 140
Mozart, Wolfgang Amadeus 7, 8, 9, 10, 44, 46, 79, 95, 98, 99, 103, 120, 127-8, 140, 142, 146, 169, 241, 243, 257, 260, 266, 276, 304, 332, 336, 345, 350, 355, 359
Mravinsky, Evgeny 119
Muffat, Georg 356

Munch, Charles 218, 260
Mussorgsky, Modeste 58, 174
Nabokov, Nicholas 155
Namara, Margaret 292
Napoleon I, Emperor 125, 208, 347, 361
Napoleon III, Emperor 233, 349
Neate, Charles 59, 148
Newton, Ivor 107
Nietzsche, Friedrich 37
Nieves, Maria 335
Nijinsky, Vaslav 282
Nikisch, Arthur 75, 323
Nina 308
Novara 265
Novello, Clara 111
Novello, Ivor 258
O'Carolan, Turlough 77
Offenbach, Jacques 32, 333
Olenin, A.A. 134
Onslow, Georges 160
Ormandy, Eugene 315
Oscar II, King 43
Paderewski, Ignacy Jan 6, 40, 47
Paër, Ferdinando 341
Paganini, Niccolò 68, 98, 99, 144, 271, 341
Paisiello, Giovanni 49, 359, 361
Palestrina, Giovanni Pierluigi da 239, 329
Palmer, Barbara, Lady Castlemaine 366
Paperno, Dmitry 119
Parke, William 178
Parker, Horatio 109, 156, 247
Parry, Hubert 170, 259
Pasta, Giuditta 76
Patti, Adelina 280, 314, 354
Paul, Prince 154
Paulsen, John 74
Pepusch, Johann (John) 29
Pepys, Samuel 366
Pergolesi, Giovanni 239
Perlman, Itzhak 293

Perlman, Shoshana 293
Persichetti, Vincent 337
Peters, C.F. 55, 74
Phelps, William 150
Philip V, King 261
Phillips, Adelaide 51, 115
Phillips, Dorothy 300
Piatigorsky, Gregor 107, 151, 152, 175
Piazzolla, Ástor 71, 335
Piazzolla, Vincente Nonino 335
Picasso, Pablo 10
Pinto, E. Roquete 27
Plato 98
Pleyel, Ignaz Joseph 14, 62
Poe, Edgar Allan 217
Polzelli, Luigia 14
Polzelli, Pietro 14
Popper, David 221
Porpora, Nicola 117
Poulenc, Francis 10, 85
Powers, Marie 231
Prescott, Richard 186
Price, Leontyne 38
Primrose, William 165, 200
Prokofiev, Sergei 108, 119, 124, 155
Puccini, Giacomo 38, 133, 149, 199, 267
Purcell, Henry 272, 317
Pushkin, Alexander 334
Quantz, Johann Joachim 344
Rabin, Michael 153
Rachmaninoff, Sergei 86, 155, 190, 209, 246, 327
Rameau, Jean-Philippe 96
Ransome, Arthur 171
Raskov (pianist) 288
Rathbone, Basil 171
Ravel, Maurice 71, 96, 138, 209, 228, 295
Reinecke, Karl 323, 350
Reiner, Fritz 67, 106
Remény, Eduard 306

Rescorla, Rick 255
Respighi, Ottorino 56
Rich, John 117
Richter, Hans 37, 221, 248
Richter, Sviatoslav 218
Ricordi, Giulio 314
Ricordi, Tito 298
Ries, Ferdinand 59, 148
Righetti-Giorgi, Geltrude 49, 50
Rimsky-Korsakov, Nikolai 58, 173, 174, 297
Ritter, Theodore 185
Rodzinski, Artur 318
Roger-Ducasse, Jean 96
Romani, Felice 21, 76
Röntgen, Engelbert 350
Roosevelt, Theodore 149, 310
Rose, Leonard 34
Rossini, Gioachino 9, 11, 13, 49, 50, 56, 79, 99, 111, 196, 229, 239, 280, 306, 341, 362
Rózsa, Miklós 318, 357
Rubinstein, Anton 215, 323
Rubinstein, Arthur 108, 142, 151, 162, 334
Rubinstein, Nikolai 187
Rudersdorff, Erminia 201
Rumbeck, Countess 146
Saillot, Félicité 53
Saint-Cricq, Caroline de 45
Saint-Régeant, Pierre Robinault de 347
Saint-Saëns, Camille 54, 194, 215, 233, 295
Salerno-Sonnenberg, Nadja 295
Salieri, Antonio 128, 243, 355
Salomon, Johann Peter 59, 62
Sarasate, Pablo de 54
Sargent, Malcolm 330
Satie, Erik 10, 85, 172, 228, 283
Sax, Charles Joseph 306
Scarlatti, Domenico 56, 261
Scheel, Fritz 12
Schillinger, Frances 289

Schillinger, Joseph 289
Schmitt, Florent 17, 27
Schoenberg, Arnold 91, 197, 253, 336
Schubert, Franz 4, 26, 57, 99, 142, 206, 260
Schumann, Christiane 212
Schumann, Clara Wieck 1, 24, 124, 181-2, 274, 350, 353
Schumann, Felix 353
Schumann, Marie 274
Schumann, Robert 1, 24, 111, 124, 130, 142, 175, 181-2, 212, 274, 309, 318, 327, 336, 350, 353
Schumann-Heink, Ernestine 296
Schütz, Heinrich 234
Schwarzenberg, Prince 30
Scott, Cyril 40
Scott, Sir Walter 206
Scriabin, Alexander 33, 75, 130, 155
Scribe, Eugène 229
Sekerina, Natalya 33
Serkin, Rudolf 175
Shakespeare, William 21, 314, 334
Shaw, George Bernard 12
Shostakovich, Dmitri 119, 166, 188, 281
Sibelius, Jean 141, 156
Siloti, Alexander 311
Simrock, Friedrich August 356
Sinclair, Upton 319
Sitwell, Edith 15
Sitwell, Osbert 15
Sitwell, Sacheverell 209
Slonimsky, Nicholas 121
Smallens, Alexander 39
Smetana, Bedřich 103
Smith, Cyril 36
Sollertinsky, Ivan Ivanovich 166
Solti, Georg 80
Sousa, John Philip 13
Spalding, Albert 54
Spohr, Louis 78, 223

Spontini, Gaspare 346
Staden, Hans 27
Stanford, Charles Villiers 16, 170, 320-1
Stark, John 331
Starker, Janos 220
Stasov, Vladimir 99
Stead, W.T. 149
Stein, Gertrude 39
Stendhal 11
Stephanie, Gottlieb 304
Stern, Isaac 34, 213
Stoeckel, Carl 156
Stokowski, Leopold 57, 157, 364
Strack, Joseph von 304
Straus, Oscar 345
Strauss, Johann, Jr. 31
Strauss, Johann, Sr. 26, 30, 31
Strauss, Richard 106, 214, 269, 313, 318, 357
Stravinsky, Igor 17, 71, 91, 96, 142, 152, 173, 282
Strecker, Willy 277
Stuart, Anne Hyde, Duchess of York 366
Stuart, James, Duke of York 366
Sudlow, Henry 203
Sullivan, Arthur 177, 322
Sutro, Ottilie 364
Sutro, Rose 364
Svendsen, Johan 43, 74
Swieten, Gottfried, Baron van 146
Swift, Jonathan 29
Szell, George 48
Szymanowski, Karel 108, 273
Taneyev, Sergei 311
Tasso, Torquato 66
Tauber, Richard 271
Tavener, John 198
Taverner, John 19
Taylor, Deems 12
Tchaikovsky, Modest 311
Tchaikovsky, Peter 141, 174, 183, 211, 311, 343

Te Kanawa, Kiri 266
Tertis, Lionel 277
Thalberg, Sigismond 35
Thomas, Ambroise 13, 233
Thomas, Theodore 122, 280, 354
Thompson. Frederick 294
Thomson, Virgil 39, 101
Thorp, Angelina Chapman 110
Thun, Countess Wilhelmine 146, 359
Thurber, Jeanette 270
Tiomkin, Dimitri 288
Toscanini, Arturo 287, 324
Toulemon, Elizabeth 172
Tovey, Donald Francis 277
Treigle, Norman 266
Tucker, Richard 38
Twining, Nathan 364
Uffenbach, Johann Friedrich Armand von 23
Uhlig, Theodor 264
Ullmann, Bernard 309
Umlauf, Ignaz 304
Valletti, Cesare 38
Van Hise, Charles 245
Varesco, Father Giovanni Battista 128
Varèse, Edgar 20
Varèse, Louise 20
Varèse, Suzanne Bing 20
Varian, John 86
Variani, Madame (soprano) 84
Vasselli, Antonio 169
Vatelot, Etienne 34
Vaughan Williams, Ralph 16, 219, 258
Verdi, Giuseppe 21, 51, 179, 239, 298, 314, 348
Victoria, Queen 30, 35, 279
Villa-Lobos, Heitor 27
Villiers, George, Second Duke of Buckingham 366
Villiers, George, Fourth Earl of Clarendon 349

Villiers, Mary Fairfax, Duchess of Buckingham 366
Vitarelli, Zenobio 49
Vivaldi, Antonio 23, 291, 365
Volkov, Solomon 152
Von Meck, Nadezhda 211, 343
Von Strack 304
Wagner, Cosima 37, 214
Wagner, Minna 216
Wagner, Richard 13, 37, 88, 96, 122, 141, 154, 167, 170, 177, 185, 194, 202, 214, 216, 221, 222, 226, 254, 264, 306, 318, 324, 339, 343, 351
Wagner, Siegfried 214
Waldstadten, Baroness von 276, 304
Waldteufel, Emil 349
Walker, Joseph C. 77
Wallis, Hal 313
Walter, Bruno 93, 318, 337
Walton, William 15, 195, 277
Warren, Leonard 38
Washington, George 186
Weber Carl Maria von 98, 102, 176, 230, 242, 339
Webern, Anton von 91, 197, 336
Weill, Kurt 244, 269
Weiner, Leo 135
Welles, Orson 101
Wesley, Samuel 97
Wiessenwolf, Countess 206
Whiteman, Paul 289
Whiting, Arthur 247
Wieck, Friedrich 181, 182
Wieniawski, Henri 187
Wilde, Oscar 199
Wilhelm Ernst, Duke 285
William III, King 272
Wilson, Woodrow 316
Wögerer, Viktor 271
Wolf, Hugo 202
Wolff, Pierre 98
Wolsey, Thomas 19

Wood, Henry 89, 90, 205, 252
Woolf, Virginia 15
Young, Cecilia 118
Ysäye, Eugène 132
Zamboni, Luigi 49
Zehetmair, Thomas 46
Zelter, Carl Friedrich 70

Zemlinsky, Alexander von 91, 336
Zimbalist, Efrem 218
Zimmer, Rudolph 333
Zirato, Bruno 318

Norman Gilliland has been a weekday voice of classical music broadcasts since 1977, first in Gainesville, Florida, and, since 1983, on Wisconsin Public Radio, where he also hosts and produces *Old-Time Radio Drama* and *University of the Air* and reads for *Chapter A Day*.

His 2002 book *Grace Notes for a Year* became the basis of daily broadcasts over public radio stations around the country. His award-winning historical novel *Sand Mansions* was published in 2005. In 2006 he and Old English scholar Dick Ringler produced the first full-cast audio version of the complete *Beowulf*.

He was one of seven cast members in the film *A Note of Triumph: The Golden Age of Norman Corwin*, which won the Oscar for Best Short Documentary in 2006. He and his wife Amanda have two grown sons, Jordan and Ross. They live in Middleton, Wisconsin.

Introduction

Genuinely funny people are hard to find. Some people are funny once in a while. Some are funny without meaning to be. A few work hard at it. But the naturally spontaneously funny person is a rare find. Such a person is Frances Weaver.

Ten years ago I was sitting in front of a dais waiting to be introduced as the director of a series of fiction workshops for the International Women's Writing Guild. A woman dressed in a rather tattered teeshirt and a skirt that had obviously seen hard service came up and sat down beside me. She was carrying a large bag with sticks and strange paper bulging out. The rest of us were gussied up to look professional on this Friday evening, and I thought perhaps this woman didn't realize that the seats at the front of the auditorium had been set aside for the workshop leaders. As tactfully as possible I tried to explain she was in the wrong seat, that she belonged back in the audience. I got a Frances Weaver smile. "I'm the kite lady," she said. "This is what kitefliers wear."

But the writing of Frances Weaver is far more than pleasant pastime reading: in every column Fran skewers the is from the ought. That is, she shows us that our expectations almost never match our hopes for the dramas in everyday existence. True comedy tells us that life is difficult and quirky, but that the salvation and safety of endurance is built on being able to laugh at how ridiculous our actions are.

Laughter is the magic medicine of survival, and we treasure those who measure out the medicine. That they are few and far between doubles the pleasure we feel in finding a genuine surgeon for the spirit. In the columns collected here there are massive doses of wit and wisdom. I recommend a column every morning before breakfast and every night before bed.

Jean Rikhof

CONTENTS

What's a Kiteflying Widowed Grandmother Doing Writing a
Weekly Newspaper Column? 7
College Prep 9
Now Where...??? 11
What Was the Tax on Mine? 13
Remember the Fat Guy? 15
"When in the Course of Human Events . . ." 17
Tethered Flight 18
Photos 19
The Late Mrs. Weaver 21
Happy Holidays, Dear Friends 23
Territorial Dispute 25
Just a Bag of Peanuts 27
The Disruptive Casting Agency 29
"Memories, Memories . . ." 31
At Last, Someone to Watch Over Me 33
Somebody's Lines are Crossed 35
Moving Conversation 37
The Rover Girls on Topless Rhodes 39
Midnight at Marmaris 41
Will the Real Cary Grant . . .? 43
Whatever Happened to Roseland? 45
Sad Sonnet for Senior Singles 45
Adirondack Equinox 46
Off Season 46
Second Season 46
Beulahland 46
Let's Clean Up the Soaps 47
"Wilt Thou Take This?" 49
China: Wingding Dynasty? 51
Chinese Fire Drill? 53
Out of a Sow's Ear, Indeed! 55
A Study of Trauma—in Cats 57
Around the World Come Hell or High Water 59
You Wanta See My WHAT??? 61

Just Drop It! 63
Get Up Off the Grass!!! 65
There Goes All the Good Stuff 67
The Merry Month 69
I Called You Grandma 71
American Gothic 72
Social Success 73
"Last Week on Number Four . . ." 75
Verbal Shorthand 77
And Then Came the Saxons 79
One of the Sights in Our Nation's Capitol 81
God Help the Queen 83
Just Give Me a Six-pack 85
Poopsie's Pet 87
All I Want Is An Atlatl 89
In the Wake of a Duck 91
Please Sign Your Name 93
Weaver's Ocean Guide to Cruising Birds 95
Tales of the South Pacific I 97
Who Will Star? 99
Are You Sure I Can't Take It with Me? 101
Good Mornin' America, How Are Ya'? 103
Did You By Any Chance See a Schnauzer? 105
Vesta 107

What's a Kiteflying Widowed Grandmother Doing Writing a Weekly Newspaper Column?

What's a wandering widow from a little mining town in the West doing in a space like this—on the features page of *The Saratogian?*

Such a question is intensely interesting to me, since I ask it about myself. There is a certain cockeyed logic to the answer; it's almost a full-circle story: My picture has appeared on these pages once before—in 1978, my first year as a kiteflier-in-residence for the Conference of Women Writers at Skidmore.

Being a kiteflier-in-residence is a relatively rare occupation, so I was interviewed and photographed as the kiteflying grandmother—local curiosity of the week—twelve years ago. That was the beginning of my writing career and my first trip to upstate New York. Like most Westerners, I pictured New York as one giant slab of asphalt. Saratoga Springs and the Skidmore campus were a new world, and I was entranced.

Two years and several *Vogue* articles later I was suddenly a widow with grown children, time on my hands, choices to make, and a point to prove. I have long been convinced that older women who find themselves bored or lonely have mainly themselves to blame—particularly those who, like me, had stuck to the traditional housewife role. A woman owes it to herself, I insisted, to develop new skills, expand interests, and broaden her own horizons in preparation for refurbishing the empty nest. I even made speeches to ladies' groups: "A woman who has no interests of her own is of no interest to anyone else," and so forth. I heard myself use phrases like, ". . .avoid stagnation of middle years." A lot of smart talk.

In 1980, Someone Up There called my bluff: "If women in their fifties and sixties can do so much, let's see you prove it!"

So here I am, happily writing columns for the Pueblo, Colo., *Chieftain* and for this newspaper in my adopted home base of the Adirondacks. The first step was to locate myself, part-time, in this area. Nobody in my hometown was ready to believe I was dedicating my life entirely to writing. Not at my age. Certainly, I had time to play bridge, run committees, make jelly for bazaars, fly kites, and be the "mayor" of Beulah as I always had done.

7

A return to college was the only answer. My bachelor's degree was almost 40 years old. Time for an overhaul. Even my mother understood my moving away to go to college. I chose Adirondack Community College.

My youngest grandchild and I started school on the same day—kindergarten and college. She's halfway through seventh grade and I'm not a sophomore yet, but that's all right. I've studied creative writing with Jean Rikhoff, taken anthropology and Spanish, and have discovered column writing, which I enjoy.

The magic of the North Country has had its way with me. I now live half-time at Saratoga Springs and boast to the folks back home about the glories of SPAC, the Adirondacks, Lake George, and Ben and Jerry's French Vanilla.

A girl like me can have a good time in a space like this.

College Prep

I should have made a tape of the lecture I received on the eve of my departure for my second college career. When my number one son offered me a cup of coffee, ushered me to the big armchair in the living room, and said, "Mother, we need to have a talk with you," I was uneasy. Then the rest of them encircled me like wagons on the prairie preparing for an attack; three sons, two daughters-in-law, and five solemn grandchildren.

I shuddered.

"Tomorrow you will be heading east for college and we want you to realize . . ."

Heavens!

It was the complete spiel—College Prep 101. "Now remember the real reason for going to school. You're not there just to have a good time with all of your friends."

I was admonished about making full use of the opportunities of college life—spend a lot of the time in the library, and take courses which will be a challenge.

"Don't take the easy stuff, Mom, you're not really a dummy, you know."

Of course I was cautioned about getting too involved in extracurricular activities too soon. What was that supposed to mean? Wait until next fall too run for Homecoming Queen? I was too stunned to speak.

Then they started on the money. Surely I would need a carefully planned budget. Cafeteria food isn't all that bad. Used textbooks were good enough for my purposes—especially since I was already laying out out-of-state tuition. Credit cards were only for emergencies. Campus dress codes were explained: "Anything goes nowadays. Not like when you were at Kansas State. For Pete's sake, Mom, don't buy a new wardrobe; you have plenty of old stuff that's good enough."

So it went—warnings about keeping up with my homework, lectures about five-year goals and being the best of whatever I might choose to be. They stopped just short of reminding me about pregnancy.

I asked why they didn't give Sarah a lecture. She was starting school, too—kindergarten. My feeble attempt at humor was not amusing to them, but Sarah climbed into my lap. That

9

made us both feel better.

My daughters-in-law came to my rescue. "Just get off your mother's back. She's going to have a good time at Lake George." Their husbands glared.

I was delighted when it was finished. In all of the years of delivering these speeches to THEM, their father and I never knew they listened, let alone memorized what we had said. Now I was getting it back verbatim.

After thanking them politely for their concern, I did remark about how proud their dad would have been to hear them quoting him so accurately. Then I headed off to upstate New York to do exactly as I wanted to—just as they had done when they went to college.

NOW Where . . . . . .???

Eyeglasses, car keys, and my purse—in that order—are driving me around the bend. There are times when I yearn for the good old days when I could neither read nor drive, and could carry all the money I needed tied in a knot in the corner of my hankie. But that was more than fifty years ago. It's been downhill ever since.

Glasses are the worst—because of the unwelcome dependence, I suppose. At first it was pride. I was a closet spectacle-wearer and left them in dark corners. In order to avoid hooking eyeglasses over my nose and around my ears in public, I carried those clever folding half-glasses—with rhinestones, no less—for reading menus and price tags. Around the house I hunted franticly for the bifocals necessary for sewing, reading, and such humdrum activities.

Better-looking glasses were suggested by my husband, (whose glasses were NEVER lost because he kept a pair in every room of the house). I tried plastic rims, "wires", sun-darkening lenses, and designer frames, all to no avail. No matter how much my new pair might suit my personality or flatter the shape of my face, it still required a full blown safari before I could open the mail or dial the telephone. I need glasses that glow in the dark and have a beeper attached.

More eye make-up might have been the solution to looking better, but I couldn't see to put it on. Then when I peered at myself through glasses, the mess I'd made was atrocious, and amazingly hard to wash off.

My son Matthew, exasperated with my lost-glasses syndrome, asked me years ago: "Why don't you hang them around your neck on that old-lady chain Dad gave you?" He had answered his own question, of course.

But I am not alone here. Watch what happens in a group of women when someone brings out pictures of the new baby. With the precision of a ballet troupe, they reach for their glasses. Some even say, "Wait 'til I get my other glasses." That's even worse than I am.

The car keys and the purse are closely related, since the keys have a habit of descending immediately into the most

11

remote corner of my bag, covered by empty breath mint boxes and rumpled Kleenex. Since I have convinced myself that matching shoes and bags are no longer fashionable—and carry only one gray slouchpouch with everything but formal evening attire—I can usually find the car keys; if I can find the purse.

The hopelessness of my case is apparent, however. In despair one day, I announced to Matthew that I was going to get contact lenses. "Great idea, Mom. Go for it! Then you'll only lose them once!"

So I'll go on hunting for a good place to keep my glasses. Maybe I'd better just hang them on my nose and leave them there.

What Was the Tax on Mine?

Listen up, Ladies, we absolutely MUST do something about the way we handle the bill when we eat out in a group. Until we resolve that problem, we can never claim true equality.

Have you ever seen six men at a table in a restaurant saying, "Now Sam had the crab salad, and that was a dollar more than my turkey sandwich,"? Have you watched the glances become glares as waiters stand around waiting for us to find out if decaf costs the same as regular coffee?

Separate checks are out of the question in anyplace ritzier than fast food chains anymore. We women are going to have to cope with the situation. Until eight of us had dinner in a classy French restaurant in Boston, I was convinced that women traveling alone can handle any problem. My faith was shaken that night.

Three of us had no cocktails, although I had mineral water—which costs much less than a martini, of course. The price spread of the entrees on the menu was ten dollars. Salad was extra. So was soup. Not everyone had dessert, but we all enjoyed watching the waiter's expertise in preparing crepes suzette for two. When the check came, amounting to just a little less than the national debt, only one of our party knew the price of her dinner. She had chicken.

I had chosen the restaurant. I could jolly well handle the finances. Without delay. The waiter patiently brought the menus back and the recital began of who had what and how much was fifteen percent of that? Charging the whole mess on a card and leaving with some semblance of aplomb would have made matters worse—trying to split up the total depended on menu prices, and the menus were much too fancy to take with us.

Bills of all denominations landed in front of me with remarks like, "That should cover mine," but were shuffled in with other stacks of money. Eventually, we had rounded up more than necessary—fifteen percent is fifteen percent, and we were

13

not going to be gauche enough to over-tip; so we started handing one dollar bills back around the table, laughing like schoolgirls at the Fair.

Believe me, the NEXT time I have dinner out with a bunch of women, I will have a notebook and pencil at the ready. I will pass the notebook around the table as each person orders, asking her to record her name and the price of her meal. If necessary, I'll send it around again when dessert and coffee are ordered, or even the second glass of wine. Quietly. Then when I have to function as Troop Treasurer, I'll be ready . . . and so will my friends.

I hope I don't forget that. It's not a bad idea.

Remember the Fat Guy?

"Who was that big fat guy? The one without a name tag?"

"Beats me! He sure seemed to remember me, but I didn't recognize him. I thought you'd know."

"He grabbed my hand like we were long-lost buddies. Was he that fat when we were in school?"

"Well, I can't think of his name for the life of me. I'll go ask my wife. Maybe she'll . . ."

I listened to that conversation without a word because I knew who the fat guy was. He was my husband doing what he likes best: attending other people's class reunions. He loved to walk into a room filled with self-conscious, often pompous "boys of the old school"—all intent upon looking prosperous, young, and fashionably undernourished—all wearing name tags.

The routine was inevitable. John, (my husband the surgeon), called everyone by name (tag). The opening gambit was something like, "Sam! You haven't changed a bit! Looks like the world's treating you just fine!" To the women he always remarked, "You're even prettier than you were in school!" The replies were equally fatuous; everyone pretended to know him. They asked about his business and whether or not he had any grandchildren. His answers varied. He left a wake of startled faces, all whispering to each other, "Who was that fat guy?"

Such harmless intrusions whenever we happened to find a reunion in progress were far more entertaining than any of our own. We would have had to be slim and successful like the rest of our crowd there. We tried one medical school reunion—in Philadelphia in the sixties. I called one of the wives we had known during the school years—the forties—to ask if she would be wearing a long dress for the gala banquet. She snarled at me: "I won't be going to your blasted reunion. Maybe George will. He's living down the road from here with his new common-law wife. I don't give a hoot WHAT you wear!"

That's when John started going to reunions of strangers.

Since I have been a widow I still avoid class reunions but I did go with my sister to hers. That was interesting. The star of the weekend was a smart-looking blonde whom everyone agreed had been "Miss Dowdy of 1944" when last seen in the old home town. She had come all the way from Mem-

15

phis on the advice of her analyst—to rid herself of girlhood frustrations and get even, I suppose. She set out to divest herself of every adolescent neurosis known to popular or medical science by ripping her astonished classmates up one side and down the other. She must have had years of assertiveness training. Her life had been virtually ruined by that high school and the snooty Sub Deb Club. She had been angry about it for forty years, but she made up for the whole traumatic experience in two days. She left raving about having had a marvelous time.

Luckily, my husband never ran into her kind when he was gate-crashing. She would have ruined his whole evening.

When I hear old grads talking now about going to reunions, I'm sure someone, somewhere, is saying to his wife: "I wonder if that fat guy will be there?"

"When in the Course of Human Events . . ."
SEPTEMBER 1982

The others my age are all talking "Retire"

While I'm just getting a start

My friends are ready to hang it all up

And I'm just shifting from PARK

My family's all shouting, "Go after it, Mom,"

My mother says, "Why should you go?"

Back off a bit, Folks, let me find my own way

It's years since I've *wanted* to grow

I'm lucky as hell just to see the brass ring

To find a direction—a role—

A way to play catch-up now my other work's done

And I'm free to consider a goal

A room of my own, as Virginia Woolf said

Where I can be thinking aloud

While my whole world looks on as I seek my own place

I just hope to God they'll be proud

17

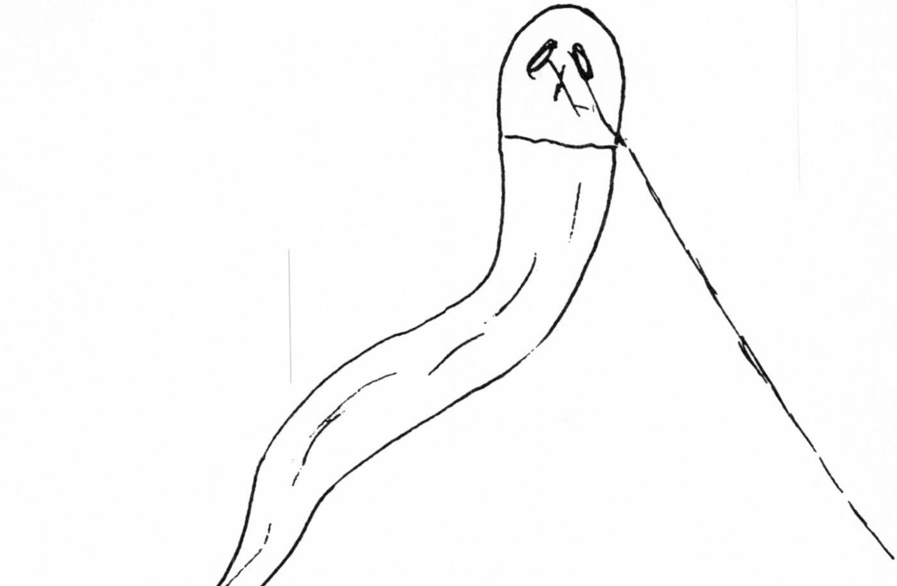

Tethered Flight

Fly!   you flippant fribbling dragons

Dance toward heaven   seek new heights

Flicker   flutter   float   you eagles

Effervescent in your flight

Soar above capricious breezes

Dart behind a low-slung cloud

Swoop!   you skittish sons of ether

Flitting   gliding   buoyant   proud

Steady as she blows, bright Phoenix

Skim above me   lively   free

Ascending as the sunlight beckons

Bait for angels   wait for me

Photos

My days as an enthusiastic photographer are numbered—not only by the two small albums of presentable pictures on my coffee table, but even more by the hundreds of yellow envelopes filled with rotten snapshots which are crowding me out of my closets. I am about to be inundated by unidentified, undated landscapes and the faces of smiling strangers.

I have unlabeled pictures of:

Long-forgotten Christmas pageants
A boy riding a headless, legless horse
Look-alike newborn babies, sleeping
People apparently flying kites
The back of my mother's head
My emu—sitting down
The 'Governor's National Oyster Shucking Championship Trophy' presented by St. Mary's Rotary Club wherever that might be
A starfish on a rock in front of somebody's bare feet
Antebellum mansions
Unrecognizable specks purported to be seals in Glacier Bay

All of these and more lurk in shoe boxes and grocery sacks; an ever-growing tidal wave of Kodak paper and Polaroid prints. Naturally, I have saved the negatives in case I need reprints.

The time has come to put this treasure trove to good use. First of all, I am going to include a snapshot with everything I mail in an envelope. Not just letters, although it is sure to be intensely interesting to my friends when I send a picture of two dogs with my thank-you notes. I intend to favor my creditors with a photo of Squirrel Creek or the Taos Pueblo when I pay my bills. My Christmas card list will have to be expanded enormously to get rid of these murky views of Chesapeake Bay and the Great Wall. I cannot simply throw them away.

Best of all, I'll have some more enlargements made. That's the most fun. I recommend it to all of my friends who share this problem: have some five-by-sevens made of your worst pictures, then show them to your guests with a straight face when the party seems to sag. They'll say insipid things like, "Oh, how nice. Is that a waterfall?" or "That baby looks just like your side of the family."

Titles add to the enjoyment of this game. My best are entitled "Two Cars and a Bush," "Man Feeding a Fish to a Bird" and "Asphalt in Portugal."

One word of warning. Do not decide to search through the boxes of yellow envelopes for material for a newspaper column.

You'll waste the whole day.

The Late Mrs. Weaver

I could be anyplace on time if I didn't have to take my body with me.

That statement is not original with me. The credit line belongs to a wise young woman named Candace, but it certainly is appropriate. Give me a deadline to write something or make an appointment for the phone—I'll be as dependable as a railroader's watch. Ask me to BE there and we both have a problem. It is somewhat cheering to know that other people are fighting this battle.

We latecomers have one common trait: no sense of the accumulation of time. It does add up. Before I start dressing to leave the house, the beds and dishes must be taken care of, naturally, AND the laundry put in the dryer and the newspapers neatened, if not thrown away. That might necessitate a trip to the trash barrel which leads in turn to hunting for a new liner for the wastebasket thence to straightening that shelf as long as the cabinet door is open—reminding me to check the paper towel supply—which often results mysteriously in a search for new bags for the vacuum cleaner and a trip to fill the bird feeder. The telephone rings. All of a sudden the forty minutes I had allotted for shampoo, shower, and turning myself into a raving beauty has disintegrated into a mad dash through the shower and make-do spritzes with the hair spray. I wind up poking myself in the eye with a mascara brush at a stoplight in the middle of town. Late again.

Had I not had a husband who was compulsively prompt, I would have missed most of my life. Now that getting me there is solely my concern, I keep trying. The best-laid plans, however . . .

Once in a while time works in my favor. This only encourages my bad habits. Case in point, one of my commuting trips from Denver to New York:

My planning had been flawless. In order to be on time without inconveniencing family or friends, I drove a rental car to Denver to spend the night at an airport hotel. I had an early flight—8:40 a.m.—to New York through Chicago. Up before six, I gave myself the entire going-to-the-city routine, had a leisurely breakfast, and returned the rental car without a hitch. THEN I checked my ticket. My flight had been 7:40.

I had misread the schedule. Story of my life: an hour late and a dollar short. I would miss the connecting flight to Albany and the limo to Lake George.

My rescue was undeserved. The agent at the United counter changed me to a direct flight to JFK. I ran to the departure gate just as the doors were closing and arrived in New York half-an-hour before my original flight through Chicago. Such providential accommodation of my sloppy behavior only makes me worse, of course.

How soon will the day arrive when I can say, "Just beam me up, George, I'll finish dressing when I get there"?

I'll probably miss it.

Happy Holidays, Dear Friends . . .

For years now, I have wanted to write an honest Christmas letter. The mailbox fills with accounts of the accomplishments of families I have not seen in years, and I have the urge to fight back.

Every roommate I had in college apparently populated the world with over-achievers from Merit Scholars to basketball heroes. The annual reports of their glories—some in verse, yet—read like certificates for the Medal of Honor:

"Peter has been promoted to first trumpet with the prestigious marching band which wins first division wherever they appear. Mary Jane is head dietician for the largest hospital west of any given point. George has been elected to his third term on the school board, and I was named Mrs. Homemaker of Northeast Kansas again."

Or they start name-dropping: "Our daughter Liz was head usher for the Perry Como concert at our Civic Center. He said she was the best he'd ever seen." Or, "Arnold Palmer played a full round at our club last summer, and admired our John's swing." Better yet, "Issac Stern complemented Lisa on her violin."

These are always accompanied by pictures of well-scrubbed perfect children whose smiles reinforce the perfection of the parents. One look tells you these youngsters never say a cross word or fail to practice their piano lessons.

My honest letter would start right out laying it on the line: "Well, we've made it through another year without suing each other or being asked to leave the neighborhood. The dogs have gotten along just fine, and—except for a couple of problems with driver's licenses—the kids are okay."

Once, in an effort to personalize the Christmas cards sent to out-of-town friends but having little to brag about, I had the brilliant idea of including something written by the children. This seemed to work well for other families. One son had produced an essay about Christmas which I thought was terrific—

funny, sensitive, just right to demonstrate the brilliance of my young Weavers. His teacher gave me the paper to have copies made. I mailed it with pride to some of those braggarts with their namby-pamby tap dancing offspring.

The enclosure was a great success. Comments came from near and far praising the genius of our clever son.

Last week he admitted to me, after more than twenty years, that he had "borrowed" that essay from *Mad Magazine*. I guess it's just as well I never sent any Christmas letters of my own.

 Territorial Dispute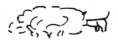

Grandchildren, diets, and dogs seem to be the most popular subjects of conversation in my circle—especially dogs. The older we get, the sillier some of us are about dogs, with good reason in most cases.

For at least thirty years our household was never without at least one dog; plus cats, rabbits, canaries, pigeons, parrots, goldfish, and even a monkey. I was never the pet lover, but I consider myself to be an expert on the subject of pet behavior.

A well-trained dog is a joy to behold. Watching the Englishwoman on PBS with her dog-training sessions is fun. The trainer has an admirable way of training the people while the dogs watch.

Sometimes that's the way it has to be—people must adapt their behavior to conform to the dog. I tried to explain that point to my cousin Pug the other day with doubtful results. Pug is a retired banker and an enthusiastic gardener. The flowers and vegetables in his yard are a sight of which he is justly proud. But Pug has a new dog, and this has him worried.

How can he reassure the new dog of his undying devotion and still keep the big-footed beast away from the sprouting bulbs and blooming begonias? His wife had suggested mothballs all over the yard, or an electric fence. Neither suited Pug. He needed advice.

My solution for him was simple enough. I have read about a scientist who had a research camp 'way out in the woods. He had trouble with wolves raising havoc with his campsite, knocking everything over and stealing his food. This very bright man convinced the wolves of his proprietary rights in his camping area by "marking" the trees and shrubbery on his chosen boundaries in the same manner used by the dogs and wolves. In other words, he used the old "If you can't whip 'em, join 'em," theory. The wolves marked THEIR boundaries. The man did just what the animals did around HIS compound. The wolves respected his claim to his own space, and left him alone. Ingenious. He even wrote a book about this discovery.

"So," I said to Pug—"Some dark night you can drink a lot of tea, then go out in your back yard and mark off what belongs to your flowers and what is available for the use of the dog. That would be better than yelling at the poor beast all summer, and probably more entertaining to the neighbors."

Somehow, Pug didn't think that was a really good idea. I had to agree it was a bit bizarre, but we have had many dogs at our house, and I never saw any other method which I could call one hundred percent effective. Pug's dog didn't seem to care one way or another.

Of course there is one conspicuous drawback: every time it rained . . . Back to the drawing board, dog-loving gardeners!

Just a Bag of Peanuts

"Why don't you write about packaging? If you're so hepped up about the problems of older women in today's world, why don't you attack those people who seal everything into plastic so tightly it hurts my hands to open the stuff? Write about this!"

The woman next door to me on the plane was furiously waving a bag of peanuts in my face. "I can't get this open. I really don't want peanuts, but it makes me furious to have to wrestle with this nasty little sack."

She was right. We all know it. Every day we struggle with heat-sealed, molded or crimped-up plastic packages before we can get to the batteries, the razor blades, the headache remedy or the salted peanuts. Every day, the problem seems more complex.

Opening anything is not my primary skill, anyway. I'm pretty good at jar lids, but I wish I had a nickel for every sardine or anchovy can I've opened with a pair of pliers because I broke off the flimsy key or the sappy flap of tin that refused to go in the slot. I have also been known to scatter laundry detergent all over the top of the machine while trying to PRESS HERE. And more milk has been lost at our house because of poorly-opened cartons than I care to admit. The days of the pickle barrel were better suited to my abilities.

Supposedly, new-fangled packages are making our life easier while cutting down on shoplifting, or some such fallacious reasoning. Freshness preservation is also listed as a big plus for all the vacuum-packing. Most of what I buy gets stale waiting for me to finish tearing apart the wrapping.

I'd like to watch one of those mechanical geniuses, the enthusiastic designers of the plastic ring carriers for soda pop, get one bottle out without shaking it up enough to make it spew all over the kitchen. Those old-fashioned cardboard carriers were good enough for me, but I suppose I'm showing my age when I say that.

The woman beside me on the plane had a lot more to say about today's maniacal packaging, but our conversation was interrupted by the flight attendant serving lunch. While trying to extricate her silverware and napkin from the plastic cocoon, tear the top of the tiny jam cup, split open the foil packet of salad dressing, and shake salt from a crushed mini-shaker, my seatmate seemed close to tears.

"See what I mean?"

I nodded and tried to help her with the pepper.

The Disruptive Casting Agency

Not everyone knows about the top-secret Disruptive Casting Agency. I verified its existence only recently, so I feel obligated to spread the word about this insidious organization to the unsuspecting public.

My discovery was made during a week-long seminar— "Irresistible Magazine Writing"—at the Smithsonian. Five minutes after the beginning of the first session a distinguished-looking, balding man in a three-piece suit interrupted Edwards Park's opening remarks. "I wish to question the title of the seminar."

Mr. Park was startled. (Magazine writers do not wear three-piece suits to seminars or workshops.) He stared at the interrupter. "What do you wish to question?"

"Just what is this supposed to mean? Are we to understand the magazine is irresistible, or the writing?"

"Well, I didn't choose that title myself . . ." The extraordinarily articulate Edwards Park was stammering.

"Let's get this straight. I am not a professional writer. I certainly don't need the money. I happen to be a retired attorney. My background is the precise use of the language . . ."

That went on for a week.

The rest of us were furious. Every hour on the hour this person would demand attention, disrupting lectures or discussion. His preface was always the same: "With my background in the legal profession, as an attorney . . ."

When I complained bitterly, my friend Dell explained: "That man was sent from Disruptive Casting. I have one of those same jerks in my crafts class—always telling the teacher how to do everything. Last week there was one of their women in line at my supermarket; she kept running back down the aisle for 'little things' then couldn't find her coupons. They're all over. It's big business."

It's true. I'm sure of that.

Somewhere out there is an office where abrasive people report for work every morning. A brawny woman in a Cecil B. DeMille outfit waves a riding crop and assigns jobs. "Whitsworth, you go to the historic preservation tours and talk about your ancestors. Gigi, you show up late at the French cooking class. Marvin, you and Shirley go to the movies— explain the story in detail and tell her how it's going to end.

Gonzales, you go to Spanish 101 and talk fast."

You'll find them everywhere.

Remember the homey-looking woman in the waiting room of the pediatrician's office whose kids had runny noses and ran wild while she diagnosed every other child in the place?

Or the man with the big voice explaining the menu in a Chinese restaurant?

Child stars from the agency are labelled "gifted" and sent off to drive each other crazy.

The Disruptive Casting Agency operates world-wide. Now that your awareness has been aroused, you will be able to identify more and more of their employees.

I'll bet I could get a job there myself.

"Memories, Memories . . ."

Experts on public television have been exploring and explaining the brain this season. This is intensely interesting to me—particularly the study of memory. However, I seem to have missed that part of the series. Forgot to watch it.

That's the story of my life. Memory has always been a problem to me—not memorizing, just memory. In my brain, at least, there's a difference. (I don't know what the experts said on the show, of course.) As a child I could memorize almost anything easily but I could not remember to wear my "leggings" home from school in the snow.

Creeping senility just makes it worse. Today I can recite the "Face on the Barroom Floor," supply the lyrics to any song popular before the sixties, list the books of the Old and New Testaments in order, get through most of the Morse Code, identify the leaf of the Japanese gingko tree, and win my share of Trivial Pursuit games; but I seldom remember to run the dishwasher or buy toilet paper or put gas in the car.

Twenty years ago my husband tried to put the household on an even keel by mounting a "daily reminder" blackboard on the kitchen wall. I constantly forgot to buy chalk.

That was when I decided to buy a book to improve my memory. Therein lies a tale: The book, *Secrets of Mind Power* was advertised in an intellectual weekly newspaper from Dow-Jones. The ad promised I would, "Become a mental wizard in one evening," but it took me three weeks to remember to cut the order blank from the paper; another fortnight to send it in. My one evening turned into three months. It was worth it.

After reading—poring over—the book, I could recite any list of sixteen things. Not ten, not twenty-two, just sixteen. It was a matter of mental images and concentration. I also learned to use image association for instant recall of names. Wonderful.

Armed with my new talent, I sat through a meeting of volunteer trainees while speakers on various subjects were introduced, each explaining his own field. My friend Betty, next to me, said, "I'll never remember who all these people are or what they do."

I undoubtedly smiled condescendingly as I replied, "Oh,

Betty, it's easy. That's Mr. Nutter. He's in physical therapy. The redhead is Mrs. Sullivan—occupational therapy . . ." and on down the line without a hitch.

Betty was properly impressed. "HOW did you do THAT?"

"I have a marvelous new book which I've been studying and . . ."

"Sensational! I certainly need that! What's the name of the book? Who wrote it?"

Stupefied, I stared at her, my mind an absolute blank. "I'll call you when I get home—if I can find the book," was all I could say.

At Last, Someone to Watch Over Me

There's a new man in my life. We've been going around together for several months now, but I don't even know his name. I call him "Walter P." He hangs out somewhere behind the dashboard of my new talking Chrysler.

I've never known a man so helpful, attentive or courteous. Walter P. cares about me. He reminds me to fasten my seat belt. He tells me when I'm about to run out of gas. He is careful about my headlights being left on. He never lets me walk away without taking the keys with me.

When Walter P. is really happy he says, "All monitored systems are functioning." A man like that is enough to gladden the heart of any woman. Sometimes when I am driving alone, feeling a bit lonely, I slow down and open the door just to hear his voice. When he says, "A door is ajar," it brightens my day.

I have been tempted to test his serenity. Nothing seems to ruffle him when he says, "Your fuel supply is low." I'd like to run it completely out of gas to find out if he'll be angry. "Dammit, I told you you'd run out if you weren't careful," or something like that. Then he'd probably say, "Thank you." He says, "Thank you," a lot.

Voices in cars are a lot like voices in cash registers—very sure of themselves. There's never any room for argument, or discussion, even. One of my friends has a Datsun which came fully equipped with a sexy lady who speaks with a little Japanese accent. Walter P. has a good solid midwestern accent like Walter P. Chrysler—a good Kansas boy.

It would be fun to do some creative meddling with these voices in cars. I'd like to make a tape to slip into someone's new Toyota which would have more interesting questions and comments:

"Where do you think you're going in THAT outfit?"

"We must be in a real hurry. Late again?"

Or, "Can't you park any better than this? We're a good

three feet from the curb."

Walter P. would never talk like that to me, of course. He smooths my frazzled nerves with his milk-and-honey voice when the lid of the trunk is not tightly shut; then says, "Thank you," when I slam it down. I'm pretty sure it is he who turns on the interior lights when I start to get in and finds FM stations while I am driving across Iowa.

He's a nice guy. I'm lucky to have such a man in my life.

Somebody's Lines are Crossed

Every day I am more confused about AT&T. Do they want my business or don't they? Now I have a letter telling me to choose one long distant company—or else! That's a blow to someone who grew up depending on "Central." The attitude of the letter is "Don't call us . . ." So why are they still paying Cliff Robertson to tell me how wonderful they are?

Becoming a customer of New York Telephone is not unlike qualifying for a seat on the Stock Exchange. When I first moved to Lake George I went to the phone company office where the woman behind the counter directed me to a phone across the room. I could call her. She then proceeded to demand information about annual income, credit cards, and bank accounts. I pointed out the obvious fact that, armed with the numbers I had just given her, she could wipe me out in ten minutes on HER phone. That seemed to please her.

The matter of the deposit of two hundred dollars was then explained. "The money will be returned eventually. Meanwhile, the company pays ten percent."

"Wow. Ten percent is okay. Can I send FIVE hundred?"

"No."

While other would-be telephone-users waited in line behind me, I had to hear the entire spiel about call-forwarding and other enhancements to my miserable life. Of course they did not have the simple brown phone I wanted. Of course, I would stay at home waiting for the installer. Of course I would be responsible for . . . I offered to settle for two soup cans and a piece of string. After twenty minutes of the haggling, the disembodied voice said, "What was the last name again?"

"Weaver."

"Can you spell it?"

"Yes."

We both hung up.

Life with the Pine Drive Phone Company in Beulah, Colorado, is much simpler. Mr. Sellers—Joe Bell to Beulah folks—has owned the system for more than forty years. His customers are not always satisfied, but we all know where we stand. Telephone service in Beulah is basic—a bit erratic, but basic. When the lines are all hooked up and the switchboard is in

35

shape—that's it.

I did have one small complaint not too long ago; one-way phone service. Receiving—not sending. I could not call out. Mrs. Sellers was as patient as ever when I went to her office on her front porch to tell her my troubles: "So, folks can call you but you can't call them?"

"That's it."

"Well, half a loaf . . ."

Life with AT&T should be so simple!

Moving Conversation

Moving is a lot like making love:
1. You hope for satisfaction when it's over.
2. Experience is worth more than advice.
3. The less conversation, the better.

Anyone with any sense moves in secret. Try to get it done while your husband is at work, your mother is in Florida, and the bridge group is involved in a charity bazaar. Don't worry about the kids. They won't notice you're moving 'til they can't find their socks. By then you can have moved their treasures to Goodwill. If they are around when you are toting heavy boxes, they'll pretend not to see you.

Should someone find you unloading your station wagon at the back door of the new house, try delaying tactics: "I'd love your help, but I'm on my way to the hairdresser. Just came by to see if the water heater is working." Then drive around the block until the well-meaning assistant is out of sight. That is, unless she has a casserole in the back seat. In that case, let her in.

Most of the Little Helpers want nothing more than a close look at your new house and your Stuff. Once inside, it is immediately apparent that your best friend thought your old house was the dump of the world. "I wondered for years how you could put up with that kitchen. This will be easier for you to keep . . . nicer floors, and not so many steps. I mean, we're not getting any younger. This house will even be okay for you alone, won't it?" What is that supposed to mean?

Friends like this come in all colors and sizes, but in the moving-in situation, they have one line of dialogue. It never varies. "I'm GLAD to help you, Dear . . . where do you want THIS?" Generally, she calls to you in a beagle voice from two rooms away, where you cannot see "THIS" or have the foggiest idea what "THIS" is. But she's your friend. She keeps the dog when you want to leave town. You drop the china compote and rush to answer her query.

Everyone talks at once. One old friend usually stops by with a total stranger in her car . . . someone she just met at a luncheon who's new in town—going to be loads of fun. The newcomer is dressed to the nines. She might even be wearing gloves. This woman has been househunting all over town. "We looked at this house," she remarks softly, "but the construction is so poor . . ."

You realize your hands smell of ammonia and you left the plumber's friend in the middle of the bathroom floor.

When you are very nearly ready to dial 911 for emergency help in clearing out the bodies after the impending slaughter, you hear the inevitable topper: "Oh, I used to have one of THESE."

Just break out the gin bottle. It's the only way to shut them up.

The Rover Girls on Topless Rhodes

A couple of Gibson Girls in Gay Nineties bathing costumes would not have been any more conspicuous.

The sky was clear, the water an unbelievable sea green shading into deepest blue. Visible on the horizon was the mountainous coast of Turkey. In close-order rows along the beach were thousands of umbrellas and lounge chairs. And there we stood wearing our standard one-piece swim suits—two middle-aged women on a topless beach.

My friend the professor and I were on Rhodes—a stunning semi-tropical Greek Island which is the Mediterranean mecca for northern Europeans, mostly sun-worshipers. All day long they lie there grilling themselves to a golden turn clad in nothing more than a G-string. We were overdressed, to say the least. We might just as well have been wearing one-piece black woolen Jantzens with red diving girls on the skirts.

Maybe we would have looked a little better without the shoes. Hot sands and rocky beaches of other islands prompted us to sport Chinese slippers—the ones that look like "Mary Janes." The professor had her Gertrude Ederle swim cap, which didn't do a lot for the image, either.

One glance up and down the beach made it chillingly clear. We had the only covered bosoms on the whole beach, a beach that stretched for at least two miles.

In forty years of practice, my gynecologist did not examine as many bare breasts as we saw on that beach in one hour. Those sauna-weary Scandinavians are the least self-conscious people I have ever seen.

My first feeling was outrage: Have they no shame? Then I tried to be cosmopolitan—cultural folkways are of interest to world travelers, I told myself. Then I remembered a class in comparative anatomy, but it was nothing like those girls parading on the sand. When I spotted women my age and older who had also shed their modesty, I gave up. Too bad they didn't.

There are many expressions about being in the minority. "Bastard at a family reunion," and such. We felt that much out of place among those nearly-naked beauties, but we persevered, determined to get a tan. That out-of-place feeling paled soon afterward when we found ourselves a part of the backpack set; but that story will have to wait for another time.

Midnight at Marmaris

There is nothing like a night in a pension in Turkey to reinforce appreciation of the Good Life. My friend the professor and I learned that lesson the hard way—trying to be Mother Good Sport to a couple of backpackers.

"Now this is going to be fun. We can put up with anything for one night; and it's cute of these kids to invite us to team up with them—a real adventure." We kept telling each other such nonsense as our new friends led us to the rooms they had found in Marmaris, a minuscule seaport of the Aegean coast of Turkey. The bus to Ephesus was full, so we were spending the night.

Our first look at the chosen pension—double rooms with shower for three dollars—should have been enough; but the girl from Chicago had said, "There are a lot of steps," in a manner suggesting we oldsters might need assistance. That was a challenge not to be ignored.

The landlady was a delight, and beside herself with the prospect of four American guests. She ran ahead—up more steps—into Number Two, motioning the professor and me to follow. Number Two was a dingy green room with four cots, no rugs, three old bedspreads tacked up for curtains, a bare bulb hanging from exposed wiring in the middle of the ceiling, and a picture of Ataturk in one corner.

The professor stared at the four cots, then at the Danish boy who had become our fellow traveler. "Oh no, Danny! Not four to a room!"

"Paula and I will be next door. Don't worry."

To find the shower, we were led through Number One back outside, down the steps, thence into a concrete cave equipped with a shower head suspended from the ceiling not two inches from another bare bulb on an extension cord. Electrocution in a Turkish shower crossed my mind. The toilet was up on our floor past Number Three—the last room. It was a gem of modern Turkish plumbing: an indoor porcelain slit trench with a bucket.

It felt like camping, but we were tired enough to sleep.

I wakened, certain it was time to get up, and tiptoed to the bathroom to look at my watch. Ten minutes after twelve. I stole a sheet from Number One for a cover and went back

41

to bed. In another two weeks it was four-thirty, and the professor said she'd dreamed she was digging a bed for herself in some dirt. Wishful thinking.

As if cots made of cardboard and sand and chill breezes were not enough; there were the noises. One demented rooster crowed all night. Donkeys brayed. Dogs fought. There were bells and whistles and motorbikes. A constant drip filled the bucket by the toilet.

The next night we checked into the most expensive hotel in Kusadasi, Turkey—a medieval fortress of great beauty and charm and modern plumbing built to be a stop for caravans in the fifteenth century. No camel driver was ever happier to hit that place than we were.

Will the Real Cary Grant . . . ?

The name mentioned most often during games of Trivial Pursuit is Cary Grant. This is not a statistical revelation; it's my own observation. Shakespeare and Arnold Palmer come close seconds, but Cary Grant is most memorable, most mentionable in the all-purpose and silver screen versions of the game, anyway. Among players of all ages, ahead of John Wayne, Gary Cooper, even Paul Newman or Robert Redford, Cary Grant is most-guessed and precipitates the most conversations.

Perhaps I simply notice his name more often than other actor's because this is almost painful to me. I'd hate to be a name-dropping bore, but I do have a Cary Grant story. It's all I can do to keep from telling it ten times during every evening. I bite my tongue a lot.

Cary Grant, his gorgeous young wife and I took a cruise together—the three of us and five or six hundred other passengers. Unlike many celebrity cruise-guests the Grants mingled with their fellow travelers and took an active part in shipboard life: sing-alongs around the piano and all that. They even played bingo and took dance lessons.

You should see him. Even in the morning he's Cary Grant. The accent, the manner, the tone of voice, the charm never slips. He was nearly 80 then—in 1983. His figure was trim, his posture perfect. He was not cutesy smiley, just pleasant.

My kites interested him. I had several with me and collected more along the way from Hong Kong to Durban. One breezy day I was on the promenade deck at the stern of the ship messing with a Chinese kite. It was a silk phoenix bird which fluttered, soared, dipped and shuddered in the combination of cross-winds and hot air from the ships engines. I would launch the kite on the port side trying to keep clear of railings, deck chairs and a few passengers. That feisty devil of a kite would dance around where I wanted him for a few minutes, dive dangerously close to the water, then invariably fly toward the center of the deck, flirting with the flagpole. For two hours or more I stayed there totally absorbed in the air currents, the challenge of the unruly kite, the varying tugs on the line. I never let it out more than two hundred feet and had a marvelous time.

Once in a while I looked back toward the upper decks

of the ship and noticed a couple leaning against the rail on the highest passenger deck. They waved at me, the stunning girl and the tanned, elegant man with snow-white hair and black-rimmed glasses. I waved back.

That evening, Cary Grant stopped at my table in the dining room. "You had a marvelous duel with that kite today. Barbara and I were fascinated watching you."

Now THAT has to be the Switch of the Century: Cary Grant was watching ME.

ARTHUR MURRAY STUDIO

Whatever Happened to Roseland?

Two nifties
Youthful fifties
Available

Superior foxtrot

Calls answered any hour
Transportation provided

Sad Sonnet for Senior Singles

My friend and I would like to dance a bit
To snuggle close in some man's gentle arms
We'd love to hear some 1940's hits
We'll captivate our partners with our charms
We're willing to provide the transportation
We'll surely be the ones to buy the drinks
Our dancing will create a huge sensation
For the guy who finds it's later than he thinks
Our jitterbug will drive the fellows mad
We'll whirl across the floor with style and grace
The dance hall owners really will be glad
When we come in to liven up the place
Six foot or more will suit us fine for height
Come one, come all, the line forms on the right

Adirondack Equinox

Colors suspended
Silent   hovering   floating
They blossom in autumn
Balloons over Glens Falls
Seasonal blossoms
Like poinsettias
Easter lilies
Jack-o'-lanterns
A hundred balloons
Followed by a thousand poems

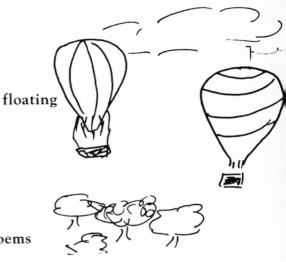

Off Season

Lake George in October
is an old man's town
They sit in the sun or
lean against expired parking meters
guarding closed shops
surveying empty streets
and the boatless lake—
talking about Florida

Second Season

Lake George in February
is the young men's town
bikes on the ice
cold parachute rides
sculpture in the snow
No one sitting in winter sun
The old men have gone—
to Florida

Beulahland

God created Beulah
so kids would have a place
to go fishing
all by themselves
without a license

46

Let's Clean Up the Soaps

Can you imagine Ma Perkins in bed with Shuffle?

Or Jack Armstrong involved in a paternity suit?

Or Helen Trent telling vicious lies after a plane crash on an unheard-of island which is suddenly over-run with outlaws, native girls, deadly enemies and the Coast Guard?

One day spent studying the soaps is enough to curl my hair. All the people look alike. They have the same trendy names on every channel—and now they all try to out-dress "Dynasty." Their family ties are so convoluted and intertwined, it's impossible to know who is the stepfather of whom, or whose mother used to be his aunt. Even a certified genealogist could not sort out the Hortons.

Writing for soaps is big business. As a writer, I took a look at the programs for a couple of days to catch up. My soap-watching time disappeared when the kids were old enough to be in school all day and I could get out of the house. I learned that soaps are written by teams and have enormous casts of characters. Each character cannot be on-screen every day, so the writers must remind the viewers through dialogue about plots and sub-plots, which makes for some pretty repetitive conversation, but does give the heroes a day off once in a while. The writers also need to thin the crowd to make way for more interesting personalities. This they accomplish with plane crashes, explosions, earthquakes, and shoves off of cliffs. Another good device is the gunshot which leaves the viewer guessing who survived. Such scenes are often followed by prolonged bouts of amnesia or flashbacks to happier days and other marriages.

If I were a cameraman, I'd die of embarrassment at some of those scenes.

Radio was different—in different days. Story lines were more simple because casts had to be small. How many people can crowd around two microphones? How many voices are THAT identifiable? The "new morality" makes the difference, too.

On radio, the most menacing situation faced by Mary Noble, Backstage Wife was the apparent theft of her diamond ring by a two-faced scoundrel called Armand.* Mary's husband's career on the stage might be ruined if news of the disappearance of the ring leaked out. That didn't make much sense, but Mary and Larry talked it over endlessly:

"I'm trying to help you in this crisis, Larry."

"I know, Mary, but you know how much this means to me."

"I'll stand by you, Larry."

"I know you will, Mary, and I love you for it."

Gone are those days of innocence. Today I suppose Amos might win a lottery and Andy would tie him up and hold him prisoner at the taxi company while Kingfish raped his wife and drugged the children. Then they would shoot each other. After that some grinning idiot of a woman would proclaim, "I feel good enough to fold the sheets."

I'm glad Ma Perkins never lived to endure television.

*Note: Two-faced scoundrels are STILL called Armand.

"Wilt Thou Take This?"

"I'm preparing a questionnaire for selecting my second wife. Any woman who wants to marry me will have to fill out an application."

A pompous little man actually said that to me. He even explained his method of screening applicants through his attorney's office. Something about a blind ad in only the best newspapers. I thought he was joking at first, but this jerk was serious. He even told me the first two questions: "How much money do you have?" and "Do you get seasick?" You can imagine the rest of the quiz.

Any woman desperate enough to fill in the blanks was also required to submit a complete medical record. Mr. Important, of course, had no intention of discussing his finances, politics, or previous sex life with the applicants. There would be no mention of HIS arthritis.

In spite of my disgust with his chauvinist attitude, I was forced to agree there is a need for older people contemplating marriage to settle some arguments before they start—establishing compatibility. After all, they won't have the first fifteen or twenty years to work out the kinks in their relationship like young marrieds can.

"Second marriage is the triumph of optimism over experience," I have read. That's not necessarily so, but after thirty-four years of the first go-round, deliver ME from any man who refuses to dance and/or play bridge—at least once in a while.

Retired couples, with so much togetherness, should have similar tastes in food, travel, and general interests. Congenial attitudes about money are essential, too. I wish now I had prepared a list of really important questions for that egomaniac:

Do you like casseroles? Brunches?

Do you consider eating out a last resort?

Is a fishing trip more important to you than a nice weekend at a fine hotel?

Do you object to pantyhose left overnight on the towel rack?

Have you ever folded sheets?

What do you feed your dog? Where does he sleep?

Will you eat leftovers? Omelets? Chinese food? Lime jello?

Did your first wife bake cookies? Make pasta? Iron?
Do you display family pictures in the living room?
Is your mother still living? Near here?
Do you watch "Masterpiece Theatre"? "Let's Make a Deal"?
Do you believe in rigid household budgets? Balancing bank
  statements to the penny?
Are you tolerant of occasional small overdrafts?
How long do you keep newspapers? Magazines? Letters?
Do you like long walks? Glenn Miller? Museums?
Perhaps I'll settle for a questionnaire for gigolos. That would
be much simpler—only a couple of questions.

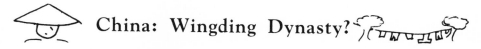

China: Wingding Dynasty?

I'm going back to China—for the same reason most tourists go to China these days—just to look at what's happening there. Much of our world I have not seen yet, but a return to China after four years seems more important than learning to get around in Paris or Brussels—or exploring the Outback of Australia. Those places will wait. China will not.

When I was there in 1981 Peking, (Beijing) was an austere city populated by millions of people in dark blue pajama-suits riding bicycles. I thought something was wrong with my Polaroid because the pictures were so drab. Then I realized there were no colors to photograph in Peking except for the neon sign at one restaurant. Peking was like a lithograph of other places; a gray, black and dirty white portrait of life. They tell me much of that feeling is changed now and one of the greatest changes is the color—the uniformity of dress of the people is disappearing. Does this indicate that Communist uniformity of thought—of life-style—is also on the way out?

Outside Peking in the communes we watched as many as fifty people with hoes, rakes, shovels and buckets working in fields of less than five acres. We saw grain thrown on the roads to be "threshed" by busses and trucks passing by. Primitive farming by our standards. One loudmouth Californian on our bus pontificated about such labor: "All they need here is one good tractor." So when you put one of these Chinamen/women on a tractor with a plow, what are the forty-nine other workers going to do? How're they gonna keep 'em down on the farm? Or will they start manufacturing Chinese Toyotas?

That's the fascination with China today. The government is trying to leapfrog that gigantic country with a billion people into the twentieth century. Already Communist restrictions on private ownership and profit-making are being relaxed. Can Communism survive, or will the entire nation be turned upside down? Will personal freedom follow Westernization? That's a staggering thought.

One of the delights of visiting Shanghai was an acupuncture-style massage administered by a grinning barber while I sat bolt-upright, fully-clothed, in a turn-of-the-century barber chair. Now that hotel has probably been replaced by an American-style tourist trap complete with sauna and hot tubs. Next will come Pizza Hut and K Mart.

A better life for the Chinese people is an admirable goal, of course. In the process, however, what happens to be venerable Chinese culture built on centuries of Oriental wisdom? China is the oldest continuous civilization in the world. Will the Chinese chuck it all in order to catch up with those of us who have learned to drive ourselves into neuroses surrounded by gadgets that buzz, ding, whirr, spin, and make funny pictures?

I'll let you know when I get back.

Chinese Fire Drill?

"Where did you go?" "Did you have a good time?"

That's all most people want to know about their friends' travels. Coming home filled with information to share with the home folks rarely makes any of us the life of the party. A funny story or two and a general description of the place will suffice. Describe getting lost in a strange city or a drunk falling down someplace, and you have their attention. Rhapsodize about the beauty of Japanese cherry trees in full bloom— yawns.

Case in point: Last summer I returned from Greece ready to discuss the early civilizations and archeological wonders. My friends asked, "How was the food?" Now I have returned from my second trip to China; same question, "How was the food?" Answer: "Chinese."

Doing my "homework" for this trip, I read a tiresome article in the *New Yorker* about the changes in China these days. One sentence stuck in my mind during my traveling from Hong Kong to Shanghai, to Xian, to Beijing, and points in between: "(The Chinese) . . . go at projects with determination and an astounding haste that frequently leads to poor planning and sloppy construction."

This is so true. Everywhere people are building fifteen- or twenty-story buildings but they are mixing the cement one wheel-barrow at a time. The quality control is shaky. So are the buildings.

The Chinese are so eager to establish cordiality with Westerners these days, the Chinese Tourist Service invited all of the passengers on our ship to dinner at the Great Hall of the People. This is an honor formerly reserved for heads of states; speeches, interpreters, Peking duck, presents, the full treatment. Our guides were relaxed, informative and friendly. The Chinese people are still curious about us, but exceedingly courteous.

We saw haphazard construction, back-breaking labor, and millions of bicycles. We saw laundry hanging everywhere. We saw a few doll-like children. We saw NO pregnant women, dogs, cats, birds, grass, or modern plumbing outside the newest hotels. Nowhere did we see farm machinery or private automobiles.

53

Relaxation of the Communist attitude toward private enterprise was in evidence. In Xian, women swarmed around us peddling quilted patchwork vests they had made. Fascinating. The vests will look strange on the streets of Saratoga Springs or Pueblo, but our tour group bought dozens of them at two dollars apiece— encouraging the women who could not make more than a dime an hour for their efforts.

I made a big speech about our being Ambassadors of Private Enterprise (beating the communist system), which I thought was excellent—a moving speech. My fellow traveler shook her head: "That kind of talk may be all right in China, but I'm damned if I'll go to Russia with you!"

Thanks for letting me tell you about it.

Out of a Sow's Ear, Indeed!

Well, I did it again, even though I swore I never would. I changed purses to go into town for lunch with some of my dressier friends. It seemed necessary at the time. My gray slouch pouch was not right at all with brown shoes. So I did it—dug out the old brown purse. The results were predictable: for days now I have been without my checkbook, carrying the wrong lipstick, unable to find my Mobil card.

I have a theory—as yet untested scientifically—that any woman asked to list the aggravations of her daily life will include purse, pocketbook, or handbag in the top ten. Most men would give handbags a high priority on their lists of frustrations with women. This does not include the backpack or African basket set. That's a sub-species unto itself.

The problems with purses are of two general categories: matching the rest of the outfit, especially shoes; and the sliding shoulder strap. Of least concern to the designers are such details as being able to find the car keys or having a make-up compartment long enough for a decent comb.

In most circles, matching handbags and shoes went out with hats and white gloves yet vestiges remain, especially when in the presence of older women. When necessary to match up, it is smart to transfer only essentials: wallet, checkbook, clean hankies, lipstick, comb, pen or pencil, driver's license and Blue Cross card. Invariably, something is lost in the shuffle and one card or another appears mysteriously between the seats of the car three weeks later.

My friend the professor has devoted approximately half of her life to the search of the perfect purse. She's still looking. Any bag big enough to hold everything weighs a ton and anything smaller than an old doughnut sifts to the bottom and stays there. Zipper compartments require two hands. Separate sections are helpful, but I invariably open the wrong one first. The only item I can always find in my purse, (any purse), is a Swiss Army knife which I have never used and cannot lose.

Which brings us to the slipping straps: Some coats or jackets having sloping shoulders—or I do. My posture is deteriorating at an alarming rate since most bags have these demonic conveniences. Catching a glimpse of myself in a store window, trudging along at an angle to stabilize my shoulder strap is a nightmare. Friends tell me they have the same problem—strangers need not say a word—we all walk alike.

Have you ever seen a woman in an airport with a magazine under one arm, her carry-on bag in one hand, tickets and boarding pass in the other hand, trying to look cool and sophisticated—a world traveler—while the strap of her ten pound handbag slides down to her elbow and the bag starts swinging against her knees as she struggles toward the boarding gate?

It was probably me.

A Study of Trauma—in Cats

"The three most perennially popular subjects currently to be found on the bedside tables of the reading public are golf, cats, and the Third Reich," according to Alan Coren. Consequently, here is the story of our Lola, the catatonic Siamese cat of Beulah.

Lola's purpose in life was to be a barn cat. At least, that was the purpose we had in mind when she was given to us.

Lola wanted something more out of life: soft sofas to lounge on, clean dishes of choice cat food served in the presence of the master, protection from the hurly-burly of the world of cats outside. Lola considered herself a lady. She made that very clear the first time she bolted from the scattered hay, stomping hooves, and rustic smells of the barn.

Whatever Lola wants . . .

She was a lady; except for her tendency to scratch incessantly—table legs, pillows, Oriental rugs, things like that. Since she refused to venture farther than ten feet from our front door, we had her de-clawed. After all, her protection was, (by her choice), our problem; and she needed protection from ME when the furniture began to show her marks.

That was the situation, a cat with no claws—about three years old—when Lola decided one day to climb a tree—a sapling just across Squirrel Creek from our terrace. She made it to the first crotch which was eight feet from the ground before she realized she could climb no higher in such a weak little tree, but lost her nerve about coming down when she looked at the ground. Lola could not get out of the tree.

She discovered that fact, then the large birds in the area sensed the truth of the matter and I found out about it when the magpies, the crows and the Stellar's jays joined forces and attacked their trapped enemy.

The caws, shrieks, and screeches of the birds were astonishing as they dived and whirled around Lola, crouched in that slingshot of a young tree without any leaves to shield her. When I rushed from the kitchen door to save her, waving a broom in the air and shouting, "Go away, you damn dumb birds!" they retreated to the surrounding pine trees, but never stopped the racket they were making. Alfred Hitchcock would have said, "I told you so!" Lola was too high for me to reach.

She didn't trust me enough to jump to me—she knew who had the claws removed—so I went back inside to call the volunteer fire department, and the attack resumed. In desperation, Lola fell out of the tree and disappeared.

Hours later, she came slinking to the door seeking shelter. Once inside, she raced upstairs and spent three days under the guestroom bed in a truly catatonic state. No water, no food, never shut her eyes.

It took weeks for Lola to recover from the bird attack. It was only tender loving rocking chair therapy from my neighbor, Neva Jo, that cured her—but she never, ever, went outside again.

Around the World Come Hell or High Water

People die on cruise ships. Passengers, I mean. The brochures never mention this, of course, but it is a fact of the Good Life: The longer the cruise, the older the crowd. Some of the fun-seeking oldsters just don't survive. My friend Sydney was on a long cruise last year when three passengers checked out before the end of the trip. One old guy had a heart attack in the pool and could not be revived. Another tumbled over the railing of the Main Staircase between Promenade and Atlantic decks and died. He appeared to have a drinking problem. The third death was a man who had the bad judgement to die in the wrong room. His wife was in the beauty salon at the time. The lady involved was embarrassed, to say the least, but the social staff took care of the matter with luxury cruise style; they put his clothes on him and carried him to another corridor before they notified his wife about the problem.

Cruise personnel are always thoroughly and efficiently trained for such emergencies. After all, what better way to go than in the lap of luxury? Deck chairs in the sun, dancing every night, excellent room service and entertainment. Mah jong and cribbage and bridge tournaments. Midnight buffets. Heaven.

On the most recent cruise I enjoyed, they tell me two people died. There was a lot of conversation on board about Mr. Morton after Mrs. Morton died from a bleeding ulcer—and no wonder.

The Mortons were traveling in real style. They had at least a suite, if not a penthouse suite. This means they had paid between forty and fifty thousand dollars per person for this ninety-day "vacation," but Mr. Morton had promised to take her around the world in style, and he meant it.

A helicopter took the ailing Mrs. Morton to Singapore just at six o'clock one Friday evening and the entire complement of passengers and crew were out on the decks to watch. The only person disturbed by the procedure with the helicopter was the rabbi because nobody came to six o'clock services— they were all out on deck. "Better they should be praying," he told me.

Two days later, the captain confirmed the latest shipboard rumor. Mrs. Morton had not survived, and Mr. Morton would be rejoining the ship at Sri Lanka. He had been flown to Singapore from Malaysia. Sympathy for the poor distraught man ran rampant.

Late one night, just out of Sri Lanka, we ran into poor Mr. Morton in the night club. He joined us gratefully for a drink. We talked. Rather, he talked. We listened. "I decided I'd just come on back and finish the trip," he said sadly. "I think they're gonna refund part of Margaret's fare . . . they Goddam well better."

We were all staring at him, I suppose. He could see the question in our eyes. "I had her cremated. Brought her back on board, too. She's in a nice Chinese jar on my dresser. After all . . . I promised her a trip around the world . . ."

I wonder if he took her to the Captain's Farewell Dinner.

You Wanta See My WHAT???

The old lady standing at the teller's window in the drive-in bank was close to apoplexy. She might just plain explode at any moment. Her hands shook. She glared at the fortyish woman behind the glass and hollered, "You wanta see my WHAT?"

"Your driver's license, Ma'am." The teller repeated for the third time.

"Just to cash this check?"

"For a check of this amount, that's the banks policy, Ma'am."

"Have you any idea how long I've been doing business with this blessed bank? For thirty years I've been . . . My husband was . . . My son was . . . I'm on the . . ." Sputtering out of control.

"Yes, Ma'am. I know. You have an old account number. We appreciate your patronage, but this is bank policy for this much cash."

That old lady stomped out of her car ready to bite somebody. You know the old lady: Me. How can this be happening, I fumed. After all these years. Then it dawned on me. I've been a fixture at that bank, not that poor gal in the drive-in teller's cage. Why in the world should she know me? The walls, the floors, the old pens on the customers' counters have been there all of my banking years. Not the people.

From the bank I made the rounds of the utility companies in Pueblo arranging new hookups for a condominium. None of those young clerks knew me either. Each required a deposit. "Now wait," I wanted to scream. "I'm an old-timer in this place."

This happens to most of us old-timers once in a while. Part of growing old gracefully is accepting the fact we've outlasted the bank tellers, retail clerks, and pharmacists who were our friends. The old gang has retired. These new folks don't know us even though we were doing business at that counter before they were born.

All of us are more comfortable being "waited on" by someone who knows our name. In one of the Pueblo supermarkets, there's a checkout clerk who was checking out my groceries before Matt was born. Matt is 27 now. I still like Connie to check out my groceries. She won't demand my driver's license.

But that's the exception which proves the rule.

According to behaviorist B. F. Skinner, old persons are often looked upon as crotchety, boastful, boring, demanding, arrogant. He claims we must all be on our guard not to fall in the same sort of behavior in our own senior years. Well, maybe nobody at his bank has asked to see B. F. Skinner's driver's license. Or maybe he's better at remembering that everyone he meets has not been around as long as he has.

That's what I'm going to try to do.

Just Drop It!

Child guidance experts and talk shows about family living are a bore for most women whose families are grown. We all did the best we could—read Dr. Spock and the *Better Homes and Gardens Baby Book*. Our children have reached maturity—more or less—in spite of the ever-changing ground rules for "personality development."

There was only one rule in our household that was never broken: Drop it. Variations abounded: Look at it and drop it. Read it and drop it. Wear it and drop it. There was some mystical penalty for putting anything back where you found it. My tirades—even the raving of their father—all failed in the end, but there was no end to the things they dropped.

At first it was the stuff shoved off the tray of the highchair or poked through the sides of the playpen; that sticky chain with the plastic discs, or half-eaten graham crackers, plus strings of beads crusted with mushy vanilla wafers . . . all on the floor.

That's to be expected, I thought.

Then it was broken Crayolas, shriveled apple cores in toy baskets, puzzle pieces, and wheels off little cars. We found most of the dropped things in those days by stepping on them.

They're just little kids, I kept telling myself.

In junior high, there was more importance to the routine. Homework, if finished, was dropped and covered by newspapers under the table in the family room. As they grew, they dropped bigger things—hammers, saws, twelve pound shot-put, garden rakes, wrenches. Or the items were smaller in size but greater in impact: eyeglasses, orthodontic retainers, contact lenses, and those infernal pins for inflating basketballs.

I found bottle caps in kitchen drawers but the opener in the basement. I fished hats and gloves from under beds, tennis shoes from the trunks of cars, ball gloves from broom closets, and jackets from the lost-and-found at Freed.

Being the family retriever was a nuisance, but I was in

great shape in those days because of the living room dash. I could clear debris from couches, tables, chairs, and the floor in less than twenty-seven seconds on the way to answer the doorbell.

Now when I visit second-generation Weaver families, I ring the bell and listen to the scurry through the house, and I hear those droppers yelling, "Pick that up!" Somehow that makes me feel good.

Get Up Off the Grass!!!

I watched the Denver Broncos play football in the snow, six inches of the stuff—slippery, wet, cold and dirty. Those players had reached a highpoint in their professional lives on Monday Night Football, and their uniforms were an absolute mess. I was sorry for their mothers.

The pros have adequate laundry facilities, I realize that—but those fellows played hundreds, maybe thousands, of hours of football before now. Most of their mothers had watched every minute. Whether in the stands in the near-blizzard or warm in front of the TV, those mothers could not help agonizing over those cold muddy pants. It becomes second nature.

One quarterback for the Washington Redskins has played professional football for nineteen years. Nineteen years! Can you imagine how pleased his mother is when he gets a game on artificial turf? The boys look so clean.

All sports are hard on mothers. In my opinion, football and wrestling are most difficult to watch. Swimming was easiest—the suits were not as much trouble. Baseball involves grass stains, but not as much mud. I always thought it would be nice if our sons would go into something dressier—like polo or riding to the hounds. Or maybe badminton.

Professional players have semi-pro mothers; no doubt about that. Those women have spent years driving Little League teams to the games, raising money for the soccer leagues, learning to call strikes and time swim meets. Fathers take part, of course, but they lean more toward advising the coaches.

How many times has each team-mother suffered through wishing her kid would tuck in his shirttail or pull up his socks? How often has she wanted to tell the coach to send her boy in—or take him out? How many detergents has she tested, spot removers has she used, only to see those white game pants covered with mud, dirt and grass stains five minutes into the first quarter?

In the sixties when the Centennial Bulldogs took to the field, I sat on Mothers' Row. We had a cheer of our own: "GET UP OFF THE GRASS!!" I don't recall their winning or losing many games. All I remember vividly was laundry tubs filled with Biz and bleach.

At least nobody was badly hurt.

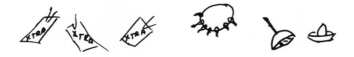

There Goes All the Good Stuff

Getting ready for a garage sale is bound to be a chore, but I am forced to face the prospect. The time has come to clear out my over-accumulation of Good Stuff. Parting with some of these treasures will be painful; nevertheless it's time to bite the bullet. I have run out of storage space and these things are much too valuable to throw away.

The most popular items in my sale will undoubtedly be the little brown envelopes marked, "EXTRA BUTTONS." I must have more than a hundred of those—each with a cunning little white string attached. None of these has ever been opened so the buttons are as good as new even though the dresses or blouses they matched hit the Goodwill sack years ago. They should bring a good price.

Another big seller will be the keys. I have keys—many on clever keyrings—which do not fit any lock in either of my houses. There are also Ford keys and Buick keys—neither of which I have owned for years. Someone ought to be able to use them. There are blue keys, red keys, luggage keys, padlock keys, skeleton keys—every kind except skate keys. Prospective buyers should be intensely interested in such a wide variety— real bargains, too.

On a larger table I will display my treasure trove of unfinished needlework. Any craft-crazy customer will go wild over the pillow cases with the adorable raccoons, (all embroidered except for the toenails and the berries on the bushes). The cross-stitch quilt might take some ingenuity to finish since I seem to have lost one of the side panels, but the pineapple design is tasteful and the sack of extra thread will come in handy. People who frequent garage sales are famous for "making do"; anyway.

I might have to sort out the yarn—some of it has tangled a bit—but I am not going to straighten out the patterns which my grandchildren played with. Each one of those pieces has a number on it. Caveat emptor on the old Simplicities. I'll just put all of the odd pattern pieces—mostly sleeves and facings—in a big box labeled: "Odds and Ends—Assorted Sizes."

Single earrings, clever T-shirts, Timex watches, potato mashers and apple peelers will round out the display of merchandise.

One more important point: I must remember to keep a careful record of who buys what at my sale—complete with addresses and phone numbers. I'll probably want to go to THEIR garage sales to buy back some of my stuff.

The Merry Month

"Grace, Grace, dressed in lace/ Went upstairs to powder her face/ How many boxes did she use?/ One, two, three..." That's a sure sign of spring—when jump rope rhymes start spinning in my head. Spring almost always meant a new jump rope when I was a kid. It certainly meant standing in a line on the playground at Roosevelt School waiting for my turn to jump. I always tried to get in line in front of Sadie Ann Gallee. She never missed, so the girls behind her never got a turn.

If you had rotten luck to be one of the rope-turners when Sadie Ann jumped, it was terrible. Your arm might fall off but she kept right on bouncing up and down—first on one foot, then both, then in a fancy skipping motion.

"Stella Stella, dressed in yella/ Went upstairs to kiss her fella . . ." Sadie Ann could jump more than two hundred kisses for Stella's fella while the rest of us stood around hoping she would accidentally hang herself. On and on she jumped through "Grace Grace" and "Stella Stella"—even "Teddy Bear, Teddy Bear"—twirling around, waving her arms and tossing her damnable cutsie curls until the bell rang. Then we'd all go in to school until recess when she'd come out and do it again. Still her turn.

Eventually jacks season began. That was better. The greatest day of the year was the day the sidewalk got warm enough to sit on. Hour after hour we sat crossed-legged over our game, bouncing an old golf ball through a set series of ever-more complicated maneuvers with the jacks. We played through "Commons," "Babes-in-baskets," "Ups," "Downs," 'til the fingernails of our right hands were filed in half. We raced back to school after lunch to get the sunniest spot on the sidewalk to continue the game.

That was grade school. Spring in junior high was even worse on the school grounds. We had girls' gym outside—an early form of adolescent torture—especially with the green rompers.

Those were the worst outfits anyone could have devised for females in puberty. My mother had looked better in her middy blouses. The rompers were seasick green. The material was some strange cotton which took forever to dry and needed ironing. The belts were always lost, and the legs of the one-piece button-front monstrosity had elastic which created a puffed effect mid-thigh. Add to this high-top tennis shoes and heavy white socks complete with name tapes; the outfit was garish. The greatest humiliation came when we had to play field hockey right under the windows of the study hall where the ninth grade boys were all watching. I have no idea how to play hockey. I endure the hour panic-stricken because the elastic might break in one leg of my rompers and make the ensemble even more devastating, one leg flapping in the breeze.

That was spring in the thirties, improved by hindsight, certainly. Some days I miss "Grace Grace" and "Stella Stella" but I don't miss Sadie Ann—or the rompers.

I Called You Grandma

"Hi, Grandma," blonde imp
parked beside the pickles
swinging sneakered feet
surveying the world
from his shopping cart
like one of my own kids
back home

"Hi, Grandma" bored with pickles
wanting a friend
to play his game
"I called you Grandma"
the clown the Big Kid

"Hey Mom, I called her Grandma
that lady see her"
Azure eyes followed me
as I found fancy mustard

"Hi, Grandma" broken record

"Hi, Kid
I called you "Kid""

At the check out
still I heard his laugh
How could he know
he'd made my day
Nicest thing that any kid could say.

American Gothic

Blest be!

I wish this young man hadn't borrowed money from my husband to pay off his mother's mortgage. Why couldn't he go to the bank like any self-respecting farm boy?

Now he can't pay the note and he has a hankerin' to go off to the city to make his fortune paintin' pictures of folks—but Henry wants payment for the hundred-dollar loan so this is what they settled on—Henry and me standin' out here in the sun having our picture painted.

Who on earth wants a picture of Henry and me?

Henry refused to put on his stiff collar so he'd look nice. Though I must say he did shave—even if it IS Thursday. Thank heaven for small favors. Course I really can't see how Henry looks since I have to stand here behind him.

Henry probably has that mean look in his eye—staring straight ahead like to see straight through the young fool while he messes around with his paints and that flimsy easel. Oh, I know that look all right.

What a lot of unnecessary commotion—and me with pickles to put down and tomatoes waitin' to be canned.

I have to give the young man credit, I guess—he IS tryin' to pay his honest debts—and he did help out his mother some.

But the pitchfork, Henry.

Why the pitchfork?

Social Success

I used to worry about being a social success as a single woman, particularly as a widow. Those fretful days are behind me know. I have discovered universal truths which can be distilled into a few simple rules to pass on to my peer group. For a mid-life single woman to be a social success, she should:

1. Be a good sport. Play ball with your host's dog and laugh merrily when he jumps on your new tweed skirt with muddy paws.

2. Never let bad weather interfere with a good time. So what if you have to picnic in the car? Tell jokes. Invent guessing games and do tricks with paper napkins.

3. Dress well—but never better than your hostess.

4. Be the life of the party—in a ladylike manner, of course. Learn new jokes of your own, three or four every week. Practice the punch lines at home. Try them out on your closest friend and the girl at the grocery check-out.

5. Stay informed about sports—at least enough to initiate a conversation. Then all you have to do is smile and nod. Any woman can get a man's attention by touching his sleeve and asking, "What do you think of the Broncos' chances?" or, "Are the Cubs really going to win the pennant?" Just be sure you have the right sport for the team name. Don't press your luck by naming home cities. Talking about Arnold Palmer is usually safe for beginners in this field.

6. Upon arrival, swear you don't mind riding in the back seat, cutting up salad, or sleeping on the couch. This creates good will.

7. Offer at least once every weekend to sit on the floor and play cards with small children. You might need to ask a grandchild to teach you games like, "Go Fish."

8. Flirt. Men expect it. But be very careful; just enough attention to the men to convince them you find them attractive, not enough to draw the wrath of over-protective wives. There are better places for arranging liaisons of any sort than your best friend's dinner table.

9. Be prepared. This applies especially for weekend visits. If you are used to a late-night snack, better carry along an apple or a candy bar to munch in your room. Should you wind up sharing bunk beds with a lippy six-year-old, you will

73

be compelled to share, then swear the kid to secrecy. Make a game of it if you can.

10. When departure time comes, don't mention the pain in your lower back or the creeping migraine. Stand tall and walk away with a noticeable spring in your step. Combine recollections of specific good times—laugh a lot on the way out—with hints of even more fun in the near future.

11. Write lots of thank-you notes, even if you had a miserable time. The next party might be better.

12. Tell yourself you are having a good time, and you will!

"Last Week on Number Four . . ."

It's childish, I suppose, but I just hate being left out; particularly being left out of the "in" crowd. That means the athletic types these days—the fitness nuts and the wilderness freaks—plus the sophisticates who lounge around the nineteenth hole or know all about what's going on at Keystone or Snowmass. I can't keep up with those folks: I'm too chicken to ski, too short-tempered to play golf, too impatient to fish, too unreliable to hunt, and too poor to have a boat. So what is left for my "set"? Simple. Look like a sport. Learn the lingo.

In another week or so, I can take the rack off my car. I don't have any skis. That's not necessary. If I remember the buzz words like "fresh powder," I can fake being a skier, so my skiing friends will at least speak to me. As soon as I get the rack off, it will be time for me to lie around in the backyard wearing one glove and some silly socks so I'll have golfer's tan. Then I'll change my vocabulary to "the back nine," or "the old number four." They won't worry about when I play, they'll at least say hello. I need that.

With the fitness crowd, it's easier. If you're like me, you never go anywhere without your support hose and your Adidas. That's the uniform of the day. Anyone can fake devotion to aerobic dancing in the aisles of the supermarket. Just do a catchy rhythmic reaching for the peanut butter, or point your toe for a little "out-in-out-in" when you pony past the green beans—then hum and jump around like you have an itch someplace when you get to the check out stand. Anyone in the know will become a kindred soul. It's even better if you do a few leg stretches pressing against the milk shelves, particularly if your cart is filled with sprouts, yogurt, and tofu, (which you plan to feed to your dog.)

There's one "in" group who is harder to fool. That's the Home Computer crowd. With them, your effort has to be concentrated. They speak their own language, as do fly fishermen or motorcycle riders, but they also ask searching questions for which a pretender has to be prepared, like: "How many K does your machine have?" or "Which word-processing software do you prefer?" Watching public television shows like "Bits and Bytes" for two weeks can usually solve these problems if you pay close attention; hard work but worth the effort in this day and age when cocktail party conversation has been known to turn into heated arguments about the relative merits of Apple Two and Commodore Sixty-Four.

One other trick I have learned about the "in" crowd which is worth passing along: Always be first to ask, "What have you been doing lately?" They'll be so interested in their own conversation, they won't notice you have been taking life easy, completely free of the stress and strain of competing on the slopes or the back nine—they WILL notice you look marvelous because of your relaxed life, and might hate you for it.

Verbal Shorthand

Returning to a college classroom after forty years is a mind-exploding adventure. In the past two years I have played "catch-up" with the subjects I had never taken time for before.

So far, my favorite course besides creative writing is cultural anthropology, which should be required for women over fifty seeking a new direction in life. I never knew it before, but anthropologists know a lot about our families, and the way we talk to each other.

Anthropologists—particularly linguists—have increased our awareness of the value and intricacies of language. Linguists write about the families of languages: Romance, Germanic, Slavic, etc. I am even more fascinated by the languages of families—yours and mine.

Families often have a special way of speaking to each other. Words carry expanded meanings, like, "Mother always said . . ."

This is a verbal shorthand. We use it in our family and it is amazingly efficient and effective. Verbal shorthand takes some of the wear and tear out of daily living and often injects some much-needed humor.

Our family had special meanings for words as I was growing up—cupcake, for instance. My sister Middy was always eager to help out when it was time to go to the grocery store. It did seem strange for a twelve-year-old who never volunteered to do anything else around the house. Mother figured it out—Middy was disappearing after returning from the store, and Mother found her behind the garage one day wolfing down some cupcakes she had bought for herself. She had a little treat on the side. To this day in my family, "cupcake" is a verb which means cheating just a little, taking more than your share.

We named our cat with verbal shorthand. She was supposed to be a barn cat, but established herself in the house with her air of superiority—no intention of dirtying herself with mice. Her name was Lola Whatever . . .

My husband John and I were in New Mexico vacationing with friends whom we had not seen for several years. All of us were talking at once, catching up on missed information and stories in mixed monologues, more talking than listening.

John signaled for silence.

"Since we all have so much to tell each other, there is a danger here of repeating the same stories or telling the same jokes. We need a signal to use in case we are repeating ourselves—something that means, 'You already told us that.'"

We all agreed. Friend Jim said, "What do you think we should say, John?"

"Shut up."

That worked just fine, and lived long after the vacation. As a matter of fact, it outlived John, so now I can say, "You know what John always said," and those friends, at least, know what I mean.

Verbal Shorthand. It happens in the best of families.

And Then Came the Saxons

Ask me anything. Go ahead. Ask me anything you've ever wanted to know about Chipping Norton or Whitney or Burford in the middle of the English countryside. Perhaps you'd prefer information about Great Tew—which almost fell down. Just ask. I'm your girl, believe me. After a fortnight, (I almost said, "two weeks,") of intensive study about Oxfordshire, I'm returning to Lake George knowing more than I ever wanted to know about such places—probably more than anyone around here wants to know. I have been saturated with rural England from pre-Roman times to today and I've enjoyed every minute of it.

Every American ought to know something first hand about our English roots if possible, I decided. That's why I signed up to go to Oxford with the Smithsonian Seminar, and opted for the course concentrating on the countryside—the life and history of the people who lived away from the cities like I do. I wanted to see thatched cottages, barns, villages, church-yards, and hedgerows. Plus arches, bridges, mullions and purlins.

With a dozen other American women I attended lectures and took copious notes. We snapped dozens of pictures of gargoyles and gables. We lunched in country pubs; all accompanied by enthusiastic historians and archeologists who were determined to teach us the differences in Roman and Norman structures and to bring alive the heritage the British cherish. I am not an Anglophile, but the experience was unforgettable.

One of our lecturers was John Rhodes, an unkempt-looking young man whose lectures were outstanding. Another was a serious young man named David Eddershaw who lived in Chipping Norton and made sense of the English pride in their countryside. They told me about the roughest part of their jobs as guardians of local history; the speeches they are expected to make to the Woman's Institute.

"The toughest part," claimed John, "is trying to keep the ladies awake. I just get started on some fascinating discourse and half of the audience nods off. Your group is more alert."

"True," said David. "I simply don't show slides anymore because the snoring gets so bad. If they DO stay awake, they start chatting with each other though, and that's worse."

"The only time they all shut up is when they force us

to judge their competitions." This was John's opinion. "Each meeting they have contest where they have arranged some little weeds and some moss in a pot and we have to say which is best. That's dangerous if you pick the wrong one. They stand around staring at you 'til you choose. Then when you've pointed to the winner they all yell at once, 'Oh dear, not Mrs. Johnson again!' Then they sing 'Jerusalem'. They always sing 'Jerusalem.'"

"Don't these ladies just love hearing more about your excavation and discoveries?" we asked.

"Oh heavens NO. They're bored to death with English history."

By now, you probably are, too.

One of the Sights in Our Nation's Capitol

Special communique from Washington, D.C.:

I saw him. And he saw me, no mistake about that. I was standing there minding my own business at the intersection in front of the Constitution Avenue entrance to the National Museum of Natural History. He was riding down the avenue in an extended Cadillac limo, headed for the National Gallery of Art.

I was alone. He was with a dozen or more cops on motorcycles, several carloads of Secret Service men, and Nancy.

Even at ten paces and thirty miles an hour, that presidential smile is extraordinary. His wave was downright enthusiastic. I waved giddily at him, of course. Then he beamed at me—standing there on the curb. Nancy didn't seem to notice but she probably has a lot on her mind.

What an addition for my Famous People page in my bulging scrapbook. I have already recorded the time when I shook hands with Will Rogers when I was five and the six-word conversation I had with Carry Grant. I wrote a long paragraph about taking a picture of the Pope since the snapshot needed explanation of the red speck in the sea of heads—to remind myself about the red biretta he wore that day.

But maybe I'd better put this recollection in the Washington pages. They're more interesting, and more important. Starting with the capitol, now half-hidden behind scaffolding, the Mall never fails to make me feel like a seventh-grader absolutely awed by the splendor of the buildings, the height of the Washington Monument, and the serenity of the reflecting pool in front of the Lincoln Memorial. Across the Tidal Basin, the Jefferson seems the classiest of all—perhaps because you can see straight through it, and he looks so dignified, so aware of architectural perfection. The newest, the Viet Nam Memorial, is stunning in its simplicity; astonishing in the silence of the people who walk slowly past the thousands of names inscribed there for posterity.

Here is one notation from the Washington pages in my scrapbook, when I was there last spring: Certainly we would visit the Iwo Jima monument. The morning—late May—was misty, cool, overcast. Those bronze Marines were dripping dark "sweat" from the fog, straining to force that flagpole into a rocky hilltop. On the terraces around their immortalized comrades real Marines, 1985 Marines, prepared for the Tuesday evening sunset formation. Drums and bugles. Files of bright young men crossing, strutting, tooting, marching, laughing, regrouping. My son the ex-Marine, his family, and I stood transfixed. "Stars and Stripes Forever" hit the air like WOW. We held hands and cried.

That's Washington. That's America.

God Help the Queen

I really felt sorry for the Queen at Andy's wedding. Here she was, beloved monarch of all she surveys—except for an egg-thrower in New Zealand—and her mother was glaring at her.

The Abbey was appropriately festive with flowers all over the place. Horses and carriages had arrived right on the dot. The guards had been properly lined up along the Mall. The clergy and guests were in their places. The singers knew the songs by heart. The Prince of Wales read from the Bible without a single mistake. Even the little kids were on their best behavior. Except for Princess Di's hat, which must of been borrowed from George Washington, everything I saw of the royal wedding on TV was just fine; an okay affair. But the Queen Mother was scowling at Her Majesty. Like she had a run in her stocking or her slip showed. Once a mother . . .

Can't you imagine a scene like this? Right after they all climbed down out of the Cinderella carriages, before they filed into the church, Queen Mum might have said something like, "Well, your father and I would never have invited Joan Rivers!"

All through the ceremony, the royal grandma watched the 60 plus Queen just in case she'd commit some faux pas which would embarrass her mother or the Empire. In that order.

Has Queen Elizabeth II ever felt like a real queen with her mother—an experienced queen—down the block at Clarence House keeping an eye on her? Is the older woman of this duo still pouting about India?

There's a message here for all of us who are mothers of middle age "children," even if we are not royals. The message is simple: Butt out. The marvels of medicine and our healthful life-styles are causing what I see as a longevity crisis. I use "crisis" in the Webster's definition of the word: "Turning point—a decisive time, stage, or event." My number one son looked as if he might faint when I suggested he might have a mother most of his entire life. Nobody wants to be mothered life-long. Nobody. We—especially widows—had better remember that. "Mother" can sound too much like "smother" sometimes.

Certainly we will always be a family; but we need a more equal footing than in years past. I have great respect for the opinions of my children—when I take the time to listen. Before our middle-age offspring weary of having us around, we'd better figure out how to make our own fun and balance our own checkbooks. We'd better work hard at keeping our noses out of their daily lives unless invited in. Next time you start to say, "Your father and I always . . ." bite your tongue, Lady. So will I. Those kids know better than we do about their fathers—and what we all used to do.

After all, during these same years when I've been learning so much, my kids have been wising up, too. I must remember they can't really be dummies. They have such a smart mother.

Just Give Me a Six-pack

Well, it's happened again. Another dream shattered. And this one hurts. I mean, this really hurts.

For years I have been clinging to the belief that I was overweight because of chocolate. My lifelong battle against obesity I have blamed on anything creamy or crunchy, nut-filled or smooth as silk, light or dark—even white—which slid across my palate and murmured "mmmm—chocolate" to my brain. One whiff from a newly opened box from Russel Stover could throw me into ecstasy which lasted as long as the candy did. Generally less than half an hour per pound.

My mother loves to tell about the time she and my dad brought a huge box of elegant chocolates when they visited John and me in Philadelphia. Within an hour the box was empty. I've tried for years to convince her that my husband ate most of that marvelous gift. She knows better. She also must know the guilt I feel about caramels, creamy centers, nougat, marshmallow Easter Eggs—even peanut clusters and covered raisins. But mostly Milky Ways. There's something about the way it lies there in your hand, promising to melt, which starts the magic. If nobody is watching, I often eat the nougat part first and save the caramel layer in one gooey limp slather of sinfulness—oh joy.

Admittedly, other treats are made from chocolate, often rivaling this miracle from Mars. Some of my friends are hooked on velvety dark mousses. Others prefer cakes or tortes. My buddy Regina remarked just the other day it's been years since she had a really good chocolate pie. People just don't seem to make it much anymore—the filling is nothing more than Jell-O pudding and the meringue tends to weep. I shared her concern even though pie has not been my chocolate of pref-erence. It's a worry.

Reflecting upon this new revelation that has shattered one

of the creeds of my life, I understand the hold chocolate has had on me. The first thing I wanted to cook was fudge—without nuts. During the war I suffered through eating runny Hershey's syrup on ice milk because the hot fudge and real ice cream had apparently gone to the boys in the trenches, along with sugar, ketchup, and butter. In those days it was all I could do to find a decent cup of cocoa.

Later in life my favorite after-dinner drink was a concoction of brandy, coffee, and chocolate ice cream. My French-chocolate mint pie was the talk of the neighborhood. When the children were little I always hid extra Easter eggs for myself. I stashed a supply to last through June.

Oh how I have loved chocolate. And it made me fat.

So what's the big disappointment? More than two months ago I was reborn into fitness. No more would I be dragging around twenty ugly pounds, I had "Bottomed out," as they say, on Milky Ways. Absolutely no more. I quit cold turkey, confident that fat would melt off my overladen frame like a you-know-what left in the Kansas sun on the fourth of July.

Ten weeks. I'm still fat as ever. It's just too much.

Poopsie's Pet

"Did you see that dog? He eats with a fork."

Finally I have seen them, the pet above all pets and the dog-lover whose boundless devotion exceeds all others. In a sweet-smelling, mouth-watering pastry shop/brasserie in Brussels, Belgium, I watched this couple. Fascinated.

My friend and I were wolfing down Belgium waffles. That's part of the compulsory gluttony while visiting this city of fine food. The waffle was perfection itself, buried under a mountain of fresh strawberries and whipped cream. We very nearly lost interest in our own gourmet experience however because of the lady seated next to us. We stared. You would, too.

This lovely lady was perfectly groomed, every shining silver hair brushed and coiffed. Her pearls and her becoming blue silk print dress were just right. This was a lady of quality, no doubt about that. Next to her on the velvet-padded seat was an ageing Pekinese. It's been years since I've seen a Pekinese— that pouting, peevish brown mop of a dog with the pushed-in face and snobbish air of superiority. This twosome carried on a conversation as they awaited their lunch. That is, the lady talked, the dog nodded indifferently, mildly amused by her little jokes. He never barked or made any effort to move away from the tasteful bowl of water which had been placed in front of him.

When their luncheon was served—fine crusty bread and a thinly sliced pâté lovingly prepared, delicately seasoned, the gracious lady cut dainty bites with her fork and fed them to the dog—with her fork. She ate the pâté too, perched on chunks of the bread. Not from the same fork, I am relieved to report. The Peke ate carefully, judging every mouthful; certainly not like some uncouth mutt scarfing down Alpo on the "Tonight Show." His smiling lady waited patiently between his bites— and hers—while he had a sip of water. She was his maid-servant. Obedient to his every whim.

We hear more all the time about pets and their importance in our ageing process, but the question here in this restaurant was clearly more than pet therapy. This appeared to be a total role reversal. That woman was her dog's pet. He allowed her to feed him and to make her little jokes, but he was in charge. He held the leash, so to speak. The dependence was astonishing, and sort of funny.

I asked to take a picture of this twosome, which pleased the old lady no end. The snapshot will be a real addition to my album of interesting moments along the way. The dog posed like some movie starlet, bored with adulation. His fashionable Belgian lady was delighted. We smiled at each other.

As my friend and I left the table the lady/pet was saying to her master/dog, "Will you say goodbye to the nice people from America? Say good-bye to Madame, Poopsie." Poopsie looked down his squashed nose at me, much too important to speak to tourists. So the lady said good-bye instead and I found myself praying that Poopsie outlasts the old lady, if only for a day or two.

All I Want Is An Atlatl

It's been a big week for the jay birds at Crow Canyon in southwest Colorado. Life might seem dull out there sometimes on those red sandstone mesas where scrub oak and piñon nuts are the real excitement—plus some rocks lying around where Indians used to live.

Perched on stubby branches, those piñon jays have had more than blue-gray juniper berries to keep them busy lately. They've been watching my Texas-style daughter and me crawling on hands and knees in the red dust, wiping sweaty brows and whooping, "WOW! Another flake!"

Not far away, acting far more grown-up, were my two 15 year-old grandsons filling wheelbarrows with sifted dirt, and paper bags with remnants of pottery a thousand years old. We have been on a dig, Folks, and a glorious time was had by all. For three years I have waited for those two boys to be 15 so we could join the Smithsonian Tour to Crow Canyon just to find out for ourselves what archeology is all about, particularly in our part of the world. "Hands on," Whitney called it, and he was right: hands and knees and elbows up to here in dirt, muddy wash water and artifacts.

There were 50 of us participating in the archeological experience. All sorts and conditions of men and women, and two teenagers. Only one or two of the crowd wanted to BE archeologists, the rest of us wanted to know what it felt like; why digging up those relics of the past is important at all. We figured it out by contact with the enthusiastic staff of professionals. Those people aren't studying things; they're studying people.

Our week was spent living in a brand-new Navajo-style hogan, eating camp-style cafeteria food, and listening to graduate school-style lectures. But that's where the style came to a screeching halt. The style of dress was nonexsistent; we were a motley crew. Everyone wore tee shirts that said something cute, shorts of varying lengths and bagginess, heavy socks and hiking boots or nine-pound brogans.

We completed the ensembles with sunglasses, bandanas, visored caps, and cotton gardening gloves. So garbed, we boarded antediluvian school buses and headed gleefully for our dig at Sand Canyon or Duckfoot. The return trip to the lodge was reminiscent of magpies discussing the day's take from campers at Mesa Verde.

We had instruction in pottery-making, weaving, and flintnapping. (That's the tedious process which turns a beautiful hunk of stone into a lethal weapon.) Learning to use these artifacts, as their inventors had long before any Europeans came to this continent, was an option which Jason and Whitney really liked. Especially spear-throwing with an ancient gismo called an "atlatl." They sailed that spear the length of a football field while the rest of us cheered happily.

This is high on my list of what-to-do-with-teenage-grandkids. We all had fun, and my two nearly-grown cherubs are the only sophomores I know who want an atlatl for Christmas.

In the Wake of a Duck

There's a very real danger in deciding you're a writer. That is, a full-time writer. It's like the cartoon of the two women at lunch. One is saying: "I've decided to marry George. I think there's a book in it." Writers run the risk on concentrating more on, "How shall I say this?" than, "How does it feel?"

Right this minute I'm floating. In an inflated 12-foot boat I am adrift in a shallow bay of Lake George. The backdrop is purple-mountains—quiet, soft Adirondack Mountains. Quiet.

There are mallards here moving across rusty-gold, maple-red or pine black-green reflections of October foliage. Ducks are gliding through white glimmers of trunks of birch trees on the surface of the lake. Eight or ten ducks are out today.

These ducks are busy bobbing for bugs on the water the way we used to bob for apples at Halloween parties. To win at apple-bobbing you really have to stick your neck out. Looks like it's the same for bug-bobbing.

On the other side, (starboard now as the breeze turns the boat), two gulls are paddling with all of the dignity any creature could muster under such circumstances: with cold wet feet; under surveillance by a goofy lady in a dinky boat. Gulls are choosier about bugs, it seems. These are bobbing only occasionally as a choice morsel lands nearby.

The Colorado-columbine blue of the sky, the hot sun, the jet trails spreading away into nothingness, floating leaves, crystal water, floating me—all adds up to a fine day.

Two crows are complaining to each other. She's probably nagging him for a boat like mine. Ducks have come closer now. I should have brought some bread. They're almost within touching distance. This is glorious. OH, what a world and how lucky I am to be here behind these eyes—inside this head. Floating.

Swimming ducks leave a miniature wake that spreads and fades as the jet trails do overhead. Their following ripples cast shadows through the clearest of water to the mossy bottom of the lake. I watch streams of light curling behind dark circles in widening patterns. Was it ever thus at Walden Pond?

It's okay to let it all end now, God. I've nothing more to ask. I've even gotten my money's worth out of this lousy boat.

Such beautiful prose, such inspired words. Carried away as I was with that masterpiece, I trotted back up to my kitchen to get the last of the raisin bread and my camera. Such serenity of nature, such purity of spirit should be recorded on film as well as distilled in my genius essay. The ducks swam courageously close, gobbling the raisin bread as I triumphantly clicked away, capturing the clarity of the lake, the silence of the moment.

At the developers I realized there was no film in the camera. And tomorrow will be cold. And the bread's gone.

Please Sign Your Name . . .

Go ahead. Make my day. Ask me to sign one of my books. After 60 years of being asked for autographs only at the gas station or when paying bills, I am ecstatic if anyone says, "Would you sign my book?" In the first place, I'm delighted they want whatever I write enough to buy the collection. That's a staggering experience. And autographs? Wow.

Celebrities on TV often complain about autograph-seekers, and I suppose it could get old; but those people have placed themselves in a public position, have accepted the admiration and support of those folks who want a signature. I want to say, "Look, Paul Newman, if your fans are such a bother, why don't you get another job? Go into some more private line of work. Be a spy. Nobody will pester you then."

Some politicians and barons of industry are almost as bad as entertainers about their demands for privacy after kicking and clawing their way into the public eye. They have been for years. I was reminded of that when I found my late husband's autograph book in the bottom of the desk drawer.

Do kids these days have autograph books? Mine never did, nor do the grandchildren. John's book, dated 1932, is stuffed with letters on tablet paper saying:

> Dear Mr. Smith,
>
> Please sign your name for my album. I am nine years old.
> Thank you,
> John L. Weaver
>
> Sign Here _____

Alfred E. Smith took time out from governing New York to write his name on his letter. Henry Ford didn't reply. FDR's private secretary, M.A. LeHand, sent the president's regrets on White House stationery. Herbert Hoover had earlier sent a fine card bearing his signature which is proudly pasted on these yellowed pages just in front of the card from Will Rogers. In this little book, even the scotch tape is antique. How times have changed the little things of our lives!

Glenn Cunningham wrote his name with a real flourish on one of the pages of the book, so John must have met him in person—probably at the KU Relays. One of the most surprising is the autograph of Ely Culbertson. Now why would a nine-year-old in 1933 want that signature? Senators Albert T. Reid and then-Congressman Frank Carlson obliged, as did the legendary Senator Arthur Capper of Kansas.

It's just a small faded book bound in green leather with black corners tooled with gold. We know more about that kid in Concordia, Kansas, ("Hoping you are a great athlete some day. [signed] All American Tackle, University of Pittsburgh, Mike Getto") than any biographer would tell us, and more about the world in the 30's just glancing through it.

I'd best put it away before I lose it.

Ah, autographs.

Weaver's Ocean Guide to Cruising Birds

The gannet is a spectacular bird, gliding over the waves at heights up to 50 feet, then plummeting like a pointed rock into the water to come up with a fish for dinner. Since Gannett is also the family name of the Saratogian, only spelled differently, I studied the behavior of these namesake birds while on my South Pacific cruise, and found them to be of great interest. In addition there were many other birds to watch, even on board the ship.

On any cruise ship there are at least five major species to be observed: the Boasters, the Whiners, the Socialites, the Dirvishes and the Laid-back Amiables. The Laid-back Amiables generally outnumber the other species but are less conspicuous because of their unruffled feathers.

Sub-species abound, particularly on a ship which offers fifty different activities daily, four or five bars and at least a dozen feeding times every day. Easiest to spot is the TWO-FISTED BARFLY. This percher stakes out a claim on the center stool of the most popular bar (usually aft, near the swimming pool), and stays in that spot for the duration. There is general disagreement about whether or not this bird ever sleeps. Apparently he never leaves his post, much like a male hummingbird guarding his sugar-water feeder. The call of the sub-species is easily recognized: "Set 'em up again, Dave," at frequent intervals.

Seldom seen at the bar is the GLASSY-EYED GLUTTON-BIRD. These gobblers spend every waking moment hovering over food—any food. Beginning with an early risers' breakfast, then a dining room breakfast, then the late-risers' breakfast, this bird follows this behavior pattern for 18 hours. He/she never misses tea, the boullion breaks, cake-decorating demonstrations or the midnight buffet. He/she waddles off the ship picking his teeth, burping and muttering about getting his money's worth.

More strenuous are the DEEP-BREATHING DECK-STRID-ERS. These on-board athletes log five or ten miles around the deck, counting laps. There is a congenital fear of smiling among these birds.

Less dedicated to exercise are the EIGHT-O-CLOCK GROAN-ERS. This is my crowd. We commiserate, bending and stretching while the macho young man who is our leader shakes his head and sighs.

GOLDEN-GRILLED SUNCATCHERS are as immobile as the DECK-STRIDERS are active. Should they move too much, they'll slide off the afterdeck; they're so drenched in oil.

BEAGLE-VOICED BITCHERS are few in number but have the strongest homing instincts. They hover around the maitre'd and swarm in clockwise gyrations surrounding the cruise director.

Strictly nocturnal are the SEQUIN-BREASTED STRUT-TERS followed by the BLACK-TIE GROUCHES. Their mating ritual consists of carefully counted cha-cha steps or Arthur Murray waltz routines. In contrast to the DECK-STRIDERS, these birds have smiles painted on.

There are other birds on board, of course, but I'd better stop before one of them recognizes himself and sues me.

Tales of the South Pacific I

Here begins the 1986 edition of "Tales of the South Pacific: According to Weaver." This will NOT be set to music for Broadway. There is no French planter/hero. But the romance of these paradise islands cannot be denied, even by a wandering grandmother from Beulah, Colorado. These are the lands of Bali Hi.

My first experience Down Under is aboard the Royal Viking Star, all set for two weeks of cruising long distances between island groups such as Fiji and Tonga with three-day stops in Sydney and Auckland. These were the places named during the War in the Pacific. American forces gathered in staging areas here, and several passengers I've met are returning to these islands after 40 years, just for old times' sake. (They exchange war stories every day before lunch around the bar.)

On our first island, New Caledonia, we docked at Noumea on the dry side of the island. That wasn't too much of a treat but we did learn a lot about the nickel industry—now principally exported to the Japanese or used in the construction of new submarines for the New Caledonians. (They already have two!)

New Hebrides became Vanuatu in 1980—an independent nation. That's where I met Rodger. I have a gut feeling I was not the first older woman alone who had hired Rodger's car for an hour or two of sight-seeing. Rodger and I inspected all of the palm trees, beaches and banana plantations, visited every one of his cousins' souvenir shops on this small island, looked at both "luxury" hotels and wound up touring out into the country so I could admire the beautiful rain forests and two vacant lots which Rodger and his brother just happened to have for sale. Being excellent carpenters, they would be glad to build me a nice little vacation house which they would manage as an income property for me. I hated to tell Rodger he was nuts for thinking I could afford a home in paradise so I said he'd have to contact my son the accountant and gave him Chris's address.

At Suva on Fiji, I enlisted Bobby to drive me to the Cultural Center at Pacific Harbor—a marvelous reconstruction of Fijian traditional life-style. Bobby was not in the vacant lot business. He wants to move to San Diego. "WHY?", I asked, "You live here where anything will grow, the beaches and trees and flowers are breath-taking. You live among people who appear to value their heritage. And certainly the future of the world now lies in the Pacific."

"The money's better in San Diego and my kids can have a better education and a better life."

Bobby made a point of driving me past a cemetery where some graves were wildly decorated with flowers and festoons of palms. "This is where our soldiers are buried who have died in Beirut. The Americans saved our necks in World War II, so when you needed help with the peace-keeping forces in Lebanon, we sent Fiji troops. We haven't forgotten."

I won't forget either, Bobby. Thanks.

Who Will Star?

If a full-length feature film were being made of the story of your life, who would you want to play the leading role?

For years now I have pondered this question. Something or other brought it to my mind the other day, and now I'm conducting a pole—an informal sampling of the way people want themselves to be seen. Or feel about their own image.

My original contention was that most women my age—in their 50s and 60s—would prefer Katherine Hepburn to portray them on the screen. I assumed all women want to be witty, sharp, well-dressed, talented, admired, ageless like Hepburn appears to be. If not ageless, she at least ages beautifully and gracefully. So far, I am dead wrong.

Regina opted for Rosalind Russell. That makes sense. Regina enjoyed a career as an executive secretary dealing with glamorous chores for big oil company bosses. Rosalind Russell always seemed to be clad in knockout tailored suits, in charge of all she surveyed, yet with enough glamour to snag the most important tycoon on the premises. Now Regina is retired, living a quiet life in the North Country. It's nice she still thinks of herself as Rosalind Russel.

My younger friend Genevieve pictures herself more as the Meryl Streep type. Meryl Streep would make a fairly good Genevieve. She has the sensitivity, the good looks—but Meryl Streep is not dynamic enough to portray my friend. At least I don't think so. Of course I have seen only one Meryl Streep picture, which tarnishes my standing as an expert on the subject.

A third friend, Mary-Arthur, the woman who keeps the Lake George Association on an even keel, says she'd like Shirley MacLaine to play the lead in her life story movie. Now there's a choice. Shirley MacLaine can do almost anything; sing, dance, act, look good, write books, win the heart of any leading man and look becomingly wistful in the process. I've never seen Mary-Arthur dance or listened to her sing but she certainly can look wistful. Maybe Cybil Shepard would be better—or Michelle Lee.

The men I know are reluctant to play this game. Maybe they're just shy about comparing themselves to John Wayne or Cary Grant or Tom Selleck—or Woody Allen. Maybe men are naturally self-conscious about such opinions. Probably they simply do not care. If I were a man, I'd want my life story acted out by Paul Newman—or Spencer Tracy if he were still around.

But nobody speaks up for Hepburn. Too smart-aleck? Too sophisticated? How do we see ourselves, and what impression do we hope to be leaving with the rest of the world?

I'll have to think of somebody in a hurry to portray me or they'll revert to typecasting and resurrect Marjorie Main. A year or so ago I might have chosen Angela Lansbury, but I don't ride a bike, so she probably wouldn't want the part. Maybe the actress I want to be me is Bea Arthur. On second thought, maybe I should offer to be in a movie about HER. That's more polite.

Are You Sure I Can't Take It with Me?

The Beulah Valley, at least Squirrel Creek Road, looked a lot like Saratoga Springs during the racing season last night. Lighted tents on the grounds, noisy people crowded around the bar, lots of food and plenty of spirited conversation. Old friends and young ones from Pueblo gathered to kick off another season: the campaign season. Number One Son is running for County Commissioner.

Out in the yard, clearing up the tag ends of trash this morning, a strange sensation hit me. I should have taken pictures of the party last night, I thought, to send them to my husband. He'd be so proud of the way this kid has turned out. Of course I can't send snapshots to John. He died more than six years ago.

What if we could "take it with us"? Weird fantasy, I know, but what if some strange being said, "You can take along one item, no more than six-by-six inches," or some such? What would I take to the great reunion in the sky—or wherever? What sort of impression would I want to make on someone who had been so much of my life? What kind of Progress Report?

How about a sort of report card? Or maybe one of the elegant pieces of glass from Venice or a small figure of the terra cotta soldiers in Xian, China? Would my over-achiever husband be more interested in my tax returns, bridge scores, dental records, insurance policies or polite notices of overdrafts? Or a picture of me in my smashing black dress after I lost 15 pounds last year, (and put them all back on this year)?

Snapshots. That's the best idea. I want my life as a single, responsible woman to be documented with pictures of me attending classes at Adirondack Community College, working at my word processor, playing miniature golf with Sarah, whale-watching with the whole family, talking to groups of old ladies about what we can do with our lives now, digging up artifacts with two 15-year-old grandsons and my good-friend daughter, taking notes in art museums, having a hail-damaged roof replaced in Colorado.

Other Kodak and Polaroid masterpieces would round out my portfolio: Chris making a speech, Donny grown up in the army, Andy and Chigger starting college, Whit playing soccer and knocking down A's, Jason giving his all on the basketball court, Miss Sarah working hard on her piano lessons. Lots more. What I want John to see would fill a big album. I'd be charged for excess baggage.

Certainly this collection would not include a portrait of Poor Me sitting alone in front of the TV waiting for one of the kids to call. That would make him furious, and we had enough cross words to last more than a lifetime already. Minnie-the-Moper poses would make him groan, "Ye gods, Frances, I'd think you'd be a grown-up by now!"

Good Mornin' America, How Are Ya'?

"Passengers will please refrain . . ."

My dad's old favorite, sung to the familiar melody of "Humoresque," rattled in my head as I stuffed too many clothes in my hanger case, shut down the heat in my digs in Lake George and headed for Colorado, my kids and Christmas. By train.

". . . from flushing toilets while the train . . ."

"Amtrak??? You're going more than halfway across the country on AMTRAK? You must be mad. I hear the trains are never on time, it costs more than flying and the food is horrid—and expensive." So said friends and well-wishers at both ends of my route.

". . . is standing at the station. I love you."

Why the train? Why 36 hours en route when any plane covers the distance in a few hours actual flying time? I thought about that. Actually, I had twice before chickened out on Amtrak reservations. This time I reflected on the hassle in and out of strung-out airports; studying blinking screens for flight numbers and boarding gates, stuffing my new English tweed coat into overhead compartments and serving my flight-time sentence strapped into a narrow seat with legroom only a jockey could appreciate, trying to eat Marriott Microwave imitations of real food without moving my elbows and jostling the fat guy next to me when I tried to unwrap my knife and fork. I recalled luggage which never slid out onto the carousel and mad dashes from one terminal at O'Hare to another. I thought it all over, folks.

"If you really think you oughta' . . ."

Perhaps, I reasoned, train travel is just the ticket for my peer group—the girls with the grandmother faces. The trip from Albany to New York City along the Hudson is a delight; why not all the way home?

" . . . you should call the Pullman porter . . ."

So here I sit comfortably in the diner, having finished breakfast while Ohio rolls by. Lake Erie is frozen. Dirty gray snow covers most of this part of the world. The young man across the table is telling me about the Trivial Pursuit™ game in the lounge car last night. Tonight there will be bingo and a movie. (We have passed the factory where crayons have been made in Sandusky since 1835.) There are a few orchards and farms now. I'll wait until we stop at Toledo before walking back to my compartment.

"When at night I dream, I dream of you." My dad knew some swell songs.

My friend Genevieve back in Glens Falls analyzed my decision to spend a weekend riding the rails: "You've been more than busy here the past few weeks and you're going home for the holidays. You'll hit the ground running. That train is a decompression chamber." Smart girl, Genevieve. From the moment I set foot on the train in Albany until I reach LaJunta, Colorado, I will be in a cocoon. The trip becomes a part of the holiday—relaxed.

All together now: *"Passengers will please refrain . . ."*

Did You by Any Chance See a Schnauzer?

Your pet can change your life. That's what some psychologists are saying these days. To most avid pet-lovers this is not news. To the rest of us it's a fascinating concept. Having a loving relationship with a dog, a cat, a bird, a llama or a friendly chimp relieves stress and sharpens the awareness of feelings. Getting in touch, so to speak.

More than one clinical psychologist keeps an amiable cocker spaniel or a warm-hearted Siamese at the ready in the office these days, providing extra comfort during consultation. My dentist has known about this for years. He has a tank of goldfish suspended above his chair where I can lose myself in their finny gyrations while he terrifies me with his medieval instruments of torture.

Lately I've learned more about pet therapy, and one aspect might change my life. That's the part about, "Having a pet can widen social horizons—generate new relationships in an otherwise lonely life." Not that I'm always lonely, but some days could use a little perking up.

Pet-owners with problems are advised to get acquainted with fellow dog or cat enthusiasts—or hamsters or parakeets—by starting conversations with the people who walk their dogs at the same time, for example. Or make frequent trips to the vet in order to get a look at other animal lovers. Great friendships can develop from such humble beginnings as a discussion of the attributes of various flea collars.

How will this enhance my own life? Traveling as much as I do, and tired as I have been of pets to care for during my kids-at-home years, would I buy even a canary just to meet a new friend? I don't have to. As in any in-crowd, the appearance and the lingo are enough.

Picture a lonely lady in an apartment. Every evening she sees a marvelous looking man on the elevator with his Golden Retriever. A gentle pair. One day she can admire the dog, ask what food keeps his coat so shiny. Next day, timed just right, she can say something about dogs being such fine companions for apartment dwellers. By now the man is smiling at her. Then she can pet the dog. Who knows what excitement might follow?

Or the supermarket. One might stand in front of the pet food shelves, reading labels until an attractive fellow stops to pick up his Friskies™ buffet or a six-pack of KalKan™. One or two questions or comments about diet and exercise for our four-footed friends might open new doors. Before you know it, it's dinner and dancing and an intimate chat about neighborhood veterinarians and truly tasteful boarding kennels.

As for me, I might be tempted to try this someday. Don't be surprised to find me knocking on your door, carrying a rhinestone encrusted leash, asking: "Have you by any chance seen a miniature schnauzer in this block?" Then get on your dancing shoes before you and I go hunting for my "lost dog."

Vesta

Whenever I buy White Cloud™ bathroom tissue I think of Vesta. Other women might have more esthetic reminders of their mothers-in-law but none more persistent than mine. There was a lot to know, criticize and/or appreciate about Vesta Weaver, but the sight of a shelf filled with toilet paper distills for me the woman, her character and her life—especially the end of her life.

In July, 1965, Vesta and I went to the grocery store together for the last time. Joe went with us—for a change. Before leaving the house Vesta prepared a list written with obvious care and effort. As I drove down Republican Street to downtown Concordia, Kansas, on that hot day, Vesta was explaining the grocery list and the process of shopping to Joe as she would to a small child with a handful of dimes.

When I parked the car in the lot next to Bogart's Market, I swallowed hard. This would not be easy. Joe Weaver was seventy years old. Until this summer he had never shopped for groceries—not in his whole life. That was Vesta's job.

"You're going to need to know how to do this, Joe," she said quietly as we got out of the car. "It can be fun. Relax."

Inside the store she pointed out the aisles of cereal, dog food, cleaning supplies and paper products. Joe walked ahead of us with the cart.

"This is the third time we've done this," she whispered to me. "Watch. He misses about half the list but he always buys toilet paper."

"Toilet paper?"

"That's it. Every time he buys more toilet paper. We must have a six-month supply from the last two trips. There he goes again."

Vesta's cotton house dress hung from her once-broad shoulders like a shroud. Her eyes shone in her bony face. Even her eyeglasses and false teeth seemed too big. She took my arm for support—then smiled.

Joe and I carried the sacks to the kitchen table. Vesta insisted that he put all the supplies away himself. "You'll need to know where things are."

Knowing where anything was had always been Vesta's job. Vesta and I talked a lot during that visit—just as we had through the 20 years we had been in-laws. She was the most pragmatic woman I shall ever know. She made a fetish of being down-to-earth—unspoiled. Having NO affectations was almost an affectation of her own.

"Cheese is cheese," she'd remark when I would proudly present a gourmet recipe. "No sense in all those fancy foreign names. We'll use good old rat trap cheese."

When the bed was unmade: "It felt good when you got out of it this morning, didn't it?"

She was Vesta to everyone in town, even her children and grandchildren. "None of that high-sounding Mrs. Weaver stuff for me or some cutesy name like Mumsie or Granny. Just call me Vesta. That's my name."

Grandkids loved to visit; rides in the country with Joe and Vesta were childhood treats, especially when Vesta would whistle or hum. Her voice was a little like a calliope but a ride over to the old family farm was reason for rejoicing so Vesta sang. When Joe's driving was too much "like Barney Oldfield" Vesta changed her tune to "Nearer My God to Thee." The children squealed—and Joe slowed down.

About a spot on a skirt or a child's uncombed hair Vesta would say, "A man on a galloping horse would never see it."

About cancer when the surgeons simply closed her abdomen with no hope of recovery: "They say one person in four is going to die of cancer. I don't know why I wouldn't be one of them."

Facing reality—even terminal cancer—was not anything her husband was ready to do. That was Vesta's job, too—facing reality. The arrangement they called marriage was a simple one: Joe worked at the post office. Vesta worked at everything else.

Growing up on a farm in Cloud County, Kansas, had not been a childhood filled with wonder and delight. Motherless at seven or eight, Vesta cared for her brother and sister and took orders from her father. After two years of college, ("Enough for any girl . . .") she married and took orders from Joe. To her that was the way life goes.

Never in her life did she wear high heels or slacks or a diamond ring. Never did she play bridge or go to lunch with the girls. Never did she go the forty miles to Salina to shop. She never had a car or a bank account of her own. Neither—

in her own mind—did she lack the absolute necessities of life. I never heard her whine. Never saw her complain.

In the summer of her 48th year of marriage she said, "I guess I should have seen to it Joe could take care of himself. It's hard for him to learn now." My insides churned and my face must have been crimson recalling the hundreds—thousands—of times I had sworn under my breath at that chauvinist sonovabitch demanding to be waited on with the same smug: "That's Vesta's job."

In those last months she showed him how to wash his clothes, do his dishes, iron shirts, pay utility bills, find socks, get the car serviced, mow the lawn and call the plumber. She taught him about frozen foods; how to operate the can opener. She demonstrated changing sheets when she could scarcely stand.

Then in August of 1965, satisfied she had done the best she could to prepare her husband for life without her, she took to her bed and died as matter-of-factly as she had lived. "Don't take me back to the hospital," she commanded, "I'll have to be here to make sure Joe gets along all right." She helped him find her good black dress—arranged for her sister to braid her hair.

So the priest came and she said her prayers and that was that.

Vesta Weaver had never considered herself "special." I don't think she had any idea of how much she was respected for her let's-just-get-on-with-it attitude. She would have been astonished by her own funeral. The church and the parish hall were filled to overflowing with her friends and admirers. The Bishop came from Topeka. Senator Carlson came from Washington. Vesta had made her point: That's the way life is.

That was quite a woman. I never really understood the way she lived but I certainly learned a lot from the way she died.

Frances Weaver is a freelance columnist whose writing career began in her 50s with the publication of an article about flying kites. Long interested in the opportunities and options open to women in their after-middle years, Frances Weaver has chosen to pursue writing as a means of exploring and sharing those possibilities with women concerned about the quality of their lives.

A Westerner by background and education, she now divides her time between residences in Pueblo, Colorado, and Lake George, New York. Her weekly column, *Midlife Musings*, appears in the *Saratogian*, Saratoga Springs, New York, and the *Chieftain*, Pueblo, Colorado. Her first collection of these columns, *Midlife Musings*, has been published in book form and as a book-on-tape in the past year.

Frances Weaver is a widow with four grown children and eight grandchildren. After the death of her husband in 1980, Mrs. Weaver chose a return to college as the vehicle for changing her life-style, living as a single for the first time in her life. She enrolled in Adirondack Community College in Glens Falls, New York, participating in workshop/conferences of the International Women's Writing Guild at Skidmore College in Saratoga Springs and developed the skills necessary for her chosen field of non-fiction writing.

In addition to keeping up with the demands of regular column production and promotion of her self-published books, Frances Weaver is a genuinely funny lady and a busy speaker, addressing civic groups and literary audiences in New York and Colorado.

Have you read Frances Weaver's other delightful books?
    As Far As I Can See . . .
    The Girls with the Grandmother Faces
    . . . books laced with wit and wisdom!

"Fran has a delightful sense of humor and it shows in her writings. In addition the hints she has for women in their sixties are not only wise but presented in a unique way which captures the readers attention."
                                        R. H. Rawlings, Publisher
                                        The Pueblo *Chieftain*
                                        Pueblo, Colorado